THE NEW BOOK OF KNOWLEDGE ANNUAL

THE
NEW BOOK
OF
KNOWLEDGE
ANNUAL

The Young People's Book of the Year

Scholastic Library Publishing, Inc.
Danbury, Connecticut

2004

Highlighting Events of 2003

ISBN 0-7172-0642-4

ISSN 0196-0148

The Library of Congress Catalog Card Number: 79-26807

STAFF

CONTENTS

CONTRIBUTORS

BLACK, Jeremy
Professor of History, University of
Exeter; Author, *European Warfare:
1600–1815; War for America; Culloden
and the '45; Eighteenth Century Europe*
(REVIEWER) EUROPE

CASILLAS, Adrian M.
Assistant Professor of Medicine, UCLA
School of Medicine
ASTHMA

GOURÉ, Daniel
Vice President, The Lexington Insti-
tute
HOMELAND SECURITY

KURTZ, Henry I.
Author, *The Art of the Toy Soldier;
John and Sebastian Cabot*
THE DISCOVERY

LEAL, José H.
Director, The Bailey-Matthews Shell
Museum
SHELLS

LOTT, Dale R.
Chairman, Department of Geography,
Jersey City State College
EUROPE

MASCIA-LEES, Frances E.
Sarah Lawrence College; Editor-in-
Chief, *American Anthropologist*; Co-
author, *Taking a Stand in a Postfeminist
World: Toward an Engaged Cultural
Criticism; Gender and Anthropology*
ANTHROPOLOGY

MURRAY, Robert D.
Director, Borden Center for Nutrition
and Wellness, Columbus Children's
Hospital; Ohio State University,
Department of Pediatrics
OBESITY

PASCOE, Elaine
Author, *South Africa: Troubled Land;
Neighbors at Odds: U.S. Policy in Latin
America; Racial Prejudice; The Horse
Owner's Preventive Maintenance Hand-
book; Freedom of Expression: The Right
to Speak Out in America*

AROUND THE WORLD

RICHARDS, Dan
Senior Editor, *Popular Photography
and Imaging*

PHOTOGRAPHY

SHAPIRO, William E.
Author, *The Statue of Liberty; Pearl
Harbor; Lebanon*

SPORTS BRIEFS

SOO HOO, Judy
UCLA Asian American Studies Center;
CD ROM editor, *The Asian-American
Experience*

ASIAN AMERICANS

TESAR, Jenny
Author, *Endangered Habitats; Global
Warming; Scientific Crime Investigation;
The Waste Crisis; Shrinking Forests; The
New Webster's Computer Handbook;
What on Earth Is a Meerkat?; Spiders*

SPACE BRIEFS

VAN RYZIN, Robert
Managing Editor, *Numismatic News,*
Krause Publications; Author, *Striking
Impressions: A Visual Guide to Col-
lecting U.S. Coins*

COIN COLLECTING

VAN VALKENBURG, Samuel
Former Professor of Geography, Clark
University; Author, *Elements of Politi-
cal Geography*

EUROPE

IN THE PAGES OF THIS BOOK . . .

How closely did you follow the events of 2003? Do you remember the people who made news during the year? What about the trends—what was in and what was out? Who won in sports? What were the top songs, films, and television shows? What important anniversaries were celebrated? All these helped to make up your world in 2003—a year that was like no other.

Here's a quiz that will tell you how much you know about your world—about what took place during the past year and about other things, as well. If you're stumped by a question, don't worry. You'll find all the answers in the pages of this book. (The page numbers after the questions will tell you where to look.)

In January, the U.S. Census Bureau released new population figures that revealed that (Asians/Hispanics/African Americans) had become the largest minority group in the United States. (*19*)

In August, the Little League baseball team from the country of _____ won the 2003 Little League World Series. (*171*)

At the 2003 Academy Awards ceremony, which movie won the Oscar for best motion picture? (*244*)

In October, (China/India/Japan) became the third nation—after Russia and the United States—to successfully send a person into space. (*36, 137*)

In March, the southeastern European nation of _____ was renamed Serbia and Montenegro. (*23*)

Which baseball team defeated the New York Yankees to win the 2003 World Series? (*168*)

In August, Italian scientists announced that they had created the world's first cloned (goat/horse/dog). (*32*)

An outbreak of a new flu-like disease called SARS infected more than 8,000 people worldwide. Researchers think the disease first appeared in the Asian country of _____. (*52*)

In March, which American skater won the World Figure Skating Championship for a fifth time? (*182*)

The United Nations proclaimed 2003 the International Year of (Freshwater/Rainwater/Saltwater). (*130*)

On the first day of summer, the fifth book in J. K. Rowling's *Harry Potter* series was released. It was called *Harry Potter and the Order of the_____.* (*29, 287*)

What famous animated-cartoon rodent with big ears celebrated his 75th birthday on November 18, 2003? (*268*)

Early in 2003, fossil hunters in China announced the discovery of the remains of a dinosaur that lived more than 125 million years ago and had four (eyes/wings/tails). (*18*)

In August, the planet _____ was closer to Earth than at any time in nearly 60,000 years. (*137*)

Which TV shows won Emmy Awards in 2003 for best comedy and drama series? (*256*)

The year's biggest game craze, which is played with trading cards, started in Japan as an animated TV show. The game is called (Whu-Nu!/Yu-Gi-Oh!/Oh-Noh-Joh!). (*235*)

The San Antonio _____ defeated the New Jersey Nets to win the 2003 National Basketball Association title. (*172*)

In 2003, a U.S. postage stamp was issued to commemorate an 1803 event that doubled the size of the United States. Can you name that event? (*152*)

On October 7, (actor David Schwimmer/former general Norman Schwarzkopf/actor Arnold Schwarzenegger) was elected governor of California. (*64*)

Singer and pianist _____ won five 2003 Grammy Awards, including one for best new artist. (*259*)

In 2003, a famous prince, who is second in line to the British throne, celebrated his 21st birthday. Can you name him? (*65*)

The United States began a four-year celebration marking the 200th anniversary of the Lewis and Clark Expedition. They began their journey to explore the West in (Michigan/Missouri/Montana). (*192*)

A summer box-office hit, which featured a cast of animated fish, was the movie _____. (*247*)

In July, for the fifth time in a row, American Lance Armstrong won the world's most famous bicycle race. Can you name that race? (*187*)

Champion Torums Scarf Michael won the Westminster Kennel Club dog show in February. He was a (black coonhound/golden retriever/Kerry blue terrier). (*96*)

The world's tallest building—called Taipei 101 because it has 101 floors—was built on what Asian island? (*36*)

In late 2003, the U.S. national debt—the total of all the government's borrowings over the years—stood at about ($1 trillion/$3 trillion/$7 trillion). (*51*)

At the age of 13, _____, a Korean-American became the youngest golfer ever to win the U.S. Women's Amateur Public Links Championship. (*187*)

Fourteen-year-old James Williams won the National Geographic Bee by correctly identifying the country that once ruled the state of Goa, now part of India, as a colony. Do you know who once ruled Goa? (*235*)

The year 2003 marked the 50th anniversary of the first climbing of Mount (McKinley/Vernon/Everest) by Edmund Hillary and Tenzing Norgay. (*110*)

The new National Constitution Center, which brings the U.S. Constitution to life, is located in the city of _____. (*270*)

In what city and country will the 2004 Summer Olympic Games be held? (*189*)

In March, U.S. President George W. Bush ordered U.S. troops to invade the country of (Iraq/Iran/Israel). (*22, 42*)

The loss of the space shuttle *Columbia* in February resulted in the deaths of seven astronauts. This was the first shuttle disaster since the _____ shuttle exploded during liftoff in 1986. (*20, 102*)

In the 2003 National Hockey League playoffs, the New Jersey Devils faced the Anaheim Mighty Ducks. Which team won? (*179*)

Thirteen-year-old Sai Gunturi won the National Spelling Bee by correctly spelling "pococurante," which means (careful/carefree/careless). (*236*)

December 17 marked the 100th anniversary of the first powered flight of an airplane invented by the _____ brothers. (*40, 210*)

THE WORLD IN 2003

With a cheering crowd looking on, U.S. Marines topple a towering statue of Iraqi dictator Saddam Hussein in the heart of Baghdad, Iraq's capital, on April 10, 2003. This picture was snapped just three weeks after forces of a U.S.-led coalition invaded Iraq to force Saddam from power. They achieved that goal quickly. But restoring order and rebuilding Iraq proved to be more difficult than U.S. leaders had expected.

THE YEAR AT A GLANCE

War in Iraq, the threat of terrorism, concern about a new disease—those problems and others produced many worrisome headlines in 2003. But the year had plenty of bright spots and memorable moments as well.

WAR IN IRAQ

The United States invaded Iraq on March 20, 2003, to remove Iraqi leader

Saddam Hussein from power. U.S. President George W. Bush justified the invasion by saying that Saddam, a brutal dictator, was a threat to world peace because he was continuing to develop weapons of mass destruction—chemical, biological, and nuclear weapons.

Saddam Hussein had been president and dictator of Iraq since 1979, and his rule had been ruthless. He had tortured and killed his political opponents, used poison gas against his own people, and launched two wars during his years in power. His invasion of Kuwait led to the Persian Gulf War of 1991, in which a U.S.-led coalition drove Iraqi forces out of that Persian Gulf country. In the peace agreement that ended that war, Saddam promised to give up his weapons of mass destruction. His refusal to allow U.N. weapons inspectors into Iraq raised suspicions that he hadn't done so.

But the United States found little international support for an invasion of Iraq. Only Britain and a handful of other countries signed up for the U.S.-led coalition that toppled Saddam's government. Bush declared victory on May 1, but the deposed dictator was still at large. Saddam was finally captured in mid-December. By that time coalition troops faced mounting violence from anti-American forces. Iraqis were growing impatient with the slow pace of rebuilding their country. And critics in the United States and abroad were questioning U.S. policies. At year's end it wasn't clear how long U.S. troops would be stationed in Iraq.

MORE WORLD EVENTS

There was little progress in the search for peace between Israel and the Palestinian Arabs in 2003. Early in the year the United States and several other countries proposed a plan that was to be a "road map" for peace. The plan set out steps leading to the creation of an independent state for the Palestinians and guaranteeing security for the Israelis. But the plan quickly became mired in the cycle of violence that had kept the Mideast conflict boiling for 55 years.

The threat of terrorism continued to stalk the world during the year. Al Qaeda, the terrorist group behind the devastating attacks of September 11, 2001, in the United States, made its presence known in a string of deadly bombings. This radical Islamic group and others linked to it were all violently opposed to the United States and other

Western countries, and they targeted sites in countries scattered around the world—in Saudi Arabia, Morocco, Indonesia, and Turkey. Scores of people were

killed in the attacks. While there was some progress in tracking down terrorists during the year, Al Qaeda's leaders were still at large. Officials warned that more needed to be done if future attacks were to be prevented.

Iran has been accused of supporting terrorism in the past, although its government has denied the charge. In 2003 there was growing concern that Iran might be developing nuclear weapons. Iranian officials also denied that charge. But they admitted to producing material that could be used to make nuclear bombs.

There was even greater concern about North Korea's nuclear-weapons program. This secretive Communist country added to worldwide jitters in 2003 by disclosing that it had at least one nuclear weapon and planned to make more. Talks involving North Korea, South Korea, the United States, Russia, Japan, and China made little progress in convincing the North Koreans to give up their nuclear ambitions.

In June, European leaders met in Greece and endorsed a draft of the first constitution for the European Union (EU). The EU is set to expand from 15 to 25 members in 2004. The goal of the constitution was to help the organization run more smoothly and establish a stronger identity. But all 25 member countries would have to formally approve the constitution before it could take effect, and there was much disagreement over its terms. A December conference aimed at ironing out the details ended with important issues, including the voting power of member nations, still not resolved.

U.S. CONCERNS

The United States was struggling to pull out of an economic recession in 2003. By late in the year, the economy seemed to be gaining strength. But unemployment remained stubbornly high. And it wasn't clear how long or how strong the recovery would be.

Meanwhile, the federal government faced the largest budget deficit in U.S. history. Just two years earlier, in 2001, the budget had a surplus—the government took in more money in taxes and other revenues than it spent. But in 2003, federal officials announced that expenses had exceeded revenues by nearly $375 billion. More stunning deficits were forecast for the years ahead. The recession, the Iraq war, and tax cuts were among the causes cited for the deficits. In 2001, President Bush had signed legislation that would cut taxes by $1.35 trillion over ten years. Now the government would have to borrow to meet its expenses, adding to the growing national debt.

The economic downturn hurt state budgets, too. Several states faced huge budget shortfalls. In California, one of the hardest-hit states, budget problems were a big factor in the state's first recall election. Opponents of California governor Gray Davis launched a petition drive to force the election, which took place on October 7. Even though Davis had been re-elected in 2002, unhappy voters were ready for a change. A majority voted to recall him. A total of 135 candidates had put their names on the ballot in hopes of replacing Davis. The winner was movie star Arnold Schwarzenegger. Although he was a newcomer to politics, he got about 47 percent of the vote.

At year's end the United States was beginning to gear up for the 2004 presidential election. Nine Democrats were seeking their party's nomination. And Bush had already raised more than $50 million for his re-election campaign—more than all nine Democrats combined.

SPACE AND SCIENCE

The United States suffered a huge loss on February 1, 2003, when the space shuttle *Columbia* broke up in the skies over Texas, killing its crew of seven. A seven-month investigation traced the disaster to a chunk of insulating foam that broke off during liftoff and damaged the shuttle's wing. But the investigators also blamed officials at the National Aeronautics and Space Administration (NASA) for underestimating the risks.

The *Columbia* disaster was a serious setback for the U.S. space program. The three remaining space shuttles were grounded until their safety could be assured. That forced a delay in the construction of the *International Space Station*, because the shuttles were the only craft that could carry parts up to the orbiting station. The accident also caused some people to question whether the benefits of manned space flight were worth the risks.

To people in China, the answer to that question was a resounding "yes." On October 15, a Chinese rocket sent the first Chinese astronaut, Yang Liwei, into space. Yang orbited Earth for 21 hours and then returned to Earth. His historic flight made China the third country (after Russia and the United States) ever to launch a person into space.

Every year has its share of natural and man-made disasters, and 2003 was no exception. On August 14 the largest power failure in U.S. history blacked out parts of eight states. People from Ohio to Vermont and lower Canada were affected. In late October, wildfires swept across some 800,000 acres (320,000 hectares) in southern California, destroying about 3,500 homes and killing 22 people. It was one of the deadliest fire outbreaks in the state's history.

Public health officials took quick action to stop the spread of a new disease. Called SARS, for *severe acute respiratory syndrome*, the disease first appeared in China and was identified in February 2003. About 8,000 cases were reported before the outbreak was brought under control in July. Most cases were in Asia, but other areas, including Toronto, Canada, were hit as well. Strict public health measures, including quarantines and travel warnings in hard-hit areas, helped stop the outbreak. Most people who came down with SARS recovered, but about 10 percent died.

ON THE LIGHTER SIDE

Movie audiences went for fantasy and fun in 2003. The year's hit films ranged from *Pirates of the Caribbean,* based on a theme-park ride, to *Finding Nemo,* an animated tale about fish. On television, however, reality ruled. Reality shows featuring ordinary people continued to get top ratings. Leading the pack was the show *American Idol,* in which amateur performers competed to win a $1 million recording contract. Several winners on the show got to live out their dreams, cutting records and then watching their songs rise to the top of the pop charts.

The recording industry fought a growing problem: file sharing. Instead of buying music on CD's, increasing numbers of fans were swapping music files over the Internet for free. In September a group representing record companies began taking file swappers to court. The goal of the legal actions was to alert people to the fact that file sharing violated copyright laws and was preventing artists, as well as record companies, from earning money for their work.

Several important anniversaries were celebrated in 2003. The United States marked the 200th anniversary of the Louisiana Purchase. In 1803, the young country doubled its size by buying a vast area known as the Louisiana Territory from France for the bargain price of $15 million, or about 4 cents an acre. The United States also began a multi-year celebration of the Lewis and Clark Expedition, which explored the American West in 1804–06. And celebrations marked the 100th anniversary of the first airplane flight. Orville and Wilbur Wright made that flight near Kitty Hawk, North Carolina, on December 17, 1903. The anniversary was a good moment to remember how dreams have fueled progress throughout history.

JANUARY

23 Fossil hunters in China announced the discovery of a four-winged dinosaur. The animal, named *Microraptor gui,* lived more than 125 million years ago. It was about 2½ feet (76 centimeters) long—the size of a large crow. Its forelimbs, hind limbs, and tail had feathers like those on bird wings. The limbs also had claws that the dinosaur probably used to catch prey. Scientists think that the creature used its wings and feathered tail to glide, like a flying squirrel. The discovery provided new evidence for the theory that birds descended from gliding dinosaurs that lived in trees.

24 Tom Ridge, a former governor of Pennsylvania, was sworn in as the first U.S. Secretary of Homeland Security. The new Cabinet-level department is responsible for protecting the nation from terrorist attacks. It brings together 22 federal agencies—including the Coast Guard, the Customs Service, and the Secret Service—that had previously been part of other departments.

28 President George W. Bush delivered his State of the Union address to Congress. Much of the speech focused on terrorism and the threat of war with Iraq. The president also spoke about the weakening U.S. economy and health care. He promised that his administration would meet these challenges with "focus, and clarity, and courage."

Government change in January: In national elections in **Lithuania,** Rolandas Pasas was elected president. He defeated Valdas Adamkus, who had been president since 1998.

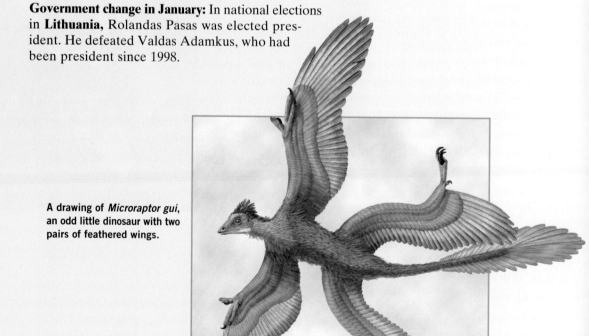

A drawing of *Microraptor gui,* an odd little dinosaur with two pairs of feathered wings.

Hispanics: The Largest U.S. Minority Group

Hispanics are now the largest minority group in the United States, according to the U.S. Census Bureau. New population figures released by the bureau in January provided a snapshot of the U.S. population as of July 1, 2001. They also illustrated how the population has changed since the last official census, in 2000.

As of July 1, 2001, the U.S. population was 284.8 million. Here's how the numbers broke down:

Non-Hispanic white: 68.9 percent
Hispanics: 13 percent
Blacks: 12.7 percent
Asians: 3.9 percent
American Indians and Alaska Natives: 1 percent
Native Hawaiians and Pacific Islanders: 0.2 percent
People of two or more races: 1.4 percent

However, the figures aren't quite as clear as they seem. One problem is the way the Census Bureau defines population groups. Hispanics are defined by language and culture. They speak Spanish or descend from people who did. The other groups are based on race. Another problem is that people can check off more than one group. They can pick Hispanic and white or Hispanic and black, for example.

Still, there's no question that Hispanics are the fastest-growing group. Two trends are behind the growth. Many Spanish-speaking people are immigrating to the United States from Latin America. And Hispanic birth rates are high. That is, Hispanic families tend to have more children than other groups.

Population experts say that the new figures mark a turning point for the United States. And they are a reminder that Americans include people from all over the world.

FEBRUARY

1 The U.S. space shuttle *Columbia* broke up during its return to Earth, killing all seven astronauts on board. The accident took place when *Columbia* re-entered the atmosphere, near the end of a sixteen-day scientific mission. The shuttle disintegrated over Texas and pieces fell to Earth in a path 100 miles (160 kilometers) long. The crew consisted of Michael Anderson, David Brown, Kalpana Chawla, Laurel Clark, Rick Husband, William McCool, and Ilan Ramon—the first Israeli astronaut to fly in space. This was the second time a space shuttle and its crew had been lost: *Challenger* exploded during liftoff in January 1986.

3 John Snow was sworn in as U.S. Secretary of the Treasury. He succeeded Paul O'Neill, who had resigned in December 2002. (The Senate had confirmed Snow's nomination on January 30.)

20 In West Warwick, Rhode Island, a fire swept through a nightclub called The Station after the heavy metal band Great White set off pyrotechnics. The fire left 100 people dead and nearly 200 others injured. The blaze began when sparks from the fireworks ignited foam soundproofing material that lined the area around the stage. It was the deadliest nightclub fire in the United States in 25 years.

Government changes in February: In national elections in **Cyprus,** Tassos Papadopoulos was elected president. He succeeded Glafcos Clerides, who had been president since 1993. . . .In the **Czech Republic,** Vaclav Klaus was chosen president. Klaus succeeded Vaclav Havel, who had been president since 1993. . . .In **South Korea,** Goh Kun was named premier. He succeeded Kim Suk Soo, who had been premier since September 2002.

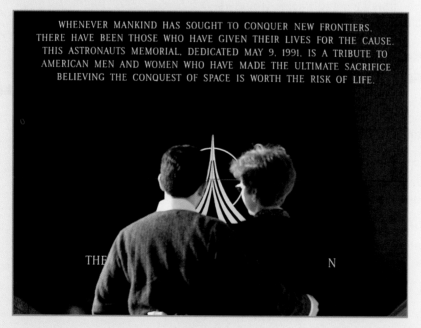

WHENEVER MANKIND HAS SOUGHT TO CONQUER NEW FRONTIERS, THERE HAVE BEEN THOSE WHO HAVE GIVEN THEIR LIVES FOR THE CAUSE. THIS ASTRONAUTS MEMORIAL, DEDICATED MAY 9, 1991, IS A TRIBUTE TO AMERICAN MEN AND WOMEN WHO HAVE MADE THE ULTIMATE SACRIFICE BELIEVING THE CONQUEST OF SPACE IS WORTH THE RISK OF LIFE.

After the tragic loss of the space shuttle *Columbia*, many people visited the Astronauts Memorial in Titusville, Florida, to pay tribute.

Rebuilding at Ground Zero

On February 26, New York City officials announced the winning plan to rebuild Ground Zero—the site where terrorists destroyed the twin towers of the World Trade Center on September 11, 2001. The design, by architect Daniel Libeskind, featured a series of glass-walled towers. The buildings would surround a deep open pit that was left after the debris of the twin towers was cleared away. The pit would be enclosed by the twin towers' concrete foundation walls. It would contain a memorial to the 2,800 people who died there on September 11.

The sloping, angular buildings that ring the pit would house offices, apartments, a museum, and a performing arts center. The tallest building would taper to a needlelike spire. It would rise to a height of 1,776 feet (541 meters), a number that represents the year of American independence. The lower floors of this building would have offices. The upper floors would have gardens—parks in the sky.

This building would be an important feature of the New York skyline. It would be the world's tallest building, a record now held by the Petronas Towers in Malaysia.

All the buildings would be designed so that light (no shadows) would fill the memorial area every September 11 between 8:46 A.M., when the first tower was struck by a plane, and 10:28 A.M., when the second tower collapsed. Although the design received the city's official stamp of approval, it wasn't clear when any of the buildings would go up. The first part built was expected to be the memorial. It might take ten years or more to rebuild the entire site.

A series of glass-walled towers will surround a deep open pit, containing the memorial. The pit will be enclosed by the original towers' concrete foundation walls, which survived the September 11 attack.

MARCH

2 The Swiss yacht *Alinghi* defeated *Team New Zealand* in five consecutive races to win the America's Cup, the most prestigious sailing race in the world. This was the first time a boat from a European country had won since the race was first run in 1851. The race was held off the coast of Aukland, New Zealand, in the Hauraki Gulf.

19 U.S. President George W. Bush declared war against Iraq and ordered American forces to invade the country. The objectives were to disarm Iraq and remove its leader, Saddam Hussein. Saddam had refused to obey a United Nations order to give up weapons of mass destruction—chemical, biological, and nuclear weapons. Britain and Australia provided military assistance to the United States. However, many other countries condemned the invasion, which hadn't received approval from the United Nations.

The United States declared war against Iraq on March 19. The war made headlines around the country—and around the world.

19–20 A two-day snowstorm shut down large parts of Colorado and Wyoming. It was Colorado's worst snowstorm in 90 years. Thousands of people were stranded in rural homes, ski resorts, and airports. Hundreds of roofs collapsed, mail delivery was suspended, and for the first time ever the Colorado Legislature was unable to convene for its regular session. In Denver, 31.8 inches (80.7 centimeters) of snow fell, the city's heaviest snowfall since 1913. Despite the inconveniences, many welcomed the late-season storm because the region had been in a long drought.

Yugoslav Airlines (JAT) is a reminder of a country that once was. In 2003, Yugoslavia was renamed Serbia and Montenegro.

Yugoslavia Becomes Serbia and Montenegro

On March 7, the parliament of Serbia and Montenegro elected Svetozar Marovic as the new nation's first president. Serbia and Montenegro were the last two republics in Yugoslavia, a nation in southeastern Europe that had been created at the end of World War I (1914–18). Until 1991, Yugoslavia was a federation of six republics. Between 1991 and 1992, four of the republics proclaimed their independence, leaving only Serbia and Montenegro in the federation.

In 2002, in response to a growing independence movement in Montenegro, the two republics agreed to a new federation pact so that each might become semi-independent. When a new constitution was approved in 2003, Yugoslavia was officially renamed Serbia and Montenegro. As part of the agreement, each state can hold a referendum in 2006 to decide if the federation should continue or be split into two independent countries.

Serbia and Montenegro is home to nearly 11 million people, most of whom are of South Slavic origin. Serbs make up nearly two-thirds of the total population. The rest is made up of Albanians, Montenegrins, Muslim Slavs, Croats, and Macedonians as well as smaller numbers of Magyars (Hungarians), Slovaks, Romanians, and Roma (formerly known as Gypsies).

Government changes in March: In **Central African Republic,** President Ange-Félix Patassé was overthrown in a military coup. François Bozizé declared himself president. . . .In **China,** Wen Jiabao was named premier. He succeeded Zhu Rongji, who had been premier since 1998. . . .In **Turkey,** Recep Tayyip Erdogan became prime minister. He succeeded Abdullah Gul, who had been prime minister since late 2002.

APRIL

16 At a ceremony in Athens, Greece, leaders of ten countries signed treaties to join the European Union (EU). The countries were Cyprus, the Czech Republic, Estonia, Hungary, Latvia, Lithuania, Malta, Poland, Slovakia, and Slovenia. The official admission was scheduled to take place in May 2004.

30 President George W. Bush signed a bill that would expand Amber Alert systems. These systems quickly distribute information about kidnapped children to the public over radio, television, and electronic highway signs. The new legislation provided money to states and communities for equipment and training to establish effective Amber Alerts.

Government changes in April: In **Burundi,** as agreed to in 2000, Pierre Buyoya, who had been president for the first 18 months of a three-year transitional government, stepped down and was succeeded by Domitien Ndayizeye. . . .In national elections in **Paraguay,** Nicanor Duarte Frutos was elected president. He succeeded Luis González Macchi, who had been president since 1999.

On April 14, scientists announced that they had completed work on decoding the human genome—the blueprint of a human being. The genome is composed of all the genes found inside body cells. Genes direct the building of body tissues, determine eye color and other individual traits, and guide the body through the life cycle, from growth to aging. Knowledge of the genome holds great promise for medicine. Researchers will be able to understand the role of genes in various illnesses. Doctors may be able to develop treatments that counter genetic flaws. Scientists may be able to correct genetic flaws before birth. And as people learn more about the way genes work, it may even be possible to slow the aging process.

After 27 years in service, the Concorde—the world's only supersonic passenger plane—will no longer be flying.

The World's Swiftest Passenger Plane Retires

On April 10, it was announced that the Concorde, the world's only supersonic passenger airplane, would stop flying. British Airways and Air France—the only airlines that operate Concordes—said they would ground the sleek needle-nosed plane by the end of 2003.

The Concorde began commercial service in January 1976. Cruising at a speed of 1,350 miles (2,200 kilometers) per hour—about twice the speed of sound—it could cross the Atlantic Ocean in just over three hours, about half the time of the fastest conventional passenger jets. This made it popular with busy executives and celebrities. But the speedy flights were expensive: A round-trip ticket on the Concorde cost as much as $13,000.

British Airways and Air France said that their decision to ground the plane was based on decreased passenger demand and increased maintenance costs. Another problem was the limited number of cities to which the airlines could offer service. The great noise of the Concorde's engines and the sonic booms it produced as it flew faster than sound ruled out regular flights over populated areas. Thus, scheduled flights only connected cities separated by vast expanses of ocean, such as London and New York or Paris and Rio de Janeiro.

The Concorde was a gas-guzzler, too. Its four engines consumed about 6,770 gallons (25,629 liters) of fuel per hour—about twice as much as a jumbo passenger plane.

MAY

1 President George W. Bush formally declared an end to major combat operations in Iraq. He delivered the speech from the deck of the aircraft carrier *Abraham Lincoln,* which was about 30 miles (48 kilometers) off the coast of California.

4 A mission to rotate crews aboard the *International Space Station* (*ISS*) ended as a Russian *Soyuz* spacecraft landed in Kazakhstan, in Central Asia. The new *ISS* crew consisted of Yuri Malenchenko of Russia and Edward Lu of the United States. The *ISS* crew returning to Earth were Kenneth Bowersox and Donald Pettit of the United States and Nikolai Budarin of Russia. It was the first time that U.S. astronauts returned from space in a foreign spacecraft and landed in a foreign country.

10 During the first ten days of May, 412 tornadoes swept through the central United States—more than had ever been seen in a ten-day period. The twisters ripped through 19 states and caused more than 40 deaths. Four states were declared disaster areas: Missouri, Kansas, Tennessee, and Oklahoma.

17–21 In Sri Lanka, the heaviest rains in 50 years caused major floods and landslides. About 250 people were killed and about 150,000 were made homeless.

In Illinois, tornadoes pushed this home off its foundation and into a pond. A woman makes her way through the rubble left behind by the destructive storms.

The Old Man of the Mountain Loses Face

Sometime on May 1 or 2, the Old Man of the Mountain—New Hampshire's most famous symbol—crumbled and fell. Year after year, this rock formation in the White Mountains had drawn thousands of tourists. Viewed from just the right angle, granite ledges on the side of Mount Cannon seemed to form the profile of an old man.

Road crews working near Franconia Notch discovered the Old Man in 1805. But it had probably been there for thousands of years. Ancient glaciers cracked the granite, and, over time, huge blocks of stone broke away. What was left behind looked like a craggy brow, nose, lips, and chin.

The Old Man came to stand for New Hampshire and the rugged independence of its people. The famous profile was featured on the state's license plates, road signs, and new state quarter. It was also a big attraction for people who visited the White Mountains each year.

Time, wind, and weather—the same natural forces that created the profile—brought it down. In the 1960's, state officials realized that the rocks were in danger of tumbling down the mountain. Workers installed steel cables and epoxy glue to keep them in place. But the efforts weren't enough.

After the rocky ledges collapsed, New Hampshire formed a government task force to see if the Old Man could be restored, or if it could be re-created in rubber, fiberglass, or some other material. But many state residents said the Old Man could never be replaced. The stone profile was real, carved by nature. Nothing people made would be the same.

21 A powerful earthquake struck the northern coast of Algeria, killing more than 2,200 people and leaving some 150,000 people homeless. It was the country's worst earthquake since 1980.

Government change in May: In elections in **Argentina,** Nestor Carlos Kirchner was elected president. He succeeded Eduardo Alberto Duhalde, who had been president since early 2002.

JUNE

3 Leaders of the major industrialized nations, known as the Group of Eight (G-8), completed three days of talks in Évian-les-Bains, France. The G-8 consists of Britain, Canada, France, Germany, Italy, Japan, Russia, and the United States. The group's discussions focused on international trade, terrorism, and the spread of nuclear weapons.

9 In the Indian state of Andhra Pradesh, rain showers brought relief from a three-week heat wave. The heat wave, with daytime temperatures as high as 126°F (52°C) in some places, claimed more than 1,400 lives.

11 Scientists announced the discovery of 160,000-year-old fossilized skulls of human ancestors. The skulls, of two adults and a child, were found buried in volcanic ash in northern Ethiopia. The scientists believe that the fossils are remains of the oldest direct ancestors of modern humans, *Homo sapiens.* This supported the theory that modern humans originated in Africa and then spread into Asia and Europe.

23 In two cases brought against the University of Michigan, the Supreme Court ruled that colleges and universities may consider a person's race in deciding which students to accept. However, the court ruled that race cannot be the deciding factor; it may only be one of many factors in admissions.

Government changes in June: In **Finland,** Matti Vanhanen became premier. He succeeded Anneli Jaatteenmaki, who resigned after two months in office. . . .In **Nepal,** Surya Bahadur Thapa was appointed premier. He succeeded Lokendra Bahadur Chand, who had been premier since late 2002.

On June 21, after nine months of work, the Eiffel Tower in Paris, France, glowed with 20,000 new lights. It was a dazzling display—one that was repeated every evening, for 10 minutes every hour on the hour. The lacy pig-iron tower, erected for the Paris Exposition in 1889, is a national landmark and popular tourist attraction. The new lightbulbs replaced 352 sodium lamps that had given the famous structure a yellow-orange hue at night.

A young reader eagerly waits to purchase *Harry Potter and the Order of the Phoenix*. About 5 million copies of the book were sold on the first day of release.

Harry Potter and the Order of the Phoenix

On June 21, the long-awaited fifth book in J. K. Rowling's *Harry Potter* series was released to much excitement and heavy sales. *Harry Potter and the Order of the Phoenix* continues the tale of skinny, bespectacled Harry Potter. In the book, which is almost 900 pages long, he is 15 and in his fifth year at Hogwarts School of Witchcraft and Wizardry. He's often moody, angry, and resentful—as teens can be.

He has plenty of reasons to be upset. Harry is haunted by mysterious dreams. A cold-hearted professor takes away his broom and kicks him off the Quidditch team. His half-giant friend Hagrid is missing. His enemy, the evil Lord Voldemort, gathers strength and becomes more dangerous. As a result, the book has a darker mood than the first four novels in the series. It even includes the death of a major character, someone close to Harry.

Harry Potter and the Order of the Phoenix shattered sales records on its first day. Fans bought about 5 million copies in the first 24 hours that the book was available. That was nearly twice as many copies as the top-selling adult novel of 2002 sold in a full year!

Many people had ordered the book before its release. Others waited in long lines at bookstores. Numerous bookstores opened at midnight on June 21 so people could get copies of the book right away. Some stores hosted parties and other events. Kids came dressed as characters from the books. The *Harry Potter* books are sold worldwide and have been published in at least 55 languages. J. K. Rowling has said that the series will include seven books in all.

JULY

12 President George W. Bush completed a five-day tour of Africa, stopping in five nations: Senegal, South Africa, Botswana, Uganda, and Nigeria. He spoke with the nations' leaders about economic growth, an end to conflicts in the region, and the fight against the disease AIDS.

13 A U.S.-appointed governing council of 25 Iraqis was formed in Iraq. The council's responsibilities were to include overseeing the drafting of a new constitution for Iraq.

24 The Congressional Committee on Intelligence released a report on its ten-month-long inquiry into the September 11, 2001, terrorist attacks on New York City and the Washington, D.C., area. The report concluded that there was no specific information that clearly indicated the attacks were coming. However, it criticized the intelligence agencies for poor communications within and among themselves. It said that beginning in 1998, U.S. intelligence agencies didn't adequately study a "relatively steady stream of intelligence indicating the possibility of terrorist attacks inside the United States." At the insistence of the Bush administration, the declassified version of the report didn't include some 28 pages said to contain information on the involvement of foreign government officials—particularly from Saudi Arabia—in supporting terrorist activity.

In Uganda, President George W. Bush greets members of a children's choir after they performed for him during a stop on his five-day African tour.

New York City's famous Central Park (*above*) spans some 50 blocks. One of the park's most famous landmarks is the Bethesda Fountain, which overlooks a lake for boating (*inset*).

Happy Birthday, Central Park

An all-day party on July 19 was the highlight of a year-long celebration marking the 150th anniversary of New York City's Central Park. The party included a giant cake in the shape of the park's most famous fountain, pet parades, croquet games, storytelling, and live music.

Central Park was the first major public park in the United States. It was born in 1853, when the New York State legislature set aside a rectangle of 843 acres (341 hectares) in the center of Manhattan for a park. At that time, it was a barren stretch of swampland. The park's designers, Frederick Law Olmsted and Calvert Vaux, turned it into a beautiful patch of country. They created sweeping meadows, wooded hills, lakes, and rocky glens. Over the years other features—playgrounds, ball fields, a skating rink, and even a zoo—were added.

Each year, 25 million visitors stroll along Central Park's 58 miles (93 kilometers) of pathways and rest on its nearly 9,000 benches. The visitors come from all corners of New York City and from around the world. It has become the city's big backyard, a perfect place for picnics, open-air concerts, birding, in-line skating, boating, jogging, sunbathing, and dozens of other activities.

Other special anniversary events during 2003 included walking tours, concerts, an auction of decorated park benches, a film festival, and exhibitions at nearby museums. And the artist Cai Guo-Qiang created a "Light Cycle" that included a sequence of huge halos floating above the park.

AUGUST

7 Scientists in Italy reported that they had created the world's first cloned horse. The horse was genetically identical to its mother. The scientists began with an egg cell from another female horse. They removed the genes from the egg cell, and replaced them with the genes from a skin cell of the mother horse. The resulting embryo was then implanted in the mother horse's womb. It developed into a healthy foal, named Prometea, which was born on May 28. The procedure may some-day enable the cloning of champion racehorses or endangered species. (On September 26, scientists in France reported that they had created the world's first cloned rats.)

14 Temperatures in Europe began to cool, ending a record heat wave that lasted for several weeks. The heat was blamed for thousands of deaths across Europe. The highest death toll was in France, where nearly 15,000 deaths were attributed to the heat.

31 A series of deadly bombings by terrorists occurred in U.S.-occupied Iraq during August. The worst occurred at the United Nations head-quarters in Baghdad and the Imam Ali Mosque in Najaf. The U.N. blast, caused by a suicide bomber who drove a truck full of explosives into the U.N. compound, killed 23 people and destroyed the headquarters. The explosion of a powerful car bomb outside the mosque—one of the holiest religious sites in Iraq—killed about 80 people.

Government change in August: In Liberia, Charles G. Taylor, who had been pres-ident since 1997, was forced to resign. (In October, Gyude Bryant took office as interim president.)

Prometea, the world's first cloned horse, stands next to her genetically identical mother. Born in a stable in Italy, Prometea joins a grow-ing list of cloned species. Sheep, cows, pigs, goats, mules, and mice are among the species that have been cloned in recent years.

The largest power failure in U.S. history left some 50 million people in the dark. Above: In a blacked-out New York City, pedestrians stream across the Brooklyn Bridge. Inset: A man in Detroit watches a battery-powered television outside his home; Detroit was especially hard hit.

Blackout!

The largest power failure in U.S. history began in mid-afternoon on August 14. Some 50 million people were suddenly left without electricity. Lights went out, air conditioners shut down, trains stopped, television screens went black, and cell phones wouldn't work.

The area affected included parts of eight states—Ohio, Michigan, Pennsylvania, New Jersey, New York, Connecticut, Massachusetts, and Vermont—as well as lower Canada. With traffic signals out, traffic snarled in and around cities. Major airports throughout the region shut down, stranding thousands of travelers. In office buildings, elevators stalled, trapping some workers and leaving the rest to trudge down long flights of stairs. In Cleveland, Ohio, electric pumps that supply the city with water shut down. National Guard troops were called in to distribute water from large tank trucks.

Most people in New Jersey, Connecticut, and parts of New York had power by the next morning. Airports were open, too. But elsewhere the power was out for more than 24 hours. In Detroit, one of the hardest-hit cities, power wasn't fully restored for three days.

Problems in the power grid—the network that shuttles electrical power from one place to another—led to the blackout. The trouble began with the failure of several high-voltage transmission lines in Ohio. As one line failed, electricity was forced into other lines, overloading them. That caused more lines to fail. Power plants automatically began to shut down to protect themselves from harmful swings in voltage.

It wasn't clear why the power failure spread so far through the eastern United States and Canada. The grid was supposed to have safeguards that would prevent such a spread. Many officials said the blackout was a clear sign that the grid needed to be upgraded.

SEPTEMBER

13 Governor Frank L. O'Bannon of Indiana died after suffering a stroke. He was succeeded by Indiana's lieutenant governor, Joseph E. Kernan.

15 Soda and junk food in school cafeterias and vending machines should be replaced with healthier drinks and snacks, according to the Center for Science in the Public Interest (CSPI). This would help combat the skyrocketing rates of obesity in children and teenagers. The U.S. Centers for Disease Control and Prevention reported that the number of children who were overweight had almost tripled over the last two decades. One in seven young people is obese (defined as more than 30 percent above ideal body weight). With obesity comes serious health problems—such as high blood pressure and diabetes—that can haunt a person throughout life. CSPI released a list of the worst drinks and snacks, along with better alternatives.

18 Hurricane Isabel struck the Outer Banks region of North Carolina, weakening into a tropical storm. It moved northwest across Virginia, West Virginia, Maryland, Delaware, New Jersey, Pennsylvania, and New York, causing more than $1 billion in damage. More than 3.3 million households were without electricity for nearly a week after the monster storm swept through the East Coast. About 40 deaths, 23 of them in Virginia, were blamed on the storm.

Schools were asked to replace sodas and junk foods with these more healthy drinks and snacks. Unhealthy food choices can lead to obesity in children and teens.

The new $20 bill includes tints of peach, blue, and green and numerous security features. The new colored backgrounds are meant to foil counterfeiters.

Colored Cash

In the fall, the U.S. Mint printed and began releasing new $20 bills with a peach-tinted background. This was a big change for U.S. currency, which had been the same color since 1862. For 141 years, nearly all bills had been printed in dull green and black ink on a neutral background—which is why U.S. bills are called "greenbacks."

The new colored backgrounds are part of an effort to stop counterfeiting. They make bills harder to copy, even with computers and other high-tech tools. Colors also make it easier for people with poor sight to recognize bills of different values. Most countries have long had colorful money for this reason. The new $20 bill has a peach background in the center, fading to pastel green at the sides. Andrew Jackson's portrait has been taken out of the oval frame used on earlier $20 bills. To the left of the portrait is a new image of an eagle, printed in a faint pastel blue. To the right are a metallic green eagle and faint blue letters spelling out "TWENTY USA."

The numeral "20" in the lower right corner is printed in color-shifting ink. It changes from copper to green when the note is tilted. On the back of the bill, small yellow 20's are scattered over the background.

Like other recent U.S. bills, the new $20's have special security features. They carry watermarks, faint pictures that are part of the paper itself and can be seen when the bill is held up to the light. They also have security threads that glow under ultraviolet light.

The U.S. Mint is planning to release tinted $50 and $100 bills in 2004 and 2005.

Government change in September: In **Guinea-Bissau,** an army coup ousted Kumba Yala, who had been president since 2000. Henrique Rosa was named president.

OCTOBER

15 China became the third nation—after Russia and the United States—to successfully send a person into space. Yang Liwei returned to Earth after orbiting Earth fourteen times during a trip that lasted about 21 hours.

17 Taipei 101, a new 101-story skyscraper in Taipei, Taiwan, became the world's tallest building. With the installation of a huge pinnacle, the building stood 1,676 feet (511 meters) tall. When it officially opens in 2004, it will house offices, a shopping mall, and Taiwan's stock exchange.

28 A mission to rotate crews aboard the *International Space Station* (*ISS*) ended as a Russian *Soyuz* spacecraft landed in Kazakhstan. The incoming *ISS* crew consisted of Michael Foale of the United States and Alexander Kaleri of Russia. The *ISS* crew returning to Earth was Yuri Malenchenko of Russia and Edward Lu of the United States. They were accompanied by Pedro Duque of Spain, who had arrived at the *ISS* eight days earlier with the incoming crew.

31 As October ended, wet weather and cool temperatures helped firefighters gain control of wildfires in southern California. The fires burned about 800,000 acres (320,000 hectares), an area almost as large as the state of Rhode Island. Some 3,500 homes were destroyed and 22 people were killed. The largest fires raged around Los Angeles and San Diego. More than 15,000 firefighters from California and several other Western states worked to contain the fires.

Taiwan, an island off the coast of China, became home to the world's tallest building. The new skyscraper, named Taipei 101 for its 101 floors, has a stepped design that's supposed to look like the sections of a bamboo shoot.

The 2003 Nobel Prizes

Chemistry: Peter C. Agre and Roderick MacKinnon of the United States, for discoveries concerning channels in the membranes of living cells. Agre was honored for his discovery of water channels in cell membranes. The channels are formed by proteins, which allow water to enter and leave but block other substances. MacKinnon was honored for his studies of ion channels. These channels allow small charged molecules (ions) to pass through the cell membrane.

Economics: Robert F. Engle of the United States and Clive W.J. Granger of Britain for methods of economic analysis. Separately, Engle and Granger focused on what economists call time series—observations over time of prices, interest rates, and other data.

Literature: John Maxwell Coetzee of South Africa, whose novels examined racial divisions in his homeland. In his early works, Coetzee examined the effects of apartheid, a rigid system of segregation put in place by white rulers in South Africa. In more recent books, he explored the ways in which people deal with moral choices.

Peace: Shirin Ebadi of Iran, for her efforts for democracy and human rights. Iran has a strict Islamic government. Ebadi, a lawyer, writer, and teacher there, has worked to promote the rights of women and children, and has defended people who spoke out against Iran's government.

Shirin Ebadi of Iran, winner of the Nobel Peace Prize.

Physics: Alexei Abrikosov of Russia and the United States; Vitaly Ginzburg of Russia; and Anthony J. Leggett of Britain and the United States, for their contributions to the theory of superconductors and superfluids. Superconductors are materials that allow electrical current to pass without resistance. Superfluidity is a bizarre state of matter that occurs when liquid helium is chilled to extremely cold temperatures. The liquid flows without friction and can even climb up the sides and out the mouth of a container.

Physiology or Medicine: Paul C. Lauterbur of the United States and Peter Mansfield of Britain, for their discoveries concerning magnetic resonance imaging (MRI). MRI produces detailed pictures of internal organs by exposing the body to a strong magnetic pulse. Lauterbur and Mansfield, working separately, were pioneers in developing MRI as a practical medical tool.

Government changes in October: In **Bolivia,** Gonzalo Sánchez de Lozada, who had been president since 2002, resigned. He was succeeded by Carlos Mesa. . . .In **Jordan,** Faisal al-Fayez became prime minister. He succeeded Ali Abu al-Ragheb, who had been prime minister since 2000. . . .In **Malaysia,** Abdullah Badawi became prime minister. He succeeded Mahathir bin Mohamad, who had been prime minister since 1981.

NOVEMBER

4   In general elections in the United States, two governorships changed hands. Republican Haley Barbour defeated Democratic Governor Ronnie Musgrove in Mississippi. And Republican Ernie Fletcher defeated Democrat Ben Chandler in Kentucky. (There were two additional changes in governorships later in the month: On November 5, Utah Governor Michael O. Leavitt resigned to head the U.S. Environmental Protection Agency; he was succeeded by Republican Lieutenant Governor Olene Walker. On November 15, in a runoff election in Louisiana, Democrat Kathleen Blanco defeated Republican Bobby Jindal for the state's top office.)

21   President George W. Bush completed a three-day trip to Britain. He and First Lady Laura Bush were guests of Queen Elizabeth II at Buckingham Palace and also spent a day in northern England. The president and British Prime Minister Tony Blair discussed the war in Iraq and stressed their determination to fight terrorism "wherever it is found." The visit was also marked by a large antiwar demonstration in London.

27   President George W. Bush made a surprise Thanksgiving visit to U.S. troops in Baghdad, Iraq. It was the first trip ever by an American president to Iraq. He spent two-and-a-half hours on the ground, meeting with about 600 soldiers and briefly helping to dish out their holiday dinner.

Government change in November: In **Georgia,** President Eduard A. Schevardnadze resigned. He had been president since 1992. Nino Burdzhanadze became acting president until elections scheduled for January 2004.

President Bush shares a platter of Thanksgiving turkey with U.S. troops during his surprise visit to Iraq. Because of concern for Bush's safety, only a handful of people knew that the president was making the trip to Baghdad.

When the side-wheel steamer SS *Republic* (*above*) sank in a hurricane in 1865, a cargo of treasure went down with the ship. Salvagers announced in November that they had discovered a cache of silver and gold coins (*right*) from the wreck.

Explorers Recover Sunken Treasure

Underwater explorers reported in November that a treasure trove of gold and silver coins had been discovered at a shipwreck in the Atlantic Ocean off the coast of Georgia. The explorers recovered more than 750 gold coins and 900 silver coins—only a small fraction of all the coins visible on the site.

The site, about 100 miles (160 kilometers) off the coast, is where the side-wheel steamer SS *Republic* sank during a hurricane in 1865. The ship was en route from New York to New Orleans, with 59 passengers and crew and a cargo meant to help New Orleans recover from the Civil War. The people made it safely off the ship and onto rafts, but some of them died before they could be rescued. The cargo sank with the ship.

In mid-2003, Odyssey Marine Exploration of Tampa, Florida, found the shipwreck 1,700 feet (520 meters) below the surface. In such deep water, objects are often very well preserved, thanks to cold temperatures and a lack of disturbance by waves or storms. After completing an archaeological survey, the company began to excavate the site, using a robot equipped with lights, cameras, and mechanical arms.

The robot retrieved the ship's bell and hundreds of jars and bottles that were labeled with everything from medicine to mustard. The glassware was in excellent condition, and it gave an idea of what people in the North thought that people in the South needed after the war.

The robot had specially designed equipment to pick up coins one at a time. It was important to lift the coins carefully from the ocean floor so that they wouldn't be scratched. At the time the *Republic* sank, its cargo of coins was reported to be worth $400,000. Today, the coins may be worth as much as $150 million, which would make the *Republic* one of the richest treasure wrecks ever found.

DECEMBER

11 Paul Martin became prime minister of Canada. He succeeded Jean Chrétien, who had been prime minister since 1993. Chrétien resigned not only as prime minister but also as leader of the governing Liberal Party, resulting in Martin's assumption of both positions. In his first major act as prime minister, Martin created a new Department of Public Security designed to deal with terrorism and disasters.

President George W. Bush nominated Alphonso Jackson to succeed Mel Martinez as Secretary of Housing and Urban Development (HUD). Jackson was Deputy Secretary of HUD. (Jackson's nomination must be confirmed by the Senate.)

13 In Iraq, U.S. troops captured Saddam Hussein, the dictator who ruled Iraq from 1979 until his government was overthrown by U.S.-led forces in April 2003. Saddam had been on the run for nearly nine months. He was found hiding in a hole at a farm near Tikrit, his hometown. The cramped underground chamber had an air vent and a fan, and it was just big enough for a person to lie down. Bricks and dirt masked the entrance to the hole. Saddam was crouched at the bottom, looking tired and scruffy, with a long gray beard and matted hair; he was captured without a shot. The discovery of his whereabouts came from intelligence tips and from information obtained from captured Iraqis loyal to him. It was expected that he would face a war crimes trial.

23 The U.S. Department of Agriculture announced that the nation's first known case of mad cow disease was found in a cow from a farm in Washington state. Efforts immediately began to track down meat from the animal. Mad cow disease is rare, but it may spread to people who eat infected beef.

Former Iraqi President Saddam Hussein was captured on December 13. He is shown here as he was found hiding in a hole in the ground, and after his beard was shaved while in custody.

2004

(calendar showing days 1–31, with "2004" in center oval)

. . . and Looking Ahead to 2004

Here are a few anniversaries that will be celebrated in 2004:

• The 250th anniversary of the start of the French and Indian War. The war, begun in 1754, was fought between France and Britain to gain control over North America. The British emerged victorious, succeeding in driving French forces from the continent.

• The 200th anniversary of the beginning of Lewis and Clark's exploration of the Louisiana Territory, purchased from France in 1803. The expedition led by Meriwether Lewis and William Clark traveled up the Missouri River, across the Rocky Mountains, and along the Columbia River to the Pacific Ocean.

• The 75th anniversary of the collapse of stock prices at the New York Stock Exchange, heralding the start of the Great Depression. The stock market crash of October 1929 occurred when a great number of people decided to sell stock at the same time, causing stock prices to fall dramatically.

• The 50th anniversary of the launch of the world's first nuclear-powered submarine. The U.S.S. *Nautilus* was launched on January 21, 1954, on the Thames River at Groton, Connecticut.

26 A powerful earthquake struck Bam, an ancient city in southeastern Iran. At least 30,000 people were killed and many thousands more were injured and homeless.

Government change in December: In runoff elections in **Guatemala**, Oscar Berger Perdomo was elected president. He succeeded Alfonso Portillo Cabrera, who had been president since 2000.

41

A shattered portrait of Saddam Hussein lies in the dust of an Iraqi military base. The United States went to war in 2003 to remove the brutal dictator from power. Late in the year, Saddam was captured by U.S. troops.

THE WAR AGAINST IRAQ

Just before dawn on March 20, air-raid sirens sounded in Baghdad, Iraq. Anti-aircraft fire lit the sky. And moments later, explosions rocked the Iraqi capital as U.S. bombs and missiles found their targets.

The air raid was the first phase of a U.S.-led war against Iraq. U.S. President George W. Bush launched the war to remove Iraqi leader Saddam Hussein from power. Saddam was a brutal dictator and a threat to world peace, Bush said, because he was continuing to develop weapons of mass destruction—chemical, biological, and nuclear weapons.

The war succeeded in toppling Saddam's government. But the tasks of bringing order to Iraq and rebuilding the country turned out to be far more difficult than U.S. officials had guessed.

THE CASE FOR WAR

Concern about Saddam Hussein went back to the 1980's, when he used chemical weapons against the Kurdish people of northern Iraq. In August 1990, Saddam invaded Kuwait, Iraq's oil-rich neighbor on the Persian Gulf. The result was the 1991 Persian Gulf War, in which a U.S.-led coalition drove the Iraqis out of Kuwait.

Under the peace terms that ended that war, Iraq was to get rid of all its weapons of mass destruction. U.N. inspectors were to tour the country to make sure this was done, and the U.N. placed stiff economic sanctions on Iraq to make sure Saddam lived up to the peace terms. But Saddam never fully cooperated with the U.N. inspectors, and in December 1998 he barred them. Although he denied having any banned weapons, many people suspected that he was hiding them.

President Bush made the case for war at the United Nations in September 2002. He said that Iraq was close to developing nuclear weapons and probably had stockpiles of chemical and biological weapons. This was a threat to other countries, he said, because Saddam might use the weapons or give them to terrorist groups such as Al Qaeda, which carried out attacks against the United States on September 11, 2001. Bush later said that if the United Nations didn't disarm Iraq, the United States would act on its own. The United States had never before gone to war unless it or one of its allies was attacked. But acting before an attack, the president said, could save lives.

In October 2002, the U.S. Congress voted to give Bush the power to strike Iraq. But nearly all foreign leaders were against military action. Russia, China, and most people in Muslim countries fiercely opposed a war. Even U.S. allies such as France, Germany, and Canada argued against it. Many Americans had questions, too. Critics said that an invasion would defy international law and increase anti-American feeling in the Middle East, leading to even more terrorism. Instead, they urged the United States to work with the United Nations.

In November, the Iraqis allowed U.N. weapons inspectors to return. Over the next few months, the inspectors searched for signs of banned weapons. They didn't find any, but they said that Iraq wasn't cooperating fully.

Who's Who

Here are some of the people who had key roles in the war against Iraq.

Colin Powell: As U.S. Secretary of State, Colin Powell advised President Bush about matters that related to foreign countries. Powell, a retired general, was formerly chairman of the Joint Chiefs of Staff, the nation's top military position. He was largely responsible for the success of the 1991 Persian Gulf War against Iraq. In 2003, one of Powell's major tasks was to win support from other nations for the U.S. action against Iraq. Another was to help mend relations with the many U.S. allies that were against the American attack.

Donald Rumsfeld: As U.S. Secretary of Defense, Donald Rumsfeld oversaw the armed forces of the United States and advised President Bush on defense and national security. Following the terrorist attacks on September 11, 2001, Rumsfeld directed the U.S. military effort against the Al Qaeda terrorists and the Taliban regime in Afghanistan. He was one of the president's closest advisers, and he strongly urged military action against Saddam Hussein. He also played a leading role in planning for postwar operations in Iraq.

General Tommy Franks: As commander-in-chief of the U.S. Central Command, General Tommy Franks headed U.S. military forces in and around the Middle East. He reported directly to Secretary of Defense Rumsfeld. Franks was a main designer of the military plan for Iraq. During the war he directed military operations from headquarters in Qatar, a small country on the Persian Gulf.

Saddam Hussein: Saddam Hussein was president and dictator of Iraq from 1979 to 2003. His rule was marked by ruthlessness, including torture and killing of his political opponents and the use of poison gas against his own people. Saddam launched two wars during his years in power—against Iran in 1980, and against Kuwait in 1990. His invasion of Kuwait led to the Persian Gulf War of 1991, in which a U.S.-led coalition drove Iraqi forces out of that Persian Gulf country.

Saddam's adult sons **Uday** and **Qusay** held powerful positions in their father's regime and were widely feared for their extreme cruelty. Qusay headed the Republican Guard and Special Republican Guard, two of Iraq's top fighting forces, as well as Iraqi intelligence services.

After Saddam's regime was overthrown in 2003, Uday and Qusay were killed in a firefight with U.S. troops in Mosul, in northern Iraq, in July. Saddam was captured in December in a village near Tikrit, his hometown.

Colin Powell

Donald Rumsfeld

General Tommy Franks

Saddam Hussein

43

Baghdad was heavily bombarded by airstrikes during the first wave of the U.S. invasion (*left*). Meanwhile, American ground troops raced from southern Iraq across the desert to seize the city (*below*).

Saying that Iraq had missed its last chance to disarm, the United States and Britain called on the Security Council to authorize war in February 2003. But the fifteen-member council was split, and only Spain and Bulgaria supported military action. Millions of demonstrators took to the streets on February 15–16 in antiwar protests. The biggest rallies were in Europe, but there were demonstrations in U.S. cities and around the world.

U.S. officials made it clear that protests and lack of U.N. support wouldn't stop the war plans. Ships, aircraft, and about 280,000 troops were already in position. Most of the troops were American, but about 45,000 were British, and 2,000 Australian. On March 17, Bush gave Saddam 48 hours to leave Iraq. The deadline passed, and the war began.

THE INVASION

Some of the first airstrikes on March 20 were aimed at a bunker in Baghdad where U.S. intelligence believed Saddam and other top Iraqi leaders were meeting. By striking at the Iraqi leaders, U.S. officials hoped to bring the war to a quick end. However, the strikes didn't succeed.

In the meantime, U.S. and British troops and tanks crossed into the desert of southern Iraq from neighboring Kuwait. The plan was to race north toward Baghdad, bypassing cities in the south. U.S. officials expected many Iraqi soldiers in the south to surrender immediately.

By March 24, American forces were just 50 miles (80 kilometers) south of Baghdad. Then the advance slowed. A fierce desert sandstorm blew in, bringing high winds and blinding clouds of dust. The coalition troops also met with stiffer resistance than expected, and they needed time to get more supplies and troops up to the front.

British forces surrounded and captured the key southern port of Basra. Meanwhile, more than 1,000 U.S. paratroopers landed in northern Iraq, in a zone controlled by the Kurds. And U.S. and British bombs continued to pound targets in Baghdad and elsewhere. Baghdad was shrouded with dark smoke from oil-filled trenches, which Iraqi forces set ablaze to interfere with the bombing.

As they neared Baghdad, U.S. troops donned masks and other gear as protection against chemical weapons. But there were no chemical attacks. By April 9, U.S. troops had encircled the city, and they moved in to take key sites. They expected stiff fighting, and they met some. But most Iraqi fighters simply melted away. The roads into the city were littered with stripped-off uniforms and abandoned tanks. U.S. troops quickly took control of several of Saddam's palaces and other important buildings.

Many people in Baghdad reacted with joy at the sight of U.S. troops. They danced in the streets, blared car horns, and tore up pictures of Saddam. On April 10, as a cheering crowd watched, U.S. Marines toppled a towering statue of the ex-dictator. It was three weeks to the day from the start of the war.

As the statue came crashing down, it was clear that Saddam had lost control. But Saddam was nowhere to be found, and other key Iraqi leaders were missing, too. The United States issued a deck of cards to soldiers showing portraits of the 55 most wanted.

U.S. officials cautioned that the war wasn't over. Even Baghdad wasn't firmly in U.S. control. Sniper fire and suicide bombings continued to be a danger. And with no local government in control, there was widespread looting. Looters stripped government offices, banks, and hospitals. At the National Museum of Iraq, they carried off priceless relics of ancient history. Aid agencies said that looting and lawlessness would hinder the delivery of badly needed food, water, and medical supplies.

Fighting continued north of Baghdad. Kurdish fighters and U.S. soldiers took control of Kirkuk, the site of important oil fields, and Mosul, the largest city in the north. Kurds, who in years past were bombed and gassed by Saddam Hussein, celebrated wildly. Meanwhile, U.S. and British planes and missiles hit Iraqi positions around Tikrit, Saddam's birthplace and a stronghold of his supporters. U.S. officials expected stiff resistance there. But Tikrit surrendered without a fight on April 14.

On May 1, Bush formally declared an end to major combat operations in Iraq. "In the battle of Iraq, the United States and our allies have prevailed," he said. Bush spoke

The Reporters— Embedded in Iraq

When U.S. and British troops went to war in Iraq, journalists went too. Some 600 reporters for television, radio, and newspapers traveled with U.S. military units. These "embedded" reporters, as they were called, were on hand as troops swept north to Baghdad. About 2,000 other journalists were on the scene independently—they weren't attached to military units. And a handful of journalists stayed in Baghdad, reporting events from the Iraqi side.

This was a big change from other recent wars. The last time journalists had free access to a war zone was during the Vietnam War. In that war, the press often pointed out gaps between official statements and actual events—which led to criticism of the military. After Vietnam, U.S. officials kept the press away from military actions.

In Iraq, the military changed its policy and invited reporters to come along. Many of the embedded reporters got some military training before the war started. Once in Iraq, they faced real danger. At least ten journalists were killed in combat situations in the war's early weeks. Embedded reporters also had to follow strict rules. They couldn't tell the exact locations of troops or targets, for example. Still, embedded reporters gave the public an on-the-spot picture of the war.

An embedded photographer uses his jacket to protect his computer from Iraq's dusty desert sands.

In an effort to find Iraq's leaders, the U.S. military gave American troops decks of playing cards with the names and pictures of "the most wanted." Saddam was the ace of spades.

from the deck of an aircraft carrier off the coast of California, standing under a huge banner that said "Mission Accomplished." But much remained to be accomplished in Iraq.

REBUILDING BEGINS

Even before major fighting ended, U.S. officials began setting up a postwar administration for the country. They met with representatives of Iraq's various ethnic and religious groups to discuss forming an interim government.

Rival groups were vying for power. They included Iraqi exiles and other longtime opponents of Saddam; the Kurds; and Shiite Muslims, who live mainly in the south and make up about 60 percent of Iraq's people. Saddam and his supporters were Sunni Muslims, and the Shiites had suffered under his rule. They weren't sorry to see him go, and thus some were willing to work with the United States. But other Shiites wanted to set up a government based on their version of Islamic law, and they opposed any U.S. role in Iraq.

An Iraqi Governing Council, with 25 members from various groups, was named on July 13. U.S. officials said a new constitution and elections would follow. Meanwhile, a U.S. ad-

ministration headed by L. Paul Bremer had the job of running the country.

For many Iraqis, daily life slowly began to improve. But lawlessness, power outages, and fuel shortages plagued a number of towns. Many Iraqis criticized the United States for not doing more to keep order and restore basic services. Anti-American protests broke out in several cities. The outlook for Iraq's economy was uncertain. Iraq has huge oil reserves, but years of United Nations economic sanctions had taken a toll. Oil production had been interrupted by the war. And anti-American forces were sabotaging oil fields and power plants, setting back efforts to rebuild.

About 150,000 coalition forces remained in Iraq. U.S. soldiers were told that they would be in Iraq for a year, to deal with the aftermath of the war. This was hard news for troops and their families. Many soldiers were reservists who had been called to active duty for what they thought would be a short time.

Guerrilla fighters continued to attack allied troops and civilians, especially Iraqis working with the Americans. U.S. officials said that Muslim terrorists from neighboring countries were joining Iraqi fighters. Terrorists exploded a truck bomb at U.N. headquarters in Baghdad on August 19. Among the more than 20 people killed was the top U.N. envoy to Iraq, Sergio Vieira de Mello, known for his work defending human rights. Another truck bomb exploded ten days later at a mosque in Najaf, south of Baghdad, killing one of Iraq's most important Shiite Muslim clerics and about 80 others.

Violence grew in late October. Anti-American forces fired rockets at a Baghdad hotel where many U.S. officials were staying and then staged a series of bombings around the city, killing 34 people. In one attack, a suicide bomber driving an ambulance packed with explosives hit the offices of the International Red Cross. Because of the violence, the United Nations, the Red Cross, and several other international groups withdrew from Baghdad. People stayed away from shops and markets, and many parents kept their children out of school.

Other attacks took place north and west of Baghdad, in areas where many Saddam loyalists lived. In separate attacks in November, anti-American forces downed several U.S. Army helicopters, killing nearly 40 American soldiers. By mid-December, more than 450 U.S. troops had died in the Iraq war. Of those, about two-thirds had died after May 1, when Bush had declared the end of major combat. More than 50 British soldiers and more than 30 soldiers and other personnel from Italy, Spain, and Japan had also died in Iraq.

HARD QUESTIONS

In October the U.N. Security Council adopted a U.S.-backed resolution recognizing

Undercover!

Special Operations Forces and intelligence agents played an important role in the Iraq war. More than 10,000 American Special Operations Forces—Navy Seals, Army Rangers, and Air Force Commandos—took part. British, Australian, and Polish special forces were also involved.

Operating in small teams, these forces worked in secret to sabotage Iraq's military and government. They helped knock out Iraqi missile launchers and other military targets. They monitored oil fields, so that Iraqi forces wouldn't set the wells on fire. U.S. special forces also led "psy-ops," or psychological operations. These were aimed at weakening the Iraqi government's hold on its military.

Coalition intelligence agents also worked in secret. Even before the war began, they were on the scene. They identified targets and told Special Operations Forces where to go. Throughout the war, intelligence agents provided up-to-the-minute information to the coalition's military leaders, allowing them to adjust strategy and even retarget air-strikes at the last minute.

The combination of military intelligence and special operations kept Iraq's military from countering the coalition invasion. And that helped keep the war short.

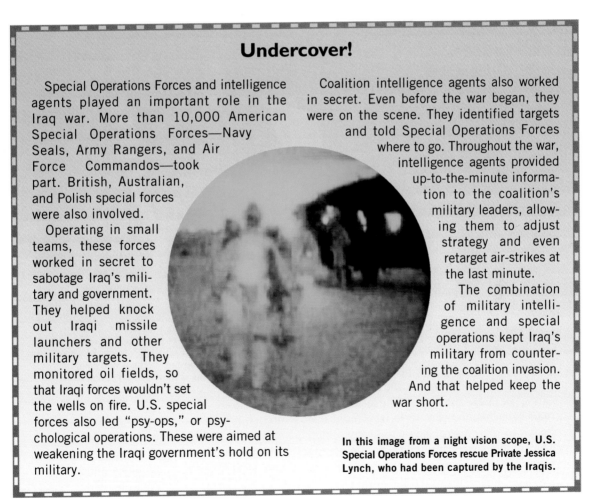

In this image from a night vision scope, U.S. Special Operations Forces rescue Private Jessica Lynch, who had been captured by the Iraqis.

the Governing Council as the interim government of Iraq. The resolution asked the Governing Council to come up with a timetable for drafting a new constitution and holding democratic elections.

The resolution also urged other countries to send troops and aid to help rebuild Iraq. But few nations stepped forward. Thus it appeared that the United States would have to bear most of the cost. In November the U.S. Congress approved $87.5 billion for operations in Iraq and Afghanistan, where U.S. forces had been stationed since 2002.

About $20 billion was for reconstruction, and the rest was to cover military costs.

Before the war, U.S. officials had said that Iraq would be able to pay for its own rebuilding through sales of its oil. But Iraq was pumping only a fraction of the oil it could produce. Officials had also predicted that Iraqis would welcome U.S. troops, and that the troops would come home quickly. Now they warned that the troops would have to stay to deal with growing violence.

Polls showed that growing numbers of Americans were questioning the Bush ad-

Secret Agents of the Deep

American and British troops got help from some unusual secret agents in the war against Iraq. The agents were marine mammals—trained dolphins and sea lions—flown to the Persian Gulf to assist with some dangerous tasks.

Two specially trained bottle-nosed Atlantic dolphins located underwater mines at Umm Qasr, an Iraqi port. Their work helped clear the way for shipments of food and other aid. The dolphins, named Makai and Tacoma, were trained to locate mines without touching them, which could cause the mines to explode. The dolphins found the mines through echolocation, a sort of natural sonar system that these animals have. Sensors mounted to their fins recorded their responses to underwater targets, telling their handlers where the mines were.

The sea lions helped protect U.S. ships in Bahrain harbor, on the Persian Gulf. The Navy brought in these animals after hearing that terrorists might use divers to attach explosives to ships' hulls. The sea lions were trained to zero in on any swimmer or diver who approached military ships or piers. They would then swim quietly

With sensors mounted on their fins, bottle-nosed dolphins helped to find mines in the waters of the Persian Gulf.

up behind the diver, slip a clamp on his leg to keep him from swimming away, and deploy a buoy to mark his position. They were also trained to flag mines and to chase intruders away by honking loudly.

Scenes from the war. Top left: U.S. Marines prepare to take over Saddam Hussein's palace in Tikrit, his hometown. Top right: Iraqi firefighters try to contain a burning oil pipeline, set ablaze by Iraqi forces. Above left: Widespread looting took place in Baghdad and other cities after the collapse of the Iraqi government. Above right: Iraqis walk past a U.S. Army tank patrolling the center of Baghdad. As the year ended, it was unclear how long U.S. military forces would remain in Iraq.

ministration's handling of Iraq. Critics raised some hard questions:

Why had no weapons of mass destruction been found? The weapons were the main reason Bush gave for going to war. And what was the plan for restoring order in Iraq and bringing the troops home? The critics warned that, by stirring up anger among young Muslims worldwide, the Iraq war had increased the risk of terrorism against the United States. And they said that Bush's "go it alone" approach had isolated the country from allies who could help in the fight against terrorism.

Bush answered by saying that the situation in Iraq was improving. In a surprise Thanksgiving visit to troops in Baghdad, he pledged that U.S. forces would "stay until the job is done."

On December 13, U.S. troops finally caught Saddam Hussein. The ex-dictator was hiding in a "spider hole"—a cramped underground chamber—near Tikrit. Saddam looked dirty, tired, and disheveled. Americans and Iraqis alike cheered his capture. It wasn't expected to bring an immediate end to fighting, but it was a huge step forward on the road to peace.

Democratic Congressman John Spratt of South Carolina uses charts to explain how the Bush administration's tax cuts have created the biggest budget deficit in U.S. history.

A WHOPPING BUDGET DEFICIT

In 2000, the U.S. government announced some good news about the federal budget. The government had taken in more money than it spent, for a record budget surplus of $236 billion. But in 2003, the budget picture was gloomy. The big budget surplus was gone. Instead, the government spent nearly $375 billion more than it took in—the largest annual budget deficit in U.S. history.

What caused the change from surplus to deficit? Economists and politicians argued about it. They debated what should be done. The growing U.S. budget deficit was part of a complex economic picture, and solving it wouldn't be easy.

FROM DEFICIT TO SURPLUS

The United States has seen budget deficits before. In fact, during the 1980's, the federal government borrowed billions of dollars every year to cover growing budget deficits. This pushed the United States deep into debt. From 1980 to 1990, the national debt (the total of all the yearly borrowings) more than tripled, rising to over $3 trillion!

Concerned about the growing debt, the government took steps to cut spending and raise some taxes. Those steps helped rein in yearly deficits during the 1990's. The 1990's also saw the longest economic boom in U.S. history. Unemployment fell, and personal incomes rose. As the economy grew, so did the taxes and other revenues collected by the government. By the end of the 1990's, the federal budget had a surplus. More surpluses were forecast for the years ahead.

Democrats and Republicans didn't agree on what to do with the surpluses. Republicans wanted to cut taxes, to keep more money in taxpayers' hands. Democrats wanted to use some of the money to pay down the national debt and some to pay for programs such as Social Security and Medicare. These programs provide retirement and health benefits for older Americans. Their cost is expected to rise sharply in coming years as the many members of the "baby boom" generation—those born soon after World War II—reach retirement age.

While Democratic President Bill Clinton was in office, the government began to pay down the national debt. But in 2001, Republican George W. Bush became president, and the policy changed.

FROM SURPLUS TO DEFICIT

In June 2001, President Bush signed legislation that would cut taxes by $1.35 trillion over ten years. But by that time, clouds were beginning to darken the budget outlook. The stock market had fallen, and many people had lost money. The U.S. economy had entered a recession, a time in which its gross domestic product (the total value of the goods and services produced) shrank. Many workers were losing their jobs. That meant the government would take in less money than had been forecast.

The terrorist attacks of September 11, 2001, were another blow. In response to the attacks, the United States beefed up domestic security and went to war in Afghanistan, to root out terrorists based there. Those were costs no one had foreseen. The combination of tax cuts, the shrinking economy, and rising expenses meant that the government once again would spend more than it took in. Once again, it would be forced to borrow.

The government took steps to try to revive the economy. The main step was to cut interest rates. Low interest rates make it easy for people and businesses to borrow money for new spending, and that helps create demand for goods and services. But recovery was slow to come. Consumers responded to the low interest rates by buying. Home sales boomed, thanks to low mortgage interest rates. But businesses held back from hiring workers and buying new equipment.

In 2003, there were some signs of growth, but unemployment was still high. And the country faced a huge new expense—war in Iraq. President Bush blamed the $375 billion federal budget deficit of 2003 mainly on the war in Iraq, national security, and the lingering effects of the recession. He held firm in support of his tax cuts, saying they would stimulate the economy. In fact, in May 2003 he signed another tax-cut package, this one worth $350 billion. His idea was that if taxpayers had more money in their pockets, they would spend it—and that would help businesses.

But Democrats said there were better ways to help the economy grow. They also pointed out that the tax cuts mostly benefited corporations and wealthy people, not average people. The richest 1 percent of the population would get 29 percent of the benefits, while the poorest 20 percent received practically nothing.

MORE BUDGET WOES

Meanwhile, most of the states faced their own budget crises. The economic downturn hurt their revenues, too. So did the federal tax cuts, because state income taxes are coupled to federal taxes. States could also expect less money from the cash-strapped federal government.

California and several other states faced huge budget shortfalls. Laws strictly limit the states' ability to borrow money, so they were forced to cut services and raise taxes. In Oregon, school officials had to let kids out weeks early for summer vacation. In California, voters were so angered by their state's budget problems that they tossed out their governor, Gray Davis, in a historic recall election. But it wasn't clear how his replacement, actor Arnold Schwarzenegger, would solve the problem.

With a presidential election coming up in 2004, politicians in both parties were leery of upsetting voters. No one wanted to raise taxes or cut popular services. The federal government continued to borrow to cover its growing deficits. Bush administration officials said this wasn't a problem—the deficits would melt away when the economy finally began to grow. But critics pointed to the mounting national debt, which stood at about $7 trillion by late 2003. As the debt grew, they warned, so would the cost of paying interest on it. The United States would be paying interest on the debt for many years to come.

SARS: A MYSTERIOUS ILLNESS

Doctors and other health-care workers around the world faced a serious threat in 2003—an outbreak of a new disease. The illness was called SARS, for *severe acute respiratory syndrome*. By the time the outbreak was declared under control, more than 8,000 people worldwide had come down with SARS, and almost 10 percent of them had died.

While the outbreak was stopped, health officials knew that SARS could return. They also knew that other new diseases could emerge at any time. Their experience in 2003 provided some lessons in how to handle future outbreaks of the disease.

THE OUTBREAK

SARS is caused by a virus, and it's a lot like the flu. Its signs include high fever, aches, coughing, and shortness of breath. In some cases, SARS causes pneumonia, a serious infection of the lungs.

Researchers think the first SARS cases probably appeared in late 2002 in the southern Chinese province of Guangdong. The virus may have hopped from animals to people, perhaps workers in farming or the food industry. Chinese officials didn't pick up those early cases, however, and SARS wasn't identified until February 2003. By that time, travelers had already begun to spread the illness. Cases of

SARS appeared in Hong Kong, Vietnam, and beyond. Health officials realized that they were dealing with a new disease—one that could spread worldwide. In mid-March, the World Health Organization (WHO) issued a global alert about SARS. Over the next few months, the illness spread to more than two dozen countries around the world.

The vast majority of cases were in China, Hong Kong, Taiwan, and Singapore. Outside of Asia, Canada was hardest hit, especially in Toronto. Canada had a total of 251 cases and 43 deaths. In the United States there were 29 cases of SARS, mostly among people returning from trips to Asia. All recovered.

FIGHTING SARS

Health workers fought the outbreak on two fronts. On one front, scientists rushed to learn more about the virus. They determined that the virus was probably a new form of coronavirus. Coronaviruses are a group of viruses that appear to have a halo or crown (corona) when viewed under a microscope. Other forms of coronavirus cause some common colds.

SARS was hard to diagnose because its symptoms resembled those of many other respiratory infections. In fact, many people who thought they had symptoms of SARS turned out to have common illnesses like colds and flu.

Young ballet dancers in Hong Kong . . . a bride and groom in China . . . travelers in Toronto: People around the world tried to take precautions against the mysterious illness called SARS in 2003.

of the illness. However, doctors doubted that these masks did much to stop the spread of the disease. The virus was so small that it was able to get through most masks. Health-care workers wore a special type of mask designed to block viruses, which offered better protection.

WHO warned travelers to avoid places hard hit by the outbreak, including Guangdong, Hong Kong, and briefly Toronto. This was the first time WHO had issued such a warning.

In those places, the SARS outbreak was hard on hotels, restaurants, and other businesses that served travelers. But the public health measures worked. WHO declared the outbreak over in July, less than four months after the agency issued its first warning.

Health officials know that SARS can still pose a threat. And they know that, with millions of people traveling by air all over the world, infectious diseases like SARS can spread fast. If another outbreak occurs, they hope to recognize and contain it quickly.

Because of this, researchers worked to develop a lab test that would identify the virus. They also hoped to develop a vaccine. Meanwhile, public health workers fought the virus on another front—trying to halt its spread.

Like cold viruses, SARS probably spreads through coughing and sneezing. People are most likely to get the virus through close contact—kissing or hugging, sharing eating or drinking utensils, talking to someone within a few feet, touching a victim, or touching a surface contaminated by droplets from a cough or sneeze.

To stop the spread of SARS, health-care workers practiced strict infection control. Patients were isolated, and those who cared for them wore surgical masks and gloves. People who had come in close contact with SARS victims were quarantined—in most cases, told to stay home for ten days—to make sure they weren't carrying the disease.

In parts of China that had many cases, schools were closed. People took to wearing surgical masks in public places. Newspapers and magazines ran pictures of people wearing the masks, so the masks became a symbol

STOP THAT GERM!

During the SARS outbreak, health officials encouraged everyone to take some simple precautions to help prevent the spread of many infectious diseases, including colds and flu. The viruses that cause these diseases spread in the tiny droplets produced when an infected person coughs or sneezes. If you're close by you may pick up the droplets directly. Or the droplets may land on an object that you touch. If you then touch your mouth, nose, or eyes, you can pick up the virus. To prevent that:

Wash your hands often with soap and water or alcohol-based hand rubs.

Avoid touching your eyes, nose, and mouth with unclean hands.

Cover your nose and mouth with a tissue when coughing or sneezing— and encourage people around you to do the same.

Terrorism was a major international concern during 2003. Above: In Saudi Arabia in May, terrorists linked to Al Qaeda attacked residential compounds for Americans and other Westerners, killing 25.

AROUND THE WORLD

Terrorism and the spread of nuclear weapons topped international concerns through much of 2003. Following is a rundown of some of the year's major events.

INTERNATIONAL TERRORISM

Deadly bombings were carried out in far-flung parts of the world by terrorists with ties to Al Qaeda, the group behind the September 11, 2001, attacks in the United States. Al Qaeda and similar groups follow a radical form of Islam. They violently oppose Western countries and anyone who tolerates Western values.

Some progress was made in the fight to stop these groups. Khalid Sheikh Mohammed, the terrorist thought to have planned the September 11 attacks and other bombings, was arrested on March 1 in Pakistan. Officials said he was a key leader of Al Qaeda who had recruited and supplied money to members, planned actions, and made sure those actions were carried out. His arrest was a blow to the group's ability to plan and carry out large-scale attacks. But two top leaders of Al Qaeda, Osama bin Laden and Ayman al-Zawahiri, remained at large. And while Al Qaeda may have been weakened, it was far from crippled.

Saudi Arabia saw several devastating attacks. Al Qaeda has roots in this oil-rich Mideast kingdom—Osama bin Laden, the terrorist group's leader, was born there, and 15 of the 19 September 11 terrorists were Saudis. Al Qaeda has long called for the overthrow of the Saudi royal family for allowing American military bases in the country. U.S. troops pulled out in 2003, but Saudi Arabia remained a terrorist target.

The most serious attacks were in Riyadh, the capital. Terrorists targeted guarded compounds that were home to foreigners. On May 12, terrorists driving vehicles loaded with explosives shot their way into three compounds where Americans and other Westerners lived. They set off the car bombs, killing 25 people including 8 Americans. Nearly 200 other people were wounded, and 9 terrorists also died. The Saudi government launched a nationwide security crackdown, and about 600 suspects with ties to Al Qaeda were arrested. But terrorists struck again on November 8, hitting a housing compound where most residents were Arabs from Lebanon. At least 17 were killed, and more than 120 wounded.

Terrorists struck in other countries, too. In the North African country of Morocco, bombs went off at a social club, a hotel, and other locations in Casablanca, Morocco's largest city, on May 16. At least 43 people died, most of them Moroccans. Again, Al Qaeda was suspected. On the other side of the world, in Indonesia, a car bomb exploded outside a hotel in Jakarta on August 6. At least ten people died in the attack, and about 150 were injured. The bombing was thought to have been carried out by a terrorist group with links to Al Qaeda.

In Istanbul, Turkey, terrorists set off truck bombs outside a synagogue (*right*), and the British consulate (*below*) in two separate incidents in November. More than 50 people died in the bombings.

Istanbul, Turkey, was the scene of shocking attacks. On November 15 terrorists set off truck bombs outside two synagogues, and five days later two trucks packed with explosives blew up near the British consulate and the headquarters of a British-based bank. More than 50 people died in the bombings. Turkish authorities arrested at least ten people, all members of extremist groups that had loose links to Al Qaeda.

Officials were also worried about the threat of attacks in Malaysia, the Philippines, and other parts of Asia, and in East Africa. They urged Westerners to avoid these regions. And they warned that attacks in Europe and the United States were possible, too.

In December a special committee of the U.N. Security Council issued a report on progress in the fight against terrorism. Security Council resolutions require countries to identify terrorist groups and people associated with them, and to take steps to keep them from crossing borders or getting money and weapons. The report warned that these efforts were being weakened by a lack of international

In Afghanistan, construction workers prepare a road for paving. Rebuilding went slowly in that war-torn country.

cooperation and, in many countries, a lack of resolve. As a result, money and weapons were still flowing to terrorists, and Al Qaeda's influence was spreading. Iraq in particular had become "a fertile ground" for the network, the report said. There, U.S. forces were still trying to establish order after overthrowing the dictator Saddam Hussein in April.

AFGHANISTAN

U.S. troops fought to drive terrorists out of Afghanistan in 2001 and 2002, and in 2003 the United States and its allies still had about 11,500 troops there. But Afghanistan's future was looking shaky.

The United States took the fight against terrorism to Afghanistan because it was Al Qaeda's base of operations at the time of the September 11, 2001, attacks. The Taliban, the Islamic militia that then ruled most of Afghanistan, sheltered the terrorist group.

After the United States and its allies drove the Taliban from power and shut down terrorist training camps, a new leader, Hamid Karzai, was chosen. And the United States and other donors pledged $4.5 billion to help rebuild the country, which had been torn by years of civil war.

But rebuilding went slowly, much of the aid money never arrived, and in 2003 Afghanistan wasn't at peace. Fighters loyal to the Taliban and Al Qaeda still roamed territory in the mountains of eastern Afghanistan, slipping back and forth across the border with Pakistan. They often attacked U.S. troops, aid workers, and Afghan officials. Except in Kabul, the capital, the Afghan government had little control. There was no true national army or police force. An international peacekeeping force was charged with keeping order in Kabul. During 2003, the North Atlantic Treaty Organization (NATO) assumed leadership of this force.

Elsewhere in the country, regional warlords were gaining power. Many of these warlords had been given arms and aid by the United States during the fight against the Taliban. But in 2003 they were fighting each other—and turning to the drug trade to raise money. Opium poppies, the source of heroin and other illegal narcotics, were a major crop.

The violence slowed the flow of aid and blocked the rebuilding of roads and schools. International agencies weren't able to do all they hoped to do. In some places, U.S. military engineers stepped in to help with rebuilding. But the main focus for the U.S. military shifted to Iraq in 2003, and the forces that remained in Afghanistan concentrated on hunting for remnants of Al Qaeda and the Taliban.

Taliban fighters stepped up their attacks in the fall, showing renewed strength. There seemed to be a growing risk that the Taliban would regain control of at least part of the country. That would mean a return to the extremists' strict religious rules, banning music and barring women from work and school.

Critics faulted U.S. policies for Afghanistan's growing problems. They said that more troops and more aid were needed to keep Afghanistan from once again becoming a sanctuary for terrorists.

ISRAEL AND THE PALESTINIANS

The conflict between Israel and the Palestinian Arabs is one of the most troublesome and long-running problems facing the world. In 2003 there were hopes that a new "road map" for peace, proposed by the United States and other nations, would lead to a solution. But it wasn't to be.

The conflict goes back to 1947, when the United Nations divided what was then the territory of Palestine into separate Jewish and Arab states. Israel was created the next year as a homeland for the Jewish people. But the Arabs of Palestine and neighboring countries didn't accept the U.N. decision. Arab countries immediately invaded Israel. Israel won the war, and some 700,000 Palestinian Arabs fled Israel for Arab-held territories. Many settled in the West Bank (on the west side of the Jordan River) and the Gaza Strip (on the Mediterranean coast). Israel gained control of those territories in 1967, during one of three later Arab-Israeli wars.

The Palestinians have long demanded an inde-

A Palestinian youth holds a smoke bomb. Violence between Israelis and Palestinians continued to erupt throughout the year.

pendent state in the West Bank and the Gaza Strip. In peace talks during the 1990's, they won partial self-rule. They set up a government, the Palestinian Authority, led by Yasir Arafat. But then talks between the Israelis and Palestinians broke down. Violence erupted in September 2000 and hasn't stopped since. Palestinian terrorists have staged bombings that have killed hundreds of Israelis. Israel has answered by sending troops into Palestinian towns.

The "roadmap" peace plan was drawn up by the United States, the European Union, the United Nations, and Russia in December 2002, but the United States put off the plan's release for four months. U.S. officials said that Arafat hadn't done enough to stop terrorists and thus stood in the way of peace. The plan had to wait for a new Palestinian cabinet, which would share power with him. That cabinet, led by Prime Minister Mahmoud Abbas, took office on April 30.

A Palestinian reads a newspaper outlining the details of the symbolic peace plan called the Geneva Accord.

The plan set out three stages on the road to peace. In the first stage, the Palestinians were to affirm Israel's right to exist in peace and security; stop terrorist attacks against Israel and do away with the groups that carry out the attacks; and hold free, open, and fair elections. Israel was to affirm the Palestinians' right to an independent state; stop building Jewish settlements in Palestinian territory; dismantle illegal settlements built since March 2001; and withdraw from areas Israeli troops had occupied during the most recent fighting.

In the second stage, the Palestinians would approve a new constitution, and an international conference would create a Palestinian state with provisional borders. In the third stage, a second international conference would give final approval to the independent state. The plan looked for that to happen in 2005.

But roadblocks popped up right away. A brief truce collapsed in August when Palestinian terrorists killed 20 people in a suicide bombing in Jerusalem. Israel canceled plans to turn over occupied cities to Palestinian control, froze high-level talks, and imposed tight security on the West Bank.

Abbas, who had vowed to control the terrorists, was unable to do so partly because Arafat remained in charge of Palestinian security forces. Abbas resigned on September 6, and it took the Palestinians two months to put together a new cabinet. A new prime minister, Ahmed Qurei, and a new cabinet finally took office in November. But Arafat was still in charge of the security forces.

With the official peace process stalled, attention turned to a symbolic peace plan drawn up by Israelis and Palestinians who didn't represent their governments. The plan's main authors were former Israeli Justice Minister Yossi Beilin and former Palestinian Information Minister Yasser Abed Rabbo. It was called the Geneva Accord because it was formally announced in Geneva, Switzerland, on December 1.

The Geneva Accord offered solutions to the thorniest issues between the two sides. It called for a Palestinian state to include the Gaza Strip, nearly all of the West Bank, and Arab neighborhoods of the city of Jerusalem, Israel's capital. Most Israeli settlers in the West Bank would have to leave their homes. Palestinians would stop demanding a "right of return" for refugees who fled Israel in 1948 and their descendants.

The plan had support from former U.S. President Jimmy Carter, and it was praised by U.S. Secretary of State Colin Powell. Arafat also praised it. But Palestinian militants rejected it, and so did Israeli Prime Minister Ariel Sharon.

IRAN

Iran has been ruled by a strict Islamic government since 1979. In 2003, opposition to that government was growing—but efforts to bring greater freedom to the country made little headway. And the United States charged that Iran was hiding terrorists and trying to develop nuclear weapons.

Iranian students link arms during a demonstration for government reform in December. The banner reads "Freedom and Equality."

Liberia's Civil War

International peacekeepers stepped in to halt a civil war in Liberia in 2003. This West African country was founded by freed American slaves in the 1800's and thus has long-standing ties to the United States. Its civil war started in 1989, when Charles Taylor led a rebellion against then-president Samuel K. Doe. Taylor took power and ran a military government until 1997, when he was elected president. All along, he fought one rebel group after another. He also stirred up conflict in nearby countries, and a U.N. court charged him with war crimes for supporting fighters in neighboring Sierra Leone.

The situation in Liberia took a sharp turn for the worse in the summer of 2003. Rebels pushed their way to the edge of Monrovia, the capital. Hundreds of civilians were killed, and refugees poured into the city. Food, water, and medicine grew scarce. The United States was asked to send troops to enforce a cease-fire, so that aid could reach the city. But U.S. President George W. Bush said that other African nations should take the first steps.

Liberians celebrate the arrival of West African peacekeeping forces (*above*) and U.S. Marines (*below*) to their country.

A West African peacekeeping force began to arrive in early August, to the cheers of war-weary civilians. A few days later a small number of U.S. Marines arrived. More Marines were standing by in warships off the coast.

Taylor resigned on August 11 and left for Nigeria, where he had been offered asylum. A week later, the government signed a peace agreement with the rebels. The two sides agreed to share power for two years, after which elections would be held. Gyude Bryant, a 54-year-old businessman, was picked to lead the government. In the fall, a U.N. peacekeeping force took the place of the West African troops.

Iran's reform movement blossomed in 1997, when Mohammad Khatami, a reformer, won the country's first free presidential elections since the Islamic republic was established. But hard-line religious leaders still held the most powerful positions in the government and controlled the courts and security forces. They used their power to block democratic reforms and jail those who spoke against them.

By 2003 many Iranians were losing faith in Khatami. They still wanted reform, but it wasn't clear how they could bring about change. In June students in Teheran, the capital, staged protests that drew thousands of supporters. Security forces arrested more than

4,000 people, throwing a chill on the reform movement. But reformers were energized in October when Shirin Ebadi, an Iranian lawyer, writer, and teacher, won the Nobel Peace Prize for her work promoting democracy and human rights. In making the award, the Nobel committee said it hoped to encourage reform in Iran and to show that Islam and human rights could go hand in hand.

Meanwhile, in May, the United States accused Iran of harboring ter-rorists and carrying on a secret nuclear-weapons program. Iran denied these charges, saying that it had arrested several Al Qaeda members and that its nuclear program was aimed only at producing electricity. But later in the year, Iran admitted that it had secretly produced small amounts of enriched ura-nium. The International Atomic Energy

Hunger: A Worldwide Threat

The biggest health threat in the world isn't a disease or a harmful habit like smoking. It's hunger. In 2003 a report from the World Health Organi-zation (WHO) ranked lack of food, especially for mothers and children, at the top of the list of health risks. The report said that lack of food caused 3.4 million deaths worldwide in 2000.

The world produces enough food for every-one, experts say. But the food doesn't always get to people who need it. One out of every seven people on Earth goes hungry at least some of the time. The problem is worst in poor countries. About 170 million children in poor countries are underweight because they don't get enough food. Often their par-ents work long hours for very low wages, sometimes less than a dollar a day. It's a strug-gle for them to get the food their children need. In contrast, many people in richer countries, in-cluding the United States, are overweight.

But hunger is still a problem in the United States. About 33 million Americans, including 13 million children, lived in "food insecure" house-holds in 2000. They weren't sure they would be able to meet their basic food needs. The threat of hunger was greatest in households headed by single mothers. When people don't get enough to eat, they suffer from poor nutri-tion. They are more likely to get sick and die. Children aren't able to grow, learn, and play as they should.

Governments, private groups, and interna-tional organizations are fighting hunger. They help get food to people hit by disasters and

other emergencies. They also help people find ways to produce and buy their own food. Kids are help-ing, too—by raising money for organizations that fight hunger and organizing food drives for local groups that distribute food to the poor.

Above: Hungry children in Africa eat food provided by a United Nations agency. Left: Junior high school students in Brownsburg, Indiana, volunteer at a local food bank.

Agency (IAEA) also determined that Iran had produced some plutonium. While Iranian officials insisted that their purpose was peaceful, these materials could be used to make nuclear weapons.

Iran promised to stop its uranium enrichment, at least temporarily, and allow the IAEA to make spot checks of its nuclear facilities. The IAEA issued a stern warning to Iran, but it stopped short of turning the matter over to the U.N. Security Council for stronger action.

NORTH KOREA

Late in 2002, North Korea alarmed the world by admitting that it had a secret nuclear-weapons program. In 2003, officials from this secretive Communist country, led by Kim Jong Il, let it be known that they had at least one nuclear weapon and were gathering material to make more. That raised a lot of concern because a nuclear-armed North Korea would be a threat to peace in Asia.

North Korea and South Korea were divided at the end of World War II. In the 1950's they fought a bitter war, in which the United States and other Western nations fought on the side of South Korea. Today South Korea is a democracy, while North Korea is a Communist dictatorship and one of the world's poorest countries.

North Korea had been developing nuclear weapons in the early 1990's, using its nuclear power plants to produce plutonium. In 1994 the country had agreed to shut down those nuclear reactors and stop the program. But in October 2002, North Korea admitted that it had revived its nuclear-weapons program.

In the spring of 2003 the North Koreans expelled inspectors from the IAEA and restarted the closed plants. They also threatened to end the cease-fire with South Korea. In April they announced that they had at least one nuclear weapon and said that their decision to test, sell, or use nuclear weapons would depend on what the United States did. They said they had gone ahead with the weapons program because they believed the United States would invade their country after finishing the Iraq war. U.S. officials

South Koreans protest North Korea's nuclear-weapons program. One demonstrator wears a mask of North Korean leader Kim Jong Il.

said there were no invasion plans and that North Korea was making nuclear threats as a way to get aid and concessions from other countries.

The crisis simmered for months as North Korea continued to develop its weapons. Officials from both Koreas, the United States, Russia, Japan, and China were involved in several rounds of talks during the year, but they made no progress toward settling the issue. At year's end it still wasn't clear whether North Korea could be convinced to end its nuclear-weapons program.

A voter in the Czech Republic casts her ballot in a referendum to approve the country's membership in the European Union (EU). Ten nations were preparing to join the EU in 2004.

THE EUROPEAN UNION: GROWTH AND CHANGE

The year 2003 was a historic one for the European Union (EU). This organization of European nations was preparing to grow from fifteen to twenty-five members in 2004. For the first time, countries of Eastern Europe would join.

The goal of the EU is to establish economic and political union among member nations. With the admission of ten new members, the EU would be the largest and richest group of nations in the world. Its population would increase by some 75 million, to about 450 million people.

BORN FROM WAR

The idea for the European Union was born after World War II, which left much of the continent devastated. Many people believed that the best hope for Europe's future lay in a union of European countries. In particular, an economic union would promote trade by eliminating barriers such as tariffs (taxes on imports) between members. Countries usually impose these barriers to protect their industries from foreign competition. But free trade among nations helps goods find a wider market, and that helps a country's economy grow.

In Europe, the first steps toward removing trade barriers were taken in the 1950's by six countries: Belgium, France, Italy, Luxembourg, the Netherlands, and West Germany. In 1951, representatives of those countries signed the Treaty of Paris. It established the European Coal and Steel Community (ECSC), which eliminated barriers to trade in coal and steel among members.

The success of the ECSC led to greater cooperation. In 1957, the six countries signed the Treaties of Rome. The treaties established the European Economic Community (EEC), or Common Market, and the European Atomic Energy Community (Euratom). The EEC sought to end the remaining trade barriers among its members by forming a single economic union, so that goods, services, labor, and capital could move freely. Euratom sought to promote the peaceful use of atomic energy. The EEC was a success, and that led to growth in its membership. Britain, Denmark, and Ireland joined in 1973, followed by Greece in 1981, Portugal and Spain in 1986, and Austria, Finland, and Sweden in 1995.

Barriers to trade didn't fall all at once, however. While many tariffs were eliminated, other barriers remained. For example, West Germany barred imported beer, while Italy kept German pasta out of the country. In the 1980's, members agreed to end such barriers. To do this, they had to take a major step: They had to give up some power. Until this point, community laws, or directives, had to be passed by all the member countries. But in 1987, the members agreed to abide by directives that were passed by just a majority. Thus, in trade matters, the community could overrule the individual governments of its member countries.

Members took another far-reaching step toward closer ties with the 1992 Treaty on European Union, better known as the Maastricht Treaty. This treaty set up the framework for a future economic and monetary union. In order to qualify, member nations had to get their national budgets under control by reducing debts and inflation.

The group became known as the European Union in 1993. Twelve of the fifteen members of the EU adopted a common currency, the euro, in 1999. The euro replaced their national currencies in 2002.

A MAJOR EXPANSION

From the end of World War II through the 1980's, the countries of Eastern Europe were under Communist rule. But Communism collapsed as the 1990's began, and these countries began developing Western-style market economies. They were eager to join the EU, as were some Western nations that had remained outside the union. A plan to increase EU membership was set out in a treaty drawn up in Nice, France, and signed in February 2001.

Fourteen of the EU members approved the Treaty of Nice that year. But the treaty hit a roadblock when Irish voters rejected it in a referendum in July 2001. However, a second referendum was held in October 2002. This time, supporters convinced Irish voters that their country would have a better future in a bigger EU. Irish voters said yes, by 63 percent to 37 percent. The EU growth plan, therefore, received a green light.

At a summit meeting in Copenhagen, Denmark, in December 2002, the EU approved the admission of ten new members: Cyprus, the Czech Republic, Estonia, Hungary, Latvia, Lithuania, Malta, Poland, Slovakia, and Slovenia. The ten members-to-be signed a treaty at a ceremony in Athens, Greece, on April 16–17, 2003. All except Cyprus later approved EU membership in referendums; Cyprus didn't hold a vote. Formal admission was set for May 2004.

The EU also endorsed a new draft constitution in 2003. The draft provides for two new

The Euro

On January 1, 2002, twelve EU members replaced their national currencies with a new common currency, the euro. The euro was introduced to bring EU members closer together. It has proved to be a particular help to travelers. They no longer have to exchange one currency for another as they travel among the participating countries.

Of the fifteen EU members, only Britain, Denmark, and Sweden didn't adopt the euro. In Denmark and Sweden, voters rejected the euro in referendums. Although Britain didn't hold a vote on the issue, polls there showed strong support for keeping the pound as the national currency.

The ten nations that are to join the EU in 2004 have said that they would like to adopt the euro. First, though, they will need to meet EU standards for budget deficits, unemployment, inflation, and other economic issues.

posts. One is a full-time president of the European Council, which is made up of the leaders of member countries and decides long-term goals for the union. The other is a foreign minister, who would direct a common foreign policy for the EU. The constitution must still be approved by the member states, and several individual countries have raised concerns about parts of it. All the same, it represents another step forward on the road to unity.

NEWSMAKERS

Action-movie star **Arnold Schwarzenegger,** a newcomer to politics, became governor of California in 2003. Schwarzenegger (above, with Maria Shriver, his wife) replaced Democratic Governor Gray Davis after a recall election held on October 7.

Early in the year, Davis's opponents launched a petition drive to force the state's first recall election. The ballot for this special vote asked two questions. Should Davis, who was re-elected less than a year earlier, be recalled? And, if so, who should replace him? The ballot listed 135 candidates. Any state resident who was a U.S. citizen, gathered 65 signatures, and paid a filing fee could run.

California voters were unhappy over the state's budget and other economic problems, and a majority chose to recall Davis. Schwarzenegger, 56, was the clear choice in the second part of the ballot. He won with about 47 percent of the vote. Lieutenant Governor Cruz Bustamante, a Democrat, came in second, with just under 33 percent.

Schwarzenegger was born in Austria and first gained fame as a bodybuilder. He won the Mr. Universe title in 1967 and then moved to California. He was featured in the 1977 film *Pumping Iron,* a documentary about bodybuilding. Five years later he landed his first big film role, as the lead in *Conan the Barbarian.* Since then he has been best known for starring roles in *The Terminator* (1984) and its two sequels.

The popular star took office in November. Californians watched to see how he would deal with the state budget and other problems in the months ahead.

British Prime Minister **Tony Blair** was America's strongest ally in the 2003 war against Iraq. Blair (here, addressing the U.S. Congress in July) backed U.S. President George W. Bush's efforts to topple Iraqi dictator Saddam Hussein, and thousands of British troops served alongside U.S. troops in Iraq. That made Blair, prime minister since 1997, the foreign leader Americans admired most. But his stand cost him support in Britain, where many people opposed the war. His popularity sank further when his government was accused of exaggerating claims that Iraq was hiding banned weapons. Those claims were the main grounds for the war.

Britain's **Prince William** turned 21 on June 21, 2003, and the royal family celebrated in a big way. More than 300 people, from dukes and earls to William's school pals, were invited to Windsor Castle for an African-themed costume party. William, a student at the University of St. Andrews in Scotland, stands second in line to the British throne. He's the grandson of Queen Elizabeth II, Britain's reigning monarch, and his father is Prince Charles, heir to the throne. His mother, Princess Diana, died in 1997. Many people say that William, with his blond hair and blue eyes, looks a lot like his mother. His natural charm has won him fans around the world.

"I only regret that I have but one life to lose for my country." Those famous last words were spoken by **Nathan Hale,** a hero of the Revolutionary War. Hale (above) was hanged as a spy by the British in 1776, and in 2003 new details of his capture turned up.

Hale, a schoolteacher who joined the Connecticut militia, volunteered to slip behind British lines on Long Island and gather information for General George Washington. What happened there is set out in the newfound account, written by a Connecticut storekeeper who supported the British. The manuscript (right) was given to the Library of Congress in 2003.

Dressed in civilian clothes and pretending to be looking for work, Hale drew the attention of Robert Rogers, a British officer. Rogers chatted with Hale and pretended that he was also an American spy. Hale was fooled and told Rogers the real reason for his trip. He was arrested and hanged. Telling his secret to a stranger showed that Hale wasn't a very clever spy—but he was a great patriot all the same.

During the 2003 war in Iraq, Americans were captivated by the story of **Private Jessica Lynch.** Taken prisoner on March 23, the third day of the war, she was rescued nine days later in what was portrayed as a daring raid by U.S. Special Forces. U.S. officials said it was the first time an American prisoner of war had been snatched from enemy hands since World War II, and it was the first time a woman had ever been rescued in that way. Lynch, 19, was hailed as a hero. But by her own account, she hadn't been in as much danger as early reports suggested. She told the real story in an authorized biography, *I Am a Soldier, Too: The Jessica Lynch Story,* which was published in November.

Lynch's unit, an Army maintenance convoy, was ambushed after taking a wrong turn near Nasiriyah, in southern Iraq. Eleven soldiers were killed, among them Lori Piestewa, Lynch's friend and the first woman to die in the Iraq war. Lynch's gun jammed, and she was unable to return fire. She was severely injured when the vehicle in which she was riding crashed, and she blacked out. She woke up hours later in an Iraqi hospital. The doctors and nurses there treated her kindly and never struck her, she said, and they put up no resistance when her rescuers arrived.

Lynch spent months recovering from her injuries. In interviews, she said she was upset by the exaggerations in reports of her ordeal and in a made-for-television movie that aired in November.

Lynch's story did put a spotlight on the growing role of women in the military. There are now more than 200,000 women in the U.S. armed forces, about 15 percent of the total. And women are taking on more military jobs than ever before.

ANIMALS

"Me first!" the frog on the left seems to be saying. These are red-eyed tree frogs, from South America. Frogs have been living on Earth for around 180 million years, but today they are in trouble. Loss of habitat, disease, pollution, and climate change are some of the many problems that have caused frogs to disappear in places where they were once common.

THE MYSTERY OF THE VANISHING FROGS

On cool spring nights, a croaking chorus of frogs is a familiar sound around many woodland ponds. Yet in many places, this froggy melody has mysteriously disappeared. Scientists investigating this trend have discovered something alarming: All over the world, the number of frogs is declining. The scientists aren't sure why this is happening, and they are hurrying to learn more about these fascinating creatures.

OUTLIVING THE DINOSAURS

Frogs are one of the oldest kinds of living things. They first appeared on Earth about 180 million years ago, and they outlived the dinosaurs and many other creatures that have disappeared. Today there are several thousand different species (kinds) of frogs and their close relatives, toads. They live in nearly all parts of the world, except the frozen polar regions and some remote islands. Frogs are amphibians—they spend part of their lives in water and part on land. Scientists think that amphibians are a link between fish, which live only in water, and animals that live only on land. They believe that amphibians developed from fish, and that reptiles and other land animals developed from early amphibians.

The life cycle of a typical frog mirrors this change from water to land. Most frogs lay their eggs in water. When the eggs hatch, tiny tadpoles swim out. A tadpole looks like a fish, with a tail for swimming and gills for breathing in water. But over weeks or months (depending on the kind of frog), the tadpole changes into a frog with four legs for hopping on land and lungs for breathing air.

Adult frogs share certain characteristics—moist, smooth skin, bulging eyes, four legs, no tail. But this basic body plan is just a starting point: Frogs have unique physical features and are among the most varied animals on Earth. In size alone, they range from tiny species just ½ inch (1.3 centimeters) long to the massive Goliath frog of West Africa, which is nearly 1 foot (30 centimeters) long. Size isn't the only characteristic that varies. Many of the differences among species of frogs have helped each adapt to its particular surroundings.

Scientists group the many kinds of frogs into about 20 families. Most widespread in North America are frogs that belong to the true frog and tree frog families. True frogs usually live in or near ponds and other bodies of water. They have long hind legs for jumping and webbed hind feet for swimming. North American true frogs include the leopard frog, green frog, wood frog, and pickerel frog. They also include the largest North American frog, the bullfrog, which can be up to 8 inches (20 centimeters) long.

Tree frogs, as you would guess from their name, live in trees. These frogs are small—about 2 inches (5 centimeters) long. Most have sticky little pads on their fingers and toes that help them cling to tree branches. North American tree frogs include the green tree frog, gray tree frog, California tree frog, canyon tree frog, and spring peeper, whose voice is a sure sign of spring in the eastern United States.

HOW FROGS LIVE

Frogs spend most of their time looking for food—or, more accurately, waiting for food to pass by. Most frogs eat insects, which they

Frogs are among the most varied animals on Earth, with each kind displaying its own unique features. Opposite page: Red-eyed tree frogs (*top*) of Central America use their bright eyes to see in the dark. The blue-skinned dumpy tree frog (*bottom*) makes its home in Australia. This page: Tomato frogs of Madagascar (*left*) are round and red—which is, not surprisingly, how they got their name. The striking colors of this yellow and black dart-poison frog (*below left*) warn predators to stay away. The bullfrog of North America (*below right*) is named for its deep, throaty call.

71

Did You Ever See a Purple Frog?

It's purple, about 3 inches (8 centimeters) long, and shaped like a jelly donut with a pointy nose. What is it? A rare frog that was discovered in India in 2003. Scientists say it's a once-in-a-century find.

The purple frog was found in the Western Ghats, a range of hills in southwestern India known for unusual wildlife. The frog has a puffy body and stumpy legs. Its head is small, with beady little eyes—and that pointy nose. It's so unlike other frogs that scientists have put it in a new, separate frog family. Its closest relatives live in the Seychelles, a group of islands in the Indian Ocean.

While the purple frog is new to scientists, it's not new to the world. Its ancestors were probably hopping around 130 million years ago, in the days of the dinosaurs. Back then, India and the Seychelles were part of the same land mass. They broke apart about 65 million years ago. After that, the frogs in the Seychelles evolved separately from those in India.

Scientists are calling the purple frog a "living fossil." They hope it will help them learn how modern frogs developed.

catch with their tongues. The long tongue flips out like a whip and traps the frog's prey with its sticky tip. But big frogs can tackle larger prey. The South American horned frog is big and strong enough to down mice, lizards—and even other frogs.

Whatever they eat, and wherever they live, frogs need water. Only one type of South American frog is known to actually drink. The rest absorb all the water they need through their skin. Thus even frogs that don't live in ponds need moist surroundings.

Some frogs have found ways to survive long periods without water. The spatulate-nosed tree frog crawls into a damp hole, plugs the opening with its broad head, and waits for rain. The Australian water-holding frog has an even more elaborate way to survive drought. This frog stores water in its body and then burrows into the ground. There it sheds its skin to form a cocoon that will pre-

Most frogs capture prey by quickly flicking out their sticky tongues like a whip. This European tree frog clings to a stem as it gobbles up a juicy damselfly.

Frogs are incredible jumpers (*above*). Some can leap forty times their body length! Male frogs, such as this barking tree frog (*left*), have sound sacs under their chin that they can puff out to make their voices sound louder—often to attract a mate.

vent water from escaping. The frog can survive for months this way. When rains finally come, it breaks out of its burrow.

Frogs in cold climates must also find ways to survive cold temperatures. Frogs are cold-blooded—their body temperature goes up and down with the temperature of their surroundings. Many frogs hibernate through winter in the mud at the bottoms of ponds. During hibernation, the frog's body systems slow down so that it doesn't need to breathe air. Instead, it absorbs oxygen from the water, through its skin. When spring temperatures warm the water, the frog wakes up, swims to the surface, and breathes air again.

JUMPERS AND SINGERS

Frogs have powerful hind legs and are fabulous jumpers. They leap to catch prey or to get out of harm's way. Some frogs can leap forty times their body length—an amazing feat. Many frogs are also good swimmers. They close their eyes underwater—but their eyelids are transparent, so they can still see.

Some frogs have unusual ways of getting around. The gliding frogs of Asia, for example, have webbed feet. By spreading the webs wide, they can glide from one branch of a tree to another. And the creeping frogs of Central and South America have weak hind legs. When danger threatens, they don't run away—they arch their backs, stretch out their legs, and pretend they're dead.

Because many frogs hold perfectly still much of the time and jump away quickly when danger comes near, it's easier to hear one than see one. Peeps and croaks are among the most common frog calls. But some frogs sound like tinkling bells, flutes, or even barking dogs. Green frogs make a distinctive loud "plunk," and bullfrogs call out "jug-jug-jug-o-rum." When you hear a frog, chances are that you are listening to a male frog calling to attract a mate. In many species females have no voice.

FROGS OF MANY COLORS

Many frogs are colored to blend with their surroundings. This helps them stay hidden

Once Upon a Frog!

Everyone knows the story of the frog prince—a prince is turned into an ugly frog by an evil spell, and only a kiss from a princess can turn him back into a man. This fairy tale is just one of many myths, legends, stories, and beliefs in which frogs have played an important part.

For example, because frogs, which must have moisture, often appear after a rain, they have been associated with rain in many cultures. One widespread belief was that frogs fell to the ground with rain. And in India, Europe, and South America, people long believed that frogs had the power to bring rain. Some South American Indians even worshipped a frog deity and presented it with human sacrifices.

Some North American Indians saw in the patterns on the moon's surface the shape of a frog, rather than the "man in the moon" that Europeans saw. And in the beliefs of some Indian groups, an eclipse occurred when a giant frog swallowed the moon.

Even after such beliefs died out, frogs continued to capture people's imaginations. In the 1800's the American writer Mark Twain wrote a famous short story about a frog-jumping contest in Calaveras County, California; today, the contest he described is re-enacted every year in Calaveras and in many other places. Also, one of the best-known characters of classic children's literature is Mr. Toad of *Wind in the Willows.* And one of the most popular characters on children's television today is a frog puppet—Kermit the Frog.

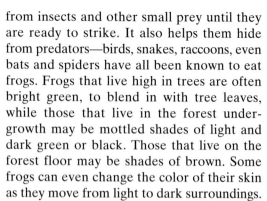

from insects and other small prey until they are ready to strike. It also helps them hide from predators—birds, snakes, raccoons, even bats and spiders have all been known to eat frogs. Frogs that live high in trees are often bright green, to blend in with tree leaves, while those that live in the forest undergrowth may be mottled shades of light and dark green or black. Those that live on the forest floor may be shades of brown. Some frogs can even change the color of their skin as they move from light to dark surroundings.

Other frogs, however, are brightly colored. They can't hide so easily—but their bright colors serve a purpose. Many brightly colored frogs have skin glands that secrete powerful poisons. The colors serve as a warning, telling would-be predators to stay away. Among these frogs are the tiny dart-poison frogs found in Central and South America. The poisons they produce affect the nervous system and muscles of an enemy, and some are extremely deadly. The poisons are so effective that they have been used by local Indians on the tips of their hunting arrows.

It helps to know something about a frog's habits to appreciate the importance of its coloring. The little red-eyed tree frog of Central America has, as its name states, bright red eyes. It also has patches of bright blue on the insides of its legs and the underside of its body. You might think that these patches would make the frog easy for predators to spot. But this frog is active only at night. When it sleeps during the day, it tucks its legs in and shows only green skin that blends with its surroundings. If a predator discovers the frog anyway, it flashes the bright blue patches. That startles the enemy and gives the frog a chance to escape.

RAISING YOUNG

Most frogs aren't very good parents. They lay their eggs in water and then leave. Many eggs are eaten by predators before they can develop into tadpoles, and many die when the water evaporates. But some kinds of frogs provide additional care for their eggs. One of these is the glass frog of South and Central America. Glass frogs lay eggs on leaves overhanging streams. The eggs are surrounded by a jellylike covering that keeps them damp. Often, a glass frog father will guard the eggs and keep them moist with water from its bladder. When the eggs hatch and the tadpoles have developed enough to swim, they drop into the water below.

Another kind of rain-forest frog, the rain frog, lays eggs in damp places on the forest floor. The mother stays nearby to guard the eggs, which look like clear bubbles. The young develop into fully formed frogs inside the giant eggs. Then they pop out and hop away.

Some frog parents carry their eggs until they hatch. Female marsupial frogs carry their eggs in pouchlike structures on their backs. In one species, the female carries the eggs until tadpoles have developed. She then heads for water, where she flexes her body, causing the pouch to open so that the tadpoles can leave and swim away. In another species, the female carries the young until they have turned into fully developed frogs. When the pouch opens, as many as 40 tiny frogs push their way out into the world.

Some frog fathers get into the act, too. Certain female dart-poison frogs lay their eggs on damp ground. When the young hatch, they wiggle onto their father's back. He becomes a walking nursery until the babies are old enough to swim. Another South American frog, the female Darwin's frog, also lays her eggs on land. They are guarded by several males for about two weeks. Then each male swallows a few of the eggs, letting them slide down into his huge vocal sac. There the eggs

Most frogs lay their eggs in water and then leave. But some frogs take greater care of their young. The female pygmy marsupial frog (*left*) tucks her eggs into special pouches on her back until they grow into tadpoles. Then the pouch opens and the tadpoles swim away. The female rain frog guards her huge bubble-like eggs (*below left*) until fully formed frogs pop out. The male Darwin's frog (*below*) swallows the female's eggs into his huge sound sac. There they grow into tiny froglets, which jump one by one out of his mouth.

Red-Legged Frogs Aren't Jumping for Joy

Mark Twain's "The Celebrated Jumping Frog of Calaveras County" is a funny short story about a California frog-jumping contest. The story made Twain famous overnight when it was published in 1865. Today it's a classic.

The town of Angels Camp, about 135 miles (217 kilometers) east of San Francisco, was the setting for Twain's tale. And every May since 1928, that town has been celebrating by holding the Jumping Frog Jubilee. Thousands of frog-jump contestants from all over the world take part in this unique event.

There are lots of frogs at the jubilee—but they're not the type that Twain wrote about. Twain's famous frogs were most likely California red-legged frogs (shown on the left in this photo). California red-legged frogs are the largest frogs native to the western United States, growing up to 5 inches (13 centimeters) long. They were common in the 1860's. But today they are rare.

The frogs' troubles started during the California Gold Rush, in the mid-1800's. Mining choked streams with mud and rock, ruining many frog habitats. Then, in the late 1800's and early 1900's, Californians developed a taste for frogs' legs. Around San Francisco and in California's Central Valley, about 80,000 frogs were killed yearly to meet the demand for this delicacy. Red-legged frogs soon became rare, so bullfrogs were brought in from the East.

That was more trouble for the red-legged frogs. Bullfrogs (shown on the right in the photo) are North America's largest frogs, much bigger than red-legged frogs. They eat insects, crayfish, other frogs, minnows, and even small snakes and young birds. And because they eat so much, they can upset the natural ecology of a site when they are introduced. In California, bullfrogs competed with red-legs for food and habitat and even preyed on the smaller frogs.

The arrival of bullfrogs was one problem for the red-legged frogs. California's growing human population was another. People were moving into areas where frogs lived. Forests were logged. Wetlands were drained. Dams were built. Livestock grazing, pesticides, and

growing towns all took their toll. The few remaining red-legged frogs were squeezed into a tiny fraction of their original range.

Since 1996, California red-legged frogs have been protected by law as a threatened species. People are working to save the wetlands where they live and to rebuild the numbers of these famous frogs.

And that's why the frogs that now line up for the Jumping Frog Jubilee are bullfrogs!

The Jumping Frog Jubilee is held at the Calaveras County Fair in Angels Camp. Frog-jump contests take place on each of the event's four days, leading up to the Grand Finals on the last day. The world-record leap was set in 1986 by a long-leaping frog named Rosie the Ribiter. Rosie jumped a whopping 21 feet, 5¾ inches (6.6 meters)!

hatch into tadpoles, which grow and gradually develop into froglets. Then, one by one, they jump fully formed out of the father's mouth.

ARE FROGS IN DANGER?

In the 1980's, scientists began to notice that there seemed to be fewer frogs. In ponds that were once filled with chirping, croaking amphibians, there were few or none to be found. Toads, salamanders, and other amphibians seemed to be vanishing, too. And the problem was occurring around the world. At a special conference held in 1990, sixteen countries on five continents reported big drops in the population of amphibians.

Why are frogs and other amphibians disappearing? Scientists aren't sure, but they think that environmental problems are to blame. Because they have thin, moist skins that readily absorb chemicals, frogs are sensitive to pollution on land and in water. Acid rain, caused by pollution from factories and automobiles, may be to blame. In some areas, frogs have been overhunted by people (frogs' legs are considered a delicacy).

But frogs are disappearing even where they aren't hunted and even in unpolluted areas, so some scientists have looked for other causes. A leading theory blames an increase in ultraviolet radiation from the sun. Normally, Earth is protected from this radiation by the ozone layer in the atmosphere. But pollution has caused the ozone layer to deteriorate, and ultraviolet radiation to increase. Research has shown that the eggs of many frogs are sensitive to one type of ultraviolet radiation, UV-B. The more UV-B the eggs are exposed to, the fewer hatch.

There are still many questions to be answered. Ultraviolet radiation can't explain the problem completely. But scientists agree that it's important to find the answers. We can't risk losing frogs, one of the oldest and most fascinating of Earth's creatures.

Frogwatch

Frogs and toads are found throughout the United States. But many people are barely aware of these animals. Now a program called Frogwatch USA is helping people learn about frogs and enlisting volunteers in the fight to save them.

Frogwatch USA is a monitoring program run by the National Wildlife Federation in partnership with the United States Geological Survey. It's modeled partly on a similar program in Canada. The program relies on volunteers to collect information about frog and toad populations in neighborhoods across the United States. Anyone can volunteer— you don't have to be a frog or toad expert. All you need is an interest in frogs and toads.

Volunteers first find out about the types of frogs that live in their area. They learn to recognize the calls of different species by listening to recordings or sound files downloaded from the Internet. Then they pick a pond or other wetland habitat in their neighborhood. They visit the site regularly to listen for frog calls, and they report the information they collect on the Frogwatch USA Web site:

www.nwf.org/frogwatchUSA/

Besides helping frogs, the program gets people involved with nature.

ODD BIRD OUT!

All these birds have traits or behaviors that make them sound too odd to be believed. But just one of them is REALLY odd—'cause it doesn't even exist! Which one is the phoney? (Solution is on page 414).

The **copterbird** gets its name from the winglike structures on top of its head, which look like the rotors of a helicopter. Scientists think that similar structures may have helped ancestors of the copterbird to hover in flight. But today the copterbird's rotors are vestigial—that is, they no longer seem to serve any purpose. These blue-jay-size birds are found mainly in the jungles of central Africa, where they feed on insects and berries. The local name for the copterbird is *ndege kofia*, which means "hat bird" or "flying hat." Images of the copterbird are frequently used in the ceremonial headdresses of the Ngbandi people.

It's easy to see how the **spoonbill** got its name. Its bill is shaped like a long-handled serving spoon. The spoonbill is a wading bird that feeds in shallow waters. The bird sweeps its partly open beak from side to side through the water, searching for small fish, insects, or other tasty treats. The bill is sensitive, so the bird knows when it has picked up something good to eat. The spoonbill also uses its bill to make loud clapping noises when it returns to its nest and greets its mate. Spoonbills live in warm, marshy areas around the world.

Like a bat, the **oilbird** spends daylight hours deep in dark caves. And like a bat, it gets around with the help of echolocation—a sort of natural sonar system. Oilbirds, which live in northern South America and the island of Trinidad, make clicking noises as they fly. The clicks bounce off the walls of the cave, and the echoes allow the bird to judge where the walls are. Adults have wingspans up to 3 feet (1 meter). Until their feathers grow in, baby birds are grossly fat, weighing up to twice as much as adults. The fat of these birds was once boiled down to make oil for torches, which is how they got their name.

Hawks, snakes, and other predators don't bother the **hooded pitohui**. This songbird, which lives on the Pacific island of New Guinea, has poisonous plumage! Its skin and feathers are laced with toxic chemicals that taste terrible, so predators leave it alone. Many insects, frogs, fish, and reptiles secrete poisons to keep predators away. But the hooded pitohui is the only bird known to have this defense. Like many other poisonous animals, the pitohui has bold coloring—which in the animal world is often a warning to predators to keep away.

The hoatzin is known as the **stinkbird**—because it has reeeally bad breath! This chicken-size bird lives in the tropical forests of South America, and it has an unusual diet. Most birds eat insects, seeds, and berries. The hoatzin eats leaves, shoots, and buds. These plant materials have fibers and chemicals that most birds can't digest. But like a cow, the hoatzin has a special chamber in its digestive tract where bacteria break down the tough plant materials. Unfortunately, the bacteria also produce smelly gasses, which the hoatzin burps up.

It isn't hard to love a hedgehog. Even though these little creatures snuffle, snort, and smell—and are far from cuddly—people everywhere seem to be captivated by them.

THE ADORABLE, PRICKLY HEDGEHOG

It snuffles and snorts. Its back is covered with prickly spines. And it smells . . . well, stinky. Yet people everywhere love the little hedgehog. Forget the snorts, the spines, the smell—hedgehogs are cute.

Hedgehogs live in the wild in Africa, Asia, Europe, and New Zealand. These small mammals aren't native to North America, however. Until recently, Americans have learned about them mainly through books, including classic children's stories such as *The Tale of Mrs. Tiggy-Winkle* by Beatrix Potter. But now some people in the United States and Canada have begun to keep hedgehogs as pets, and everyone wants to know more about these little creatures.

SPINY SNUFFLERS

With its turned-up snout, round body, and short legs, a hedgehog looks a little like a pig. But despite the name, a hedgehog isn't a hog. Nor is it a porcupine, although porcupines also have spines. The hedgehog's closest relatives are moles and shrews.

There are about fourteen different kinds, or species, of hedgehogs. All are small, ranging anywhere from 4 to 12 inches (10 to 30 centimeters) long. African hedgehogs are smaller than European hedgehogs. They have cream-colored fur around the face, while the European hedgehog's face is brown.

The stiff, spiky spines that cover a hedgehog's back are actually modified hairs. Unlike a porcupine's quills, the hedgehog's spines aren't barbed—and also unlike a porcupine, a hedgehog can't "fire" or release its spines to drive off a predator. But the hedgehog's spines are sharp, and they are a good defense. When a predator comes near, the hedgehog rolls up in a tight ball, with its spines sticking straight out all around. An animal that tries to bite this prickly ball gets a painful surprise. Badgers, foxes, polecats, and large birds of prey, such as owls and eagles, are the only predators that get through the hedgehog's defenses.

Hedgehogs have one habit that's really strange. When a hedgehog encounters something with a new or unusual scent, it may lick or chew the smelly object until it begins to foam at the mouth. Then the hedgehog uses its long tongue to spread the foamy saliva all over its back and sides. Scientists call this behavior self-anointing, but they don't know why hedgehogs do it.

A HEDGEHOG'S LIFE

Hedgehogs are nocturnal (active at night). During the day, they curl up to sleep under a bush, in a leaf pile, or in some other protected place. When the sun goes down, they come out to hunt for food. And since hedgehogs don't have to worry very much about predators, they aren't very quiet as they go about their business. They make a lot of noise snuffling around in the dirt, searching for snacks.

Hedgehogs are mainly insect eaters, but they aren't picky—they'll also eat earthworms, snails and slugs, small mice and frogs, eggs, carrion (dead meat), some plant material, and whatever else they find. A hedgehog may cover a mile in its nightly search for food. As dawn nears, it may return to its old sleeping place or find a new one.

Most hedgehogs spend their entire lives in the same territory, making their nightly rounds. In Britain these animals are often found along the

When a hedgehog feels threatened, it curls itself into a tight little ball with its spines sticking straight out.

edges of woodlands, in the hedgerows that line farm fields, and in suburban yards—all places where they can find food. Unlike most wild animals, hedgehogs aren't very afraid of people. Gardeners welcome the little animals because they help get rid of slugs and other garden pests, and people often put out food to attract "hedgies" to their yards. But without meaning to, people sometimes harm hedgehogs. Many hedgehogs are killed in traffic as they cross roads at night. Others are caught in drains, tangled in wire, or harmed by garden chemicals.

The hedgehogs that are native to Britain and other places with cold winters hibernate through the coldest part of the year. In November, the hedgehog makes a special nest of leaves in a protected place—under a compost pile or a log, for example. It curls up and goes into a dormant state in which its heart rate and breathing slow down. In this state it uses very little energy, so it doesn't need to eat or drink. The hedgehog

If a hedgehog discovers a strange scent, it licks the smelly object until it foams at the mouth. Then it spreads the saliva all over its body. This behavior is called self-anointing.

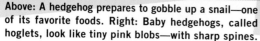
Above: A hedgehog prepares to gobble up a snail—one of its favorite foods. Right: Baby hedgehogs, called hoglets, look like tiny pink blobs—with sharp spines.

may wake up several times over the winter and may even move to a new nest, but it doesn't become active again until the weather warms up in spring.

In Africa and other places where the climate is warm all year, hedgehogs don't hibernate. But African hedgehogs enter a similar dormant state, called estivation, during hot summers in desert areas.

Hedgehogs are solitary—they don't hang out together. After breeding, females and males separate. The female gives birth to anywhere from two to seven young, called hoglets. The hoglets are little pink blobs at first, but their spines begin to poke out soon after they are born. The mother nurses them for about three weeks, and then they are ready to switch to insects and other grownup-hedgehog food. By eight weeks, the hoglets are ready to snuffle off on their own. At six months, they are considered adults.

Hedgehogs are becoming more common as pets in the United States and Canada. But people must carefully consider the pros and cons of keeping a hedgehog before bringing one home to stay.

In the wild, hedgehogs often live only two or three years. But in captivity, with good care and no risk of predators, hedgehogs may live eight to ten years.

PRICKLY PETS

Hedgehogs are protected in Britain, and it's illegal to trap them there without a special permit. It's also illegal to import hedgehogs to the United States. But little African hedgehogs (also called pygmy hedgehogs) are being raised and sold as pets in the United States.

Hedgehogs make cute pets, but they aren't for everyone. Here are the pros and cons:

St. Tiggywinkles to the Rescue

In the early 1900's, Beatrix Potter created a group of wonderful fictional animals in her books for children. One of them was Mrs. Tiggy-Winkle, a kindly hedgehog that took care of Peter Rabbit and the other wildlife characters by washing and ironing their clothes. Today, a special animal hospital named for Mrs. Tiggy-Winkle takes care of wildlife in another way— by nursing sick and injured animals back to health. Located in Aylesbury, England, this unusual hospital is called St. Tiggywinkles.

St. Tiggywinkles was started in 1978. Since then, the hospital has cared for countless animals, from toads and snakes to badgers, deer, and swans. St. Tiggywinkles doesn't take dogs, cats, or other pets—just wild animals. Besides healing sick and injured wildlife, workers at the hospital hand-raise orphaned baby animals. Before the animals are released, they spend time in outdoor pens so that they can adjust to life in the wild.

The hedgehog ward is the hospital's busiest wing. More than 3,000 hedgehogs turn up at St. Tiggywinkles every year. Some have been injured. Some are sick. Many are brought to the hospital in winter because they are too thin to survive hibernation. They are cared for until spring, when they can return to the wild.

St. Tiggywinkles also teaches veterinarians and veterinary nurses how to care for injured wildlife. In fact, it was the world's first wildlife teaching hospital. After learning the most modern ways to heal injured wild animals and return them to the wild, students have gone on to run wildlife rescue centers all over Europe.

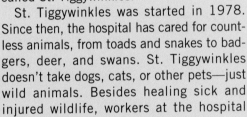

Pros: Hedgehogs are fun to watch. And because they are solitary, you only need one. A hedgehog can be happy in a big cage, as long as it has a wheel or some other way to exercise. It doesn't need brushing. Besides providing food (commercial hedgehog food) and water, and cleaning the cage, hedgehogs don't require a lot of care.

Cons: Hedgehogs are nocturnal, so your little pet will sleep during the day (when you're awake) and be busy all night (while you're trying to sleep). Hedgehogs aren't very trainable, and they don't care to be petted or cuddled. If you handle your hedgie when it's feeling threatened, you will need to wear gloves to protect your hands from its spines. African hedgehogs can't tolerate cold and need temperatures of 72°F (22°C) or more. And it can be hard to find a veterinarian to care for a sick hedgehog, because they are such unusual pets.

If you're thinking of getting a pet hedgehog, be sure to check all the regulations in your city and state. Some areas in the United States and Canada don't allow these animals to be kept as pets, and some require special permits for them. Officials in these areas are worried that if pet hedgehogs were to escape into the wild, they might compete with local wildlife.

A gray squirrel takes a snooze in an airy leaf nest perched high in the treetops. Like all animals, squirrels build homes to provide shelter and protection for themselves and their young.

ANIMAL ABODES

A nest perched high atop a tree. An underground burrow. A timber and mud lodge in the middle of a pond. A hive that can accommodate 50,000 bees. A termite nest that rises skyscraper-like into the sky. These are but a few of the many kinds of homes, or abodes, built by animals. At this moment, animals are building new homes for themselves. They are hard at work digging, cutting, carrying, spinning, weaving, chiseling, cementing, gluing, and plastering. They build for the same reason humans do: to provide shelter and protection for themselves and their young.

An animal is guided by instinct when it builds. It inherits its construction skills from its parents, just as it inherits the shape of its body. Almost every animal can build the right kind of home the first time it tries.

MAMMAL HOME-BUILDERS

The gray squirrel has two different homes. During the winter, it lives in a snug tree hole, where it sleeps on a mattress of shredded bark and leaves. In spring, it moves outside and builds an airy leaf nest high above the ground.

It may steal a bird's nest and put a roof of twigs and leaves over the top. Or the squirrel may lay its own foundation by wedging sticks and twigs into the crotch of a tree. It builds a roof by lacing smaller twigs and leaves into the foundation, and it shingles the roof with large leaves to keep out the rain. When the nest is finished, it looks like a ragged cluster of leaves the size of a basketball. A small hole on one side serves as a doorway. Inside the nest, the hollowed-out living chamber is lined with grass and moss.

Anyone can see squirrels' leaf nests perched in the treetops of woods or city parks. The nests of mice and other small rodents are just as common, yet few people notice them because they are carefully hidden. A white-footed mouse builds a typical nest. Working with tooth and paw, it fluffs out strands of shredded grass and weaves them into a hollow ball the size of an apple. The inside of the nest is padded with the softest bedding available, such as milkweed floss or cattail down. The nest may be hidden just about anywhere—between rocks, in a hollow log, in a knothole. White-footed mice often move into cabins in the wilderness, where they build nests of shredded rags, cotton, or newspaper among the rafters or in empty boxes or drawers.

The underground burrow is the most popular type of home used by small mammals. This kit fox is using it as a nursery den.

Many other kinds of mice live in underground burrows. In fact, the burrow is the most popular type of home used by mammals. Wolves, foxes, and coyotes dig burrows as temporary nursery dens. Their pups are born in a chamber at the end of a tunnel. When the pups are big enough to keep up with the adults, the den is abandoned.

Ground squirrels, chipmunks, gophers, woodchucks, and many other mammals live in burrows all year long. A woodchuck (or groundhog) may occupy the same burrow for several years. It constantly enlarges and remodels its underground home, digging through soil with its heavy claws, cutting away roots with its sharp teeth. The burrow has an entrance hole surrounded by a mound of excavated soil and two or more emergency exits. Underground, a network of tunnels connecting several rooms may extend for 50 feet (15 meters) or more. During the winter, the woodchuck hibernates in a grass-lined sleeping chamber several feet underground.

The most accomplished mammal architect is the beaver. Beavers use their sharp teeth to cut down trees and trim off branches and twigs. They build dams across marshes and

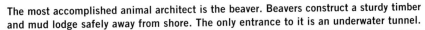

The most accomplished animal architect is the beaver. Beavers construct a sturdy timber and mud lodge safely away from shore. The only entrance to it is an underwater tunnel.

Master Nest Builders

Weaverbirds are master nest builders. The males build the nests, and they do it to attract females. When a female sees a really good nest, she mates with the male and settles in to lay eggs and raise chicks. There are 126 differ-

ent kinds of weaverbirds, found mostly in Asia and Africa, and each builds its own kind of nest.

A male grosbeak weaver starts his nest by tying two plant stalks together with blades of grass (top). Weaverbirds are so clever that they can actually tie knots, using their beaks and their feet! The bird keeps working until he has built a ring of woven grass, small twigs, and other plant ma-

terial between the two stalks. This ring will become the opening to the nest. The bird keeps weaving, making a grassy basket that hangs from the opening ring (above and right). When the nest is complete, the male weaver calls out to females. He wants a female to stop by and check out his work. And he hopes she'll like it enough to move in.

streams by piling up this timber and cementing it together with mud and stones. A well-constructed beaver dam will last for many years.

As water backs up behind a beaver dam, a pond is formed. In the middle of this pond, safely away from the shore, the beavers construct a sturdy timber and mud lodge. Its walls are plastered with plenty of mud to make them waterproof. The top of the roof isn't plastered, leaving ventilation holes that allow air to circulate.

The only entrance to a beaver lodge is a narrow underwater tunnel. It leads to a circular room. The floor of this room stands a few inches above water level. Raised above the floor is a sleeping shelf lined with shredded wood.

During the winter, snow covers the lodge and locks in the heat given off by the beavers' bodies. Warm air rises to the ceiling, escapes through the ventilation holes in the roof, and forms vapors of steam that look like smoke rising from a chimney.

BIRDS AND THEIR NESTS

Some people think that birds sleep in their nests, or that they use their nests as hiding places. A few birds, such as owls and woodpeckers, actually do live in their nests. But most birds live in the open. They build nests only during the breeding season and use them for one purpose—as a sheltered cradle for their eggs and young.

The location of a nest reveals a great deal about a bird's young. Ground-nesting birds, like ducks and geese, usually have chicks that run about soon after they hatch. If danger threatens, the chicks can tumble out of the nest and run for safety. Birds whose young are born blind and helpless usually avoid the open ground. They try to build their nests out of sight or out of reach.

Cliff swallows build nests of mud mixed with their own sticky saliva. They smear the mud against the face of a cliff or the wall of a building and shape it into a neat little pottery jug with a round opening at the top. The inside is filled with grass, moss, and

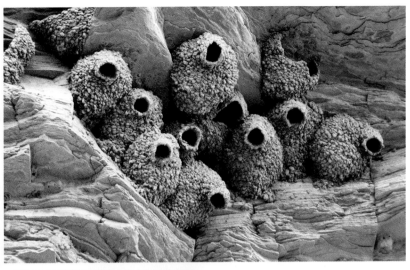

A hummingbird's nest (*above left*) could fit in a teaspoon. Cliff swallow nests (*above right*) look like little pottery jars. A woodpecker's nest (*left*) is a hole carved in a tree trunk.

feathers to cushion the eggs. These nests are always placed beneath overhanging ledges, so that rain won't soften the mud and wash the nest away.

A hole in a tree provides an ideal nesting site. Woodpeckers have an advantage because they can drill their own nesting holes. Abandoned woodpecker holes are in great demand. Birds like wrens, swallows, bluebirds, and starlings will sometimes fight noisily over the possession of an empty woodpecker hole.

Crows, hawks, and eagles carry branches and sticks to the tops of trees and cliffs, where they build large platform nests. Eagles can airlift branches as big around as a person's arm. They sometimes line their nests with pieces of trash, such as old brooms and tablecloths. Eagles return to the same nest year after year, adding more branches, twigs, and grass. As the nest grows older, it also grows bigger. One bald eagle's nest, atop a longleaf pine near St. Petersburg, Florida, was 20 feet (6 meters) deep, 9½ feet (3 meters) across, and weighed several tons.

A hummingbird's nest, made from moss and plant floss bound together with cobwebs, measures barely an inch (2.5 centimeters) across the top. It is small enough to fit into a teaspoon, yet big enough for the hummingbird's two pea-sized eggs.

Many common songbirds build little cup-shaped nests. A goldfinch weaves its cup-shaped nest from strands of grass, strips of moss, and bits of plant fiber. The nest is lined with thistledown and feathers.

In the tropics, small perching birds such as weavers often build hanging nests that are completely covered to keep out tree-dwelling enemies. The nest of one kind of African weaverbird hangs by a loop from the branch of a tree. It may contain more than 300 strands of grass woven tightly into a ball. Inside the nest, the weaverbird hollows out a nesting chamber. The most inventive of the weavers are the social weavers, who join together to build a giant nest that resembles an apartment house. Some of these structures are 10 feet (3 meters) high and 15 feet (4.5 meters) across and can accommodate 300 pairs of birds.

If a bird can't find the building materials it usually uses, it will seek the best substitute it can find. In New York City, a street-wise pigeon fashioned a nest from wires, nails and paper clips. In Switzerland, a sparrow built its nest entirely of small watch springs. In California, a warbling vireo used Kleenex for its nest. And in Bombay, India, a pair of crows constructed their nest with gold eyeglass frames that they stole from an open shop window.

collects bits and pieces of water plants, squirts them with a sticky fluid released by his kidneys, and glues the pieces together. Pressing against the pile with his body and snout, he forms a neat, tunnel-shaped nest with a front entrance, a rear exit, and a stream of water flowing through it.

When the nest is ready, the stickleback leads several females into the tunnel. After they deposit their eggs, he chases them away. The male stays behind to guard the eggs. He fans fresh water through the tunnel so the eggs will get plenty of oxygen.

Some of the most interesting underwater structures are built by newly hatched insect

Caddis worms build some of the most interesting underwater structures—caselike dwellings, where they can live until they become adult caddis flies.

BUILDING UNDERWATER

A surprising number of fish build simple nests at the bottoms of lakes and streams. The nest is often constructed by the male, who may also watch over the eggs and the newly hatched fry. A smallmouth bass is typical. He uses his mouth to loosen gravel and debris at the bottom of a lake and to carry off larger stones. Then he turns around and uses his tail to scoop out a nesting hollow.

The most skillful nestbuilders among fish are sticklebacks, found in North American ponds and streams. A three-spined stickleback is about the size of your little finger. The male

larvae called caddis worms. Caddis worms hatch from eggs laid in cool mountain ponds and streams. As soon as they wriggle out of their eggs, they begin to build sturdy, caselike dwellings where they can live until they leave the water as adult caddis flies.

There are many kinds of caddis insects, and each kind prefers certain building materials. Caddises that hatch in quiet ponds and lakes usually build cases of wood, bark, pine needles, and other lightweight materials.

In swift mountain streams, caddises construct heavy stone cases that won't be tossed about by the currents. A stone case may be

Above left: This paper wasp nest is covered by a protective paper envelope. Above: A close-up shows how the wasps form the paper in swirls. Inset: Inside the nest, eggs are laid in paper cells.

Paper Houses

Have you seen a nest like this hanging from the branch of a tree or the eaves of a house? The nest is made of paper, and the insects that made it are paper wasps.

Like the paper of this page, the paper of the nest begins with wood pulp. Worker wasps nibble bits of old wood and plant stems. They chew the material, mixing it with their saliva, until it's mashed into pulp. Then they add it to the nest in thin layers, which dry to form paper.

The outer paper covering, or envelope, protects the nest from weather. Inside, the wasps build a network of hexagonal (six-sided) cells. The queen of the colony lays her eggs in the cells. The eggs hatch into larvae, which stay in the cells until they mature. Workers feed and care for them.

Some paper wasp nests contain thousands of cells. Others have just a few cells. But the goal is the same. Dozens of wasps work together to build a safe home for their young.

---

shaped like a tube, a trumpet, a coiled snail's shell, or a domed turtle's shell. The caddis worm picks up tiny pebbles and grains of sand in its mouth. It cements these building stones together with a sticky silk that pours out of its mouth and hardens in water.

The caddis starts by building a ring of stones around its body. It adds more and more stones, gradually forming a hollow tube. The rear of the tube is sealed with silk, but the front is left open so the caddis can climb part way out. As it crawls along the stream bed looking for food, it drags its stone case behind it. If danger threatens, it retreats inside.

INSECT CITIES

Only a small percentage of Earth's insects build nests, yet they construct some of the architectural wonders of the animal world.

The nests of bees, ants, and termites are populous insect cities that may last for many generations.

Honeybees usually build their hives in hollow trees or in wooden boxes provided by beekeepers. The interior of the hive contains row after row of neat, six-sided cells, made of wax that oozes from the abdomens of worker bees. The cells at the center of the hive are nurseries for the developing eggs and young. Surrounding these brood cells are storage cells for honey and pollen.

A flourishing beehive has a population of perhaps 50,000 bees. Guards stationed at the entrance to the hive will attack and sting any outsider. Inside the hive, worker bees constantly build new wax cells, repair old ones, and carry away refuse.

The brood cells must be kept at a very high temperature, or the eggs and larvae cannot

Honeybees build hives containing rows of six-sided cells, made of wax oozing from the abdomens of worker bees.

The African termite constructs an architectural wonder— a towering mound that rises like a skyscraper into the air. The walls of this insect nest are as hard as concrete.

develop successfully. In cool weather, the bees cluster by the thousands on top of the brood cells, keeping them warm with the heat of their bodies. In hot weather, the bees cool the hive by fanning their wings. If fanning isn't enough, the bees carry drops of water into the hive and spread a thin film of moisture over the brood cells. They continue to fan their wings, and the nest is cooled as the moisture evaporates.

Most ants live underground. An ant hill is made of soil that the insects have excavated and is actually an extension of the nest. Beneath an ant hill, the ground is riddled with tunnels and nursery chambers. A large nest may penetrate 15 feet (4.5 meters) into the earth, cover an area larger than a football field, and contain several million ants. Worker ants shuttle back and forth from one nursery chamber to another, carrying eggs and larvae in their jaws. During the day, workers carry the brood to sun-warmed nurseries in the upper parts of the nest. In the evening, they carry the brood back down to deep underground nurseries, where heat has accumulated during the day. The entrances to these nurseries are sealed to keep out the cool night air.

Some of the strangest insect nests are the towering, air-conditioned mounds built by African termites. Constructed of soil that the termites chew and mix with their own saliva, these insect skyscrapers may rise 20 feet (6 meters) into the air. Their thick, sun-baked walls are as hard as concrete.

the "attic." Between the cellar and the attic stands the nest itself, where the termites live in perpetual darkness.

A network of air channels is built into the walls of the mound. These channels absorb fresh air from outside the mound. As air seeps into the tunnel, it rises up to the attic and flows down to the cellar. The nest in the center of the mound is surrounded on all sides by endlessly moving streams of air. Termites are constantly at work inside the air channels,

A Makeshift Mouse House

Game, set . . . mouse? You wouldn't expect a mouse to pop out of a tennis ball, but some animals will make their homes in surprising places. And in Britain, used tennis balls—including some balls from the famous Wimbledon tennis tournament—are being turned into homes for tiny harvest mice.

Harvest mice are Europe's smallest mice, and their numbers have been shrinking in recent years. The mice live in tall grass and reeds, where they weave little round nests from the stalks. But they're happy to nest in tennis balls, too.

To turn a tennis ball into a mouse house, a hole about half an inch across is cut into the ball. Then the balls are put on stakes so that they are several feet off the ground, like the natural nests that the mice make. British wildlife officials hope that more nest sites will help the harvest mouse population grow.

The soft, pale bodies of termites dry out quickly in open air, causing them to shrivel and die, so they must avoid the sun. If temperatures drop too low, they become paralyzed. They need darkness, moisture, and warmth to survive. In Africa, they create the special conditions they need by building climate-controlled mounds.

At the base of the termite mound is a "cellar," a large hollow space below ground level. Tunnels branch out from the cellar to underground sources of food and water. At the top of the mound is another large hollow space,

opening and closing them to regulate the flow of air. When the nest is too warm, new channels are opened to bring in fresh, cool air from the outside. When the nest isn't warm enough, some of the channels are closed.

Some of the African termite mounds look like giant mushrooms or miniature pyramids. Others resemble towers or craggy mountain peaks. Each species of termite follows its own architectural blueprint—the blueprint of its ancestors. Guided by their instincts, termites have been building climate-controlled nests for millions of years.

CHOOSE ME!

Spring is the time when birds pair up to raise their families. And male birds go all out to attract females—dancing, showing off their feathers, and doing all sorts of stunts. Male birds will do almost anything to get a mate! Here are a few of their tricks:

Feed a Treat: How does a male lovebird say "I care"? By feeding a female a tasty morsel of regurgitated food! That may not seem like a treat to you, but it's a hit in the bird world. Once lovebirds (*top left*) pair off, the male and female are never far apart. They do everything together, and the bond lasts for their whole lives. That's why they are called lovebirds!

Show Off: A peacock wows a female with his beautiful plumage (*right*). He spreads his gorgeous tail feathers in a huge fan, rattling his quills and shrieking in his harsh, raucous way. If his show meets with the peahen's approval, they will mate.

Puff Up: A male frigatebird has a red throat pouch that's barely noticeable most of the time. But when a female comes near, he inflates his pouch like a red balloon to catch her eye (*top left*). Then he spreads his long wings, shakes them, and sends out a call that sounds like a whinny. The female can't resist!

Give Gifts: A male great blue heron brings his mate a stick (*top right*). It may not seem like much, but it's his way of showing that he can help build a good nest. Herons are large birds, and the male will need to gather a lot of sticks for the pair's big nest. The parents will take turns keeping the eggs warm until hatching, and then they'll share the work of feeding the young.

Dance: A blue-footed booby (*left*) dances for his mate. He hops, rocks, and struts around, flapping his wings and whistling as he dances. It's quite a show! If the female likes his dance, she rubs her beak on his neck to show that she accepts him.

ANIMALS IN THE NEWS

A guinea pig the size of a buffalo? It may sound like a bad dream, but creatures like that once roamed the swamps of South America. In September 2003, scientists announced that they had found a fossil skeleton of a **giant rodent** that lived about 8 million years ago. The animal was something like a guinea pig with a large tail—but it weighed about 1,500 pounds (680 kilograms).

The official name of the giant rodent is *Phoberomys pattersoni,* which means "Patterson's fearful mouse." The scientists who found the skeleton nicknamed it Goya. Teeth of this animal had been found before, but this was the first skeleton. It was discovered in Venezuela, west of Caracas, the capital. This area is dry today, but when Goya lived it was covered with lush swamps. A plant eater, Goya grazed on grasses. Like other rodents, it had teeth that grew continually and were continually worn down as it gnawed on its food.

Goya looked something like a gigantic chipmunk. It was about 9 feet (3 meters) long, with small round ears. But while chipmunks and guinea pigs move in a crouched position, with their legs bent, scientists think Goya stood with its legs straight. The furry animal could also stand up on its hind legs to scout for danger, using its large tail for balance. It had to worry about some serious predators, too. The swamps were full of crocodiles that were 30 feet (9 meters) long, birds of prey that were 9 feet (3 meters) tall, and lion-sized meat eaters called marsupial cats.

Modern rodents can't begin to match Goya in size. Goya's closest living relative is the pacarana, a rare plant-eating rodent of South American forests. It weighs about 30 pounds (13 kilograms). Even the largest living rodent, the South American capybara, weighs a mere 110 pounds (50 kilograms).

Penguins at the San Francisco Zoo made a splash in the winter of 2002–2003. Zoo visitors were startled to see all 52 birds swimming together in circles, for hours at a time! It started when six new birds joined the zoo's flock of Magellanic penguins. The new birds wanted to swim, and within hours they had the whole flock in a swimming frenzy. The penguins kept up their daily water show for weeks, whirling through the water like a group of tuxedos in a washing machine. Zookeepers think the birds were mimicking natural migration behavior.

Granny, a Holstein cow in Wisconsin, set a new U.S. record for lifetime milk production in the spring of 2003. This 17-year-old cow had produced 429,132 pounds (194,650 kilograms) of milk. That's enough milk to fill 50,000 1-gallon (3.8-liter) jugs—or 1,000 bathtubs! And Granny, the star cow at the Koepke Dairy Farm, was still being milked three times a day. The Koepke family threw a party for their prize cow in April. Of course, they served milk and cheese.

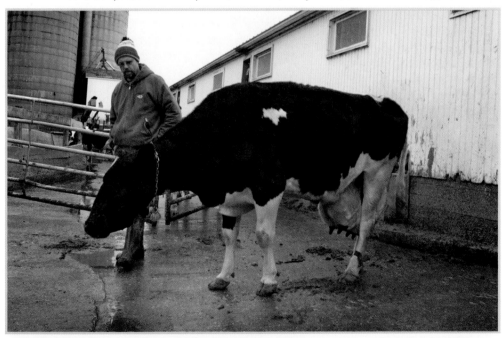

Champion Torums Scarf Michael, a Kerry blue terrier, won top honors at the 2003 Westminster Kennel Club show in New York City in February. Westminster is the most famous dog show in the United States. And Mick, as he's known to his friends, is one of the winningest dogs ever. He had won top awards at 112 other shows in the United States and Britain. Kerry blue terriers like Mick are lively, friendly dogs with wavy, blue-gray coats. They were first bred in Ireland.

Your dog is barking. Did he see a cat? Does he want to play? A device that arrived in U.S. stores in 2003 can help you find out—or so the manufacturer claims. Called **Bow-Lingual,** the device comes with a wireless microphone that clips onto a dog's collar. The microphone sends the dog's barks and howls to a palm-size receiver that translates woofs into words—everything from "I'm sorry" to "I feel like dancin'!" Bow-Lingual was a big hit in Japan. Its Japanese manufacturer figured that Americans, who spend $30 billion a year on pet products, would also bite.

The poodle is one of the smartest dogs. The Labrador retriever is one of the friendliest. Both breeds are popular pets. So it was no surprise that the star of the pet world in 2003 was the smart, friendly **labradoodle** (above). This cute lab-poodle cross was developed in Australia. There, labradoodles are popular as service dogs, as well as pets. Oodles of other poodle crosses are popular, too.

The cockapoo is a cocker spaniel and poodle cross. The schnoodle is a schnauzer-poodle mix. The peke-a-poo is a cross between a Pekinese and a poodle. The American Kennel Club doesn't recognize the crosses as true breeds, but that hasn't stopped dog lovers from taking the dogs into their hearts and homes. Some of the most popular crossbred puppies sell for as much as purebred pups.

Fans say the crossbred dogs are healthier than purebreds and combine the best of both breeds—for example, the easy-going attitude of a lab and the intelligence and non-shedding coat of a poodle. But dog experts say that crosses don't always work out as planned. Some labradoodles do shed, and not all are as laid back as labs or as smart as poodles.

The tiny **cactus ferruginous pygmy owl,** which measures less than 7 inches (18 centimeters) from beak to tail, was at the center of a big fuss in Arizona in 2003. Land developers were in an uproar over a plan to protect the little bird, which wildlife officials say is in danger of dying out.

Once common in southern Arizona, the pygmy owls have been on the U.S. Endangered Species list since 1997. It's illegal to kill or harm them—but despite the protection, their numbers have kept falling. In 1999 there were 41 adult pygmy owls in Arizona. In 2001, there were just 18. The problem, wildlife

officials say, is development. Southern Arizona is growing fast. People are taking over wild areas where owls live for housing and other uses.

The U.S. Fish and Wildlife Service proposed a plan to help the owls. Putting out nest boxes, moving owls into suitable habitats, and raising owls in captivity are some of the steps. In addition, the service proposed setting aside 1.2 million acres in southern Arizona as "critical habitat" for the owls. People who wanted to develop this land would need to show that their actions wouldn't affect the owls. It was this part of the plan that caused the fuss. Builders said that it would unfairly bar development of the land, which is mostly privately owned. And they said that the owls weren't in such great danger. The pygmy owl's natural range extends into Texas and Mexico, where many more of these owls live.

In August a federal court ruling added strength to the developers' case. The court said that wildlife officials hadn't shown that the Arizona owls were significantly different from the pygmy owls in northern Mexico. Thus, the Arizona owls might not be entitled to special protection.

But the controversy didn't end there. The deserts of southern Arizona are home to many unique plants and animals. Environmentalists say that protecting the desert habitat may be the only way to keep many species, not just the pygmy owl, from dying out. The growth of towns and cities—"urban sprawl"—is the biggest threat many of these species face.

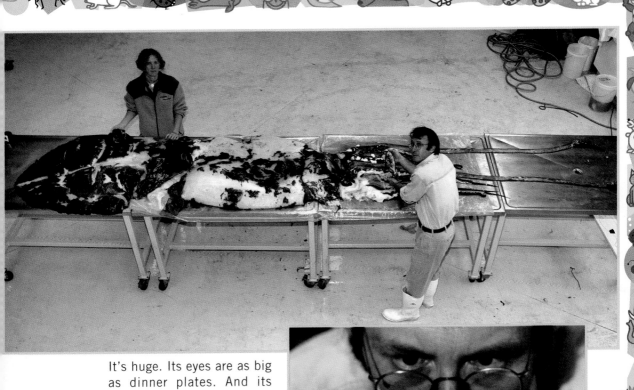

It's huge. Its eyes are as big as dinner plates. And its long, powerful tentacles have razor-sharp hooks for snagging prey. That's a description of a rare ocean animal known as the **colossal squid** (above). Fishermen netted one of these giant predators off Antarctica in March 2003. It was only the second complete specimen ever found. The squid was dead when it was hauled up by the crew of a New Zealand fishing boat. It had been feeding on the fishermen's catch. Researchers don't know why it was so close to the surface, because squids live in deep, cold ocean waters.

The squid was probably not full grown, researchers said. The body, or mantle, was about 8 feet (2.4 meters) long, and the barbed tentacles measured about 16 feet (5 meters). As adults, colossal squids are thought to grow to be more than 13 feet (4 meters) long, even bigger than the better-known giant squid. But no one has ever found a living squid of either species, so little is known about them.

Colossal squids prey on fish. Their tentacles are lined with suckers and hooks that can rotate in any direction (inset). Once in the grip of this predator, fish don't escape. But sperm whales are known to prey on colossal squids.

Steve O'Shea, a New Zealand marine biologist who examined the colossal squid specimen, said: "When this animal was alive, it really had to be one of the most frightening predators out there. It's without parallel in the oceans."

SCIENCE

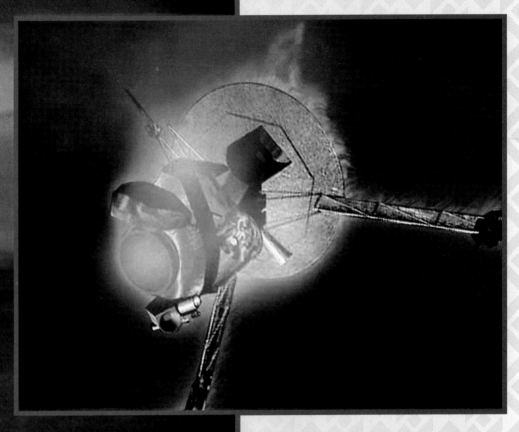

Galileo *was one of the longest-running, hardest-working spacecraft ever launched by the United States. This unmanned craft was sent on a mission to Jupiter in October 1989. Over the next fourteen years,* Galileo *made many discoveries. The craft orbited Jupiter for twice as long as anyone expected, and it sent back amazing pictures of the giant gas planet and its moons. But in 2003,* Galileo *finally began to run out of power, and scientists at the National Aeronautics and Space Administration (NASA) decided to bring its long mission to an end. On September 21, the spacecraft made a planned dive into Jupiter's dense atmosphere and burned up (inset).*

"THE *COLUMBIA* IS LOST!"

On the morning of February 1, 2003, the space shuttle *Columbia* broke up in the skies over Texas as it returned to Earth. All seven astronauts, including the first Israeli in space, were killed. "The *Columbia* is lost," said President George W. Bush, in an address to the nation five hours later. "There are no survivors."

The tragic accident stunned the nation. As people mourned the loss of the shuttle and its crew, investigators tried to find out what had gone wrong. The *Columbia* disaster led some to question the way the National Aeronautics and Space Administration (NASA) ran the shuttle program and even whether manned space flights should continue in the future.

COLUMBIA'S LAST FLIGHT

Most recent shuttle missions have focused on building the *International Space Station* (*ISS*). But *Columbia* was on a strictly scientific mission—the first such mission in three years. The crew carried out more than 80 experiments during the sixteen-day flight. They studied everything from the effects of microgravity (near weightlessness) on cancer cells to the effects of dust storms on Earth's climate. Students sent up several experiments. For example, students from Syracuse, New York, sent up an experiment called "Ants in Space" to see how ants would adapt to microgravity.

The mission seemed normal until the last day. Then, at 8:45 A.M. Eastern Standard Time, *Columbia* entered Earth's atmosphere, 75 miles (120 kilometers) up. It began to undergo stress as friction with the air created temperatures as high as 2000°F (1093°C). Controlled by computers, the craft descended like a glider, making the first of several sweeping S-turns that would help slow its speed.

The first sign of trouble came at 8:53, when gauges

People everywhere mourned the loss of the space shuttle *Columbia* and its seven astronauts. The tragedy stirred a debate on whether sending humans into space was worth the risk.

showed rising temperatures around the left landing gear. Five minutes later, temperatures on the left wing dropped "off scale," meaning that sensors weren't working. The crew and ground controllers saw the problem but didn't realize how serious it was. Then, at 8:59, something began to create a drag on the left wing. This caused the craft to roll left. The flight computers tried to correct the roll, but within moments ground controllers lost contact with the craft.

Columbia was sixteen minutes away from its scheduled landing at Cape Canaveral in Florida when it broke up. People on the ground heard a sound like rolling thunder and a loud boom, and pieces of the craft streaked across the sky like meteors. Flaming debris fell to Earth in a swath 100 miles (160 kilometers) long.

Ground controllers knew at once that the crew was lost. Although *Columbia* had an escape system that would have allowed astronauts to eject, it could be used only when the craft was flying level, at altitudes below 20,000 feet (4 miles) [6,096 meters; 6.1 kilometers]. The shuttle was more than 200,000 feet (40 miles) [60,960 meters; 61 kilometers] above Earth and traveling at a speed of Mach 18 (18 times the speed of sound) when it broke up. No one could have survived the accident.

This was the second time a space shuttle and its crew had been lost. *Challenger* had exploded during liftoff in January 1986. In 2003, as in 1986, the tragedy raised important questions.

THE INVESTIGATION

Investigators appointed to find the cause of the disaster spent seven months interviewing people, studying tapes and other data from the doomed flight, and running tests. They collected more than 84,000 pieces of debris, enough to reconstruct more than a third of the shattered craft. Their report blamed technical problems and human error for *Columbia*'s loss.

The seeds of the disaster were planted on January 16, as the shuttle lifted off. A chunk of insulating foam broke off the shuttle's huge external fuel tank and struck *Columbia*'s left wing. The foam probably weighed only about

The *Columbia* Crew

The crew for *Columbia*'s last mission was led by Commander Rick Husband, 45, a U.S. Air Force colonel, and Pilot William McCool, 41, a U.S. Navy commander. The payload commander, Michael Anderson, 43, was one of a handful of African Americans who have become astronauts. Also on board were three mission specialists. David Brown, 46, a U.S. Navy captain and a medical doctor, was making his first space flight. Laurel Clark, 41, was also a medical doc-

The *Columbia* crew: Front row—Rick Husband, Kalpana Chawla, William McCool. Back row—David Brown, Laurel Clark, Michael Anderson, Ilan Ramon.

tor as well as an astronaut. Kalpana Chawla, 41, was an aerospace engineer who was born in India but became a U.S. citizen. The crew's seventh member was Ilan Ramon, 48, a colonel in the Israeli Air Force. Ramon was the first person from his country to fly in space, and he was a national hero in Israel.

"These men and women assumed great risk in the service to all humanity," President George W. Bush said to the nation. "Because of their courage and . . . idealism we will miss them all the more."

In one of many memorials to the crew, seven asteroids have been named for the seven astronauts. The asteroids are among thousands of space rocks that orbit the sun between Mars and Jupiter.

2 pounds (1 kilogram). But because the shuttle was roaring skyward at twice the speed of sound, it hit with tremendous force.

The blow was enough to punch a hole in the leading edge of the wing, and that proved fatal when *Columbia* re-entered the atmosphere. For protection from the extreme heat of re-entry, *Columbia* had a heat shield made of ceramic tiles. A material called reinforced carbon carbon (RCC) protected the leading edges of its wings. It was this material that was damaged. The hole allowed hot gases to enter the wing, and the heat melted the wing's aluminum supports and burned through electrical wiring. The left wing began to come apart, and the shuttle went out of control.

If anyone had seen the damage during liftoff, the shuttle could have made an emergency landing right then. But engineers didn't even know the foam had hit the shuttle until they reviewed videotapes of the launch the next day. Even then, no one understood how serious the problem was. Some engineers were worried and urged that spy satellites be used to check *Columbia*'s wing for damage. NASA officials dismissed those concerns, believing there was little risk. The hole was never detected.

Even if the hole had been spotted, it's not likely that *Columbia* could have been saved. The crew had no tools for repairing the wing. *Columbia* didn't have enough fuel to reach the *ISS* or the equipment for docking with the station. And no other shuttle was ready to be launched on a rescue mission.

LOOKING AHEAD

The investigators' final report criticized NASA for allowing risks to be underestimated. They said the space agency had failed to learn from past mistakes, such as the *Challenger* disaster. NASA's handling of *Columbia*'s final flight, they said, reflected "missed opportuni-

GO COLUMBIA!

Columbia: First of Its Kind

Columbia was the very first space shuttle, or reusable spacecraft. Before its first flight, on April 12, 1981, astronauts went into orbit in space capsules that were launched on rockets and splashed down into the ocean. When the mission was finished, so was the capsule.

Like the capsules, *Columbia* was launched by rocket power. It escaped Earth's gravity with a pair of rocket boosters and a huge external fuel tank. These were cast away as the shuttle rose, leaving just the orbiter with its swept-back wings. But when the orbiter returned to Earth, it coasted down like a glider and landed like an airplane on a runway. Then it could be sent into space again.

Columbia proved that a winged, reusable spacecraft could be built. NASA built four more shuttles: *Challenger* (which exploded after launch in 1986), *Discovery*, *Atlantis*, and *Endeavour*. They became the workhorses of the space program, carrying science experiments, satellites, research tools such as the Hubble Space Telescope, and parts for the *International Space Station*.

Columbia was lost on its 28th mission. Its previous flights included the longest space-shuttle mission ever, in November–December 1996, lasting 17 days, 15 hours, 53 minutes, 18 seconds.

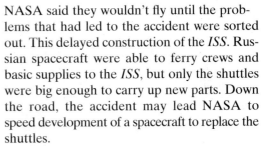

To help pinpoint the causes of the disaster, more than 84,000 pieces of the space shuttle *Columbia* were arranged on the floor of a huge hangar at the Kennedy Space Center in Florida. Inset: After months of study, investigators released their report in August.

ties, blocked or ineffective communications channels, flawed analysis and ineffective leadership." If such problems weren't fixed, they warned, the scene was set for another accident. The report had some specific recommendations for shuttle flights. Among them were these:

⚠ Shuttles should have cameras that can take pictures of the orbiter and fuel tank and send the pictures to the ground.

⚠ Spy satellites should be used to inspect shuttles during flight.

⚠ Astronauts should have equipment that would let them repair damage during a flight.

⚠ Wing panels should be inspected more thoroughly between flights.

The three remaining space shuttles were grounded after the *Columbia* accident, and

Shortly after the accident, these Georgia students participated in a simulated shuttle mission. For many people, the loss of *Columbia* has only strengthened their belief in the importance of manned space flight.

NASA said they wouldn't fly until the problems that had led to the accident were sorted out. This delayed construction of the *ISS*. Russian spacecraft were able to ferry crews and basic supplies to the *ISS*, but only the shuttles were big enough to carry up new parts. Down the road, the accident may lead NASA to speed development of a spacecraft to replace the shuttles.

The accident revived an old debate on whether manned space flights are worth the risk. On one side are those who say that manned missions aren't worth the cost in lives and dollars. Most of the knowledge and benefits gained in space exploration, they say, have come from unmanned flights.

On the other side are those who compare astronauts to explorers of long ago. Exploration is dangerous—many ships were lost when people first began to cross the oceans, they say. And astronauts, not space probes, have inspired people to reach for the skies.

COLOR: More Than Meets the Eye

Why do you choose certain colors? Perhaps you think blue is a good color for your clothes because it matches your eyes. Maybe you think a sunny yellow would be the best color for the walls of your bedroom.

In fact, your reasons for choosing colors may be a great deal more complex than this. Color can affect your moods and behavior, and it can even affect other people's responses to you. Color choices can be so important that businesses from clothing manufacturers to car makers to restaurant decorators often hire special color researchers to help them with these decisions.

HOW WE SEE COLOR

The color of your clothes or the walls of your room is really nothing more than reflected light. Light is made up of waves of different lengths, and we see the different wavelengths as colors. Light that contains all the wavelengths appears white to us. But it actually contains wavelengths in three basic colors—red, green, and blue—called primaries.

A red shirt appears red because it absorbs most of the wavelengths but reflects the red ones. A green car is green because it reflects green light. Most of the colors we see are mixtures of the primaries. Yellow, for example, is a blend of red and green light.

When light waves of any color enter your eyes, they stimulate special cells called cones at the back of the eye. The cones send signals along nerves to the brain, and you identify the color. But many researchers say that this isn't all that happens. Part of your response to color takes place on a deeper, unconscious level and can have a direct effect on the way you feel. Thus, our reactions to color seem to be a complicated mixture of inborn and learned responses.

ULTRASIGHT

Did you know that there are "colors" that you can't see, but that birds and insects can see? What we know as visible light is just a small part of a broad range, or spectrum, of electromagnetic waves emitted by the sun and stars. You see only part of the spectrum because your eyes are sensitive to certain wavelengths and not others. But birds and insects can see very short wavelengths, called ultraviolet (UV) waves, that are invisible to you.

We can't know exactly what these creatures see, but we can take pictures with UV-sensitive cameras. Such pictures show that certain insects have bold markings that are visible only in ultraviolet light. So do some flowers that depend on birds and insects for pollination. The UV markings may help birds and insects find food and mates, and help flowering plants reproduce.

Right, top: This is how *you* see the flower. Right: This is how birds and insects view it, because they can see the very short wavelengths called ultraviolet light.

THE LANGUAGE OF COLOR

Some colors seem to prompt a response almost from birth. Babies react to the color red, for example, just a few days after they are born. Attraction to red continues throughout life. Color researchers say that when a restaurant has a red decor, customers stay longer and eat more. Men seem to prefer yellow-based reds—a tomato color or a bright, attention-getting fire-engine red. Women tend to choose blue-based reds, such as raspberry.

Pink seems to have a calming effect. In one study, conducted at a prison, convicts who became angry or upset were put in a bright pink room. They calmed down quickly. Other studies have shown that candy, pastries, and other sweet foods seem to taste better when they come out of a pink box or are served on a pink plate. But the rule doesn't hold for foods that aren't sweet.

Blue also has a calming effect. Deep, true blues seem to send a message of strength and trust, and pale blue is said to encourage daydreaming. Bright yellow often has the opposite effect—it can make people nervous and anxious. Studies have shown that babies cry more, and adults lose their tempers more easily, in yellow rooms.

There are also certain colors and color combinations that repel people. Orchid can prompt feelings of nausea. Most people also dislike muddy bronze and yellow-ocher shades. And the combination of black and yellow seems to act as an alarm, perhaps because many poisonous creatures in nature sport these colors. Whatever the reason, the reaction makes the combination useful for traffic signs.

Besides these and other unconscious reactions, color choices depend on many other factors. In fact, color preferences can be quite complicated. You may learn to value a certain color because your parents or your friends like it, because your favorite movie star or singer wears it, or because a popular television show features it.

Color can also be a way to make another statement about yourself. For example, many people like green—because most of nature is green, it's perceived as a restful, natural color. But true forest green appeals to only about three percent of people, and they tend to be people who have a lot of money. Social and economic differences play a part in other color choices, too. In general, people high on the ladder go for deeper and more complex colors, perhaps as a way of advertising their status.

Colors send other social messages, especially in clothing and cars. Black signals power and sophistication; gray, business success; brown, trust; and blue, authority and sincerity. To most people in Western societies, white is associated with purity.

Children like bright, simple colors until they reach their teens, when they begin to prefer more complicated shades. Color preferences depend on geography, too. Because the quality of sunlight varies from northern regions to southern regions, the same color can appear different depending on where it's seen.

WHICH HUE FOR YOU?

All these differences are interesting, but to many business people the question of color choice is very important. The color scheme of a workplace can affect the way people work, for example. Gray and beige seem to encourage creativity, while an all-white workplace promotes precision. In one case, changing

A DIFFERENT WORLD

To people who are color blind, the world looks very different than it does to people who see all colors. Many color-blind people see blues and yellows well, but reds and greens appear as shades of gray. Others confuse green and gray with certain blues, or have trouble distinguishing any pastel shade. Some see everything in shades of gray—all colors are the same to them.

Why does this happen? In the eyes, there are three kinds of cone cells. Each contains a different pigment that's sensitive to a different color—red, green, or blue. People who suffer from color blindness are missing one or more of these pigments.

Some forms of color blindness result from injury or disease. But in most cases color blindness is an inherited trait. It affects about 8 million Americans—about 8 of every 100 men, and about 1 of every 200 women. The reason that more men are color blind is that two of the three genes controlling color vision are linked to the genes that determine sex. (Genes are chains of protein inside body cells that carry codes for all physical traits and are passed from parents to children.) Women who have normal vision can still carry the color blindness trait, however, and pass it along.

classroom walls from orange and white to blue led to higher test scores and better behavior from students.

On supermarket shelves that are crowded with products, the color of a package can affect sales. For example, orange seems to be associated with good value. Research has shown that laundry detergent sells best in a blue and orange box—the colors signal a combination of strength and low cost. Manufacturers also try to develop "signature" colors that shoppers will automatically associate with their products.

Manufacturers often hire color consultants when they are developing new products. The consultants help them determine such things as the range of colors for new cars, home furnishings, clothing, house paint, and even toys, as well as packaging. In fact, a U.S. organization

Red makes food taste better, so we eat more. Babies react to red a few days after they are born.

Pink has a calming effect on people. Sweets seem to taste better when they come out of a pink box or are served on a pink plate.

Yellow is the first color the eyes see. It signals caution. Splashes of it are cheery; too much make people nervous.

Green makes people feel safe and secure, perhaps because most of nature is green. Dark green appeals only to about 3 percent of people, many of whom are rich.

Blue is most people's favorite color. Blue is calming. Dark blue signals authority and knowledge. Pale blue encourages daydreaming. People eat less from blue plates.

The same picture is shown as it is seen by people with normal color vision (opposite page, first photo) and by people with the three major types of color-blindness.

Many people who are color blind don't realize that they have a problem. This is especially true of young children—they assume that everyone sees the world the same way they do. But there are simple tests that can determine color blindness.

Scientists haven't yet found a cure for color blindness. Sometimes wearing special contact lenses helps. But researchers are working on the problem because color is more and more important in everyday life—in everything from primary school (where many teaching materials are color-coded) to computer technology (in which color is important in operating many programs).

called the Color Marketing Group, made up of consultants and color specialists from various industries, meets twice a year to coordinate colors for upcoming seasons.

Color consultants earn thousands of dollars for their advice. But now that you know something about color, you can put some of their ideas into practice. What color should your bedroom be? A calming blue or pink may help you relax there more easily. Pink is a good choice for bathrooms, too, because it looks good next to bare skin. A neutral gray or beige would be a good color choice for the area where you do your homework. Want to lose weight? Try eating off a blue plate—researchers say that people eat less around this color. Want your friends to open up to you? Try wearing brown, the color of trust. Whatever the situation, you can make color work for you.

Fifty years after Edmund Hillary and Tenzing Norgay (shown in 1953, above) first scaled Mount Everest, climbers are still lured to stand on Earth's highest peak.

MOUNT EVEREST: THE TOP OF THE WORLD

You're standing on a narrow ridge of wind-blasted snow and rock. The air is so cold that it bites, and so thin that you need an oxygen mask to breathe. On each side of you the ground drops away with terrifying steepness—one bad step, and you'll plunge thousands of feet to an icy death. Looking out over vast spaces, you see ridge after ridge of snow-covered peaks. The only sound is the wind.

Welcome to the top of the world—the summit of Mount Everest, the highest place on Earth. Everest was first scaled on May 29, 1953, by Edmund P. Hillary and Tenzing Norgay. They were hailed as heroes for conquering the mountain. And in 2003, the world celebrated the 50th anniversary of their feat.

Since 1953, more than 1,200 people have struggled to the top of Mount Everest. Today, with better equipment and experienced guides, climbing the world's tallest mountain isn't as impossible as it seemed before Hillary and Norgay's success. But Everest is still a daunting place!

THE MOUNTAIN

Mount Everest towers 29,035 feet (8,850 meters) above sea level. It belongs to the Himalayas, the massive mountain range that lies between China and the Indian subcontinent. Everest itself stands on the border between Tibet, which is controlled by China, and Nepal, an independent kingdom north of India.

The summit of Everest isn't only the highest place on Earth, it's also one of the most severe. In winter, the temperature averages about –33°F (–36°C). Even in summer, it never rises above freezing. Winds often reach hurricane force, carrying snow off the peak in a great plume that stretches out like a flag. Violent snowstorms can buffet the summit in any season. Climbers usually wait for "weather windows" in spring and fall, when winds die down and snowstorms are less likely.

The huge peak is named for George Everest, who surveyed the Indian subcontinent for Britain in the mid-1800's. It was he who first determined that this mountain is the highest in the world. But the people who live near the mountain have other names for it. In Tibet, it is *Chomolungma*—Goddess Mother of the World. In Nepal, it's *Sagarmatha*—Goddess of the Sky.

Traditionally, Nepalese and Tibetans have considered the peaks of the Himalayas to be the homes of the gods. The mountains were thought to be sacred, and local people had no interest in climbing them. Mountain climbing was a Western sport. And for many years, both Nepal and Tibet were closed to foreigners—putting Everest off limits for climbers. But that only made the idea of climbing the world's tallest peak more tempting. For mountaineers, Everest became the ultimate challenge.

TO THE TOP

In 1920, Tibet opened its borders, and soon after that a group of British mountaineers tried to climb Everest's north side. Led by George Leigh Mallory, they were forced to turn back. On Mallory's third attempt, in 1924, he and a climbing companion came within 800 feet of the summit. Then they disappeared, victims of Everest's extremes.

Everest became notorious for its dangers—high winds, extreme cold, and avalanches that thundered off the peak, carrying climbers to their deaths. The lack of oxygen at high altitudes could make climbers light-headed and even cause death. Climbers carried oxygen tanks, but some still died from the effects of "altitude sickness."

Through the 1940's, there were nine attempts to climb Everest from the north. Then China took control of Tibet, and that route was closed. But in 1950, Nepal was

Mount Everest Record-Setters—2003

Fastest Ascent

Most Ascents

Oldest

Youngest

A record number of climbers tried for the summit in 2003, in time for the anniversary of the first ascent. Many were forced to turn back by the mountain's notorious winds and weather. Others broke records:

Fastest ascent: Lhakpa Gulu Sherpa of Nepal, 10 hours and 57 minutes, on May 26, 2003

Youngest person to make the ascent: Mingkipa Sherpa of Nepal, 15 (female), on May 22, 2003

Oldest person to make the ascent: Yuichiro Miura of Japan, 70, on May 22, 2003

Most ascents: Appa Sherpa of Nepal, 13th ascent on May 26, 2003

Today's high-tech equipment has made Everest easier to climb. But the mountain is still a dangerous place.

on the mountain, each one higher than the last. At each camp, a few climbers stayed behind while the rest continued up. There were just two climbers at the last camp, at 27,900 feet (8,500 meters)—Hillary, who was a New Zealander, and Tenzing Norgay, who was a Sherpa (a member of one of the hill tribes that live near Everest).

On the morning of May 29, Hillary and Norgay strapped heavy oxygen tanks to their backs and set out for the summit, picking their way up steep slopes and across unstable snowfields. The last stretch of the climb took them along the edge of a narrow ridge, with breathtaking drops on each side. At last, exhausted and together, they reached the summit. Everest had been conquered.

Hillary and Norgay won lasting renown. Hillary was knighted by Queen Elizabeth II of England. Before long, other climbers followed in their footsteps. In 1956, following the same route as Hillary and Norgay, four Swiss climbers "summited" Everest. In 1963 an American expedition put six men on top. Four climbed by way of the South Col, and two blazed a new west ridge route.

opened to foreigners, and mountaineers switched their efforts to Everest's south side.

In 1953, the British mounted their tenth expedition to Everest. They went by way of the South Col, which is a pass between the peaks of Everest and Lhotse. The expedition members, ten in all, set up a series of camps

Cleaning Up Mount Everest

Mount Everest is not only the world's highest mountain—it's also the world's highest garbage dump! As more and more climbers have scaled the mountain, they have left the slopes littered with food cans, oxygen canisters, plastic bottles, magazines, clothes, ropes, and even tents.

Climbers are supposed to carry down whatever they take up. But many mountaineers are so exhausted by the climb, they leave behind what they can.

Japanese mountaineer Ken Noguchi has brought down tons of garbage from Everest.

The situation is worst at the South Col, the most popular route to the summit. Climbers often camp there for days, waiting for the weather to clear. The South Col has more garbage than any other place on the mountain.

Now the Nepalese government and teams of foreign climbers are working to clean up the mess. Since 1996 teams from Nepal, Japan, and the United States have brought down thousands of tons of garbage from the mountain.

Fiftieth anniversary celebrations. an Everest marathon (*above*); Hillary at a parade in Nepal (*right*).

FIFTY YEARS LATER

Climbers who attempt Everest today have an easier time than Hillary and Norgay did. That's partly because they have better equipment. Tough, lightweight synthetic materials are used for everything from clothes and boots to ropes and tents. Climbers pack dehydrated foods and energy bars, and they carry oxygen tanks that weigh much less than earlier models. They also benefit from high-tech weather forecasting, better training and mountaineering techniques, and satellite communications.

Experienced Sherpa guides also give today's climbers an edge. Since 1953, mountain trekking has become an important source of income for the Sherpas. Most expeditions would never reach the top of Everest without these guides. The guides climb ahead of the main group, securing ropes and laying lightweight aluminum ladders over deep crevasses in the ice. They set up tents at the next camp, and then they go back to guide the climbers up.

Even with help, climbing Everest is extremely difficult and dangerous. Yet more and more people have set out to conquer the mountain each year. Experienced mountaineers have also raised the bar by trying new routes and setting new challenges. People have reached the top by climbing without oxygen, climbing in winter, and climbing solo. Climbers have even skied, snowboarded, and paraglided from the summit!

The May 29 anniversary was celebrated with many special events. Among them were a marathon race on the mountain's lower slopes and a special ceremony to honor the more than 175 people who have died trying to climb Everest. Hillary was on hand for a parade and a gathering of Everest "summiters" in Katmandu, Nepal's capital. He had maintained close links with the Sherpas over the years, helping to bring hospitals and schools to their region.

Norgay died in 1986, but his son, Jamling, represented him at the celebration. Jamling said of his father and Hillary, "They took a step farther into the unknown. They made known that it was possible for us to climb this mountain."

113

100 YEARS OF
WILDLIFE REFUGES

One hundred years ago, tiny Pelican Island (*above*) was the last breeding ground for brown pelicans along the entire east coast of Florida. These magnificent birds, along with beautiful herons, egrets, and spoonbills, had been hunted nearly to extinction for their feathers, which were wanted for women's hats. But because people cared, the birds were saved—and Pelican Island became the first National Wildlife Refuge (NWR).

The year 2003 marked the 100th birthday of the U.S. National Wildlife System, which today protects more than 95 million acres (38,445,000 hectares) across the United States. Hundreds of animal species, many rare and endangered, are sheltered in these natural havens. National Wildlife Refuges are administered by the U.S. Fish and Wildlife Service, and many are open to the public.

Pelican Island first came to national attention thanks to the efforts of Paul Kroegel, a German immigrant who stood guard to protect the birds that nested on the island from hunters. His brave actions drew notice from conservationists and from President Theodore Roosevelt, who declared the island a National Wildlife Refuge on March 14, 1903.

More than 540 such reserves have been created across the United States and its territories since then. Here are snapshots from just a few of them.

The black-footed ferret has been one of the most endangered mammals in North America for many years. Now a group of these rare animals is thriving at the Charles M. Russell National Wildlife Refuge in Montana.

Black-footed ferrets prey on prairie dogs and live in prairie dog burrows. As the Great Plains were settled and large tracts of wild prairie were plowed for farmland, habitat was destroyed for prairie dogs and ferrets alike. But since 1994 black-footed ferrets have been reintroduced at several sites, including the Russell NWR. This vast refuge extends 125 miles (200 kilometers) up the Missouri River, above Fort Peck Dam, and contains about 1,100,000 acres (445,000 hectares). Within its boundaries are native prairies, forested gullies, river bottoms, and badlands. The refuge is named for Charles Russell, the Western artist who often portrayed this wild landscape in his paintings.

Seals stretch out to sun themselves on the rocks at Farallon National Wildlife Refuge in California. The refuge is made up of islands in the Pacific Ocean about 30 miles (48 kilometers) off San Francisco. It's the site of the largest seabird breeding colony on the Pacific coast south of Alaska. More than 300,000 gulls, auklets, and other birds nest there during the summer.

Nesting seabirds such as this Atlantic puffin are protected on the islands of Petit Manan National Wildlife Refuge in Maine. Petit Manan is a 3,335-acre (1,350 hectare) refuge that includes land on Petit Manan Point, Petit Manan Island, and portions of two other islands, Bois Bubert and Nash. It's part of a complex of refuges that span 200 miles (320 kilometers) off the Maine coast.

The main focus at Petit Manan is restoring and managing colonies of nesting seabirds. Besides Atlantic puffins, islands in the refuge provide habitats for common, Arctic, and endangered roseate terns; razorbills; black guillemots; Leach's storm-petrels; and other species. Over the last 25 years, the Fish and Wildlife Service has worked to reverse a decline in the population of these birds. Many species have returned to nest on islands where they had disappeared.

Moose graze the grasslands at Agassiz National Wildlife Refuge, in northwestern Minnesota. With more than 60,000 acres (24,280 hectares), this refuge includes evergreen forests, tallgrass prairie, and the "prairie pothole" wetlands of the Red River Valley. Besides moose, it is home to black bear, gray wolves, and bald eagles. Its wetlands are habitat for migrating waterfowl.

A leatherback sea turtle digs a hole for her eggs at Sandy Point National Wildlife Refuge, in St. Croix in the U.S. Virgin Islands. The beach at Sandy Point, which is more than 3 miles (4 kilometers) long, is an important nesting site for these endangered turtles. More than 350 leatherback nests are dug each breeding season. Hawksbill and green sea turtles also nest on the beach. Inland, the refuge has more than 360 acres (145 hectares), including the largest salt pond in the Virgin Islands. It is home to many birds, including rare West Indian flamingos.

Endangered whooping cranes wade through the ponds and saltwater marshes at Aransas National Wildlife Refuge, along the Gulf of Mexico in Texas. One of the rarest creatures in North America, whooping cranes nest in Canada during the summer and return to winter at this coastal refuge each year. With its grasslands, live oaks, and redbay thickets, the Aransas refuge is also home to alligators, deer, and many other kinds of animals.

Flocks of migrating snow geese swoop in for a landing at Bosque del Apache National Wildlife Refuge, located along the Rio Grande river in New Mexico. Tens of thousands of birds—sandhill cranes, snow geese and other geese, and many kinds of ducks—winter here. Bosque del Apache is at the edge of the Chihuahuan Desert. Its 13,000 acres (5,260 hectares) of wetlands, fed by the river, are a green oasis in the dry surrounding lands. The refuge also preserves thousands of acres of desert wilderness.

About 3,000 Kodiak brown bears are at home in Kodiak National Wildlife Refuge in Alaska. The bears are a subspecies of grizzly bear found only on the islands of the Kodiak Archipelago, and the refuge was established in 1941 to protect their habitat. It covers nearly 2 million acres (809,000 hectares), including two-thirds of Kodiak Island and all or part of several nearby islands. The refuge can be reached only by boat or float plane. At least 600 pairs of bald eagles nest within its borders.

Alligators lurk in the dark pools of Okefenokee National Wildlife Refuge, on the border between Georgia and Florida. More than 10,000 of these reptiles live in the huge freshwater Okefenokee Swamp, which extends 38 miles (61 kilometers) north to south and 25 miles (40 kilometers) east to west. Its name comes from Indian words meaning "land of trembling earth." Deep peat deposits cover much of the swamp floor. The peat is so unstable that in some places just stamping the ground causes nearby trees and bushes to tremble.

Surefooted desert bighorn sheep clamber among the rocks at Cabeza Prieta National Wildlife Refuge in the Sonoran Desert of Arizona. This desert wilderness is as big as the state of Rhode Island. It includes rugged mountains and desolate valleys where saguaro cacti stand like lonely sentinels. The sheep, like the other wild animals that live here, have adapted to harsh desert life. They can go for weeks at a time with only the moisture they get from food or from puddles of rainwater.

People have always been intrigued by the beauty of snowflakes. Now, with the use of computers, scientists are learning how these delicate ice crystals are created.

SECRETS OF SNOWFLAKES

Have you ever caught a snowflake on your sleeve? If you looked closely at it, you know how beautiful these delicate ice crystals are. But you would need a microscope to see the full range of their beauty. Each snowflake has a delicate six-pointed shape. And each snowflake is different from the next.

Snowflakes are full of secrets. What causes them to form? Why do they always take six-sided shapes? What creates their delicate patterns? And why is it that no two snowflakes look exactly the same? Scientists have puzzled over these questions for years. Now, with the help of computers, they are finding answers.

FROZEN STARS

Snow forms as much as 6 miles (10 kilometers) above Earth's surface, where temperatures are cold. The cold causes water vapor to condense into tiny droplets, forming clouds. And if the temperature is below freezing, the droplets may form ice crystals. The structure and electrical charge of water molecules cause ice crystals to have a hexagonal (six-sided) shape. If the temperature is extremely cold—below −40°F (−40°C)—the droplets freeze instantly into ice crystals. But if the temperature is slightly warmer, the water needs a "seed"—a speck of dust or other matter—to freeze around.

A snowflake begins its short life when ice forms around a seed. It grows as it picks up more ice crystals. The new crystals collect on the six corners of the hexagon because the corners stick out farthest. If conditions are right, the corners begin to grow into six arms, each with branches. These arms are called dendrites.

The ice crystals that make up snowflakes are clear. But snowflakes appear white because the surfaces of the ice crystals reflect light and scatter it in all directions. Snowflakes reflect the full spectrum of light, which we see as white.

A snowflake becomes heavier as it grows, so it starts to fall. It picks up more crystals as it falls, so it continues to grow. But on its way to the ground, it meets many changes in the temperature and moisture content of the air. These changes affect its pattern of growth. No two snowflakes take exactly the same path to the ground, so each meets slightly different conditions. That's why each snowflake looks different.

NO TWO ALIKE

Snowflakes get larger and more complex as the amount of moisture in the air increases. Temperature is important, too. In cold, moist air, snowflakes tend to form lacy stars with sharp tips. In drier air, they may become flat, six-sided plates, columns, or needle-like crystals. If the air is warmer, snowflakes clump together as they fall to the ground. These clumps can be an inch (2.54 centimeters) across and contain thousands of snowflakes.

Because tiny changes in weather conditions can produce almost infinite variations in the shape of snowflakes, no one has ever seen two that are exactly the same. It might be possible for identical snowflakes to form, mathematicians say. There may be 18 million snowflakes in a cubic foot of snow, and snow has been falling for a couple of billion years. It's possible—even likely—that at some point a snowflake formed that was just like one that had formed before. But you're still not likely to see two identical flakes.

Still, snowflakes have enough similarities that they can be divided into groups. Scientists have identified nine classes of snowflakes—including dendrites, plates, needles, columns, and prisms—and 30 subclasses. They're using computers to figure out how snowflakes form, and they're also experimenting with ice crystals formed

SNOWFLAKE BENTLEY

You've read that no two snowflakes are exactly the same. But how did that fact become known? Wilson Bentley, a Vermont farmer, was the first to figure it out.

Bentley was fascinated by snowflakes as a boy. As he grew older, he began to study them scientifically. Using a camera attached to a microscope (above), in 1885 he became the first person to photograph the crystal structure of a snowflake. He eventually photographed more than 5,000 snowflakes.

"Every crystal was a masterpiece of design, and no one design was ever repeated," Bentley wrote. "When a snowflake melted, that design was forever lost. Just that much beauty was gone, without leaving any record behind."

Bentley's pictures and articles were published in scientific journals. He became known as "Snowflake" Bentley for his work. You can read more about him and see his pictures at: www.snowflakebentley.com

in the lab. They're interested in finding out how snowflakes interact with the atmosphere. Some research suggests that snowflakes may help clean the air of some polluting chemicals as they fall to the ground.

When snowflakes reach the ground, they change their shape. If temperatures are warm, they melt. Even if snowflakes don't melt, evaporation and condensation soon change them into tiny, smooth-sided granules. All too soon the beautiful patterns disappear, taking the snowflakes' secrets with them.

is to take a piece of dark cloth outside while it's snowing. Spread the cloth where snow will fall on it, and use a magnifying glass to see the snowflake patterns before they melt.

It's also possible to capture a print of a snowflake that can be viewed under a simple microscope. For this, you'll need a microscope slide, a box with a lid, and a can of clear acrylic spray. When snow is forecast, put the slide, box, and can of spray outside overnight. They must be cold, or the snowflakes you capture will melt instantly.

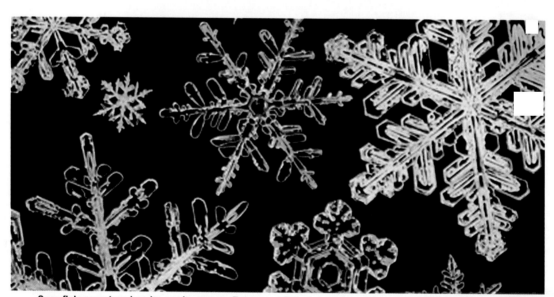

Snowflakes captured under a microscope: Every snowflake has a six-pointed shape, and each is unique.

At the poles and on mountain peaks where snow never melts completely, the snowfalls of thousands of years have built up in thick layers. The weight of these layers, along with alternating patterns of freezing and thawing, turns the snow into ice sheets and glaciers.

CATCH A FALLING SNOWFLAKE

To see a snowflake's beauty, you need to look closely—and quickly. One way to do this

To catch a snowflake, spray the slide with a light coating of acrylic. Hold the slide face up, so snowflakes will land on it. Then quickly put it in the box, and cover it with the lid. Leave the box outside until the spray is completely dry and hard. Then take the slide inside. The snowflake will melt, but it will leave a ghostly impression on the slide. You'll have an image of its beautiful pattern to keep and study whenever you want.

Make a Paper Snowflake

Beautiful one-of-a-kind snowflakes form high in the sky, where it's very cold. But you can create some fake flakes in the warmth and comfort of your home. All you need are scissors and some square sheets of white paper.

1. Begin with a square sheet of paper.

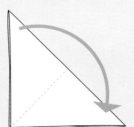

2. Fold it in half on the diagonal, so you have a triangle.

3. Fold the paper in half again, to make a smaller triangle.

4. Fold the smaller triangle in thirds: Bring the left side over so the edge is two-thirds of the way to the right, and fold down. Then fold the right side over the left.

5. Trim the unfolded edge of the paper straight across.

6. Make a full cut anywhere along the folded side of the paper.

7. Cut a design, leaving some of the folded edges uncut. Unfold your snowflake!

The car of tomorrow will be smarter, safer, and easier to operate—and more fun to travel in.

THE CAR OF TOMORROW

A beep from the microwave tells you that your popcorn is ready. You take it out, grab a soda from the mini-refrigerator, and flick on your palm computer to check your e-mail. Then, as you settle back in your massaging seat and pop a DVD into your personal player, you glance out the window. Trees and houses are flying by as your family car rolls along at a steady 55 miles an hour.

That scene may be commonplace in the not-too-distant future. High-tech gadgets are making cars smarter, safer, and simpler to operate. The car of the future may even be able to drive itself, cruising along on autopilot. Meanwhile, the family car is becoming more and more like a family room on wheels, designed to coddle and entertain passengers.

SMART CARS

Thanks to computers, cars have been getting smarter every year. Today's new cars have onboard computers that monitor mechanical conditions, fuel consumption, weather conditions, and even tire pressure. Computerized navigation systems are also available. These devices make use of the satellite-based Global Positioning System (GPS). The car picks up signals from satellites orbiting Earth, and an onboard computer uses the information to plot the car's exact position. At the same time sensors record your car's every movement and change of direction.

To use the system, all you do is enter your destination in the control unit. The computer figures out the best route and displays a map on a video screen. Because it would be dangerous for a driver to look away from the road to study a map while the car is moving, the computer also announces each turn as the car approaches it.

In the years ahead, improvements will make navigation systems even easier to use. Engineers are working on systems that can respond to voice commands, gather information on traffic and road conditions, and suggest alternate routes when conditions ahead are bad. Some cars already have reflected map displays that seem to float like holographs in front of the driver, so that the driver doesn't have to look to the side to see the map.

Similar "heads up" displays can float the car's speed and other essential information in front of the windshield, so the driver never has to stop looking at the road. A few cars even have a sort of night vision. Infrared detectors mounted on the front of the car pick up the heat created by animals and other objects before they appear in the car's headlights. The image of the object ahead is projected onto the windshield, giving the driver advance warning of the danger.

Tomorrow's cars may even be smart enough to recognize their drivers. One system would use sensors on the steering wheel to recognize the driver's fingerprint. Then the car's computer would use stored information to adjust the seats, steering wheel, mirrors and the like to suit that driver's preferences.

On the other hand, cars of the future may not even have steering wheels—or brake pedals. One idea is to replace the current controls with joysticks. Drivers would be able to steer, brake, and accelerate by using a pair of joysticks, one on each side of the driver's seat.

SAFER CARS

Most cars have blind spots—areas to the side and behind where the driver can't see everything. Today's cars have side and rear-view mirrors to help. A few have small video cameras, mounted to the rear of the car, that monitor what's behind. Images from the cameras appear on the car's navigation screen. In the future, more cars may have these cameras, and they may be placed to cover the sides as well as the rear of the car. That would eliminate dangerous blind spots by giving the driver a full view of everything around the car.

Radar is being adapted to create crash-avoidance systems for cars. One such system is a variation of cruise control, a system that maintains the car's speed without any attention from the driver. Cruise control has been available for a long time, but the latest version uses

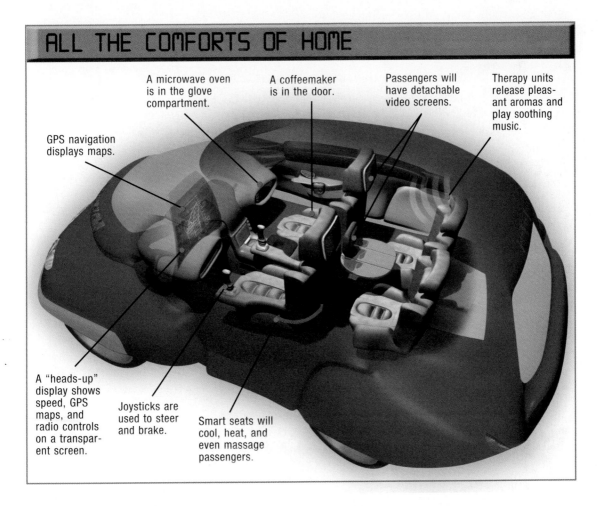

ALL THE COMFORTS OF HOME

A microwave oven is in the glove compartment.

A coffeemaker is in the door.

Passengers will have detachable video screens.

Therapy units release pleasant aromas and play soothing music.

GPS navigation displays maps.

A "heads-up" display shows speed, GPS maps, and radio controls on a transparent screen.

Joysticks are used to steer and brake.

Smart seats will cool, heat, and even massage passengers.

Rear Seat Monitor	Fingerprint Identification	Navigation Screen	Keyless Go	Night Vision
Watch DVD's, play video games, tune in your favorite TV show.	Place a finger on a sensor to make your seat adjust to your favorite position.	Display a GPS map to plan the best travel route.	You don't need a key—just the press of a button starts the engine.	Infrared sensors detect heat from an unseen obstacle and displays the image on the windshield.

radar to sense the speed of the vehicle ahead. Then it automatically adjusts the car's pace to make sure the two cars don't get too close for safety.

Another future system would sense when a car is swerving out of its lane, as may happen when a driver falls asleep at the wheel. Tiny video cameras mounted in the rearview mirror might even take note if the driver's eyelids start to close. The system would sound an alarm and cause the steering wheel and seats to vibrate, waking the driver. Farther down the road, car-makers hope to create an autopilot system for

cars. Using long-range cameras, the system would see what's ahead and automatically accelerate, brake, and steer the car.

The roads that cars travel may be smarter and safer, too. Cameras and sensors may keep watch over intersections, sending radio signals to cars. This system could warn drivers of approaching vehicles and might even stop cars from running red lights.

HIGH-TECH FUN

Drivers aren't the only ones who will bene-fit from high-tech changes. Passengers will be

Rearview Display

A rear-mounted camera shows the view behind the car.

Satellite Radio

A portable unit can move from the house to the car.

Active Cruise Control

Radar sensors adjust your pace to the speed of the car ahead.

watch a different DVD or show. Or passengers may plug in individual video headsets—but so far engineers haven't been able to design a video headset that doesn't make the wearer carsick when the car is in motion.

Wireless Internet connections will allow people to check their e-mail on the road. They'll even be able to send answers just by speaking, using voice-recognition software. Mood lighting and soothing scents are some of the other ideas that designers have on their drawing boards. Storage compartments may be reconfigured to hold foldaway tables and appliances like mini-refrigerators, coffee-makers, and microwave ovens.

Many of these high-tech gadgets share a problem: They're distracting. DVD's and microwave popcorn

able to enjoy all the comforts of home. In fact, with seats that heat, cool, massage, and cradle passengers, cars may even be more comfortable than home!

Video monitors already allow backseat passengers to watch DVD's or play video games. Satellite radios allow cars to tune in static-free broadcasts. Now engineers are working on systems that will allow cars to pick up satellite television broadcasts or download games, audio files, and movies via satellite, too.

In the future, each seat may have its own little video screen, allowing each passenger to

may be fine for passengers. But if they distract the car's driver, the result could be an accident. It's also possible that drivers may be distracted by all the heads-up displays, navigation screens, and other devices designed to help them.

Statistics show that similar distractions, such as talking on cell phones, already account for one-fourth of all crashes. Researchers are studying this problem, to see how much information drivers can handle at one time. Meanwhile, new technology keeps making cars smarter, safer—and more fun.

CELLULAR CAMOUFLAGE

The next time you pass a really tall tree on the road, look closely at it. It might be a fake, put up to camouflage antennas for cellular phones! Cell phones are everywhere these days. And so are the antennas that make cell phones possible. There are about 128,000 cellular antenna sites in the United States. Of those, about 25 percent are hidden or disguised.

Cell phones work like two-way radios. They send and receive radio signals.

Antenna towers located at base stations relay the signals. Each base station covers a small area called a cell.

As long as your cell phone is within range of a base station, you can make and receive calls. If you're driving around, your phone automatically switches from one station to the next as you move from cell to cell. But if you're out of range, your phone won't work.

People want to use their cell phones wherever they go. So phone companies are building many more

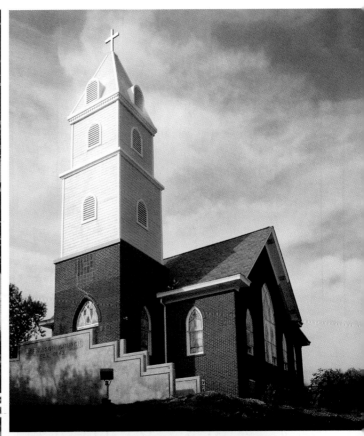

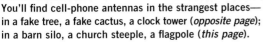
You'll find cell-phone antennas in the strangest places—in a fake tree, a fake cactus, a clock tower (*opposite page*); in a barn silo, a church steeple, a flagpole (*this page*).

cell-phone stations. Towers are sprouting all over the landscape. And in some places, people are objecting. A cell tower bristling with antennas isn't a pretty sight.

That's where camouflage comes in. In places where a cell tower would be an eyesore, companies are designing the towers to look like something else.

Flagpoles and trees are favorite disguises. Antennas can be hidden inside an extra-wide flagpole or the trunk of a giant fake tree. Fake clock towers and chimneys have also been built to screen antennas. In the southwest, antennas are hiding inside giant fake cacti!

Antennas are also being tucked inside existing buildings, such as church steeples and farm silos. These hidden antennas are helping calls go through—without spoiling the view!

EARTH WATCH

Water and soil, people, animals, plants—they all interact on our fragile planet Earth. And, as scientists noted yet again in 2003, not always in good ways. The main culprit? People. During the year, scientists continued to devise ways to combat the negative effects that people have had on the land, water, and living things of our planet.

Water, Water—It's Not Everywhere. People in the United States are used to having all the water they need. Open the tap, and fresh, drinkable water rushes out. But in many other parts of the world, clean water is scarce. To call attention to this problem, the United Nations proclaimed 2003 the International Year of Freshwater. Special events spread the word about water problems and encouraged people to take action.

Everyone, everywhere, needs water. People can't live without it. Neither can plants or animals. People also use water for growing crops, for transportation, and for industry. But there's only so much freshwater on Earth. In fact, just 3 percent of Earth's water is fresh (not saltwater). And two-thirds of that is frozen in ice sheets and glaciers. As the world's population grows, more water is used. In addition, people waste huge amounts of water and pollute water sources with chemicals and wastes.

According to the U.N.:

• Four out of every ten people worldwide live in areas where water is scarce. The problem is greatest in the Middle East, North Africa, and South Asia.

• By 2025, two-thirds of the world's people may be short of water.

• One-sixth of the world's people don't have safe drinking water. Some 6,000 children die every day from diseases associated with unsafe water and poor sanitation.

• One flush of the average Western toilet uses as much water as the average person in the developing world uses for a whole day's washing, drinking, cleaning, and cooking.

World leaders have pledged to cut in half the number of people without safe drinking water by 2015. They have set a similar goal for improving sanitation. But much more needs to be done—by governments, private groups, and individuals. The United Nations is encouraging people to start at home and take steps to save water.

Many people around the world don't have clean, drinkable water. Left: In New Delhi, India, people are washing their clothes on the banks of the river Yamuna. This polluted river is one of the major sources of drinking water for the people who live there.

Louisiana's coastal marshes (*above*) are sliding into the Gulf of Mexico. Around New Orleans, some homes are settling and cracking (*right*).

Louisiana Sinking. Tilted houses, dying trees, water where fields and forests once stood—those are signs of a big problem in Louisiana. The ground along the Louisiana coast is sinking into the Gulf of Mexico, at a rate of about 30 square miles (78 square kilometers) every year!

The land here has actually been settling for thousands of years, as part of a natural cycle. Most of North America rests on bedrock. But the New Orleans area stands on silt that's been carried down the Mississippi River. In the Mississippi River delta region, where the river meets the gulf, this silt slowly compacts under

CACTUS RUSTLERS

In the Old West, ranchers had to look out for cattle rustlers who might steal their herds. But now there's a new kind of rustler in the West. These rustlers ride in pickup trucks, not on horseback. They carry shovels, not six-shooters. And they aren't after cattle. They're stealing cacti!

Why would anyone steal a spiny cactus? In parts of the Southwest, people want to plant cacti in their yards and gardens because these plants need little water to survive. That's important in dry areas from Nevada to Texas.

Big cacti bring big prices. A full-grown saguaro can cost $5,000! But cacti grow very slowly. They take many years to reach full size. So instead of growing cacti, some landscapers

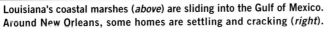

have become rustlers. They are going into the deserts and digging up barrel cacti (shown at left), wild saguaros, prickly pears, and other plants. Rustlers are rounding up rare kinds of cactus, too, to sell to collectors.

One hard-hit area is the Chihuahuan Desert of western Texas and Mexico. Some of the world's rarest cacti grow there. There's concern that some of the rare species won't survive if rustlers keep stealing them. Even digging up less-rare cacti has harmful effects on wildlife. Many desert animals depend on these plants for food and shelter. Some states have set up special cactus patrols to protect the plants. But the patrols are small—and the deserts are huge. Catching cactus rustlers isn't easy.

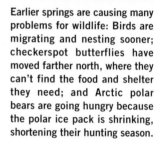

Earlier springs are causing many problems for wildlife: Birds are migrating and nesting sooner; checkerspot butterflies have moved farther north, where they can't find the food and shelter they need; and Arctic polar bears are going hungry because the polar ice pack is shrinking, shortening their hunting season.

its own weight. In the past, spring floods delivered more silt, which built up the ground and balanced the sinking. However, people broke that natural cycle by building levees to protect the land from floods.

The levees have prevented new soil from flowing in. But the old layers of soil have continued to settle. Drilling for oil and gas and natural erosion have added to the sinking problem. And as the land sinks, saltwater creeps into coastal marshes, killing freshwater plants. The roots of the plants no longer hold the soil in place, so it washes away.

Around New Orleans, houses and roads are tipping and settling. Some towns are becoming islands. Water is lapping at people's doors. Roads, shipping and industrial sites, the state's seafood industry—even supplies of drinking water—are threatened.

Louisiana officials came up with a $14-billion plan to slow the land loss. New channels will be dug to carry water and silt from the Mississippi River to threatened parts of the delta. And marsh grasses will be planted to hold the soil. No one knows if the plan will work, and stronger measures may be needed. Louisiana may one day have to build seawalls like those in the Netherlands to keep back the waters of the Gulf of Mexico. And in the areas most at risk, people may have to move to higher ground.

Early Springs . . . Endangered Wildlife. Birds fly north and build nests. Frogs wake up and begin to croak. Plants put out new leaves and flowers. Those signs of spring are always welcome. But spring has been arriving earlier in recent years, and scientists are worried. Many spring events are taking place an average of 2.3 days earlier every ten years!

Early springs are one sign that the world's climate is growing warmer. Studies published in 2003 outlined some of the effects of this warming on wildlife. In spring, birds migrated and nested sooner, and trees flowered earlier. In some cases, the warmer climate forced many plants and animals to shift their ranges to cooler regions. On average, ranges are shifting by 4 miles (6 kilometers) every ten years. The ranges of some butterflies have shifted north by 60 miles (96 kilometers) in recent decades.

CENSUS OF MARINE LIFE

The oceans teem with life, and to find out more about that life, 300 researchers in more than 53 countries began a ten-year project in 2000—the first Census of Marine Life. They hope this census will give them a picture of the past, present, and future of life in the oceans.

There are millions of different living things in the ocean, and each one plays a role in keeping the ocean ecosystem healthy. But the ecosystem is being damaged by pollution, overfishing, and other threats. How is ocean life coping with these threats? Scientists are hoping that the marine census will help them find out.

The census is focusing on a range of ocean habitats, from the Pacific Ocean shore to the Atlantic Ocean floor. The researchers are looking for unknown kinds of plants and animals. They have already found hundreds of new species (including the new species of scorpion fish shown above). And scientists predict that as many as 5,000 new fish species may be lurking in the oceans, along with thousands of previously unknown plants and animals such as worms and jellyfish.

Scientists are also reviewing historical records and other sources to find out what lived in the oceans many years ago. And they are learning about known species, such as large fish, whales, and seals (shown at left). They've attached tags to some of these animals, so they can be tracked by satellite.

The results of the census will help identify endangered species and provide information for the fishing and shipping industries. But mainly, scientists hope the census will show how the ocean ecosystem has changed in the past, and how it may change in the future.

These climate changes disrupt ecosystems—communities of plants and animals that depend on each other for food and in many other ways. For example, if trees flower too early, there may not be enough insects around to pollinate the flowers. And if butterflies move north, they may not find the plants they normally feed on.

The world's climate is now changing much faster than in the past. Many scientists believe that the burning of fuels such as oil and gas pumps carbon dioxide and other gases into the air. These gases trap heat the way glass traps heat in a greenhouse. And that's causing the climate to warm.

These climate changes are taking place with just a 1 degree increase in average world temperatures in the last 100 years. If people don't reduce the amounts of heat-trapping gases they pump into the air, scientists say, temperatures will go up another 2 to 10 degrees in the next 100 years. That will have even bigger effects on wildlife and could even cause some species to die out.

Left: An army of little clay warriors was recently unearthed in China. The figures are about 2,000 years old and include horses and chariots as well as soldiers. Above: The round-faced soldiers are all just 1 foot (.3 meter) tall. They are positioned as if they had been carrying various weapons.

CHINA'S LITTLE CLAY ARMY

Villagers in eastern China were out planting trees one day in 2002 when they made an amazing discovery. They put their shovels into the earth and turned up an ancient army of warriors—all 1 foot (.3 meter) tall and made of clay!

The clay soldiers were buried about 2,000 years ago, at a tomb site near Weishan Mountain, 300 miles (483 kilometers) south of Beijing. Now archaeologists are exploring the Weishan site. So far they have found hundreds of the little soldiers, along with little horses, chariots, and other figures. And they think that the site may hold many other treasures.

TINY WARRIORS

The Weishan site dates from the first half of the Han dynasty. Members of this dynasty ruled China for more than 400 years, from 202 B.C. to A.D. 220. Under the Han, China became a great empire, expanding into Korea and Central Asia. Archaeologists aren't sure who was buried at the site, but it's most likely the tomb of a member of the ruling family or an important noble. During the Han dynasty, sculptors often made small clay dancers, servants, dogs, and other figures to accompany the dead in the spirit world. Only someone very important, however, would have been sent into the afterlife with a military escort.

The statues are made of a type of fired clay called terra cotta and painted in bright colors. They were placed in the ground in marching order. At the front were the cavalrymen—soldiers mounted on sturdy horses painted with colorful decorations. Then came decorated chariots, pulled by more horses. Behind the chariots were rows of infantry soldiers, marching on clay feet. Alongside them were several figures representing musicians, including one with a brightly painted drum.

Some scholars think that the order of the figures mimics the order in which Han armies went into battle. Others aren't so sure. The figures may have represented the sort of honor guard that would have accompanied a prince when he traveled, to show his power and importance, rather than a battle group. Similar honor guards are shown in paintings of the time.

BURIED TREASURES

Near the pit with the clay soldiers, archaeologists found a tomb with gilded crossbows, arrows, and stone carvings. They don't know who was buried in this tomb, but they are fairly sure it isn't the main tomb at the site. The burial site seems to be spread over a large area, perhaps as much as 10,000 square feet (930 square meters). Archaeologists think that it may contain other tombs and many pits like those that contained the clay soldiers. If so, many more figures may be found, as well as other artifacts.

The Weishan warriors aren't the first such figures to be found in China. In the 1970's, researchers dug up more than 7,000 life-size clay soldiers and horses at the 2,200-year-old tomb of Emperor Shi Huangdi near Xian, in central China. Another clay army was later found in the same region. That site, the tomb of Emperor Jingdi and Empress Wang (157–141 B.C.), had some 40,000 figurines, including farm animals as well as soldiers. The Weishan discovery suggests that the Chinese may have made a regular practice of providing rulers and nobles with military escorts for the afterlife.

As the figures are dug up, the archaeologists are rushing to preserve them before their bright painted colors fade in the air. They are being taken to a nearby museum for restoration and conservation. Eventually China hopes to build a special museum to house them.

A Life-Size Clay Army

In 1974, Chinese farmers digging wells near the city of Xian made one of archaeology's greatest discoveries—a life-size terra-cotta army that had been buried for more than 2,000 years. The clay soldiers were guarding the tomb of one of the most important figures in ancient Chinese history, the Qin ruler who unified China in 221 B.C.

After defeating the rulers of other Chinese states, the Qin ruler proclaimed himself Shi Huangdi, which means "first emperor." He created the first centralized government of China and established uniform laws, weights and measures, and writing throughout his realm. He also began construction of a series of walls to keep invaders out of the country.

When Shi Huangdi died in 210 B.C., a complete army of more than 7,000 terra-cotta pieces—archers, foot soldiers, mounted troops, and chariots—was buried outside his tomb to guard him through the ages. With the soldiers were thousands of real swords, spears, and bows and arrows. Beautiful objects of gold and jade were also found.

Three years after Shi Huangdi's death, a civil war broke out and swept away his dynasty. But today his life-size terra-cotta army is one of China's biggest tourist attractions.

SPACE BRIEFS

Both disaster and achievement marked the exploration of space during 2003. On February 1, disaster struck when the U.S. space shuttle *Columbia* broke up during its return to Earth, killing all seven astronauts on board. Flights of other U.S. space shuttles were halted as scientists and engineers studied the tragedy.

Meanwhile, achievements were realized on other fronts. China sent its first person into space, unmanned probes were launched toward Mars and the moon, and a new space telescope trained its eyes on the universe.

THE *INTERNATIONAL SPACE STATION*

Suspension of U.S. space shuttle missions had an important impact on the *International Space Station* (*ISS*). It slowed work on construction of the *ISS* and affected the astronauts and cosmonauts who live on the station for months at a time. Without the space shuttle, crews began to travel to and from the *ISS* aboard Russian *Soyuz* craft. These craft were launched from and returned to Earth in Kazakhstan in Central Asia. Russia also sent a succession of unmanned *Progress* ships to the *ISS*. These

craft kept the crews supplied with water, food, fuel, and basic equipment.

The Expedition 6 crew of two U.S. astronauts and a Russian cosmonaut, which arrived at the *ISS* in November 2002, remained there until May 2003, when they were replaced by the Expedition 7 crew. The new crew was the first to have only two members, a U.S. astronaut and a Russian cosmonaut. They remained at the *ISS* until October, when another U.S.-Russian crew of two, Expedition 8, replaced them.

While in orbit, the crews maintained the *ISS* and carried out scientific experiments. In August, an exciting first-of-its-kind event took place. Cosmonaut Yuri Malenchenko married Ekaterina Dmitriev, a Russian-American, in the first space wedding. The groom said his vows in orbit, 240 miles (386 kilometers) above Earth. The bride said hers at the Johnson Space Center in Houston, Texas. A video hookup made the ceremony possible.

CHINA JOINS THE SPACE CLUB

On October 15, a powerful rocket lifted into the sky over the Gobi Desert in north-

All aboard the *ISS*. Below: Cosmonaut Alexander Kaleri and astronaut Michael Foale boarded the space station in October. Right: Ekaterina Malenchenko poses with a cardboard cutout of her new husband, cosmonaut Yuri Malenchenko—after the first wedding in space, in August.

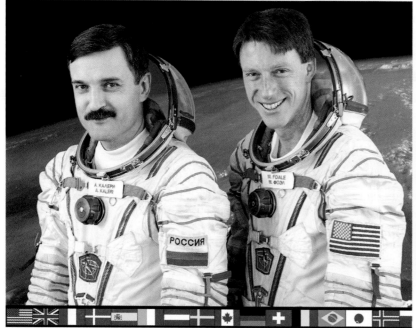

A hero's welcome: In October, Yang Liwei became China's first "taikonaut" when he orbited Earth 14 times in his spacecraft *Shenzhou 5*.

western China. On top of the rocket was the *Shenzhou 5* spacecraft, carrying Chinese astronaut Yang Liwei. Yang orbited Earth 14 times in his spacecraft. Then, after 21 hours in space, he returned to Earth, landing in the grasslands of Inner Mongolia. Thus China became only the third country ever to launch a person into space, joining Russia and the United States.

Yang had trained for years to be China's first "taikonaut." ("Taikonaut" is a nickname based on the Chinese word for space, *taikong.*) He was busy throughout his mission, but he took short breaks to nap and eat Chinese food designed for space travel.

The technology that sent Yang into orbit was similar to the systems that first sent Russians and Americans into space more than 40 years ago. The *Shenzhou 5* spacecraft was based on the *Soyuz,* with some improvements. It had three parts. In the back was a propelling module, to maneuver the craft. In the front was an orbiting module, designed to be left in space.

Close Encounter With Mars

On August 27, Mars was closer to Earth than at any time in nearly 60,000 years. It was "only" 34.6 million miles (55.7 million kilometers) away. The next time it will be this close will be in August 2287.

The close approach made Mars the second brightest object in the sky. Only the moon was brighter. Professional and amateur astronomers trained their telescopes on the planet, observing mountains and desert basins, and hoping to learn something new. The

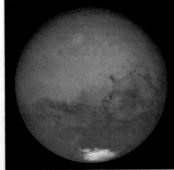

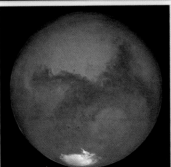

Hubble Space Telescope snapped the sharpest views ever taken of Mars from our planet. These included photos of the southern polar cap of dry ice—solid carbon dioxide—which gradually melted away as summertime arrived in the Martian south.

These two views of Mars up-close were snapped by the Hubble Space Telescope eleven hours apart. Mars completed almost half a rotation during that time. Thus the pictures show opposite sides of the planet.

New Eye on the Universe

On August 25, the United States launched the *Space Infrared Telescope Facility* (Sirtf, pronounced SIRT-ef), which picks up infrared light invisible to human eyes. (Although you cannot see infrared radiation, you can feel it—as heat.)

Sirtf is the last of the nation's Great Observatories, four space-based telescopes that study the sky across the energy spectrum. The most famous of these observatories is the Hubble Space Telescope, which sees visible light. The other two are the Compton Gamma Ray Observatory and the Chandra X-Ray Observatory.

Sirtf is designed to pick up infrared waves that travel through the dust that clouds parts of the universe. Scientists expect it to reveal new information about galaxies and stars. Sirtf will also help scientists see the universe as it was billions of years ago. Light from the most distant objects in the universe reaches Earth as infrared radiation. The infrared waves have taken billions of years to travel through space, and they show objects as they were in the earliest days of the universe.

In the middle was a re-entry module, to carry Yang back to Earth. Before re-entry, this part separated from the others. It protected the astronaut from the extreme heat created by friction with the atmosphere during the return trip. As it neared the ground, its parachutes opened to slow its fall.

It was a big moment for China, and many other countries sent congratulations.

NEW MISSIONS TO MARS

Most scientists think that the surface of Mars is too harsh a place for life. Life as we know it needs water, and the only water on the Martian surface is in the form of ice. But was Mars once a milder, wetter place? Could life have developed there at one time? During 2003, three spacecraft raced toward Mars in the hope of answering these questions.

The first to reach the Red Planet was the European Space Agency's *Mars Express*, launched on June 2. Upon its arrival in mid-December, it released a landing craft called *Beagle 2*, then went into orbit around Mars. *Mars Express* will beam radar at the Martian surface, looking for pools of hidden underground water. It will also gather information about the climate and minerals on Mars. However, by the end of 2003, *Beagle 2*—which carried a device to collect soil samples—had not yet been heard from and scientists were uncertain of its fate.

The United States launched a pair of identical robot explorers, the *Mars Exploration Rovers (MER's)*. The first rover, called *Spirit*, was launched on June 10, and touched down on the planet on January 3, 2004. The second, *Opportunity,* was launched on July 7 and was scheduled to arrive about three weeks after *Spirit*. Each traveled inside a protective shell. Once at Mars, parachutes would slow the spacecraft's descent. Then a cocoon of airbags would inflate around the spacecraft to cushion the shock of landing. After the spacecraft turned itself upright, the airbags would deflate and the shell would open so that the rover could roll out.

The twin rovers are about the size of golf carts and can travel about 100 yards (90 meters) a day. Each carries cameras and

Above: Identical U.S. robot explorers—named *Spirit* and *Opportunity*—were expected to reach Mars early in 2004. Right: The robots were named by 9-year-old Sofi Collis, the winner of a name-the-rovers contest.

tools for analyzing soil and rocks. They will explore two sites, on opposite sides of the planet, where scientists think water once flowed.

Spirit and *Opportunity* were named by 9-year-old Sofi Collis, a third-grader from Scottsdale, Arizona. She won a contest sponsored by NASA and the LEGO toy company. Kids submitted some 10,000 possible names for the twin rovers. The judges decided that the names Sofi suggested best suited the bold Mars mission.

BRIEF BRIEFS

Mission to the Moon. On September 27, the European Space Agency launched the unmanned *SMART-1*. "SMART" stands for *S*mall *M*issions for *A*dvanced *R*esearch and *T*echnology. It was the first European space craft to go to the moon.

The main purpose of the mission was to test a new solar-electric propulsion system, or ion engine. This system is ten times more efficient than a chemical rocket. In the future, such systems could be used for missions into deep space.

An ion engine doesn't burn fuel as chemical rockets do. Instead, solar panels on the spacecraft convert sunlight into electricity. The electricity is used to give a charge to atoms of xenon gas. The electrically charged atoms, or ions, speed away from the spacecraft, driving it forward.

SMART-1 is using its ion engine to spiral out from Earth until the moon's gravity catches it. Then, sometime in early 2005, it will enter a polar orbit around the moon. The spacecraft's instruments will peer at the dark parts of the moon's south pole, which have never been studied in depth. And it will hunt for frozen water in the craters of the moon's poles.

Stardust and Cassini. Two U.S. space probes are to begin important research in 2004.

Stardust, launched in 1999, will meet Comet Wild-2 in January, passing within some 90 miles (145 kilometers) of the iceball. Its mission is to collect interstellar dust and tiny particles from the glowing cloud surrounding the head of the comet. Then the craft will return the samples to Earth. If successful, the mission will be the first ever to bring back extraterrestrial material from beyond the moon.

Cassini, launched in 1997, is the largest interplanetary spacecraft ever built. It's scheduled to begin orbiting Saturn in July. Its mission will be to send back photographs and data about the giant planet's atmosphere, rings, and moons. It will deploy a probe, named Huygens, to explore Titan, Saturn's largest moon.

MAKE & DO

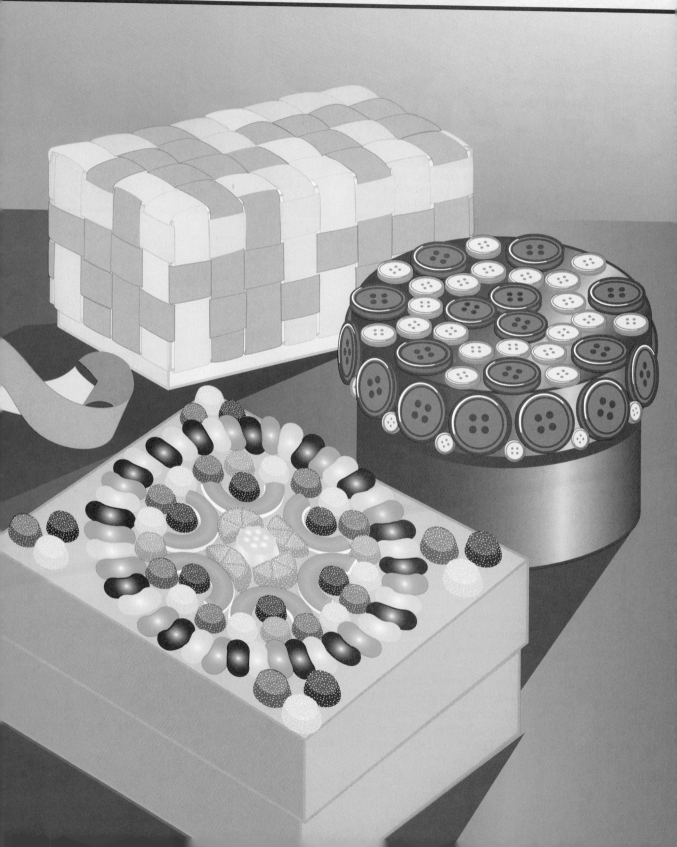

Here's an easy way to change an ordinary box into one that's pretty—and pretty unusual! Create your own unique design by decorating a box with ribbons, lace, buttons, candies, shells, macaroni, and other materials. Use your art box to hold your small treasures, or fill it with candy or gifts to give to your friends.

READ ALL ABOUT IT!

- ► Local Student Wins Science Scholarship!
- ► Drama Club Auditions for New Play!
- ► Home Team Champs Go to State Tourney!

Your life is filled with stories like these. Would you like to share them with your friends and relatives? You can do this by creating your own newsletter. A computer and some special software will make it easy.

What would you like to write about? Who will read your newsletter? What will you call it? How will you distribute it? When you've made these decisions, you can begin to design your newsletter.

Start with the masthead—this is the display at the top of the first page that gives the name of the newsletter. The masthead should be the same from one issue to the next. You should also try to arrange the text consistently from page to page and from issue to issue.

You might consider printing your newsletter on colored paper. This will help make it more appealing to readers. And adding graphics will make it especially eye-catching. Many computer programs provide clip art—images stored on disk that you can electronically "clip out" and "paste into" your newsletter.

The newsletters shown on these pages contain additional pointers on how to make them exciting and informative.

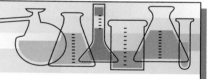

SCIENCE CLUB NEWS

Newsletters are a great way to get the word out about clubs, sports leagues, religious groups, and school and community events. Do you belong to a science club? Members of the club, as well as other students in your school, will enjoy a newsletter that gives information about upcoming science fairs, describes members' activities, and provides tips on how to conduct experiments.

To be successful, a newsletter must give readers what they need and want, so choose your subjects carefully. Try to be up-to-date. Don't worry if other publications, such as local newspapers, cover the same subjects. Your challenge is to provide coverage that's different and more complete. For example, a newspaper may present a brief account of a science fair. Your newsletter can devote several pages to the event, listing participants from your club, describing award-winning projects, and reporting interviews with judges. Hint: Always double-check the spelling of people's names!

Henry Smith received top honors last weekend at the County Science Fair. Read all about his project on page 3.

BLOOMING BLURBS

Spring Edition
50 cents

What's your favorite hobby? Woodworking? Gardening? Listening to popular music? Collecting baseball cards? Whatever it is, you can combine your favorite hobby with publishing to create a newsletter.

If your favorite hobby is gardening, for example, you'll need to get your newsletter to other people with a similar interest. Environmental organizations and scouting groups might be eager to have copies—especially if the newsletter provides lots of how-to information. If your local library has a "free literature" display, ask permission to include your newsletter there. And perhaps garden shops in your neighborhood might be interested.

Will your newsletter be free? Or do you want to sell it? If you decide to sell it, you should indicate the price on the front page of the newsletter, near the masthead. The price should be high enough to cover your expenses, including paper, printing, and distribution.

The price should include a profit, too. You could use the money to buy supplies or additional clip art. Many clip-art disks come with a wide variety of flowers and other botanical subjects.

Camp Chatter
Your Official Camp Newsletter

Do you go to summer camp? If you do, ask if you can use one of the camp's computers to publish a camp newsletter. This would be helpful to your fellow campers, and it would be a great way to let everyone back home know what you are doing. If you save all the issues, you'll also have a wonderful record of your summer camp stay.

What should a camp newsletter include? You could write about hiking trips. You could do articles on camp safety—how to build a campfire or what to do if you get lost in the woods, for example. You could even draw a comic strip about camp life.

Most people love to read about themselves. So write about your fellow campers. Spice up the articles by using quotes from the people you're writing about. You might also ask them—and counselors and other camp staff members, too—to submit poems or stories for publication. Encourage people to come to you with article ideas.

Make sure you give contributors a byline—a line right under the title of the article with the writer's name. And make sure to put your name and cabin and bunk number in the newsletter, so people can get in touch with you.

Tug-of-War

Teams for the tug-of-war contest will be chosen today at 4 p.m. in the dining hall. Make sure you're there on time!

Pet Talk

Cats. Dogs. Rabbits. Hamsters. Parakeets. Fish. It seems that there's a pet for everyone, and that pet owners enjoy reading about pets. So try publishing a pet newsletter!

Make sure the articles are varied and interesting. Make sure, too, that you design an attractive layout. This is easy to do with special software programs.

First, give every story a headline, or title. The headline should be in large letters and in bold-face type, as shown below. Next, using your software programs, set the text in neat columns. You might place a short article in a diamond-shaped or circular box with an interesting border. Put a graphic in the center of a page and wrap text around it. Have fun experimenting!

It's the Law!

Do you have a cat or a dog? If so, obey the law!

Our state requires that cats and dogs receive annual rabies vaccinations. This protects the animals—and you!—against rabies, a deadly disease caused by a virus. The virus is passed from one animal to another in saliva. For example, an infected animal might bite your pet and give it the disease.

Contact your vet today and make sure your pet is up-to-date on all its shots.

Finicky Feline

Nothing is more important to your cat's health than good nutrition. A cat won't thrive on human food—just as you wouldn't stay healthy if all you ate was cat food.

Veterinarians recommend that quality commercial cat foods should make up the major portion of your cat's diet. But the cat might also enjoy an occasional treat, such as a little cottage cheese or cooked egg. Some cats even like string beans and other vegetables.

Life in a Bowl

"It's much more fun than watching television!" says Dave Morse about raising and caring for fish. We interviewed Dave at Fish Tales, a new store at 53 Maple Avenue. Dave has two aquariums at home, and he was at Fish Tales to buy a pair of fish to breed. "I can't decide whether to buy pearl gouramis or harlequin fish. Both are beautiful!"

Barbara Diaz, owner of Fish Tales, offers some advice to people interested in keeping an aquarium: "Buy a wide rectangular tank. It has more water surface open to the air than a globe or a tall, narrow tank. The water can take in more oxygen, a gas that's very important to the health of fish. "It's also important to place the aquarium in a healthy location in your home. It shouldn't be placed in direct sunlight or near a radiator or other source of heat. Nor should you put it in a drafty spot. Sudden changes in temperature can kill fish."

Dave, by the way, bought the gouramis. Ms. Diaz told him that they are peaceful fish, although they jump when frightened. They like habitats with lots of plants. When the gouramis are ready to mate, the male builds a large bubble nest between floating plants. He also looks after the eggs until they hatch. Then, Dave should place the male in another tank—despite the gouramis' peaceful nature, the male might eat the baby fish!

Neighborhood News

ISSUE NUMBER 5

Block Party

Our annual block party will be held on Saturday at 1 P.M., with a fantastic picnic. The Caseys will grill hot dogs and burgers, and the Browns will provide drinks. Everyone else is asked to bring a salad or a dessert. You can call Mr. Casey (555-5555) for more information.

A neighborhood newsletter could be a wonderful way to bring your neighbors together and keep track of events in your community. How often should you publish it? Professional newspapers and magazines have a regular publication schedule. They come out daily or weekly or monthly. Try to publish your newsletter on a regular basis, too, perhaps once a month. Remember, writing an issue can be time-consuming!

Do you need article ideas? Look at the calendar. Holidays are always good subjects. What costumes will the kids in your neighborhood be wearing on Halloween? How will people celebrate Valentine's Day? What's the recipe for that relish your neighbor makes at Thanksgiving? You can even devote an entire issue to one subject: back-to-school or summer vacation.

When writing about upcoming events, include the names and telephone numbers of people who can provide additional information. But first get permission to list their names.

LOOKING FOR A JOB?

Most teens are interested in ways to earn money, so a newsletter about jobs should find a wide readership in your school and community. In addition to listing job openings and opportunities, your newsletter can provide tips on how to write résumés, how to dress for interviews, and how to answer telephones. You can publish interviews with local business employers, too. The interviews could cover such matters as the kinds of jobs available, educational and other requirements, salaries, and working conditions. You can also ask them to describe the kinds of people they feel would make the best employees.

FLASH:

Ace Car Experts and Henry's Supermarket need full and part-time workers.
See our "Help Wanted" listings on Page 3.

Software programs have many special features that can help you produce a professional looking newsletter about jobs. For example, most programs come with a variety of type fonts. A font is a complete set of letters, numbers, and punctuation marks of a particular size and design.

This "Looking for a Job?" newsletter uses five different type fonts. Some fonts are suitable for regular text. Others are perfect for headlines and other attention-getters. Try experimenting with various mixes of type fonts. Create a design that's exciting but doesn't look too busy.

Yard Work

A job taking care of lawns and gardens can be profitable. Many professional lawn services are eager to hire summer workers. Look in the yellow pages for services in your area. If you're experienced and own the necessary equipment, you may prefer to line up your own customers.

BANGLES & BEADS

Bangles and beads make an eye-catching addition to any outfit—and they never go out of style. Try your hand at these simple crafts made with beads, safety pins, and scraps of fabric. You'll have striking accents for your wardrobe. They make great gifts, too—give the glittery bracelet to your mom, and the fancy necklace to a friend!

BANGLES

Dazzle your friends with an armful of colorful bracelets—each made with safety pins that have been filled with beads.

Lay forty safety pins in a row, with the heads facing up. (Use more pins for a large wrist, fewer for a small wrist.) Open the pins and fill with beads. Follow one of the patterns shown, or create your own design. Close the pins, and securely fasten them.

Next, place forty empty pins in between the beaded pins. The heads of the empty pins should be facing down. (If you are using tiny beads, even *these* pins can be filled with beads.)

Use two strands of elastic thread to connect the pins. Be careful: As you connect the pins, make sure they all open outward, not toward your wrist! Pass one piece of elastic through the top holes in the row of pins—through the heads of the beaded pins and through the tails of the empty pins. Bring the ends together and knot. Repeat the process for the bottom of the row of pins. Place a drop of glue on the knots to prevent them from loosening.

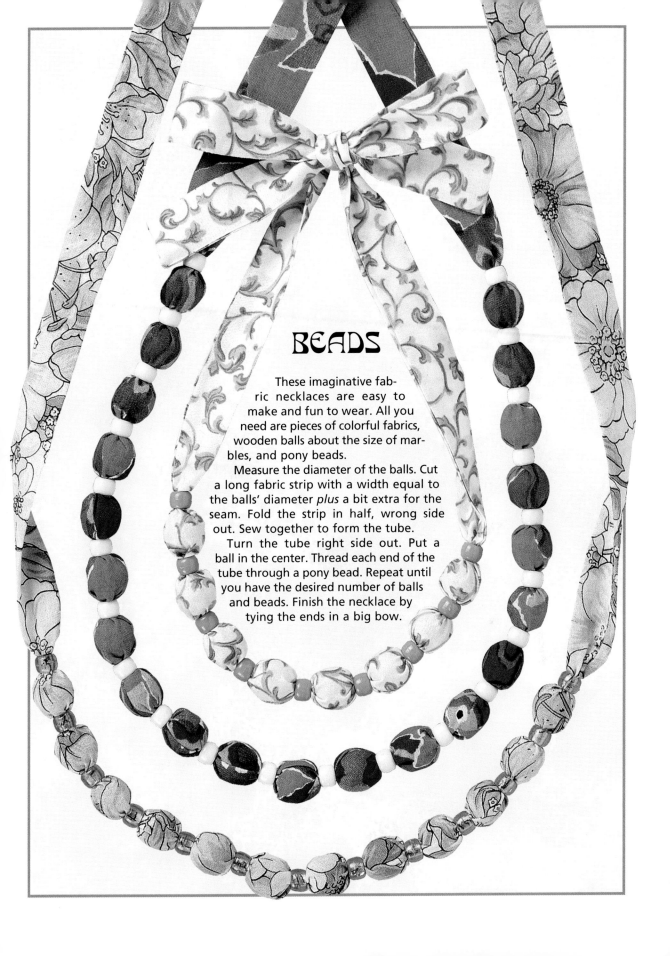

BEADS

These imaginative fabric necklaces are easy to make and fun to wear. All you need are pieces of colorful fabrics, wooden balls about the size of marbles, and pony beads.

Measure the diameter of the balls. Cut a long fabric strip with a width equal to the balls' diameter *plus* a bit extra for the seam. Fold the strip in half, wrong side out. Sew together to form the tube.

Turn the tube right side out. Put a ball in the center. Thread each end of the tube through a pony bead. Repeat until you have the desired number of balls and beads. Finish the necklace by tying the ends in a big bow.

ORIGAMI: PAPER SCULPTURE

Origami is the art of folding paper into decorative objects. The name "origami" comes from the Japanese words *oru* (to fold) and *kami* (paper). With a few folds, a square piece of paper can be transformed into an intricate design!

Traditional origami is always done without cutting or pasting. In creative origami, which is a more recently developed art, scissors and even paste can be used to help form more complicated designs. People usually begin with the traditional designs.

To get started, you need paper that's thin and crisp enough to hold the folds and creases well, yet strong enough to give body to the designs so they will stand. Use inexpensive paper, such as photocopy paper, to practice with. Once you gain confidence, you may want to use colored paper, which makes more interesting designs. Thin Japanese paper, called *washi,* is usually brightly colored on one side and plain on the other.

The paper for your design must be a perfect square. Start practicing with one that

How to Make a Helmet

Here's an easy origami project. Try making a helmet that's large enough to wear.

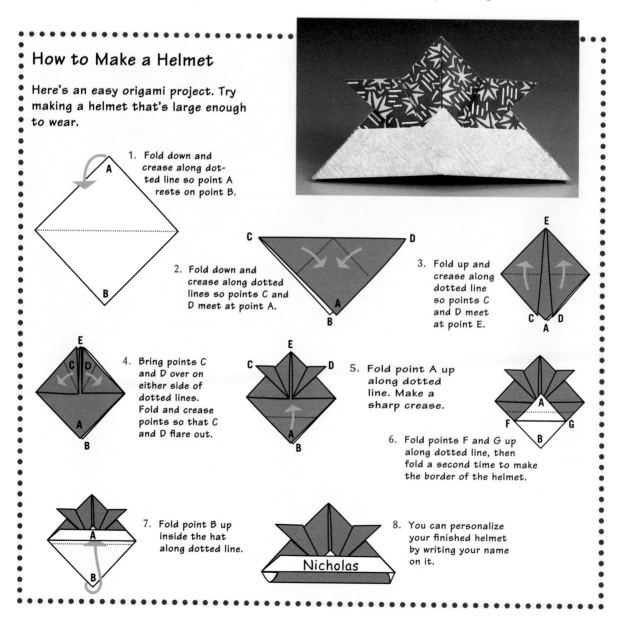

1. Fold down and crease along dotted line so point A rests on point B.

2. Fold down and crease along dotted lines so points C and D meet at point A.

3. Fold up and crease along dotted line so points C and D meet at point E.

4. Bring points C and D over on either side of dotted lines. Fold and crease points so that C and D flare out.

5. Fold point A up along dotted line. Make a sharp crease.

6. Fold points F and G up along dotted line, then fold a second time to make the border of the helmet.

7. Fold point B up inside the hat along dotted line.

8. You can personalize your finished helmet by writing your name on it.

Nicholas

How to Make a Swan

The swan is a classic origami design. Use a large square to create a mother swan and smaller squares to create her young.

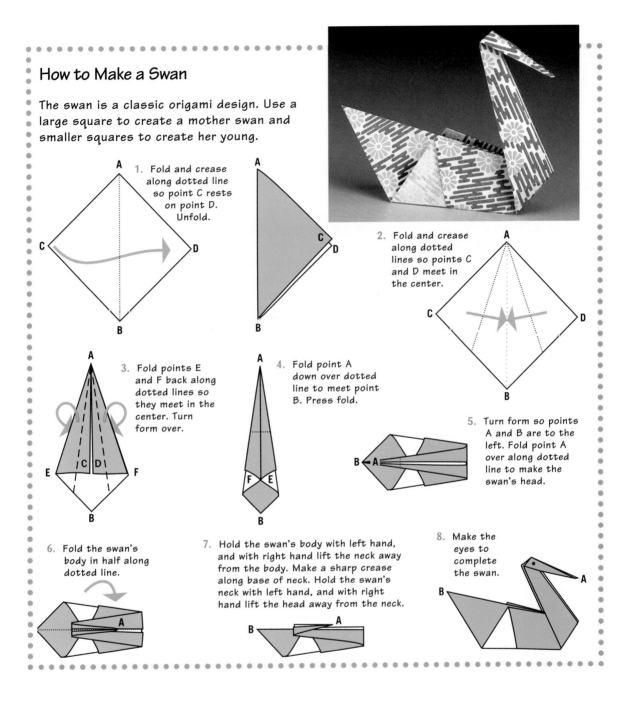

1. Fold and crease along dotted line so point C rests on point D. Unfold.

2. Fold and crease along dotted lines so points C and D meet in the center.

3. Fold points E and F back along dotted lines so they meet in the center. Turn form over.

4. Fold point A down over dotted line to meet point B. Press fold.

5. Turn form so points A and B are to the left. Fold point A over along dotted line to make the swan's head.

6. Fold the swan's body in half along dotted line.

7. Hold the swan's body with left hand, and with right hand lift the neck away from the body. Make a sharp crease along base of neck. Hold the swan's neck with left hand, and with right hand lift the head away from the neck.

8. Make the eyes to complete the swan.

measures 8 inches (20 centimeters) square. Work on a hard, flat surface, such as a table. Directions and diagrams should be placed so you can easily read them while you fold.

Here are some tips and suggestions:

● Start simple. Practice the basic, traditional forms.

● Be patient. At first you may find the instructions a little difficult to follow, but don't give up.

● Make accurate folds. Correct folds and creases are very important, so follow the directions carefully and don't skip steps.

● Make firm folds. By pressing your thumbnail along the fold, you will get a sharp crease, and this will keep your fold in place.

● Be creative. Draw eyes on your origami animals with a black marker. Make a hat out of newspaper. Draw a pond and fill it with origami swans of different colors and sizes.

TWO BROTHERS MAKE HISTORY

In 2003, the world celebrated the 100th anniversary of powered flight. On December 17, 1903, Wilbur and Orville Wright arrived at a sandy hill near Kitty Hawk, North Carolina. They started the engine of the plane they had built. Orville lay down on the lower wing to pilot the plane. He pushed a lever and the plane lifted into the air. It flew about 120 feet (36.5 meters) before touching down.

The brothers flew three more times that day. Then Orville went into Kitty Hawk and telegraphed home the triumphant news. Where was home? To learn where the brothers were born, you need a pencil and sheet of paper. Carefully follow the directions given below. Hint: It will be easier if you rewrite the complete words at each step. (The solution is on page 415.)

1. Print the words KITTY HAWK, NORTH CAROLINA.

2. Combine the first two words. Then combine the last two words. (Leave the comma and space between the two remaining words.)

3. Eliminate every K.

4. Change the first letter of the first word to an O.

5. Take out the CAR.

6. Find the seventh letter from the left. Change it to a D.

7. Find the I and put it between the H-O combination.

8. Reverse the order of the first two letters of the first word.

9. Remove the first four letters from the right.

10. Find the Y. Remove the letter to its left and the letter to its right.

11. Remove the first letter of the second word and insert it after the first vowel of the first word.

12. Delete the R-T combination.

13. Reverse the order of letters 4, 5, and 6 of the first word. Then place them at the beginning of the first word.

Although most people think of Kitty Hawk as the birthplace of aviation, the Wright Brothers' flight actually took place 4 miles (6.4 kilometers) south, from the base of Kill Devil Hill.

JACKS OF ALL TRADES

Our language is populated with JACKS. There are real people, such as JACK Nicholson and Jesse JACKson. And fictional people, such as JACK Sprat and that nimble young lad who jumped quickly over the candlestick. There are also the games of JACKs and JACKstraws.

Use the following clues to complete more words and names that contain JACKs.

1. A short coat   JACK _ _

2. Seventh U.S. president   JACK _ _ _

3. A couple who went to fetch water   JACK _ _ _ _ _ _ _ _

4. A male donkey   JACK _ _ _

5. A worker who cuts down trees   _ _ _ _ _ _ _ JACK

6. A pop-up toy   JACK- _ _ - _ _ _ _ - _ _ _

7. The top prize   JACK _ _ _ _

8. A large hare   JACK _ _ _ _ _ _ _

9. Florida city   JACK _ _ _ _ _ _ _ _ _

10. A carved pumpkin   JACK- _ '- _ _ _ _ _ _ _ _

11. A leather-covered hand weapon   _ _ _ _ _ _ JACK

12. Person symbolizing freezing weather   JACK _ _ _ _ _ _

13. A wild dog   JACK _ _

14. A machine used to drill rock   JACK _ _ _ _ _ _ _

15. Wildflower that grows in damp places   JACK- _ _ - _ _ _ _ - _ _ _ _ _ _ _ _

16. Valley in Wyoming   JACK _ _ _ _ _ _ _ _

17. Person who works on very tall buildings   _ _ _ _ _ _ _ _ JACK

18. A small crow   JACK _ _ _ _

19. A person who can do many things   JACK- _ _ - _ _ _ _ - _ _ _ _ _ _

ANSWERS: 1. jacket; 2. Jackson; 3. Jack and Jill; 4. jackass; 5. lumberjack; 6. jack-in-the box; 7. jackpot; 8. jackrabbit; 9. Jacksonville; 10. jack-o'-lantern; 11. blackjack; 12. Jack Frost; 13. jackal; 14. jackhammer; 15. jack-in-the pulpit; 16. Jackson Hole; 17. steeplejack; 18. jackdaw; 19. jack-of-all-trades.

STAMP COLLECTING

History, heroes, and holidays were among the many themes featured on stamps in 2003. Many of the year's most attractive stamps featured animals, a subject that's always popular with young collectors. But countries around the world presented a huge range for collectors to choose from.

U.S. STAMPS

The year 2003 marked the 100th anniversary of the first powered airplane flight, achieved by Orville and Wilbur Wright on December 17, 1903. The U.S. Postal Service marked the anniversary with a 37-cent commemorative showing the Wright brothers' plane, the *Flyer,* soaring over the dunes at Kill Devil Hill, on the coast of North Carolina. The self-adhesive stamps were issued in sheets of ten, with a photograph of the Wright brothers and a description of their achievement on the back of the sheet.

Other historical events marked by U.S. stamps included the 200th anniversary of

the 1803 Louisiana Purchase, in which the United States bought the vast Louisiana Territory from France. A 37-cent commemorative showed representatives of the two countries signing the treaty for this great land deal, which doubled the size of the young United States.

The U.S. flag has been featured on many stamps. But a group of five 2003 stamps gave this theme a new twist by showing unusual folk-art objects that incorporated the flag in their designs. The objects ranged from a folding fan to a carving of Uncle Sam on a bicycle. The stamps were sold only in special souvenir booklets and weren't available in all post offices.

Other U.S. stamps showed famous Americans, from early football heroes to U.S. Supreme Court Justice Thurgood Marshall. A new entry in the Legends of Hollywood series honored Audrey Hepburn, who charmed audiences in films from the 1950's through the 1970's. The stamp showed her as

**2003 STAMPS
FROM AROUND
THE WORLD**

she appeared in 1954 in one of her best-known films, *Sabrina*.

A coiled scarlet kingsnake was one of five animals in a group of stamps depicting American reptiles and amphibians. The scarlet kingsnake is harmless, but it closely resembles the poisonous coral snake. Other animals in the group were the reticulate collared lizard, ornate box turtle, blue-spotted salamander, and ornate chorus frog.

An elegant brown pelican was featured on a stamp marking the 100th birthday of Pelican Island National Wildlife Refuge in Florida. Pelican Island was the first of the more than 540 protected areas that today make up the National Wildlife Refuge system.

A colorful ram, based on a cut-paper design, decorated a new stamp in the U.S. Happy New Year series. In the Chinese lunar calendar, 2003 was the Year of the Ram. And for its Christmas stamps, the postal service released new designs showing fanciful Santas and reindeer playing musical instruments.

STAMPS AROUND THE WORLD

Hockey stars, tourist attractions, and the Year of the Ram were among subjects for 2003 stamps from Canada. Volunteer firefighters were honored on a 48-cent commemorative. The stamp showed a firefighter rescuing a child, against a background of smoke and flames from burning buildings.

The Canadian Rangers were honored on another new issue. These part-time military reservists keep watch over Canada's coasts, borders, and remote areas and take part in search-and-rescue missions. The stamp showed a ranger peering through binoculars, with the view reflected in the binocular lenses.

Classic children's games were featured on stamps from several countries. The Cayman Islands showed kids jumping rope, spinning tops, dancing around a maypole, playing hopscotch, and shooting marbles. Argentina depicted two games everyone knows—hide-and-seek and tag—and two traditional Argentine games.

Swashbuckling pirates figured in the history of the Bahamas, and in 2003 this Caribbean island nation featured five different pirates on stamps. The figures ranged from the legendary Blackbeard to Anne Bonney, one of the few female pirates. Tunisia, in North Africa, issued a series of stamps showing characters from myth as depicted in ancient mosaics.

Among the most unusual animal stamps was a set of four from Singapore. They showed cartoon-style illustrations of animals that are nocturnal (active at night), and the pictures glowed in the dark! The animals were the tarsier, a tiny primate from Indonesia and the Philippines; the barn owl, found worldwide; the clouded leopard of Asia; and the babirusa, an Indonesian animal that looks like a pig with tusks.

Valentine's Day brought a bouquet of "love" stamps. Slovenia's stamp was shaped like a heart—and smelled like a rose! Belgium's stamp showed hearts flying out of a bird cage, part of a set honoring caring professions such as nursing. Israel celebrated marriage on a stamp. A heart shape was used for the designs for a set of four stamps from Taiwan (Republic of China); they illustrated love for society, family, the Earth, and animals.

The Pacific island nation of Samoa produced one of the year's most unusual issues. Its Samoa on the Move set showed colorful buses on stamps that were shaped like buses. New Zealand honored the 50th birthday of its Royal New Zealand Ballet with a group of five stamps showing scenes from some of the dance company's productions.

Britain's Secret of Life set took a light-hearted look at a scientific milestone—the discovery in 1953 of the structure of DNA, the protein that carries the genetic code of all living things. The five stamps in this set marked the 50th anniversary of the discovery with cartoons. One stamp showed a scientist climbing a ladderlike molecule of DNA, in a new version of the old board game Snakes and Ladders. It illustrated the ups and downs that scientists have faced in trying to crack the genetic code.

A TOPICAL COLLECTION OF CAT STAMPS

People in Britain had fun with design-it-yourself stamps that were like the classic Mr. Potato Head game. The Fun Fruit & Veg stamps showed ten different fruits and vegetables. On the same sheet were 76 stickers showing features—eyes, noses, mouths, mustaches, ears, glasses, ties, hats, and shoes—that could be mixed and matched to turn the fruits and veggies into comical characters.

Pictures of spring and summer wildflowers, based on 19th-century watercolors, graced six stamps from the Netherlands. These stamps were semi-postals—that is, they carried a small extra charge to raise money for a cause. In this case, the cause was aid for the elderly. French Andorra continued its popular Legends series with a stamp depicting the Legend of the Margineda pine.

Poster art was the theme for the 2003 Europa stamps. These stamps are issued by member countries of PostEurop (the Asso-ciation of European Public Postal Operators). More than 50 countries took part. Among them, Luxembourg showed a reproduction of a colorful 1950's poster for the national lottery, while Portugal featured a jazz musician.

A TOPICAL COLLECTION

Cats are popular pets all over the world. In the United States, there are more cats than dogs. Naturally, cats are also popular subjects for stamps. And that makes cats a great focus for a topical collection—a collection built around a single theme, covering any year and any country.

Stamps from many countries spotlight the different kinds of cats, wild and domestic, that are found around the world. Other stamps highlight the playful antics and charming behaviors that make these animals so delightful. A collection of these stamps is a great reminder of the joy that cats can bring.

MANY FRIENDS COOKING

BANANA SMOOTHIE
from Kenya

Blend two bananas, and make some great shakes. Here's a refreshing drink to share with a friend on any picnic or safari.

INGREDIENTS

2 bananas
1 cup plain yogurt
1 cup orange juice
4 tablespoons honey

EQUIPMENT

knife
blender or jar with lid
measuring spoons
measuring cups
2 tall glasses

HOW TO MAKE

1. Slice the bananas. If you don't have a blender, mash the bananas with a fork.
2. In the blender or jar, blend the bananas with the rest of the ingredients.
3. Pour into two tall glasses. Add ice if you like a cold smoothie.

This recipe serves two people.

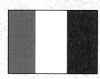

HERO SANDWICH
from Italy

A hero sandwich is called by many names, depending on where it's made. On the West Coast, it's called a submarine; in New England, it's known as a grinder; in Pennsylvania, it's a hoagie; and in New Orleans, a muffuletta. But no matter what you call it, try this tasty sandwich made with foods that originally came from Italy—salami, mozzarella and provolone cheeses, and Italian bread.

INGREDIENTS

1 Italian sandwich loaf or ½ loaf of Italian bread
4 lettuce leaves
2 tablespoons salad oil
1 teaspoon vinegar

8 slices of salami
6 slices of tomato
6 slices of cheese, such as provolone or mozzarella

EQUIPMENT

knife
paper towels

measuring spoons
small bowl

HOW TO MAKE

1. Cut the bread in half the long way.

2. Wash the lettuce leaves and pat dry with paper towels.

3. Lay the leaves on the bread. Sprinkle the lettuce with oil and vinegar.

4. Lay the other ingredients on top in any order you wish.

5. Cut into two sandwiches and serve.

For a hot hero, wrap the sandwich in foil and warm in a 250° F. oven for ten minutes.

This recipe serves two people.

EXPLORING UNKNOWN WORLDS

People have always been explorers of the unknown. They have traveled across land and water to distant places. They have gone deep beneath the surface of oceans, to the tops of the highest mountains, and into outer space. They have peered through telescopes at distant stars and through microscopes at tiny creatures.

What motivates explorers? Some seek fame or fortune. Others want to conquer new lands. Still others are simply curious.

The names of 19 people who made important discoveries are listed below (in the left column). Match each person to his or her achievement (in the right column). One of them celebrated the 50th anniversary of his feat in 2003. Can you figure out who it is?

1. Amundsen, Roald	**a.**	First European to see the Pacific Ocean (1513)
2. Armstrong, Neal	**b.**	Discovered penicillin (1928)
3. Balboa, Vasco Núñez de	**c.**	He and Matthew Henson were the first people to reach the North Pole (1909)
4. Columbus, Christopher	**d.**	Led the first circumnavigation of the world (1519–22)
5. Cook, James	**e.**	Discovered the belts of radiation that surround Earth in space (1958)
6. Curie, Marie	**f.**	First person to walk on the moon (1969)
7. Dias, Bartholomeu	**g.**	Discovered X rays (1895)
8. Fleming, Alexander	**h.**	Discovered mountains on the moon (1609)
9. Galileo	**i.**	First European to visit the Hawaiian Islands (1778)
10. Hillary, Edmund	**j.**	Discovered the planet Pluto (1930)
11. Magellan, Ferdinand	**k.**	First European to land in Florida (1513)
12. Mendel, Gregor	**l.**	First person to reach the South Pole (1911)
13. Peary, Robert	**m.**	First European to discover Manhattan Island and the Hudson River (1524)
14. Ponce de Léon, Juan	**n.**	Together with Tenzing Norkey, first to reach the summit of Mount Everest (1953)
15. Priestley, Joseph	**o.**	First European to sail around the southern tip of Africa (1488)
16. Roentgen, Wilhelm	**p.**	Discovered the basic laws of heredity (1860's)
17. Tombaugh, Clyde	**q.**	First European to reach the New World (1492)
18. Van Allen, James	**r.**	With her husband, discovered radium (1898)
19. Verrazano, Giovanni da	**s.**	Discovered oxygen (1774)

ANSWERS: 1.l; 2.f; 3.a; 4.q; 5.i; 6.r; 7.o; 8.b; 9.h; 10.n; 11.d; 12.p; 13.c; 14.k; 15.s; 16.g; 17.j; 18.e; 19.m.

Next, go on a hunt. The last names of all 19 people are hidden in this word-search puzzle. Try to find them. Cover the puzzle with a sheet of tracing paper. Read forward, backward, up, down, and diagonally. Then draw a neat line through each name as you find it.

A	N	O	E	L	E	D	E	C	N	O	P	E	B
M	R	P	Y	T	H	E	A	S	N	R	C	P	A
U	I	M	A	G	E	L	L	A	N	Y	E	I	U
N	L	E	S	N	T	A	Z	S	E	A	R	M	L
D	Y	S	I	T	O	A	R	D	R	A	C	C	I
S	H	E	C	B	R	E	C	Y	I	M	U	W	D
E	E	V	L	R	C	O	R	O	N	A	D	O	G
N	L	A	E	T	O	J	N	F	N	C	I	B	X
Y	B	V	R	K	S	O	O	G	E	O	F	E	B
R	O	A	O	L	G	E	N	Y	N	L	S	U	D
A	E	N	E	E	N	D	I	A	S	U	Q	D	E
L	L	A	N	H	I	Z	Z	R	O	M	R	I	U
L	I	L	T	G	M	U	R	K	P	B	R	L	W
I	L	L	G	M	E	N	D	E	L	U	E	K	N
H	A	E	E	C	L	N	U	Q	C	S	B	N	O
K	G	N	N	J	F	T	O	M	B	A	U	G	H

Liven up your summer wardrobe by making this necklace, earrings, and bracelet trio.

POPULAR CRAFTS

"I made it myself!" What a wonderful feeling! It's a feeling of satisfaction that appeals to people of all ages and all levels of ability. Even if you've had little experience in working with your hands, you can create things that are attractive and useful.

Here are five projects for you to try. You can copy them—or change them. In the world of crafts, there are always opportunities to express your imagination and to create objects that are uniquely yours!

CITRUS JEWELRY

Jewelry-making is one of today's most popular crafts. It's fun to do, and you can liven up your wardrobe by wearing jewelry that you have fashioned yourself.

There are many different techniques you can use to create jewelry. One option is to buy and decorate special jewelry "blanks." The summertime necklace and earrings shown above are made with plastic jewelry blanks; the bracelet is made of wood. A hole-punch was used to make holes in the necklace pieces.

Start by covering the pieces with a special white, gritty, pastelike substance that creates a textured appearance. (You can buy this in a craft store.) After the pieces have thoroughly dried, paint the tops with acrylics in the cool colors of peaches, lemons, and limes. Blend the colors where they meet.

When the tops are dry, paint the backs of the necklace and earrings yellow. Paint the inside of the bracelet yellow, too. Let dry. Then lightly dab white paint onto all the surfaces, to give the jewelry a frosted appearance. Let dry. Cover all surfaces with several coats of clear acrylic gloss.

Your bracelet is completed. To create the earrings, all you have to do is glue the pieces onto metal backings.

Make the necklace from six strands of satin cord. Holding the cords together, make a single knot at one end and two knots an inch (2.5 centimeters) apart at the other end. Tie five knots, evenly spaced, in the center of the necklace. Put white glue on each knot to prevent it from loosening. Let dry.

Attach a jump ring to each "citrus slice." Then slip each ring through one of the five center knots. To put on the necklace, slip the single-end knot into the cords between the double-end knots.

Now you're ready to model your citrus jewelry. It's so delectable you might want to wear it on your next picnic!

CLOWNING AROUND

Children love to laugh at the antics of clowns. And a clown doll can bring back happy memories of visits to the circus. So if you enjoy sewing, try your hand at making this giant clown. It's as big as a young child—the perfect size to be cuddled or placed on a chair in a corner of a room.

Buy a pattern for a giant doll at a craft store. Follow the directions for cutting out the pattern, sewing the fabric, and stuffing the

If you like to sew, try making this big cuddly clown.

doll. However, before you assemble the head, make the face. Use black paint or large black buttons for the eyes, add a nose, and sew on a red felt smile.

Make lots of curly hair by wrapping several loops of different-colored yarn around two fingers. Stitch the curls all around the clown's head.

Now make a clown suit, hat, and shoes—either by using ready-made patterns or by creating your own. Use a variety of colorful fabrics. Make big pom-poms in bright colors and sew them onto the suit and hat.

Don't forget to make a couple of pockets for your clown's costume. You can hide lots of sweet treats and little toys in them!

A DOLL OF A TEACHER

With two wooden dowels and various accessories, you can make this whimsical doll for your favorite teacher.

First, drill a hole through the larger dowel. Insert the smaller dowel through the hole, to create arms. Apply glue where the dowels meet.

Paint the body and arms with flesh-colored acrylic paint. When dry, paint on eyes, a nose, and a smiling mouth. Rub pink powder blush onto the cheeks.

Cover a large wooden heart with black paint. Glue it to the bottom of the large dowel so the doll can stand.

Make a dress by shaping pieces of blue paper twist and gluing them onto the dowels. Add a bow and belt of red plaid ribbon, and five red buttons. Make a pair of glasses by twisting a piece of thin steel wire. Glue the glasses onto the head. Use doll hair, available at craft stores, to create the hair style.

Create or buy little apples, rulers, chalkboards, and other items a teacher might have. With white paint, put messages onto the chalkboards. Make a series of loops in a long piece of thick steel wire. Wrap the ends of the wire around the hands. Use glue, clips, and ribbons to attach the apples and other objects to the wire.

Your dowel doll of a teacher is now ready to decorate any classroom!

WASHCLOTH SUN AND FUN

The cheerful sun on the facing page is made from bright yellow washcloths. It can add a bright accent to a kitchen or bathroom wall. (And it can later be taken apart and used.)

You need ten yellow washcloths, a plastic-foam ball 6 inches (15 centimeters) in diameter, a pair of children's red sunglasses, a heavy cardboard circle 8½ inches (21 centimeters) in diameter, and both straight pins and T-pins.

Begin by making the sun's face. Cut the foam ball in half. Cover the rounded side of one of the halves with a washcloth. Use straight pins to hold the edges of the cloth to the back of the foam. Use T-pins to attach the face to the center of the cardboard.

Fold and knot the remaining nine washcloths as follows: Diagonally fold each washcloth in half. Fold the bottom

Create this doll of a teacher with wooden dowels and an assortment of accessories.

162

Let the sunshine in with this washcloth craft.

point of the triangle to the top of the fold. Fold the cloth again in the same direction, forming a long strip. Knot the washcloth in the center. Fold one tail end to the back side of the knot.

Arrange the nine knotted washcloths around the outside edge of the face, with the front of the knots facing upward and the tails pointing outward. Gently fan out the tails until they form a halo of "sun rays." Use T-pins to attach the cloths to the cardboard.

Take the ear pieces off the sunglasses by removing the screws, and position the sunglasses on the face. Insert straight pins into the screw holes to hold the glasses in place. Make the smile from the curved ends of the two ear pieces. Cut the ends to size, glue their cut edges together, then glue the smile onto the sun.

Your washcloth creation will bring a splash of sunshine wherever it's displayed.

NOTEWORTHY NOTEBOOKS

Use dimensional paints and your imagination to turn an ordinary cloth-covered binder into a one-of-a-kind notebook. It will be a great place to keep your schoolwork.

Lightly draw a design onto the cover. Or draw your design on paper, changing it until it's exactly the way you want it; then use carbon paper to trace it onto the cover. Or you can try to find an appropriate design in a magazine and trace it onto the cover.

Work slowly and carefully. Let each paint dry completely before working with another paint. Special painting tips can be purchased to use with dimensional paints, to create a variety of effects. For example, on the binder shown here, a tri-line painting tip was used with red dimensional paint to create the three-part zigzag line.

Your fancy binder is sure to be the talk of your class!

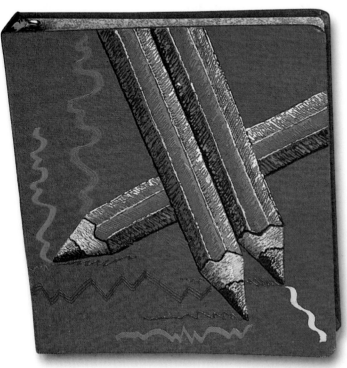

Use dimensional paints to turn a cloth-covered binder into a fancy work of art.

163

COIN COLLECTING

Coin collectors had plenty of attractive choices in 2003. With subjects that ranged from wild animals to movie characters to the first powered airplane, new coins offered something for everyone.

U.S. COINS

As it has each year since 1999, the U.S. Mint issued five new state quarters in 2003,

Meriwether Lewis and William Clark's epic journey to explore the American West was the theme of Missouri's new quarter. The explorers were shown traveling down the Missouri River on the return leg of their 4,350-mile trip. The Lewis and Clark Expedition began in 1804 near St. Louis, Missouri, traveled to the Pacific Ocean, and ended in 1806 back in St. Louis.

U.S. state quarters representing Illinois, Alabama, Maine, Missouri, and Arkansas.

as part of its 50 State Quarters program. First up was Illinois, which honored President Abraham Lincoln. Lincoln practiced law in Illinois before becoming the nation's 16th president. The new quarter showed a young Lincoln, carrying his law books, at the center of an outline of the state. Also depicted were a farm scene and the Chicago skyline.

The inspirational story of Helen Keller, who overcame blindness and deafness, was captured on Alabama's quarter. Keller, born in Alabama in 1880, was shown seated in a chair with a book in her lap. Keller's name appeared on the coin in English and Braille, the system of raised dots that allows the blind to read by moving their fingers across the page.

Maine chose to honor one of its landmarks—Pemaquid Point Light in New Harbor. Since it was built in 1835, this lighthouse has safely guided ships through the waters at the entrance to Muscongus Bay and Johns Bay. The lighthouse was shown atop a granite cliff, with a schooner sailing just off the coast.

U.S. gold coin commemorating the 100th anniversary of the first powered flight by the Wright brothers, in 1903.

Arkansas released the final new quarter for 2003. Arkansas is known as the Natural State for its many natural resources, and the coin featured three of them. A diamond was in the center of the design. Crater of Diamonds State Park in Arkansas contains the only active diamond mine in North America. To the right, a mallard duck flying over a lake represented the state's wildlife and natural areas. To the left were several stalks of rice, one of the state's most important crops.

As part of its annual commemorative coin program, the U.S. Mint also struck gold $10, silver dollar, and copper-nickel half-dollar coins honoring the 100th anniversary of the first powered flight. Orville and Wilbur Wright successfully flew their plane, the *Flyer,* at Kill Devil Hill near Kitty Hawk, North Carolina, on December 17, 1903. The reverse sides of all three coins showed the *Flyer.* The obverse of the gold and silver coins showed the Wright brothers, while the half-dollar showed the Wright Memorial at the town of Kill Devil Hills.

Canadian coins honoring
Canada Day, marquis wheat,
and the Year of the Sheep.

CANADIAN COINS

The big coin news in Canada was a new image of Queen Elizabeth II of Britain. The queen's image appears on all Canadian coins. The new design, the first since 1990, presented a modern view of the queen. She was shown uncrowned, wearing simple clothes and a single strand of pearls.

Colors and holograms enlivened new coins in Canada's Natural Wonders collection. Niagara Falls, on the Niagara River between Lake Erie and Lake Ontario, was featured on a new silver $20 coin. A hologram showed the falls as seen from the air. A view of the snow-capped Rocky Mountains was shown in color on another $20 coin. In Canada, the Rockies run along the border between Alberta and British Columbia, extending south to the U.S. border. A third $20 coin carried a hologram showing the Northern Lights, the colorful nighttime sky display that's often seen over northern Canada. Holograms also appeared on Canada's 2003 Maple Leaf bullion coins.

Canada Day was celebrated on a new 25-cent coin designed by 14-year-old Jade Pearan of Kelowna, British Columbia. The design showed a polar bear blowing maple leaves into the air. Endangered Atlantic walruses frolicked on Canada's four-coin platinum set for 2003. A wildflower—the white trillium—and hardy marquis wheat were shown on gold coins. And a daffodil appeared in gold-relief on a silver 50-cent coin. The Royal Canadian Mint and the Canadian Cancer Society jointly issued the coin as part of the fight against cancer.

WORLD COINS

Characters from the popular *Lord of the Rings* movies battled their way across coins

The Isle of Man's coin featuring *The Snowman*.

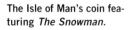

from the Isle of Man and New Zealand. The Isle of Man issued a set of gold coins showing characters from the films, including Frodo, Aragorn, Gandalf, Gimli, and Legolas. New Zealand, where the movies were filmed, released a 48-coin set.

It was the Year of the Sheep in the Chinese lunar calendar, and countries from Canada to China issued coins featuring this animal. Wild animals were popular subjects for other coins. The southern black rhinoceros was featured on coins from South Africa, as part of that country's ongoing wildlife series. South

The Isle of Man's coins depicting Gandalf and Frodo from *The Lord of the Rings* movies.

Africa also honored the lion on four gold coins. A silver dollar from Australia featured the Jirrah-Watty, or "big kangaroo," in a design by Aboriginal artist Ray Thomas.

Festivals and holiday traditions were celebrated on coins from many lands. Gibraltar released the 16th in its series of 50-pence Christmas coins. It showed Mary and Joseph arriving in Bethlehem. And the Isle of Man closed out the year with a 50-pence Christmas coin showing a scene from the classic children's story *The Snowman*, about a boy named James who builds a snowman that comes to life.

ROBERT VAN RYZIN
Editor, *Coins* magazine

SPORTS

Lance Armstrong did it again! On July 27, 2003, the U.S. cyclist (in yellow) scored his fifth consecutive victory in the Tour de France, the most famous bicycle race in the world. Armstrong thus became the fifth person ever to win this grueling race five times, and only the second to win it five times in a row. Armstrong's first Tour de France victory, in 1999, marked an amazing comeback after a battle with cancer. He promised to be back in 2004 to try for an unprecedented sixth win.

The Florida Marlins beat the New York Yankees 4 games to 2 to win the World Series. Pitcher Josh Beckett (*right*) was named MVP of the Series.

BASEBALL

Experience and youth combined in 2003 to lead the Florida Marlins to the championship of major league baseball. The experience belonged to Jack McKeon, who at 72 became the oldest manager in the game's history to win a World Series. The youth was that of pitcher Josh Beckett; the 23-year-old right-hander shut out the New York Yankees to win the sixth, and deciding, game of the 2003 Fall Classic.

The baseball season began poorly for the Marlins. Through early May, the "Fish" were swimming near the bottom of the Eastern Division of the National League (NL). McKeon wasn't even managing Florida at the time. After a 16–22 start (16 wins, 22 losses), the Marlins fired Jeff Torborg and hired McKeon—and soon the Fish began to fly.

With McKeon as manager, Florida went 75–49 and finished the regular season second in the NL East, behind the Atlanta Braves. Holding the best second-place record in the NL,

the Marlins qualified for the playoffs as the league's wild-card team. The San Francisco Giants, the Western Division leader, and the Chicago Cubs, who finished first in the Central Division, were the other two NL teams to reach the playoffs.

In the first round of the playoffs, the NL Division Series, the Marlins cut down the Giants, three games to one. The Cubs, meanwhile, bested the Braves, three games to two. Then, in the National League Championship Series (NLCS), Florida dashed the hopes of long-suffering Chicago fans by eliminating the Cubs in seven games. Marlin catcher Ivan (Pudge) Rodriguez was named Most Valuable Player (MVP) of the NLCS. He slugged two home runs and collected 10 runs batted in (RBIs).

The American League (AL) Division champions were the Yankees in the East, the Minnesota Twins in the Central, and the Oakland A's in the West; the Boston Red Sox captured the wild card. New York dropped Minnesota in four games, and Boston ousted Oakland in five, in the AL Division Series. Baseball's ancient rivals, the Yankees and the Red Sox, then tangled in a seven-game AL Championship Series. New York emerged victorious. The MVP was Yankee reliever Mariano Rivera, who recorded one win and two saves.

Few people gave the Marlins much chance against the mighty "Bronx Bombers" in the World Series. But Florida won Game 1, played in Yankee Stadium, by the score of 3–2. Marlin center fielder Juan Pierre rapped out two singles and drove in two runs.

Yankee left-hander Andy Pettitte pitched his team to a 6–1 triumph in Game 2, also contested in New York. Yankee Hideki Matsui clobbered a three-run homer, and Alfonso Soriano added a two-run shot.

Pro Player Stadium in Miami was the scene of Games 3, 4, and 5. Florida's Beckett and New York's Mike Mussina hooked up in a

2003 WORLD SERIES RESULTS

		R	H	E	Winning/Losing Pitcher
1	Florida	3	7	1	Brad Penny (W)
	New York	2	9	0	David Wells (L)
2	Florida	1	6	0	Mark Redman (L)
	New York	6	10	2	Andy Pettitte (W)
3	New York	6	6	1	Mike Mussina (W)
	Florida	1	8	0	Josh Beckett (L)
4	New York	3	12	0	Jeff Weaver (L)
	Florida	4	10	0	Braden Looper (W)
5	New York	4	12	1	José Contreras (L)
	Florida	6	9	1	Brad Penny (W)
6	Florida	2	7	0	Josh Beckett (W)
	New York	0	5	1	Andy Pettitte (L)

Visiting team listed first, home team second

AL Rookie-of-the-Year laurels went to Angel Berroa of the Kansas City Royals; the shortstop batted .287. The top rookie in the NL was Florida pitcher Dontrelle Willis; the left-hander posted a 14–6 won-lost record.

During 2003, Roger Clemens notched his 300th victory. The New York Yankee right-hander completed his celebrated career with a 310–160 lifetime won-lost record; 4,099 strike-outs, third on the all-time list behind Hall-of-Famers Nolan Ryan and Steve Carlton; and six Cy Young Awards, two more than anyone else.

pitchers' duel in Game 3. The contest was close until the Yanks exploded for four runs in the ninth inning to win, 6–1. New York was up, two games to one.

But the Marlins wouldn't lose again. They took Game 4, 4–3, in extra innings. Florida shortstop Alex Gonzalez led off the last of the twelfth with a game-winning homer.

The Marlins won Game 5 by 6–4. Third baseman Mike Lowell's two-run single in the fifth inning provided the winning margin.

Back in New York for Game 6, Beckett was back on the mound for the Marlins. The powerful hurler went the full nine innings and held the Yankees to five hits. For his complete-game, Series-ending, 2–0 shutout, Beckett was honored as the 2003 World Series MVP.

San Francisco's Barry Bonds was named NL MVP of the regular season for the sixth time and for the third straight year—both record-setters. He batted .341 and hit 45 home runs. Bonds also stole his 500th base in 2003, becoming the first player ever to reach or exceed that number in both steals and home runs. The AL MVP was Texas Ranger short-stop Alex Rodriguez, who batted .298, knocked in 118 runs, and clubbed 47 homers.

Right-handed pitcher Roy Halladay of the Toronto Blue Jays won the Cy Young Award as the AL's top hurler; he compiled a 22–7 won-lost record and a 3.25 earned run average (ERA). Righty reliever Eric Gagne of the Los Angeles Dodgers won the Cy Young Award in the NL; he recorded an astounding 55 saves in 55 opportunities and a tiny 1.20 ERA.

The World Series Turns 100!

Here are some interesting facts about the World Series, which celebrated its 100th anniversary in 2003.

• From 1903 through 2003 there were 584 World Series games with a total attendance of 26,158,685.

• Ticket sales in 1903 were $50,000; in 2003 they were $41 million.

• American League teams have won the World Series 58 times, and National League teams have taken the crown 41 times. The New York Yankees hold the record with 26 World Series titles.

• The World Series wasn't played in 1904 because the manager of the National League champion New York Giants refused to let his team compete against the "inferior" American League champion Boston Red Sox.

• The World Series wasn't played in 1994 because the players went on strike and the Series was canceled.

MAJOR LEAGUE BASEBALL FINAL STANDINGS

AMERICAN LEAGUE

Eastern Division

	W	L	Pct.	GB
*New York	101	61	.623	—
Boston	95	67	.586	6
Toronto	86	76	.531	15
Baltimore	71	91	.438	30
Tampa Bay	63	99	.389	38

Central Division

	W	L	Pct.	GB
Minnesota	90	72	.556	—
Chicago	86	76	.531	4
Kansas City	83	79	.512	7
Cleveland	68	94	.420	22
Detroit	43	119	.265	47

Western Division

	W	L	Pct.	GB
Oakland	96	66	.593	—
Seattle	93	69	.574	3
Anaheim	77	85	.475	19
Texas	71	91	.438	25

*League Championship Series winners

NATIONAL LEAGUE

Eastern Division

	W	L	Pct.	GB
Atlanta	101	61	.623	—
*Florida	91	71	.562	10
Philadelphia	86	76	.531	15
Montreal	83	79	.512	18
New York	66	95	.410	34½

Central Division

	W	L	Pct.	GB
Chicago	88	74	.543	—
Houston	87	75	.537	1
St. Louis	85	77	.525	3
Pittsburgh	75	87	.463	13
Cincinnati	69	93	.426	19
Milwaukee	68	94	.420	20

Western Division

	W	L	Pct.	GB
San Francisco	100	61	.621	—
Los Angeles	85	77	.525	15½
Arizona	84	78	.519	16½
Colorado	74	88	.457	26½
San Diego	64	98	.395	36½

MAJOR LEAGUE LEADERS

AMERICAN LEAGUE

Batting
(top 10 qualifiers)

	AB	H	Avg.
B. Mueller, Boston	524	171	.326
M. Ramirez, Boston	569	185	.325
D. Jeter, New York	482	156	.324
V. Wells, Toronto	678	215	.317
M. Ordonez, Chicago	606	192	.317
G. Anderson, Anaheim	638	201	.315
A. Pierzynski, Minnesota	487	152	.312
I. Suzuki, Seattle	679	212	.312
A. Huff, Tampa Bay	636	198	.311
C. Beltran, Kansas City	521	160	.307

Home Runs

	HR
A. Rodriguez, Texas	47
C. Delgado, Toronto	42
F. Thomas, Chicago	42
J. Giambi, New York	41
R. Palmeiro, Texas	38
A. Soriano, New York	38

Pitching
(top qualifiers, based on number of wins)

	W	L	ERA
R. Halladay, Toronto	22	7	3.25
J. Moyer, Seattle	21	7	3.27
A. Pettitte, New York	21	8	4.02
E. Loaiza, Chicago	21	9	2.90
D. Lowe, Boston	17	7	4.47
M. Mussina, New York	17	8	3.40
R. Clemens, New York	17	9	3.91

NATIONAL LEAGUE

Batting
(top 10 qualifiers)

	AB	H	Avg.
A. Pujols, St. Louis	591	212	.359
T. Helton, Colorado	583	209	.358
B. Bonds, San Francisco	390	133	.341
G. Sheffield, Atlanta	576	190	.330
E. Renteria, St. Louis	587	194	.330
J. Kendall, Pittsburgh	587	191	.325
M. Giles, Atlanta	551	174	.316
L. Castillo, Florida	595	187	.314
M. Loretta, San Diego	589	185	.314
M. Grudzielanek, Chicago	481	151	.314

Home Runs

	HR
J. Thome, Philadelphia	47
B. Bonds, San Francisco	45
R. Sexson, Milwaukee	45
A. Pujols, St. Louis	43
J. Lopez, Atlanta	43
S. Sosa, Chicago	40

Pitching
(top qualifiers, based on number of wins)

	W	L	ERA
R. Ortiz, Atlanta	21	7	3.81
M. Prior, Chicago	18	6	2.43
W. Williams, St. Louis	18	9	3.87
J. Schmidt, San Francisco	17	5	2.34

Members of the Tokyo, Japan, and East Boyton Beach, Florida, teams parade around the stadium after the Little League World Series championship game. Japan won, 10–1.

LITTLE LEAGUE BASEBALL

Baseball is big in Japan; and baseball is "little" in Japan, too—young athletes from that country have won the Little League World Series three times in five years: 1999, 2001, and 2003. In the final game of the 2003 Series, played August 24 in South Williamsport, Pennsylvania, the international champions, from Tokyo, Japan, defeated the United States champs, from East Boynton Beach, Florida, by a 10–1 score.

The contest was scoreless through three innings. But in the fourth, Tokyo loaded the bases with two outs. Batter Eito Ono was hit by a pitch, sending the first run home. Boynton Beach's pitcher Michael Broad walked the next batter, Kazumasa Sakamoto, and Tokyo led, 2–0. Then Hokuto Nakahara stepped to the plate; swinging on Broad's first offering, he clobbered the ball over the centerfield fence, a grand slam home run, propelling the youngsters from Japan to a 6–0 lead. A moment later, they made it 8–0 on a two-run roundtripper by their pitcher, Yuutaro "The Tank" Tanaka.

In the top of the fifth inning, Tokyo extended its margin to 10–0; Hirofumi

Superstar Yuutaro "The Tank" Tanaka

Yamazaki contributed a one-run homer. In the meantime, hurler Tanaka was handcuffing the Boynton Beach batters with curves and fastballs. Boynton Beach collected its sole tally in the bottom of the fifth when Richie DeJesus singled home Devon Travis.

When the game was over, both teams charged into the outfield—Tokyo to celebrate, Boynton Beach to congratulate. Win or lose, the kids had fun. Tokyo pitcher Tanaka struck out 14 Boynton Beach batters and gave up only three hits. In their six games of the World Series tournament, the Japanese youths outscored their opponents by 59–9 and smacked a record-tying 15 home runs.

The other international teams in the tournament hailed from Curaçao, Netherlands Antilles; Glace Bay, Nova Scotia, Canada; Dhahran, Saudi Arabia; Agana, Guam; Zulia, Venezuela; Mexico City, Mexico; and Moscow, Russia. The other U.S. teams came from Saugus, Massachusetts; Tallmadge, Ohio; Richland, Washington; Wilmington, Delaware; Eldridge, Iowa; Chandler, Arizona; and Richmond, Texas.

171

Led by Tim Duncan (#21), the San Antonio Spurs beat the New Jersey Nets for the NBA championship. Duncan won the MVP award for both the playoffs and regular season.

BASKETBALL

The San Antonio Spurs won the National Basketball Association (NBA) title in 2003. In the playoff finals in June, San Antonio defeated the New Jersey Nets, four games to two.

Throughout the 2002–2003 season, the Spurs were sparked by forward/center Tim Duncan. He and center David Robinson—both seven-footers—made a formidable pair in the frontcourt. In addition to the "big guys," the squad included guard Tony Parker and guards/forwards Stephen Jackson and Bruce Bowen. And San Antonio's Gregg Popovich collected NBA coach-of-the-year honors.

At the end of the regular season, the Spurs and the Dallas Mavericks stood atop the Midwest Division of the NBA's Western Conference, tied for the league's best record. The other Western Conference teams qualifying for the playoffs were the Minnesota Timberwolves; the Utah Jazz; the Sacramento Kings, who led the Pacific Division; the Los Angeles Lakers; the Portland Trail Blazers; and the Phoenix Suns.

In 2003, all playoff series became "best of seven" (the first team to win four games advances). In round one, the Spurs outshone the Suns, eliminating them in six games. In round two, San Antonio defeated Los Angeles, the defending NBA champs, also by four games to two. And in the Western Conference finals, the Spurs dropped Dallas, again in six games.

San Antonio center David Robinson—one of the sport's all-time stars—retired after the Spurs' winning season.

NBA FINAL STANDINGS

EASTERN CONFERENCE

Atlantic Division

	W	L	Pct.
New Jersey	49	33	.598
Philadelphia	48	34	.585
Boston	44	38	.537
Orlando	42	40	.512
Washington	37	45	.451
New York	37	45	.451
Miami	25	57	.305

Central Division

	W	L	Pct.
Detroit	50	32	.610
Indiana	48	34	.585
New Orleans	47	35	.573
Milwaukee	42	40	.512
Atlanta	35	47	.427
Chicago	30	52	.366
Toronto	24	58	.293
Cleveland	17	65	.207

WESTERN CONFERENCE

Midwest Division

	W	L	Pct.
San Antonio	60	22	.732
Dallas	60	22	.732
Minnesota	51	31	.622
Utah	47	35	.573
Houston	43	39	.524
Memphis	28	54	.341
Denver	17	65	.207

Pacific Division

	W	L	Pct.
Sacramento	59	23	.720
L.A. Lakers	50	32	.610
Portland	50	32	.610
Phoenix	44	38	.537
Seattle	40	42	.488
Golden State	38	44	.463
L.A. Clippers	27	55	.329

NBA Championship: San Antonio Spurs

COLLEGE BASKETBALL

Conference	Winner
Atlantic Coast	Wake Forest, (regular season) Duke (tournament)
Atlantic Ten	East: St. Joseph's West: Xavier (regular season) Dayton (tournament)
Big East	East: Boston College, Connecticut West: Syracuse, Pittsburgh (tied, regular season) Pittsburgh (tournament)
Big Ten	Wisconsin (regular season) Illinois (tournament)
Big 12	Kansas (regular season) Oklahoma (tournament)
Big West	UC Santa Barbara (regular season) Utah State (tournament)
Ivy League	Pennsylvania
Missouri Valley	Southern Illinois (regular season) Creighton (tournament)
Pacific-10	Arizona (regular season) Oregon (tournament)
Southeastern	Eastern: Kentucky Western: Mississippi State (regular season) Kentucky (tournament)
Southwestern Athletic	Prairie View A&M (regular season) Texas Southern (tournament)
Western Athletic	Fresno State (regular season) Tulsa (tournament)

NCAA, men: Syracuse
women: Connecticut

NIT: St. John's

In the Eastern Conference, New Jersey finished first in the Atlantic Division, and was joined in postseason competition by the Philadelphia 76ers; the Boston Celtics; the Orlando Magic; the Detroit Pistons, the Central Division winners; the Indiana Pacers; the New Orleans Hornets; and the Milwaukee Bucks. The Nets felled the Bucks in six games in round one of the playoffs, and then swept the next two rounds, ousting both Boston and Detroit in four straight. Entering the finals, the Nets had won ten consecutive games; but the Spurs put an end to that. Playing at home, San Antonio captured Game 1 by 101–89, as Duncan scored 32 points. New Jersey took Game 2, 87–85, as their All-Star guard Jason Kidd notched 30 points.

The finals moved to East Rutherford, New Jersey, for the next three contests. San Antonio won Game 3 by 84–79; Tony Parker poured in 26 points and Duncan added 21, plus 16 rebounds. Game 4 went to the Nets, 77–76. But in Game 5, Duncan amassed 29 points and 17 rebounds to power San Antonio to a 93–83 victory.

Back home in Texas, the Spurs clinched the NBA title with an 88–77 triumph in Game 6; Duncan totaled 21 points and 20 rebounds, and David Robinson chipped in with 13 points and 17 "boards." Afterward, the Spurs said "farewell" to Robinson, one of the sport's all-time stars. The center retired after fourteen years in the NBA, all with San Antonio. Robinson averaged 21.1 points and 10.6 rebounds per game during his career. Another basketball great, Michael Jordan, also retired—for the third and, no doubt, final time.

Tim Duncan was named Most Valuable Player (MVP) of the finals. He was also MVP of the regular season for the second straight year, averaging 23.3 points and 12.9 rebounds per game. Orlando's Tracy McGrady led the NBA in regular-season scoring with 32.1 points per game. Rookie of the Year was Phoenix forward Amare Stoudemire.

WNBA. In 2003, the Detroit Shock went from "worst to first": After a last-place fin-ish the previous year, they won the championship of the Women's National Basketball Association (WNBA) in September. In the three-game playoff finals, Detroit, coached by former NBA star Bill Laimbeer, topped the defending champion Los Angeles Sparks, two games to one. Shock center Ruth Riley was voted MVP of the finals.

College Play. Coach Jim Boeheim piloted Syracuse University to the National Collegiate Athletic Association (NCAA) men's title. In the final game of the NCAA tournament, played on April 7, the Orangemen beat Kansas, 81–78. Syracuse's fabulous freshman Carmelo Anthony was named most outstanding player of the "Final Four." The University of Connecticut gained the NCAA women's crown for the second consecutive year. Coached by Geno Auriemma, the Huskies defeated Tennessee in the April 8 final, 73–68. Elected most outstanding player of the Final Four was UConn's All-American junior guard Diana Taurasi.

The Huskies Set a College Record

On January 18, the University of Connecticut made women's college basketball history. The Huskies downed the Georgetown Hoyas, 72–49, to win their 55th game in a row (shown at left after the game). The previous record—54 games in a row—had been set by Louisiana Tech during the 1980–82 seasons.

The Huskies continued to roll, but their winning streak ended at 70. On March 11, they were stopped by the Villanova Wildcats, 52–48, in the Big East tournament final.

In 2003, running back Jamal Lewis (number 31) of the Baltimore Ravens rushed for 2,066 yards—the second highest single-season total ever—and set an NFL single-game record of 295 yards on September 14.

FOOTBALL

In 2003, the Tampa Bay Buccaneers proved the old sports saying "Offense wins games; defense wins championships." Tampa Bay gave up fewer points than any other team in the National Football League's 2002–03 regular season, and then proceeded to shut down the Oakland Raiders' offense in the 2003 Super Bowl. This resulted in the first NFL title for the Buccaneers. In the Canadian Football League (CFL), the Edmonton Eskimos won the 2003 Grey Cup. And the number-one ranking in U.S. college football became a matter of controversy.

THE NFL PLAYOFFS AND SUPER BOWL XXXVII

Jon Gruden made his first year as Tampa Bay's head coach a memorable one. During the regular season, he piloted the Bucca-neers to first place in the Southern Division of the NFL's National Conference (NFC). The other NFC division leaders were the Philadelphia Eagles, the Green Bay Packers, and the San Francisco 49ers; the New York Giants and the Atlanta Falcons qualified for the playoffs as wild-card teams.

Atlanta eliminated Green Bay, 27–7, in the first week of the playoffs, while San Francisco edged out New York in a wild 39–38 contest. The following week, the Buccaneers' defense squelched the 49ers, 31–6, and the Eagles soared over the Falcons, 20–6.

In the NFC title game, Tampa Bay topped Philadelphia, 27–10. So the Buccaneers set sail for the Super Bowl—their first ever.

Joining Oakland as American Conference (AFC) 2002–03 division champs were the

New York Jets, the Pittsburgh Steelers, and the Tennessee Titans; wild cards went to the Cleveland Browns and the Indianapolis Colts.

In the opening round of the playoffs, the Steelers stopped the Browns, 36–33, and the Jets jolted the Colts, 41–0. A week later, Oakland felled New York, 30–10, while Tennessee nipped Pittsburgh in overtime, 34–31.

Oakland's powerful offense ran up 41 points in the AFC title game, while Tennessee mustered only 24; the Raiders were on their way to their fifth Super Bowl, but only their first since 1984.

Super Bowl XXXVII, played at Qualcomm Stadium in San Diego, California, on January 26, 2003, was largely a one-sided affair. Tampa Bay's defense clamped a lid on Oakland, and the Buccaneers held a 20–3 lead at halftime.

In the third quarter, Tampa Bay extended its margin to 34–3. Oakland mounted a second-half rally, scoring 18 straight points, but it wasn't enough. The Buccaneers scored the last two touchdowns of the game with less than two minutes left, both on interceptions. The final score was 48–21. Named the Super Bowl's Most Valuable Player (MVP) was Tampa Bay defensive safety Dexter Jackson, who snared two interceptions in the first half.

THE 2003 REGULAR SEASON

Tampa Bay didn't make the playoffs in the 2003 regular season. The NFC division champs were Philadelphia, Green Bay, the Carolina Panthers, and the St. Louis Rams. Wild cards went to the Dallas Cowboys and the Seattle Seahawks. The AFC division leaders were the New England Patriots, the Baltimore Ravens, the Kansas City Chiefs, and Indianapolis. Tennessee and the Denver Broncos captured the wild cards.

Two quarterbacks—Tennessee's Steve McNair and Indianapolis's Peyton Manning—were co-winners of the NFL MVP Award for 2003.

THE CANADIAN FOOTBALL LEAGUE

On November 16, 2003, at Taylor Field in Regina, Saskatchewan, the Edmonton Eskimos won the CFL title, besting the Montreal Alouettes, 34–22, in the Grey Cup. Edmonton's Jason Tucker caught seven passes, two for touchdowns, and was named Grey Cup MVP.

COLLEGE FOOTBALL

Competing polls ranked different teams at the top of college football. LSU (12–1, regular-season record) defeated Oklahoma (12–1) in the Sugar Bowl; USC (11–1) beat Michigan (10–2) in the Rose Bowl; Miami (10–2) overcame Florida State (10–2) in the Orange Bowl; and Mississippi (9–3) dropped Oklahoma State (9–3) in the Cotton Bowl. Following the Bowl games, LSU finished first in the Bowl Championship series, and USC was first in the Associated Press college-football poll.

Oklahoma senior quarterback Jason White won the Heisman Trophy. During the regular season, he passed for 3,744 yards and 40 touchdowns.

Quarterback Peyton Manning led the Indianapolis Colts to first place in the AFC South Division in the 2003 NFL regular season.

University of Oklahoma quarterback Jason White won the 2003 Heisman Trophy as the best college player.

COLLEGE FOOTBALL

Conference	Winner
Atlantic Coast	Florida State
Big Ten	Michigan
Big Twelve	Kansas State
Pacific-10	USC
Southeastern	Louisiana State
Western Athletic	Boise State

Cotton Bowl: Mississippi 31, Oklahoma State 28
Fiesta Bowl: Ohio State 35, Kansas State 28
Gator Bowl: Maryland 41, West Virginia 7
Orange Bowl: Miami 16, Florida State 14
Rose Bowl: USC 28, Michigan 14
Sugar Bowl: Louisiana State 21, Oklahoma 14

Heisman Trophy: Jason White, Oklahoma

2003 NFL FINAL STANDINGS

AMERICAN CONFERENCE

East

	W	L	T	Pct.	PF	PA
New England	14	2	0	.875	348	238
Miami	10	6	0	.625	311	261
Buffalo	6	10	0	.375	243	279
N.Y. Jets	6	10	0	.375	283	299

North

	W	L	T	Pct.	PF	PA
Baltimore	10	6	0	.625	391	281
Cincinnati	8	8	0	.500	346	384
Pittsburgh	6	10	0	.375	300	327
Cleveland	5	11	0	.312	254	322

South

	W	L	T	Pct.	PF	PA
Indianapolis	12	4	0	.750	447	336
Tennessee	12	4	0	.750	435	324
Jacksonville	5	11	0	.312	276	331
Houston	5	11	0	.312	255	380

West

	W	L	T	Pct.	PF	PA
Kansas City	13	3	0	.812	484	332
Denver	10	6	0	.625	381	301
Oakland	4	12	0	.250	270	379
San Diego	4	12	0	.250	313	441

NATIONAL CONFERENCE

East

	W	L	T	Pct.	PF	PA
Philadelphia	12	4	0	.750	374	287
Dallas	10	6	0	.625	289	260
Washington	5	11	0	.312	287	372
N.Y. Giants	4	12	0	.250	243	387

North

	W	L	T	Pct.	PF	PA
Green Bay	10	6	0	.625	442	307
Minnesota	9	7	0	.562	416	353
Chicago	7	9	0	.438	283	346
Detroit	5	11	0	.312	270	379

South

	W	L	T	Pct.	PF	PA
Carolina	11	5	0	.688	325	304
New Orleans	8	8	0	.500	340	326
Tampa Bay	7	9	0	.438	301	264
Atlanta	5	11	0	.312	299	422

West

	W	L	T	Pct.	PF	PA
St. Louis	12	4	0	.750	447	328
Seattle	10	6	0	.625	404	327
San Francisco	7	9	0	.438	384	337
Arizona	4	12	0	.250	225	452

Mike Weir:
Master of the Masters

"This is an unbelievable feeling," said 32-year-old Mike Weir, "something that I have been dreaming of a long time." Weir's dream-come-true was his victory in the 2003 Masters tournament, one of the most prestigious events in the world of golf. Not only did he win the Masters, Weir was the first Canadian and the first left-hander ever to do so.

The Masters was Weir's third win on the Professional Golf Association (PGA) tour in 2003 and his sixth PGA win overall. But none of his victories came easy. In each one, he made a comeback after being behind on the final day of play. And the Masters was no different. After trailing by three strokes, Weir came back to tie the tournament on the last hole. He then went on to win on the first hole of the sudden-death overtime.

Weir is no newcomer to the sports spotlight. He was twice named Canada's Male Athlete of the Year.

GOLF

PROFESSIONAL		AMATEUR	
	Individual		**Individual**
Masters	Mike Weir	**U.S. Amateur**	Nick Flanagan
U.S. Open	Jim Furyk	**U.S. Women's Amateur**	Virada Nirapathpongporn
Canadian Open	Bob Tway	**British Amateur**	Gary Wolstenholme
British Open	Ben Curtis	**British Ladies Amateur**	Elisa Serramia
PGA	Shaun Micheel	**Canadian Amateur**	Richard Scott
U.S. Women's Open	Hilary Lunke	**Canadian Ladies Amateur**	Lisa Meldrum
Ladies PGA	Annika Sorenstam		
			Team
		Walker Cup	Britain/Ireland

Goalie Martin Brodeur of the New Jersey Devils makes a save against the Anaheim Mighty Ducks in the Stanley Cup finals. New Jersey beat Anaheim, 4 games to 3. Brodeur won the Vezina trophy as top goaltender.

HOCKEY

Two opposing goaltenders dominated the National Hockey League (NHL) playoffs in 2003. One collected the playoffs' Most Valuable Player (MVP) honors; but the other's team captured the Stanley Cup. Goalie Martin Brodeur and his teammates won the New Jersey Devils' third NHL title in nine years. In the playoff finals, they defeated the Anaheim Mighty Ducks, anchored by netminder and MVP Jean-Sebastien Giguere, four games to three. Each team won every game on its home ice.

New Jersey was piloted by coach Pat Burns, in his first year with the Devils. In the regular season, they topped the Atlantic Division of the NHL Eastern Conference with 108 points (46 wins, 20 losses, 10 ties, 6 overtime losses). New Jersey was followed into the playoffs by the Philadelphia Flyers (107 points) and the New York Islanders (83). Other Eastern Conference teams qualifying for postseason play were, from the Northeast Division, the Ottawa Senators (with an NHL-leading 113 points), the Toronto Maple Leafs

(98), and the Boston Bruins (87); and from the Southeast Division, the Tampa Bay Lightning (93) and the Washington Capitals (92).

The Devils bounced the Bruins in the first round of the playoffs, winning the series four games to one. New Jersey also needed only five games to eliminate Tampa Bay in round two. In the Conference finals against Ottawa, the Devils took a three-games-to-one lead but then had to hold on to oust Ottawa in seven.

In the Western Conference regular season, Anaheim, coached by Mike Babcock, finished second in the Pacific Division with 95 points, behind the Dallas Stars (111). The other Western Conference playoff teams were, from the Central Division, the Detroit Red Wings (110) and the St. Louis Blues (99); and from the Northwest Division, the Colorado Avalanche (105), the Vancouver Canucks (104), the Minnesota Wild (95), and the Edmonton Oilers (92).

In the first round of the playoffs, Anaheim defeated Detroit in four straight games, though two of the victories required overtime. In

Most Valuable Players: Anaheim's Jean-Sebastien Giguere (*left*) collected the playoff honors. Colorado Avalanche center Peter Forsberg (*above*) was named MVP of the regular season.

round two, Anaheim fought off Dallas in six games; Game 1 went to five overtimes before the Mighty Ducks finally won. In the Western Conference finals, Anaheim swept Minnesota in four straight—the first three contests were shutouts, and the Wild managed only one goal against goalie Giguere in Game 4.

Playing on their home ice at Continental Airlines Arena in East Rutherford, New Jersey, in late May, the Devils won Games 1 and 2 of the Stanley Cup finals by identical 3–0 scores. In each game, Anaheim managed only 16 shots, all deflected by New Jersey goalie Brodeur. The Devils' goals in Game 1 came off the sticks of left wing Jeff Friesen (who had previously played for Anaheim), right wing Grant Marshall, and Friesen again. In Game 2, centers Patrik Elias and Scott Gomez scored in the second period, and Friesen notched his third goal of the finals in the third.

In Games 3 and 4, contested at Arrowhead Pond arena in Anaheim, California, the Mighty Ducks tied the series. Anaheim won Game 3 by the score of 3–2 at 6:59 of overtime on a goal by defenseman Ruslan Salei. Scor-

ing the Mighty Ducks' earlier goals were center Marc Chouinard and defenseman Sandis Ozolinsh. Game 4 also required a sudden-death overtime for Anaheim to win, 1–0. Only 39 seconds of the extra period elapsed before the Mighty Ducks' right wing Steve Thomas netted the puck off a rebound of a shot by Samuel Pahlsson. Giguere stopped all 26 New Jersey scoring attempts for the shutout.

The series returned to New Jersey for Game 5; both defenses went "on vacation," as the two teams combined for nine goals. The Devils prevailed, 6–3, as right wing Jamie Langenbrunner notched two goals in the third period to put the victory on ice.

Back home in California, the Mighty Ducks won Game 6 by the score of 5–2. Anaheim captain and forward Paul Kariya contributed two assists and a goal, despite being briefly knocked unconscious by a thunderous check from New Jersey's Scott Stevens.

In Game 7, contested on June 9 in New Jersey, goalie Brodeur set the NHL record of seven playoff shutouts in one year. The Devils won, 3–0, as rookie forward Mike Rupp

NHL FINAL STANDINGS

EASTERN CONFERENCE

Atlantic Division

	W	L	T	OL	Pts.
New Jersey	46	20	10	6	108
Philadelphia	45	20	13	4	107
N.Y. Islanders	35	34	11	2	83
N.Y. Rangers	32	36	10	4	78
Pittsburgh	27	44	6	5	65

Northeast Division

	W	L	T	OL	Pts.
Ottawa	52	21	8	1	113
Toronto	44	28	7	3	98
Boston	36	31	11	4	87
Montreal	30	35	8	9	77
Buffalo	27	37	10	8	72

Southeast Division

	W	L	T	OL	Pts.
Tampa Bay	36	25	16	5	93
Washington	39	29	8	6	92
Atlanta	31	39	7	5	74
Florida	24	36	13	9	70
Carolina	22	43	11	6	61

WESTERN CONFERENCE

Central Division

	W	L	T	OL	Pts.
Detroit	48	20	10	4	110
St. Louis	41	24	11	6	99
Chicago	30	33	13	6	79
Nashville	27	35	13	7	74
Columbus	29	42	8	3	69

Northwest Division

	W	L	T	OL	Pts.
Colorado	42	19	13	8	105
Vancouver	45	23	13	1	104
Minnesota	42	29	10	1	95
Edmonton	36	26	11	9	92
Calgary	29	36	13	4	75

Pacific Division

	W	L	T	OL	Pts.
Dallas	46	17	15	4	111
Anaheim	40	27	9	6	95
Los Angeles	33	37	6	6	78
Phoenix	31	35	11	5	78
San Jose	28	37	9	8	73

Stanley Cup: New Jersey Devils

OUTSTANDING PLAYERS

Hart Trophy (most valuable player)	Peter Forsberg, Colorado
Ross Trophy (scorer)	Peter Forsberg, Colorado
Vezina Trophy (goalie)	Martin Brodeur, New Jersey
Norris Trophy (defenseman)	Nicklas Lidstrom, Detroit
Selke Trophy (defensive forward)	Jere Lehtinen, Dallas
Calder Trophy (rookie)	Barret Jackman, St. Louis
Lady Byng Trophy (sportsmanship)	Alexander Mogilny, Toronto
Conn Smythe Trophy (Stanley Cup play)	Jean-Sebastien Giguere, Anaheim

scored the first goal and assisted on the next two, both by Jeff Friesen. The Stanley Cup belonged to New Jersey. Anaheim goaltender Giguere, however, won the Conn Smythe Trophy as the playoffs' Most Valuable Player (MVP). Colorado center Peter Forsberg was named MVP of the NHL 2003 regular season; he was the first Swedish player to be so honored. He was also the first Swedish player to lead the league in scoring, with 106 points on 29 goals and 77 assists.

Martin Brodeur won the Vezina Trophy as the NHL's top goaltender, Detroit's Nicklas Lidstrom garnered best-defenseman laurels, and defenseman Barret Jackman of St. Louis was voted rookie of the year.

College Play. On April 12, 2003, the University of Minnesota won the men's ice hockey championship of the National Collegiate Athletic Association (NCAA) for the second straight year. Coached by Don Lucia, the Golden Gophers bested the University of New Hampshire in the final game of the NCAA tournament by the score of 5–1. Thomas Vanek, a freshman from Austria, registered the game-winning goal and was named tournament MVP.

The Bulldogs of the University of Minnesota-Duluth, coached by Shannon Miller, were the women's NCAA champs for the third consecutive year. In the tournament final on March 23, they defeated Harvard University, 4–3, in double overtime. Bulldog Nora Tallus tallied the game-winner after 4 minutes, 19 seconds of the second extra period.

Michelle Kwan Wins World Gold—Again!

The 2003 World Figure Skating Championships were held in Washington, D.C., in March. American skater Michelle Kwan (left) won the gold medal. Elena Sokolova of Russia finished second.

It was Kwan's fifth world championship. That made her the first woman in 43 years to win the world title for a fifth time. And just two months earlier, she had won her seventh U.S. figure-skating championship! "It's like, 'Wow,'" the 22-year-old skater said. "I have no words."

The audience cheered Kwan so loudly during the last minute of her performance that her music was almost drowned out. The cheering was for good reason. In her exciting long program, she landed six triple jumps, two of them in combination.

ICE SKATING

FIGURE SKATING

World Championships

Men	Evgeni Plushenko, Russia
Women	Michelle Kwan, United States
Pairs	Xue Shen/Hongbo Zhao, China
Dance	Shae-Lynn Bourne/Victor Kraatz, Canada

United States Championships

Men	Michael Weiss
Women	Michelle Kwan
Pairs	Tiffany Scott/Philip Dulebohn
Dance	Naomi Lang/Peter Tchernyshev

SPEED SKATING

World Championships

Men	Gianni Romme, Netherlands
Women	Cindy Klassen, Canada

SKIING

WORLD CUP CHAMPIONSHIPS

Men	Stephan Eberharter, Austria
Women	Janica Kostelic, Croatia

WORLD ALPINE CHAMPIONSHIPS

Men

Downhill	Michael Walchhofer, Austria
Slalom	Ivica Kostelic, Croatia
Giant Slalom	Bode Miller, United States
Super Giant Slalom	Stephan Eberharter, Austria
Combined	Bode Miller, United States

Women

Downhill	Melanie Turgeon, Canada
Slalom	Janica Kostelic, Croatia
Giant Slalom	Anja Paerson, Sweden
Super Giant Slalom	Michaela Dorfmeister, Austria
Combined	Janica Kostelic, Croatia

SWIMMING

Michael Phelps: In the Swim of Things

For 18-year-old Michael Phelps of Baltimore, Maryland, 2003 went swimmingly! In July, at the World Swimming Championships in Barcelona, Spain, 14 world records were broken—and Phelps accounted for five of them. And in August, at the U.S. National Championships in College Park, Maryland, he became the first man ever to win five individual titles at one Nationals. Altogether, in 2002 and 2003, Phelps set 12 world records (11 of them individual records) and won four world titles!

Phelps began to attract attention in 2000. Only 15, he was the youngest member of the U.S. Olympic swimming team—and the youngest male Olympian since 1932. The following year, he was named Swimmer of the Year by *USA Swimming*.

In the 2003 World Championships, his five record-shattering wins were in the 100-meter and 200-meter butterfly, the 200-meter individual medley (twice), and the 400-meter individual medley. And with his win in the 200-meter individual medley at the Nationals, he broke the world record for that event for the fourth time in just six weeks!

What's next for Phelps? The 2004 Olympics in Athens, Greece. Not surprisingly, he'll be considered the top American swimmer.

TENNIS

Men's tennis in 2003 witnessed the appearance of several new young stars, and the departure of Pete Sampras. But there wasn't one dominant player. Four different men won Grand Slam singles titles—none of whom won in 2002. Among the women, Serena Williams's winning streak was broken. She was still dominant, but not invincible. And late in 2003, she was no longer ranked first.

At the **Australian Open** in January, American Andre Agassi collected his eighth Grand Slam singles championship, and his fourth Australian title. He beat Rainer Schuettler of Germany in a lopsided final by scores of 6–2, 6–2, 6–1. As the year developed, fans wondered if this Grand Slam title would be the 33-year-old Agassi's last.

In winning the women's Australian Open, Serena Williams won her fourth Grand Slam in a row—following the 2002 French Open, Wimbledon, and U.S. Open. In all of them, her opponent in the finals was her sister Venus. The 2003 Australian Open was the first of the four in which Serena even dropped a set to Venus, ultimately winning by 7–6 (4), 3–6, 6–4. It seemed as if the 21-year-old Serena sat securely atop the women's world rankings.

Belgian Justine Henin-Hardenne won the women's singles titles at the French Open and the U.S. Open (*above*).

TOURNAMENT TENNIS

	Australian Open	French Open	Wimbledon	U.S. Open
Men's Singles	Andre Agassi, U.S.	Juan Carlos Ferrero, Spain	Roger Federer, Switzerland	Andy Roddick, U.S.
Women's Singles	Serena Williams, U.S.	Justine Henin-Hardenne, Belgium	Serena Williams, U.S.	Justine Henin-Hardenne, Belgium
Men's Doubles	Michael Llodra, France/ Fabrice Santoro, France	Mike Bryan, U.S./ Bob Bryan, U.S.	Jonas Bjorkman, Sweden/ Todd Woodbridge, Australia	Jonas Bjorkman, Sweden/ Todd Woodbridge, Australia
Women's Doubles	Venus Williams, U.S./ Serena Williams, U.S.	Kim Clijsters, Belgium/ Ai Sugiyama, Japan	Kim Clijsters, Belgium/ Ai Sugiyama, Japan	Virginia Ruano Pascual, Spain/ Paola Suarez, Argentina

Davis Cup Winner: Australia

But at the **French Open** in June, 21-year-old Justine Henin-Hardenne of Belgium eliminated Serena Williams in the semifinals. She then captured her first Grand Slam crown by defeating another Belgian, Kim Clijsters, 20, in the final, 6–0, 6–4.

The men's French Open Winner, Juan Carlos Ferrero, 23, of Spain, also took his first Grand Slam. In the final, he outmatched Martin Verkerk of the Netherlands, 6–1, 6–3, 6–2.

Still a different young man triumphed at the **Wimbledon** championship in July. Switzerland's Roger Federer, 21, claimed his first Grand Slam singles title. He pounded out a three-set victory in the final over Australia's Mark Philippoussis, 7–6 (5), 6–2, 7–6 (3).

The Williams sisters were back in center court at the Wimbledon final. Serena needed three sets to dispatch Venus in the final, 4–6, 6–4, 6–2.

But neither of the Williamses competed at the **U.S. Open** in August/September. Both were injured, and fans saw an all-Belgian final in the women's competition. Henin-Hardenne again topped Clijsters, 7–5, 6–1. Henin-Hardenne's victory was especially sweet—the previous night, she had fought a grueling three-set semifinal match with American Jennifer Capriati. It had lasted into the early morning, and Henin-Hardenne seemed utterly tired. But she recovered for the final and won convincingly.

The men's U.S. Open winner was yet another first-time Grand Slam champion. American Andy Roddick, 21, with a power serve reminiscent of Pete Sampras, dropped Ferrero, 6–3, 7–6 (2), 6–3. Roddick, like Henin-Hardenne, also had to survive a tough semifinal to qualify for the final.

At the U.S. Open, 32 year old Pete Sampras announced his retirement. The legendary Sampras had been the number-one-ranked men's player for six straight seasons (1993–98). He had won fourteen Grand Slam singles titles—more than any man in tennis history.

Andy Roddick: Rising Tennis Star

With the retirement of Pete Sampras in 2003, and with Andre Agassi nearing the end of his tennis career, tennis fans began to ask: Who will be the next American men's tennis star?

By defeating Spain's Juan Carlos Ferrero in overwhelming fashion in the final of the U.S Open, the 21-year-old Andy Roddick gave every sign that he could be the one. En route to victory, Roddick smashed 23 aces (unreturnable serves). His opponent was unable to break his serve. The day before, Roddick staged one of the great comebacks in U.S. Open history. In an exhausting semi-

final match against David Nalbandian of Argentina, he overcame a two-set deficit and a match point to win in five sets.

Roddick grew up in a family that excelled at sports. He played basketball in high school but later followed his older brother, Lawrence, into tennis. In 1999–2000, he was the number-one junior player in the United States. And in 2000, after becoming the number-one junior player in the world, he turned professional. Since then, Roddick has won about a dozen singles titles. And his star is still rising.

SPORTS BRIEFS

A number of sports stories received special attention during 2003. Women golfers made headlines—and history—by competing against men. But women's soccer fell on hard times with the end of the Women's United Soccer Association (WUSA) and the failure of the U.S. women's soccer team to win the World Cup.

There were, however, many notable sports champions, including bicyclist Lance Armstrong in the Tour de France and musher Robert Sorlie in the Iditarod. Notable, too, was teenage sailor Sebastian Clover, who became the youngest person to sail solo across the Atlantic Ocean.

And as 2003 ended, sports lovers looked forward to the 2004 Summer Olympic Games, and to the Summer and Winter Games that will follow in the years ahead.

WOMEN'S GOLF: MAKING HISTORY

Tiger Woods, Vijay Singh, Ernie Els—move over! Annika Sorenstam, Suzy Whaley, Michelle Wie—it's the women golfers who grabbed the headlines in 2003!

Annika Sorenstam was considered the best woman golfer in the world. In 2003, she won the Ladies Professional Golf Association (LPGA) Tournament and the British Open, completing a career Grand Slam. She had earlier won the two other major tournaments that make up a Grand Slam: the U.S. Open and the Nabisco Tournament. This made her only the sixth woman to complete a career Grand Slam.

But Sorenstam wasn't satisfied with playing just on the LPGA tour. In the spring, she was given special permission to compete against male golfers in a Professional Golf Association (PGA) event, the Colonial Tournament. Sorenstam failed to make the cut, so she didn't play the two final rounds. But the thousands of fans who watched her were happy with her performance.

In July, Suzy Whaley also played against male golfers, in the Greater Hartford Open. Like Sorenstam, she failed to make the cut. But she was the first woman to actually qualify for a PGA event since the great Babe Didrikson Zaharias did it in 1945.

Two women golfers grabbed attention in 2003 by competing against male golfers in Professional Golf Association (PGA) events: Annika Sorenstam (*left*) at the Colonial Tournament, and Suzy Whaley (*below*) at the Greater Hartford Open.

Michelle Wie: Teenage Golf Superstar

In 2003, Michelle Wie was a typical 9th-grader. She read Harry Potter books and listened to music by Missy Elliott, Eminem, and Aaliyah. But that's where the comparison with other teenagers stopped. In June, when she was still 13, Michelle became the youngest golfer ever to win the U.S. Women's Amateur Public Links Championship.

Michelle, who is from Honolulu, Hawaii, has taken the pro golf world by storm. Other players have been impressed by her fluid swing, near-300-yard drives, and her total confidence. She stands nearly 6 feet (189 centimeters) tall and has been playing golf since the age of 4. Her parents, who were born in South Korea, are her biggest fans. Her father, B. J. Wie, a professor at the University of Hawaii, is her caddy and coach.

Michelle finished ninth in her first major Ladies Professional Golf Association (LPGA) tournament, the Kraft Nabisco Classic, in March. During the summer, she played in other tournaments, including the U.S. Women's Open. Wherever she played, she

drew attention. Her long-term goal is to win the Masters, the most prestigious tournament in golf. It doesn't worry her that women have never before played in that event.

WE ARE THE CHAMPIONS!

Three champions overcame great challenges in exciting races in 2003.

Cyclist Lance Armstrong: In July, 31-year-old American cyclist Lance Armstrong won his fifth straight victory in the Tour de France. He defeated some 200 other cyclists in the most famous bicycle race in the world.

The Tour de France is an extremely difficult race. The contestants must cycle around France for more than 2,000 miles (3,200 kilometers). And some of the course runs up and down the steep slopes of the towering Alps and Pyrenees mountains. Armstrong finished the race in 83 hours, 41 minutes, 12 seconds—just 61 seconds ahead of the second-place finisher.

Armstrong was the fifth person ever to win this grueling race five times, and only the second to win it five times in a row. He won his first Tour de France victory in 1999, after

making an amazing comeback from a battle with cancer. Will Armstrong become the first to win the race six times in a row? "I love cycling," he said, "I love my job and I will be back for a sixth."

Musher Robert Sorlie: On March 13, Robert Sorlie rode his eight-dog dogsled into Nome, Alaska, and became the winner of the 2003 Iditarod Trail Sled Dog Race. A Norwegian firefighter, Sorlie was only the second person born outside the United States to win this grueling race since it began in 1973.

The Iditarod is known as "The Last Great Race on Earth." It's an exhausting 1,100-mile (1,770-kilometer) dogsled race across the ice and snow of Alaska. The temperatures along the trail are frigid, and the winds are blistering.

The race usually begins in Anchorage, in south-central Alaska, and ends in Nome, a city on the Bering Sea just 15 miles (24 kilo-

Top athletes: Lance Armstrong (*above*) in the Tour de France; Robert Sorlie (*above right*) in the Iditarod; and Sebastian Clover (*right*), the youngest person to sail across the Atlantic.

meters) south of the Arctic Circle. But in 2003, unseasonably warm temperatures left the Anchorage area without enough snow. As a result, the starting point of the race was moved 350 miles (563 kilometers) north to Fairbanks.

When the race began, Sorlie faced 63 other mushers. His victory, in 9 days, 15 hours, 47 minutes, gave him the $68,571 first-place prize money.

Sailor Sebastian Clover: On January 12, 15-year-old Sebastian Clover of Britain sailed into the record books by becoming the youngest person ever to sail solo across the Atlantic Ocean.

Seb, as he is known, raced his father, Ian, nearly 3,000 miles (4,828 kilometers) across the ocean. The two set out on December 19, 2002, in separate yachts from Tenerife, in the

Canary Islands, off the northwest coast of Africa. Seb, who lives on the Isle of Wight, along the southern coast of England, was well-prepared for the race. His father teaches sailing and navigation, and he had been training for the race for three years. His 32-foot (10-meter) yacht was equipped with a satellite navigation system.

Still, the trip was hard. He had to struggle with broken rigging. And he had lonely moments, and frightening ones. But there were exciting moments, too. A highlight was a group of killer whales that followed his boat for part of the way.

After 24 days at sea, Seb finally reached the finish line—English Harbor, on the Caribbean Island of Antigua. His father had beaten him by one day. But Seb didn't mind. His dad may have won the race, but Seb set a world record.

WOMEN'S SOCCER: DASHED HOPES

Women's soccer in the United States suffered a double blow in 2003. In September, the Women's United Soccer Association (WUSA) folded. The WUSA—the first women's professional soccer league in the world—played its first season in 2001. But attendance at WUSA games was low, and the eight-team league couldn't come up with the millions of dollars needed to start its fourth season in 2004. The players hoped that commercial sponsors would get involved and enable a new league to be formed, perhaps in 2005.

In October, the U.S. Women's World Cup team lost to Germany in a semifinal match, dashing their hopes for another World Cup victory. After defeating the U.S. team, Germany went on to beat Sweden to take the title. The American women came in third, and the Canadians fourth.

THE OLYMPICS ARE COMING

The International Olympic Committee has selected the countries that will host the Olympic Games through the year 2010. Maybe you'll be lucky enough to travel to one of these cities to watch the exciting competitions.

The next Summer Olympic Games will be held in 2004 in Athens, Greece, the country where the Olympics originated more than 2,700 years ago.

The 2006 Winter Olympics will be staged in Turin, an ancient city in northwestern Italy that's flanked on the north and west by the towering Alps.

The 2008 Summer Games will be in Beijing, the capital of China, the world's most populous nation.

The 2010 Winter Games will be held in Vancouver, British Columbia, a beautiful city in southwestern Canada that has majestic snow-capped mountains on its northern fringes.

LeBron James: From High School to NBA

"He's the best talent I've seen come out in years," said Larry Bird, famed Boston Celtic basketball player and now president of basketball operations for the Indiana Pacers. He was talking about 18-year-old LeBron James, the phenomenal high-school basketball player who made his National Basketball Association (NBA) debut in October 2003 as a forward for the Cleveland Cavaliers.

In that debut, against the Sacramento Kings, LeBron recorded 25 points, 9 assists, and 6 rebounds. He was equally impressive in his second game, against the Phoenix Suns: 21 points, 8 assists, and 12 rebounds. The Cavs lost both games, but that didn't take away from James's extraordinary play.

James is 6 feet, 8 inches (203 centimeters) tall and tips the scale at 240 pounds (108 kilograms). And he's incredibly talented. In his senior year at St. Vincent-St. Mary High School in Akron, Ohio, he was named USA Today's High School Basketball Player of the Year. It isn't surprising, then, that he was the No. 1 pick in the 2003 NBA draft!

LIVING HISTORY

Meriwether Lewis and William Clark led a band of explorers across the American West in 1804–06, traveling all the way to the Pacific Ocean and back. Among those who helped guide them was the Shoshoni Indian woman Sacagawea, shown with the explorers in this picture. Lewis and Clark encountered many hardships, from grizzly bears to snow-covered mountain passes, but they paved the way for later explorers and settlers. In 2003, the United States began a four-year celebration marking the 200th anniversary of their expedition.

In 2003, the United States began a four-year celebration of the famed Lewis and Clark Expedition (1804–06). Meriwether Lewis (*left*) and William Clark (*right*) explored the uncharted lands of the western United States. Their journals described in great detail everything they saw—and even included drawings.

LEWIS AND CLARK: A VOYAGE OF DISCOVERY

In 1804 a band of explorers set out across the uncharted lands of the western United States. Back then, no one knew what lay beyond the Mississippi River. The Lewis and Clark Expedition traveled all the way to the Pacific Ocean, overcoming great hardships on the way, and returned with tales of a rich and wonderful land.

In 2003, the United States began a four-year celebration marking the 200th anniversary of that grand adventure. Through 2006, special events are being held along the route the explorers took. The Lewis and Clark Expedition was a key event in American history—the first of many explorations that would open the West to settlement.

PLANNING THE JOURNEY

The expedition was the idea of President Thomas Jefferson, who had long urged Americans to explore the West. When he took office in 1801, most of the U.S. population lived along the Atlantic coast. But Jefferson looked to the future. He

The praire dog was one of the strange new animals discovered by Lewis and Clark. They sent a live specimen back to President Thomas Jefferson.

The Louisiana Purchase has been called the best real-estate deal in history. For the bargain price of $15 million, or about 3 cents an acre, the United States doubled in size.

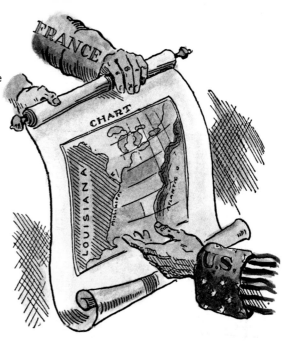

LOUISIANA PURCHASE - 1803

knew that if the country was to grow, Americans would have to explore and settle the West before others did. In January 1803, he asked Congress for $2,500 to fund the expedition. Later that year the United States bought the vast uncharted Louisiana Territory from France, making exploration even more important.

Jefferson asked his private secretary, Meriwether Lewis, to lead the Corps of Volunteers for North West Discovery, as the expedition was officially called. Lewis chose William Clark as co-leader. The president outlined several goals for the explorers—

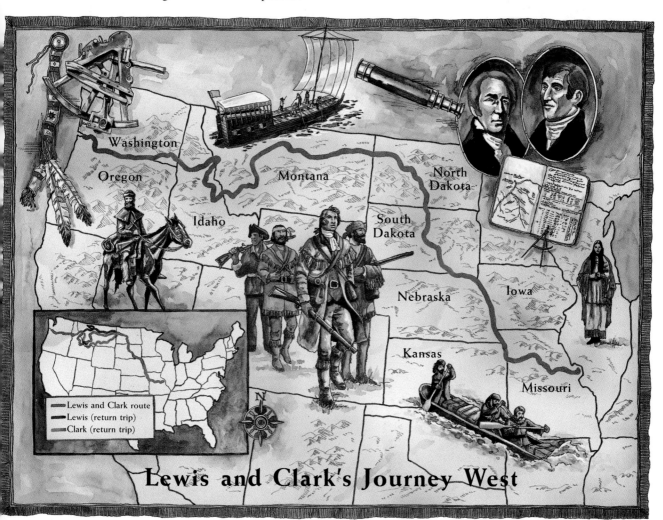

Lewis and Clark route
Lewis (return trip)
Clark (return trip)

Lewis and Clark's Journey West

Meriwether Lewis

Meriwether Lewis was born in 1774 near Charlottesville, Virginia. His father died when he was just 5 years old, and his mother remarried and moved the family to Georgia. It was there that he learned frontier skills. At 13 he returned to Virginia to study, and at 20 he enlisted in the army, where he reached the rank of captain.

In 1801, Lewis was hired as private secretary to President Thomas Jefferson. With Jefferson, he planned an expedition to explore the West. Jefferson then asked him to lead it. Lewis spent months preparing, studying with scholars and scientists. He learned how to navigate by the stars, treat illnesses and injuries in the field, and preserve natural specimens.

The expedition was a huge success, but Lewis's life ended sadly. After his return, he was appointed governor of the Louisiana Territory. But by 1809, he faced growing political and financial problems. He died in September of that year, a probable suicide.

establish good relations with American Indians; find an all-water route to the Pacific Ocean; follow the Missouri River to its source; and collect information about the plants, animals, climate, and terrain of the West. He wrote, "We shall delineate with correctness the great arteries of this great country: those who come after us will fill up the canvas we begin."

Lewis and Clark spent the winter of 1803–04 at Camp Dubois (also known as Camp Wood), near St. Louis, Missouri. They recruited about 30 soldiers and bought supplies. The corps would be well provisioned, with kegs of flour, salt pork, salt, a thick beef paste called portable soup, and parched meal (corn toasted in hot ashes and then ground into powder). But they couldn't hope to carry all the food for a trip that would last more than two years.

Instead, they planned to live off the land and barter with Indians as much as they could. Their muskets, powder, and shot were their most prized possessions, along with goods such as beads, mirrors, and cloth that could be used in barter. The explorers also packed tools, instruments for surveying and mapping, cloth for making tents, extra clothes, and medical supplies, They took maps, science books, and even a four-volume dictionary.

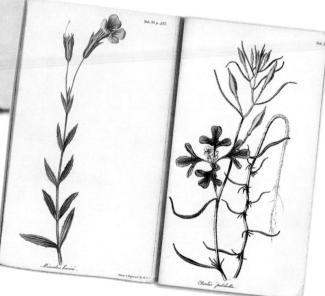

Lewis and Clark found many new plants in the West. These two plants were named for them—*Lewisii* (*left*) and *Clarkia* (*right*).

Lewis and Clark gave medals like this to Indian leaders. The medal shows President Thomas Jefferson on one side. The other side shows a handshake of friendship.

All the gear was loaded into a 55-foot (17-meter) keelboat and two smaller boats called pirogues. Then, on May 14, 1804, the Corps of Volunteers for North West Discovery set out up the Missouri River.

THE JOURNEY BEGINS

By July the expedition had followed the Missouri deep into the Plains. Lewis and Clark both kept journals of the trip, and Clark described the country: "I had an extensive view of the surrounding plains, which afforded one of the most pleasing prospects I ever beheld: under me a beautiful river of clear water about 80 yards (73 meters) wide, meandering through a level and extensive meadow, as far as I could see."

The men left the boats often to hunt, explore, and collect plant and animal specimens. They were on the lookout for Indians but saw none until early August, when they met with several Oto and Missouri chiefs near present-day Council Bluffs, Iowa. The expedition suffered its only death on August 20, when one of the soldiers, Charles Floyd, died, probably from a ruptured appendix.

Soon after that, the corps entered territory controlled by the powerful Sioux tribes. Lewis and Clark held a council with chiefs of the Yankton Sioux, near present-day Yankton, South Dakota, on August 30. They smoked a pipe together, and the explorers presented the Sioux with a flag and other gifts. But not far upriver, the Teton Sioux proved far less friendly. The explorers just managed to avert a fight when the Tetons demanded that they pay a toll to continue up the river.

On October 26, the expedition reached the villages of the Mandan and Hidatsa tribes, in present-day North Dakota. Lewis and Clark decided to winter there, and the soldiers built Fort Mandan, across the river from the villages. Here the explorers met Toussaint Charbonneau, a French-Canadian trapper, and hired him as a guide. Sacagawea, Charbonneau's Indian wife, also joined the expe-

William Clark

Born in 1770, William Clark was the younger brother of a hero of the Revolutionary War—George Rogers Clark. The Clarks moved to Kentucky when William was 14, and he grew up on the frontier. He joined the army in 1792 and became a captain. It was in the army that he met Meriwether Lewis. When Lewis asked him to be co-leader of the Corps of Discovery, William Clark wrote in reply, "I will cheerfully join you... and partake of the dangers, difficulties, and fatigues."

Clark drew all the maps of the expedition's route, producing the most complete picture of the West to that time. After his return, he married and settled in St. Louis. He was superintendent of Indian affairs for the Louisiana Territory and, later, governor of the Missouri Territory. He died in 1838.

Lewis and Clark were astonished by the bighorn sheep's ability to climb steep cliffs to avoid "the pursuit of the wolf, bear, or even man himself."

Sacagawea

Sacagawea was the only woman on the Lewis and Clark Expedition. A member of the Shoshoni tribe, she was captured by a Hidatsa Indian raiding party when she was 11 years old. Later, the Hidatsa sold her to a French-Canadian trader, Toussaint Charbonneau, who made her his wife. The name Sacagawea means "Bird Woman."

In 1804, Lewis and Clark hired Charbonneau as a guide, as much for Sacagawea's skills as for his own. She was just 18 and expecting her first child (her baby was born in February 1805). But she spoke several Indian languages, knew the country, and would be able to help the expedition get horses from the Shoshoni. Sacagawea helped in another way, too. Indians who might have been hostile reasoned that, with a woman and a baby along, the expedition had to be a peaceful one. And they let the explorers pass.

Sacagawea and Charbonneau returned with the expedition as far as present-day North Dakota, where they had joined it. Little is known of her life after that.

dition. On February 11, 1804, she gave birth to a son, Jean-Baptiste, nicknamed Pompy by Clark.

ACROSS THE MOUNTAINS

On April 7, 1805, the explorers loaded their boats and set out again. Lewis wrote: "We were now about to penetrate a country at least two thousand miles in width, on which the foot of civilized man had never trodden; the good or evil it had in store for us was for experiment yet to determine, and these little vessels contained every article by which we were to expect to subsist or defend ourselves."

Danger and hardship lay ahead. Near the end of April, Lewis and his men met a pair of grizzly bears while exploring on shore. They fired on the bears, but one chased Lewis almost 80 yards (73 meters) before it was brought down. This was the first of several encounters with grizzlies, and the explorers soon learned to respect the bears. Lewis wrote that he would "rather fight two Indians than one bear." Bears were only one of the troubles the explorers faced. They were bitten by mosquitoes and stabbed by thorns. Their feet blistered. A lot of the time, they were hungry, damp, and cold. On May 14, strong winds tipped one of the pirogues on its side, dumping precious journals, medicines, and other supplies into the river. Sacagawea acted quickly, reaching into the water to save as much as she could. Lewis praised her action in his journal.

Almost two weeks later, the corps came within sight of the Rocky Mountains. They were thrilled, knowing that the mountains must mark the source of the Missouri River. But the snowcapped peaks would be a daunting barrier on their way to the Pacific Ocean. In fact, the way became harder even before they reached the mountains. In June the explorers reached the Great Falls of the Missouri River, a series of five waterfalls. It took them more than a month to portage (carry their boats and gear) around this obstacle.

At least there was plenty to eat. The explorers fished in the rivers and gathered fruits such as wild grapes and plums. Game was plentiful. "We eat an immensity of meat. It requires 4 deer, an elk and a deer, or one buffalo, to supply us plentifully 24 hours," Lewis wrote. Sometimes they dried or "jerked" meat for later use.

By mid-August the expedition had reached the territory of the Shoshoni, Sacagawea's people. She was reunited with her brother, the Shoshoni chief Cameahwait. Lewis and Clark now had to leave their boats to cross the Rocky Mountains, and Sacagawea helped them obtain horses from the Shoshoni. The Shoshoni also provided a guide for the hazardous trip through the mountains.

The explorers set out on August 31 with 29 horses and one mule. By September 11 they had reached the Lolo Pass, high in the Bitterroot Range. The trail wound along the sides of steep cliffs where a misstep would be fatal. Snow covered the ground. Food supplies ran low. When hunters returned empty-handed, the explorers were forced to eat a horse. But they survived the crossing.

REACHING THE PACIFIC

West of the mountains, the expedition paused to trade for supplies with the Nez Percé Indians and to make five dugout canoes. Then they headed down the Clearwater River, which joins the Snake River and then the Columbia River. Paddling with the

Lewis and Clark often called the coyote "prairie wolf." They thought its howls sounded like dogs barking.

York

York was the only African American on the Lewis and Clark expedition. He was a slave, willed to William Clark by Clark's father in 1799, and he had been Clark's servant and companion since childhood.

Tall and very strong, York was an important member of the expedition. Clark's journal shows that he helped pole the keelboat, paddle canoes, build shelters, and hunt game. When the expedition members voted to pick a campsite for the winter of 1805–06, York's vote was counted with the rest.

After the expedition, however, York received scant thanks. He hoped to get his freedom, but Clark refused his request. Clark did allow York to go from St. Louis to Louisville, Kentucky, to visit his wife, who belonged to a family there.

York's life after that is a mystery. According to Clark's account, he was finally freed in 1815, failed in business, and died of cholera sometime before 1832. But in 1832 a fur trader reported that a black man claiming to be York was living with the Crow Indians. It's possible that York escaped and returned to the West.

current, they sped along. But they were forced to portage around some dangerous rapids and falls.

On November 7, they heard the roaring waters of the mouth of the Columbia River and thought they had reached the Pacific. But they were actually still 20 miles (32 kilometers) away. On November 15, they finally arrived at "this great Pacific Ocean," as Clark wrote in his journal, "which we have been so long anxious to see."

The expedition voted to camp for the winter on the south shore of the Columbia. All members took part in the vote, including Sacagawea and York, the only African American on the voyage. The men built wood shelters at a site they named Fort Clatsop, for the Indians in the area, and they spent the winter storing food and repairing equipment and clothes.

Winter at Fort Clatsop was damp and dismal. At one point Clark wrote: "The fleas were so troublesome last night that I made but a broken nights rest, we find great difficulty in getting those troublesome insects out of our robes and blankets." And on Christmas: "Our dinner consisted of poor elk, so much spoiled that we ate it through mere necessity, some spoiled pounded fish, and a few roots."

The explorers were eager to set out, and on March 23, 1806, they left Fort Clatsop and headed for home.

THE TRIP HOME

Going up the Columbia River through rapids and falls proved difficult, and on

Lewis and Clark called the henlike sage grouse the "Cock of the Plains." The birds' showy mating dance was imitated by some of the Plains Indian tribes.

April 12 one canoe was lost. No one was hurt, but the remaining canoes were now overloaded.

Lewis and Clark decided to obtain horses from Indians and strike out overland, leaving the canoes behind. But when they reached the Bitterroot Range, they found the pass blocked by snow. They were forced to wait until late June to cross.

Once through the pass, on July 3, Lewis and Clark split up to explore more territory. Clark's group followed the Yellowstone River. They lost half their horses to Crow Indian raiders and were plagued by hordes of mosquitoes. On July 25, Clark reached a large rock pillar overlooking the river. He named it Pompy's Tower, for Sacagawea's son, and carved his name and the date in the stone.

Lewis followed the Missouri River. Taking a loop north to explore the Marias River, a tributary of the Missouri, his party skirmished with Blackfoot warriors on July 27. Two Indians were killed, and Lewis and his men rode full out back to the Missouri. They met up with Clark and his group near the junction of the Missouri and Yellowstone rivers on August 12. But Lewis had been shot—one of Clark's men, hunting for game,

Seaman: The Four-Legged Explorer

When Lewis and Clark set out in 1804, Clark wrote that their expedition was made up of "46 men, 4 horses and 1 dog." The dog was Seaman, a big black Newfoundland. Lewis had bought the dog some months earlier for $20, a high price in those days. Newfoundlands are known for their strength, swimming ability, and intelligence, and Seaman turned out to be a valuable member of the expedition. He warned the explorers of prowling bears and once defended the camp from a charging buffalo. He helped hunt game. This was dangerous work. Once Seaman was bitten so badly by a beaver that Lewis feared he might die, but the dog recovered.

Pictures from an 1811 book depict events along the trail: A bear chases a hunter up a tree (*above left*); The explorers build huts (*above right*); Lewis and Clark meet with Indians (*left*); A canoe tips over (*below*).

had mistaken him for an elk. Luckily, the shot only hit his thigh, and he survived.

Two days later the expedition reached the Mandan villages. Charbonneau, Sacagawea, and Jean-Baptiste took their leave, and Lewis and Clark continued down river. Finally, on September 23, they arrived in St. Louis, where they were greeted as heroes.

Lewis and Clark didn't find a water route to the Pacific, but they achieved the expedition's other goals. They traveled 4,350 miles (7,000 kilometers) to the Pacific Ocean and back. They encountered many Native American tribes, and established good relations with most.

Thanks to these explorers, Americans began to imagine a United States that stretched from the Atlantic to the Pacific.

Today, the route Lewis and Clark followed has been designated the Lewis and Clark National Historic Trail. It winds for 3,700 miles (5,954 kilometers) through eleven states.

LEWIS AND CLARK TRAIL

CALL IT A DAY!

Did you ever wonder why a week has seven days, or how the days got their names? The answers lie far back in history, in the times when people first developed calendars to keep track of the days as the year passed.

Many ancient calendars were very different from ours. The Chinese, for example, developed a calendar with sixty-day months and ten-day weeks. The Mayan Indians of Central America had thirteen-day weeks. But in ancient Mesopotamia, the Babylonians used a seven-day week. Their calendar was based on observations of the night sky, and they named each day for a different heavenly body. The ancient Hebrews also chose the seven-day week. For them, it mirrored the biblical story of creation, which says that the world was created in six days and that the seventh day was a day of rest.

The calendar of the Romans, who conquered much of the ancient world, originally had months but no weeks. But the Romans eventually adopted the seven-day week, and this custom gradually spread through their empire. The Romans named the days for the sun, the moon, and the gods that they associated with the five planets that can be seen with the naked eye.

Since our calendar is based on the Roman one, the seven-day week is still with us. And perhaps because the seven-day week is so old, each day has a tale of its own.

Sunday

In the Roman calendar, Sunday was named *dies solis*—the day of the sun. As the Romans expanded their rule into Europe, they conquered tribes who spoke Germanic languages. These tribes adopted the Roman calendar, but they changed the names of the days to follow their own language. *Dies solis* became *Sunnandag* (sun's day). Over many years, that name developed into the modern English Sunday.

In the Christian tradition, Sunday is the Sabbath—a day of rest and worship. And as Christianity spread throughout the Roman Empire, the Romans changed the name of the first day of the week to *dies dominicus,* or day of the Lord. Thus languages that can trace their roots to Latin, such as French and Spanish, have different names for Sunday: *dimanche* in French, *domingo* in Spanish.

Today, schools and many businesses in most places are closed on Sunday, and people spend the day as they please. But in the past, observance of the Sabbath was often strictly enforced. The Puritan colonists who settled in New England, for example, had rigid rules: There could be no work and no play. People spent the day at the meetinghouse, praying and listening to sermons, and

Monday

The Romans called the second day of the week *dies lunai,* or day of the moon. Modern languages that come from Latin have similar names—*lundi* in French, and *lunes* in Spanish. But the groups that spoke Germanic languages substituted their own word for the moon and came up with *monandag,* which developed into the modern English Monday.

In ancient times, Monday was considered an unlucky day—perhaps because there were many superstitions about the moon. Some people even thought that gazing at the moon could drive a person insane. (In fact, the word "lunacy" comes from the Latin word for moon.)

Monday was unpopular for another reason in days gone by. It was washday—and washing all a family's clothes by hand was a lot of work. Even today, Monday is an unpopular day. This has less to do with superstition than with the fact that Monday marks the end of the weekend. After two days off, most people have to wake up early and head back to school or work. But some Mondays are better—in the United States and a number of other countries, many holidays fall on Mondays. And that gives everyone a three-day weekend.

even simple activities such as running, cooking, cutting hair, and kissing, were banned.

Tuesday

The Romans named the third day of the week *dies Martis,* for Mars, the god of war. It is still known as *mardi* in French and as *martes* in Spanish. The Germanic people used the name of their own war god, Tiu—giving us the name Tuesday.

A few Tuesdays have special importance. The Tuesday after the first Monday in November is Election Day in the United States. Most people go to the polls to choose the officials who will run the government.

In the Christian calendar, Shrove Tuesday comes right before Lent, the 40-day period of prayer and fasting that leads up to Easter. It's the last chance for people to eat, drink, and make merry. In days gone by, people tried to use up all the butter and other fats they had on this day because they would have to give up fats during Lent. Rich, buttery foods became a Shrove Tuesday tradition. So this day is also known as Pancake Tuesday, and as Fat Tuesday (or *Mardi Gras,* in French).

Today some cities still hold Mardi Gras parades and festivals. The Mardi Gras celebration in New Orleans is one of the most famous. But most Tuesdays are just ordinary days. And Tuesdays of the past were pretty dull: Just as Monday was washday, Tuesday was ironing day.

Wednesday

The ancient Romans named the fourth day of the week after Mercury, the messenger of the gods and guardian of the spiritual life. Their *dies Mercurii* became *mercredi* in modern French and *miercoles* in Spanish.

The Germanic people chose a different god to honor on this day: Woden (or Odin), the chief of their gods and, like Mercury, the ruler of the spiritual life. In English, Woden's day became Wednesday—the name that's used today. But Wednesday goes by still another name in modern German: *Mittwoch,* or midweek. As the fourth of the seven days, Wednesday marks the midpoint of the week.

In some places, Wednesday was traditionally a market day. Farm families went to town to sell their produce and buy the supplies they needed. Since they traveled by horse and wagon, the trip usually took all day.

Thursday

In ancient Rome, Jupiter (or Jove) was honored on *dies Jovis,* the fifth day of the week. Thus this day is called *jeudi* in French and *jueves* in Spanish. Jove was the Roman god of thunder and lightning, so Germanic tribes named the day after their own god of thunder—Thor. That gave us the modern English Thursday.

In Muslim countries, Thursday is the traditional day for weddings. Because Friday is the Muslim Sabbath, everyone will be off on the day after the wedding.

One of the most important U.S. holidays falls on the fourth Thursday in November:

Friday

Venus, the goddess of love and beauty, was honored by the Romans on the sixth day of the week. Their *dies Veneris* became *vendredi* in French and *viernes* in Spanish. Germanic people chose another goddess: Frigga, the wife of Woden. That gave us Friday, the English name for this day.

In the past, Friday was considered an unlucky day. Perhaps this was because Friday was hangman's day—the day when public executions were held. And because the number thirteen was also considered

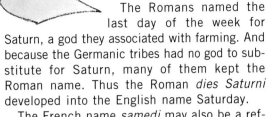

Thanksgiving. The first Thanksgiving feast was held by the Pilgrim settlers of New England in 1621. It lasted three days. After that, Thanksgiving gradually became a traditional way to celebrate the harvest. But every town chose its own day until 1863, when the feast was declared a national holiday.

In those days, a Thursday holiday was a welcome break from routine. Thursday was sweeping day in many homes. Furniture was dusted, floors were swept, and rugs were dragged outdoors and beaten to knock the dirt out. Before the days of vacuum cleaners, cleaning the house was a lot more work.

The Romans named the last day of the week for Saturn, a god they associated with farming. And because the Germanic tribes had no god to substitute for Saturn, many of them kept the Roman name. Thus the Roman *dies Saturni* developed into the English name Saturday.

The French name *samedi* may also be a reference to the god of farming. It probably developed from *semer*, the French word for sowing. But the names used in some languages have a different origin. Saturday is the Jewish day of worship, and in the Bible the seventh day of the week is referred to simply as "sabbath." Thus Saturday is *sabado* in Spanish and *lordag* (Lord's day) in Swedish.

Traditionally, Saturday was bath day. Before homes had indoor plumbing, bath water had to be drawn from a well, carried indoors, and heated over a fire. Once a week was considered quite enough for this work, so every Saturday people cleaned up and got ready to begin a new week.

unlucky, any Friday that was also the thirteenth day of the month was thought to be especially bad. Even today, some people are superstitious about Friday the Thirteenth.

For most people, however, Friday is one of the best days of the week. In Western countries, it's the last day of work and school—people look forward to the weekend. And in the Islamic religion, Friday is a day of worship. Thus schools, shops, and offices in Muslim countries are closed on this day.

QUILTS: STITCHES IN TIME

Princess Feather, Wild Goose Chase, Hovering Hawks, Wandering Foot—the names of classic quilt patterns are as colorful as the quilts themselves. Quilts have a practical purpose, keeping sleepers warm on cold nights. But handmade quilts are also beautiful. And they are wonderful examples of folk art, created by individuals and, sometimes, groups working together.

In classic patterns or one-of-a-kind designs, quilts have always reflected the skills and creativity of those who make them. Older quilts are like windows into the past,

offering a glimpse of the lives women led in the early days of the United States. And today the craft of quilting is enjoying a revival.

QUILTS IN EARLY AMERICA

A quilt is like a fabric sandwich—two layers of cloth, with a layer of padding in between. The layers are sewn together with tiny stitches, often in intricate patterns. The craft

Handmade quilts offer a colorful picture of America's past—and remain a popular craft today. Two common quilt styles are appliqué (*top*) and patchwork (*bottom*).

of quilting is very old. In medieval Europe, knights wore quilted clothing under their armor. In the 1600's, women wore quilted petticoats for warmth. And, of course, warm quilts were made to cover beds.

European settlers brought the craft of quilting to North America. The quilts they preferred were whole cloth quilts, not patchwork. They were made of all white or solid-colored fabrics and quilted with tiny stitches in elaborate geometric patterns or designs of flowers or other forms.

By the 1700's appliquéd quilts were popular. In appliqué, pieces of fabric are cut out to form a design and sewn onto a larger piece of fabric. Floral designs were most common. But during the Revolutionary War, women stitched patriotic quilts that featured symbols of the new nation and honored the heroes of the war.

Making elaborate quilts such as these took many hours. For wealthy women who had the time, quilting was a way to demonstrate their

In appliqué, pieces of fabric are cut out to form a design and are sewn onto a larger piece of fabric. Floral designs are often used for appliqué quilts.

skill with a needle. Poorer women had little time for this work—they had to spin, weave, and make clothes for their families. What quilts they made were often pieced together from leftover fabric scraps and worn-out clothing. These early patchwork quilts were the poor cousins of the fancy whole-cloth and appliquéd quilts.

That began to change in the mid-1800's, after machine-made fabrics became available and affordable. The popularity of quilting took off. There was an explosion of new quilt designs, and many were popularized by women's magazines that were first published at this time.

PATCHWORK PATTERNS

From their humble beginnings, patchwork quilts blossomed into an American art form in the 1800's. Instead of using leftover scraps and worn-out clothing, women began to stitch these quilts from fabrics that they bought just for this purpose.

The simplest patchwork quilts were made up of square fabric pieces stitched together into larger squares. Young girls learned to sew by

Patchwork quilts are made by stitching pieces of fabric together into large squares (*left*). The haphazard crazy quilt (*below*) is a more complicated patchwork design.

In pioneer days, friendship quilts were often made as gifts for women who were moving west with their families. Each square was made by a different woman.

making simple quilts such as the nine patch, in which each square was made up of nine pieces. Squares were sewn together into strips, and then the strips were joined to make the top of a quilt. Sewing and other forms of needlecraft were important skills for women, and training started early. Many girls completed their first quilts by age 5!

As they became more skilled, sewers could try their hands at more complex patterns. Dozens of new patchwork patterns appeared during the 1800's. Most of these patterns were geometric, made up of stars, circles, and squares. But they often had names that mirrored nature (Autumn Leaf, Ocean Wave, Flying Geese), daily life (Wedding Ring, Flower Garden, Log Cabin), and the Bible (Jacob's Ladder, Job's Trouble). Some quilt patterns went by different names at different times and in different parts of the country.

Among the most popular designs were friendship and album quilts. These quilts were usually made by groups of women, rather than by individuals, with each woman making a square.

Quilting Bees

In the 1800's a woman usually worked on her own to create the patterns that made the top layer of her quilt. But when it was time to put the layers of a quilt together, women often came to-gether for a quilting bee. A quilting bee could be a small gathering of a few friends and family members or a big social event, bringing women for miles around. Either way, the idea behind the gathering could be summed up in the old saying, "Many hands make light work."

The quilting was done on a large wood frame, which was often supported by four chairs. The layers—backing, filler, and top—were stretched over the frame. The pattern for the quilt stitching was traced onto the top. Then the women sat around the frame and stitched the layers together, using fine running stitches. As they sewed, they exchanged news, recipes, and gossip. The hostess always provided food. And sometimes, when the work was done, men joined the gathering for a meal and a dance in the evening. Especially on the frontier, a quilting bee was a welcome break from daily routine.

Friendship quilts often had simple designs made from fabric scraps. During pioneer days many of these quilts were made as gifts for women who were moving west with their families. Friends and family members would each make a square and add their names and the date to the design, using indelible ink or embroidery. These quilts became treasured keepsakes, reminding pioneer women of the people they had left behind.

Album quilts were more elaborate, but the idea was similar. These quilts were generally made for special occasions, such as weddings, or in memory of someone who had died. The squares often had appliquéd designs showing flowers, animals, or patriotic symbols, and they were usually made with new fabrics. As with friendship quilts, the women who contributed the squares often signed them. Sometimes small sketches and verses or sayings were added to the squares. Fine album quilts were kept for display, and many have been handed down through generations.

The most complicated patchwork quilts were crazy quilts. These designs first appeared in the 1870's, and they were popular until about 1910. As applied to quilts, the term "crazy" meant broken or cracked. It described the splintered, haphazard look of the design. Crazy quilts were made up of irregularly shaped pieces sewn onto a muslin backing. Although the designs seem random, they were actually carefully planned. Each piece in the quilt was bordered with fancy embroidery stitches. Many of these quilts were made with fine fabrics such as velvet and brocade. They were display pieces, meant to show off the maker's skill and creativity.

STITCHES IN TIME

Quilts were part of American life in the 1800's. For the pioneers, quilts were much more than bed coverings. Quilts were packed around china and other breakables for the journey west. Folded quilts cushioned the hard board seats in covered wagons. In the simple sod homes that settlers built on the plains, quilts were used as door coverings. Quilts even served as makeshift coffins for those who died on the trail west.

Some people say that Log Cabin quilts were often hung in windows to indicate a safe house for slaves who were escaping through the Underground Railroad.

Women everywhere made quilts to mark the important events of their lives, such as weddings and the birth of children. When a family member died, they might make a memorial quilt that included fabric from that person's clothes. Some women made quilts to mark important events in the community or the nation, too. And quilts were a form of expression for women. Sometimes they stitched their opinions into the designs of their quilts. In the north, for example, women made quilts with inscriptions about the evils of slavery. Since women couldn't vote in the 1800's, quilting was a way to make their views known.

Some people say that quilts helped guide runaway slaves through the escape network known as the Underground Railroad. A Log Cabin quilt hanging in a window would indicate a safe house, where an escaped slave could find food and shelter. Other patterns were said to hold clues to the route to freedom. Historians say there is little evidence that quilts were used in this way, but there are many stories about it.

In the South, large plantations had skilled sewing slaves who did quilting and other

To raise money for Confederate forces, Southern women made appliquéd quilts in a style called broderie perse (*above*). Women supporting the temperance movement made quilts in a pattern known as Drunkard's Path (*right*).

needlework. Slaves made quilts for their own use as well as for their masters. They did this work at the end of the day, after their plantation work was done, and they often had to make do with scraps and feed sacks for fabric. Few slave quilts survive because most were worn out through long, hard use.

Slaves and free African-American women used many of the popular quilt designs of the day. They also created their own designs, including appliquéd quilts in which each square told a story. Among the most famous examples are the story quilts created by Harriet Powers, who was born a slave in 1837.

QUILTING FOR A CAUSE

During the Civil War, quilting was one of many ways in which women of the North and the South supported the soldiers of their respective sides. Northern women donated thousands of cot-size quilts for soldiers. Some of these quilts were made by cut-

ting full-size quilts in half, while others were made from scratch. Early in the war, Southern women raised money for Confederate forces by making and selling quilts. Some of these quilts were appliquéd in a style known as broderie perse, in which pieces of printed fabric were arranged in intricate floral designs.

After the war, other groups took up quilt making as a way to raise money for various causes. One such cause was the temperance movement, which sought to end drunkenness. Members of the Women's Christian Temperance Union made blue and white quilts in a pattern known as Drunkard's Path and raffled them to raise funds. Quilts were also made and sold by women crusading for suffrage, or the right to vote.

American women won that right in 1920 with the passage of the 19th Amend-

The AIDS Memorial Quilt—with more than 44,000 panels— is often displayed to raise awareness of the disease.

The Quilts of Gee's Bend

Quilts from the tiny Alabama community of Gee's Bend were the toast of the art world in 2003. Seventy of these striking quilts were on view in an exhibition touring U.S. cities. The exhibition featured quilts created by 45 women from the 1920's to the 1990's.

Gee's Bend, which is about 30 miles (48 kilometers) south of Selma, began as a cotton plantation. Most of the 750 people who live in the town today are descendants of the slaves who worked on that plantation. The little community was largely cut off from the rest of the world, and its women carried on a tradition of making striking quilts from fabric scraps and worn-out clothes. Their quilts began to gain recognition in the

1960's after a cooperative, the Freedom Quilting Bee, was organized to earn money for the community by selling handcrafts.

The Gee's Bend quilts (left) look a lot like modern abstract paintings. Actually, they owe their geometric designs and bold colors to quilting traditions that go back many generations. The patterns are original, but they remind many people of African textile designs.

In 2003, the Quilts of Gee's Bend exhibit was at the Whitney Museum of Art in New York City, the Mobile Museum of Art in Mobile, Alabama, and the Milwaukee Art Museum in Milwaukee, Wisconsin. It will be touring a number of other U.S. cities through 2006.

ment to the Constitution. By that time, more and more women had entered the workforce. Fewer women needed or wanted to spend many hours sewing, and young girls were no longer required to practice needlework by making patchwork. But the craft of quilting didn't die.

QUILTS TODAY

Although anyone can buy machine-made quilts in stores today, people still value the beauty and workmanship of handmade quilts. Antique quilts sell for thousands of dollars. Some of the finest examples are considered works of art and hang in museums.

Meanwhile quilt making is growing in popularity once again. Nearly 20 million Americans—including many children—enjoy the craft today. Special quilt shops cater to their needs and offer classes for quilters of varying skills.

Quilts are still made for causes, too. The AIDS Memorial Quilt is an example—a really big example. This quilt has more than 44,000 panels, each honoring the life of a person lost to AIDS. Portions of the quilt are displayed in different parts of the country, to increase awareness of the disease and raise money for services to victims.

Many modern quilters enjoy re-creating old-fashioned designs such as Log Cabin and crazy patchwork. These designs provide a link to the past. But today's quilters are also inventing new designs of their own. Today as in the past, quilts reflect the creativity of their makers.

The Wright brothers, Orville (*right*) and Wilbur (*far right*), proved that powered flight was possible when they made their historic flight (*above*) on December 17, 1903. The 100th anniversary of that flight was widely celebrated in 2003.

THE WRIGHT BROTHERS—FLYING HIGH!

December 17, 1903, was a cold and blustery day on the Outer Banks, the string of islands off the North Carolina coast. But to two men who had camped on a desolate strip of sand near the village of Kitty Hawk, the weather was perfect. Wilbur and Orville Wright were there to test an invention they hoped would be the world's first powered flying machine, and the wind would help lift it into the air.

The brothers positioned their machine on a wooden track they had built on a windswept dune. They started the engine. Orville stretched out in the pilot's cradle, on the lower of the craft's double-decker wings. He pushed a small lever, and the machine began to roll down the track, into the wind. Wilbur ran alongside, holding a wing to keep the plane balanced. The machine lifted off the track and soared into the air.

That first flight lasted only twelve seconds, but it changed history. Orville and Wilbur Wright proved that powered flight was possible, fulfilling one of the oldest human dreams. They and others would go on to improve the airplane, making flight a practical means of transportation.

The year 2003 marked the 100th anniversary of the Wright brothers' famous flight. It was a time to celebrate their achievement and everything that made it possible.

DREAMS OF FLIGHT

People have dreamed of flying since the earliest times. But they didn't get off the ground until 1783, when a hot-air balloon carried two passengers into the sky over Paris. The balloon was designed by two Frenchmen, Joseph Michel and Jacques Étienne Montgolfier, and it marked the start of the age of flight. The Montgolfier balloon rose because it was lighter than air. Other people experimented with heavier-than-air craft. Among them was Otto Lilienthal, a German, who built a series of gliders that he controlled by shifting his weight. Lilienthal was killed in a crash in August 1896, but his experiments laid the groundwork for later inventors.

Balloons and gliders had serious drawbacks. Balloons went wherever the wind took them. And gliders were like planes without engines; they could stay aloft only as long as air currents would support them. To fly farther, people needed a machine that could be steered and would fly under its own power. Building such a machine became the goal of many inventors. Among them were Orville and Wilbur Wright of Dayton, Ohio.

At first glance the Wright brothers seemed unlikely inventors. Neither Wilbur (born in 1867) nor Orville (born in 1871) graduated from high school, although both completed their courses. But they were fascinated by everything mechanical, and they were great tinkerers. When he was still in his

WEST SIDE NEWS.

The Wright brothers published this weekly newspaper at their printing press in Dayton, Ohio, in the late 1880's.

teens, Orville built a printing press and started a successful printing business in Dayton. Wilbur joined him in the business. In 1893, the brothers started a second business—repairing bicycles, which were then becoming more and more popular. Soon they began to build and sell bicycles, too.

But what really fascinated the brothers was the problem of flight. Inspired by Lilienthal and others, they built their own glider in 1900. It was made of muslin cloth stretched over a lightweight wood frame. There was no place near Dayton to test it, so they decided to take it to the North Carolina coast. There, strong winds and wide-open beaches would provide the right conditions for takeoff—and few people would be around to watch.

In the fall of 1900 the Wright glider made several flights at Kill Devil Hill, a stretch of dunes near Kitty Hawk. The glider was a disappointment—it was hard to get off the ground and hard to control. The brothers returned to Dayton and built another. The next summer they were back at Kill Devil Hill, where they built a shed that became

Left: The brothers tested their gliders at Kill Devil Hill, a sandy stretch of beach in North Carolina. Below: To help design their glider, they built this wind tunnel to test different kinds of miniature wings.

Wilbur Wright sits at the controls of an early Wright airplane. The brothers demonstrated their flying machines in cities throughout the United States and abroad.

the base for their experiments. But the second glider was disappointing, too.

In designing their gliders, the Wrights had relied on published calculations about lift and other factors affecting flight. They began to wonder if these figures were wrong, so they decided to do their own tests. Back in Dayton that winter, they built a wind tunnel to test miniature wings of different sizes and shapes. The experiments told them how to lengthen and curve their glider's wings to get the lift they needed. They also added two fixed tail fins to the design.

The Wrights took their third glider to their camp at Kill Devil Hill in the fall of 1902. By this time they were well known to the locals, who thought they were a pair of crazy but harmless fools. The new glider flew much better than the earlier models, but it had an alarming habit of spinning out of control. The brothers were stumped. Then Orville had a flash of inspiration: If the glider had a moveable rudder instead of fixed tail fins, the pilot could use the rudder to keep the craft stable. They tried it, and it

worked. In late October, the glider traveled more than 600 feet (183 meters) and stayed aloft almost half a minute—a record.

AN IDEA TAKES OFF

The Wrights had built a craft that flew well and could be steered. Now they needed an engine to give it power. No engine light and powerful enough was made, so they designed their own. They also designed the propellers that the engine would turn.

In September 1903 the Wright brothers took their powered flying machine, the *Flyer,* to Kill Devil Hill for its first test. Bad weather and mechanical problems delayed a flight attempt until December 14. On that first try, Wilbur was at the controls. He made a mistake in adjusting the elevators, flaps at the front of the plane that helped lift the nose. The plane shot into the air—and then flopped into the sand.

But three days later, the *Flyer* soared over the beach in its first flight, landing about 120 feet (37 meters) away. The brothers made three more flights that day, taking turns at the controls. In the last flight, Wilbur stayed aloft for almost a minute, flying 852 feet (260 meters).

The Wright brothers had made history, but few people realized it at the time. The brothers took their *Flyer* back to Dayton and went to work improving it. In 1905, in a stretch of prairie near Dayton, they tested a new *Flyer*—one that could take off and land repeatedly and stay aloft until it ran out of fuel. It was the first practical airplane.

Within a few years the brothers were demonstrating their machines in flights over New York, Paris, and other cities. They won a contract to make airplanes for the U.S. Army, and in 1909 they formed the American Wright Company to manufacture airplanes. But others soon took to the air with flying machines of their own. The Wrights began to spend more and more time suing inventors who, they claimed, had stolen their designs.

Wilbur died of typhoid fever in 1912. Orville lived until 1948, and by that time the importance of their invention was clear.

Celebrating 100 Years of Flight

The 100th anniversary of the first airplane flight was celebrated in many ways in 2003, but three places held major events.

Dayton, Ohio, held a 17-day celebration in July. Among the attractions was a simulator that gave people a sense of what it was like to fly an early Wright plane. Visitors could also see the workshop where the brothers developed many of their early ideas.

North Carolina held events through the year. At the Wright Brothers National Memorial, which includes Kill Devil Hill, a new pavilion filled with special flight-related exhibits was opened. The memorial was the end point for interstate air races and fly-ins, and it was the focus of a six-day celebration in December that featured a working reproduction of the Wright *Flyer.*

In Washington, D.C., "The Wright Brothers & The Invention of the Aerial Age" opened at the Smithsonian Institution's National Air and Space Museum in October. This exhibition, scheduled to run for

Top left: Dancers at the opening ceremonies of the Dayton, Ohio, celebration. Top right: The Wright Brothers National Memorial in North Carolina. Above: The original 1903 *Flyer* on display at the National Air and Space Museum in Washington, D.C.

several years, includes full-size reproductions of gliders built by the brothers and re-creations of their home and bicycle shop. The original 1903 *Flyer,* part of the museum's collection, is displayed at eye level for the first time. In December, the museum celebrated with another big event. It opened a sprawling new center at Washington Dulles International Airport, in Virginia, to house most of its huge collection of airplanes and spacecraft.

The ability to fly changed everything—travel, mail delivery, access to goods from distant places, even military strategy. Less than 60 years after the *Flyer* rose into the air at Kill Devil Hill, astronauts were orbiting Earth. Flying drew people closer together and gave them a new sense of their place in the universe.

mountains; and in water—in wells, deep forest pools, swamps, rivers, and lakes. These legendary creatures share a love for jewels and treasure. But they take many forms. Some have horns, sharp spines along their backs, or barbs on the ends of their tails. Most have legs and claws—two legs, like eagles, or four, like lions. Many have batlike wings and can fly. Some are more like snakes—legless, wingless, or both.

The reason dragons vary so much is simple: They are mythical creatures, so they take any form that the imagination gives them. There is no evidence that real dragons ever lived on Earth. But that hasn't stopped people from dreaming up fantastic tales about them.

EARLY DRAGONS

Monsters of many kinds figured in the tales told in ancient times, especially in stories of the world's creation. Often it's not

TALE OF THE DRAGON

A huge, scaly, lizardlike creature, baring its sharp fangs and spitting fire—you know at once what this is. Of all the mythical beasts that leap, crawl, and fly through ancient tales, none is more famous than the dragon. Dragons appear in stories from all over the world. In some tales, especially those of medieval Europe, dragons are evil creatures that prey on people. In others, especially Chinese myths, they are powerful but kind, even helpful.

The stories say that dragons live in many places—under the ground, in caves, on high

214

A glazed brick relief of a dragon is displayed on a mural created by an ancient Middle Eastern civilization.

clear what these monsters were supposed to look like, but some are thought to have been dragons.

Dragons first appeared in art thousands of years ago in Mesopotamia, where the civilizations of Sumer and Babylon arose. A creation myth from those ancient times features a dragonlike goddess called Tiamet. It tells that at the dawn of the universe, Tiamet led the forces of evil and chaos. The sun god, Marduk, defeated her, using the wind as his ally. When the dragon opened her gaping jaws to devour him, he drove the wind into her mouth so that she couldn't close it. Then he shot an arrow down her throat to her heart—a dragon-slaying method used by many later heroes—and killed her.

The ancient Egyptians told of a huge serpent, Apophis, who was the enemy of their sun god, Re. Each night the sun god disappeared into the underworld to fight this monster. Each morning, having won the battle, he reappeared.

Our word "dragon" comes from the Greek word *drakon*, which was used to refer to any type of snake. Many Greek tales tell of heroes who defeated dragonlike monsters. The god Apollo, for example, slew the serpent monster Python. The hero Perseus killed a sea dragon to save Andromeda, a beautiful maiden.

The Roman writer Pliny believed that dragons lived in far-off lands such as India. Some dragons, he wrote, had huge crests on their heads that acted like sails, allowing the dragons to fly thousands of miles to hunt. Pliny's descriptions were accepted as fact for hundreds of years, and they convinced many people that dragons were real.

In late Roman times, dragons became a symbol of evil. Early Christians gave stories of dragons a new twist: Christian saints replaced gods as dragon slayers. One such hero was St. George. The original George was a soldier and martyr who was beheaded around A.D. 303. After his death, many stories were told about him. The most famous involved a dragon that terrorized a city in North Africa.

Every day, according to the tale, the dragon appeared at the city gates, demanding food. At first the people gave it sheep. But it soon demanded men, and then young maidens. To satisfy its horrid appetite, the king of the city ordered that all the maidens

Dragons can take many forms—but they are usually described as scaly, snake-like creatures. They often have huge claws, sharp spines along their backs, and monstrous wings.

According to medieval legend, St. George slew a dragon to save the daughter of a king. This story was hugely popular in England, which claimed St. George as its patron saint.

DRAGONS OF EUROPE

The tale of St. George and the dragon was a favorite in medieval Europe, and especially in England. But St. George was only one of many heroes who battled dragons in medieval legend.

European dragons were always causing trouble. If a well went bad, the reason was doubtless that a dragon was living in it. If a fire broke out in the middle of the night, dragons flying overhead had caused it with their fiery breath.

Even when dragons didn't cause calamity, they were linked to it. Viking raiders carved dragon heads on the bows of their ships, striking fear in their victims. Sightings of dragons were often reported just before disasters such as invasions or outbreaks of plague. Such reports were

draw lots each day to see which would be sacrificed. The lot finally fell to his daughter.

Sick at heart, the king watched her as she walked through the city gates to face her death. But suddenly, St. George appeared. Sword drawn, he spurred his horse at the horrible beast and battled it until it fell to the ground. Then St. George cut off the dragon's head.

The Vikings carved dragons on the bows of their raiding ships. The sight of these fearsome vessels on the horizon caused terror among their enemies during the Middle Ages.

common in Europe through the 1600's, and preserved "dragon babies"—usually stitched together from lizard skins and bat wings—were sold.

Europeans believed there were several distinct types of dragons. The wyvern was a fierce, flying dragon that carried the plague. The amphiptere was a legless dragon that lived in Egypt and Arabia, where it guarded trees that produced the fragrant resin called frankincense. The lindworm had no wings and lived in Central Asia. The guivre had no wings or legs and lived in forests and wells. Most fantastic of all was the vouivre, a dragon that lived in the French Alps and was covered head to claw with jewels.

There were many famous individual dragons. One of the best known in Norse mythology was Fafnir, who began life as a giant. Fafnir killed his father to gain a hoard of gold and a magic ring. Then he changed into a dragon to guard his treasure better.

Fafnir was a famous dragon in Norse mythology. Once a giant, he turned into a dragon to guard his treasure. Fafnir spread destruction until he was slain by the hero Siegfried.

Fafnir ravaged the countryside until the hero Siegfried came along. Siegfried, like many other dragon slayers, used brains as well as brawn to defeat his scaly foe. He dug a pit along a path the dragon used and waited in it. When the dragon came down the path and passed over him, he drove his sword into the monster's unprotected underside.

If the number of tales is an indication, Britain must once have crawled with dragons. Among them was the Laidly Worm of Northumberland—a princess who was changed into a dragon by her wicked stepmother. Her brother returned from overseas, changed her back with a kiss, and turned the stepmother into a toad.

Russians who listened to fireside tales knew that it was unwise to strike a bargain with a dragon. One famous tale told of Gorynych, a dragon with several heads and even more tails that lived near Kiev. He was defeated in battle by Dobrynja Nikitich, who agreed to let him live if he would stop destroying the countryside and carrying off young maidens. But that was what European dragons did best—so it wasn't long before Gorynych swooped down on Kiev and snatched a beautiful princess. Dobrynja pursued the dragon to his lair, where he freed the princess and dispatched the monster once and for all.

CHINESE DRAGONS

The Chinese believed that dragons were powerful, magical, and friendly beings—not evil monsters to be slain. Dragons were honored and feared because they had great powers over the forces of nature. Just by flying up into the sky, they could bring gentle rains to make crops grow. Chinese farmers would beat gongs to frighten the dragons into the air when they needed rain. But when dragons were angry, they caused floods, windstorms, and destruction.

Many Chinese scholars separated dragons into four types, each with its own job. The Celestial Dragon supported the palaces of the gods in heaven. The Spirit Dragon governed wind and weather. It was said to be a lazy dragon that always tried to hide from work. The

In China, dragons were magical symbols of good luck and were even thought to have healing powers. Dragons often appear in Chinese art.

Dragon of the Earth had power over rivers and streams. Every river was said to have its own dragon lord, who lived in a palace beneath the water. The fourth type was the Dragon of Hidden Treasure, who guarded all the precious minerals underground.

Other Chinese writers grouped dragons according to differences in their color or appearance. Blue dragons were said to be omens of spring. Red and black dragons fought in the clouds and produced storms. Yellow dragons were the most honored and were symbols of intelligence and virtue. But some people said dragons could change color if they chose.

The Imperial Dragon had five claws and was a symbol that could only be used by the emperor. Other dragons were thought to look like, and be related to, fish or horses. Nine dragons with different traits were believed to protect objects ranging from bells and swords to gates, bridges, and rooftops. Some tales told that dragons could assume human form and even shrink themselves to the size of mice.

The Chinese believed that dragons hatched from huge, jewel-like eggs. These eggs lay

Living Dragons

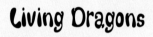

It doesn't breathe fire, hoard treasure, or fly. But the Komodo dragon is probably the closest thing on Earth to the dragons of myth and legend.

The Komodo dragon is the world's largest lizard, growing up to 10 feet (3 meters) long and weighing up to 300 pounds (135 kilograms). It's found only on Komodo and several other remote islands of Indonesia, in Southeast Asia.

This giant lizard is a meat eater, armed with long claws and powerful jaws studded with sharp teeth. It usually eats carrion (dead animals). But it is big, strong, and fast enough to catch and kill goats, pigs, deer, water buffalo—even, at times, people.

Could living Komodo dragons have inspired dragon stories like the tales of Perseus or Siegfried? It's not likely. Western explorers didn't discover the lizards until 1912.

near riverbanks for as long as 1,000 years before the young, snakelike creatures emerged. The young dragons immediately began to grow, taking 3,000 years to reach their final form. Along the way, they passed through various stages, sprouting scales, shaggy manes, claws, horns, and wings.

Parts of a dragon's body were thought to have healing powers. Chinese apothecaries (pharmacists) sold powders that were said to be ground dragon's bone (for fevers and paralysis) or teeth (for madness and headaches). Dragon's blood was said to turn into amber when it touched the ground.

Most important of all was the dragon's pearl, which it kept in its mouth or in a fold of skin under its jaw. The pearl was said by some to symbolize wisdom and by others to stand for the sun, the moon, or life itself. But by all accounts, the pearl possessed great magic.

One Chinese story tells of a poor boy who finds a dragon's pearl lying in a field. He takes it home to his widowed mother and puts it in a rice jar. In the morning, the jar is full. The boy and his mother find that the pearl will provide them not only with rice but with all the food they need, as well as silk and money. They keep it secret, and their wealth grows.

Other people grow jealous, and the village headman goes to their home to investigate. The boy puts the pearl in his mouth to hide it. But he swallows it by mistake—and is changed into a fire-breathing dragon.

THE LEGEND LIVES

In Chinese culture today, the dragon remains an important symbol. Images of dragons are associated with prosperity and good luck. At Chinese New Year celebrations, crowds gather to watch the Dragon Dance, a colorful parade in which dancers carry a long paper dragon through the streets.

Why do dragons turn up in so many stories, from so many parts of the world? Some people have suggested that dragons represent a distant memory of dinosaurs. But dinosaurs died out long before humans appeared on Earth. Still, it's likely that people found fossil bones of dinosaurs and extinct mammals, such as giant cave bears, in ancient times. Those fossils could have given rise to dragon tales.

The Dragon Dance is always an exciting part of the Chinese New Year celebration.

Most dragons are something like certain living creatures, such as crocodiles and large lizards. It's possible that these creatures inspired dragon stories. Another theory is that dragons represent predators—lions, big snakes like boa constrictors, and birds of prey—that the earliest ancestors of humans instinctively feared. Some of that prehistoric fear survives in legends of dragons, this theory holds.

Today, people accept the fact that dragons never existed. But we still enjoy reading the old tales. And dragons turn up in new stories, such as J. K. Rowling's *Harry Potter* series. Dragons may have lived only in legend, but their legend lives on.

These kids aren't playing firefighter. They are firefighters! The Dragon Slayers, a group of kids ages 13 to 18, make up about half of the only emergency rescue squad in rural Aniak, Alaska. They are all Yupik Inuit or Athabascan Indians, and until recently they were all girls. The teen volunteers get about 400 hours of training in firefighting and rescue work each year. When a fire breaks out or a hiker is injured, they're on the scene—even if that means rushing from school.

ENVIRONMENTAL CAREERS

Today people are more and more worried about threats to the environment. How can we stop pollution? How can we conserve natural resources? How can we save wilderness areas and endangered animals? Everyone needs to do his or her part. But if you are really concerned about these questions, you may want to consider a "green-collar" career—a career that will allow you to work full-time to help the environment.

Environmental careers cover a wide range of different kinds of work, from scientific research to public health work to education and publicity. That's because environmental concerns touch so many aspects of our lives today. And, since environmental concerns are still relatively new, these careers also include many new specialties within traditional fields—such as engineering and biology. With the need to solve serious environmental problems growing all the time, demand for people in these specialties seems likely to be high in years to come. Both government and private businesses have need for environmental specialists of many different kinds.

ENVIRONMENTAL PROTECTION

One of the biggest general areas of environmental work is that of public health and environmental protection. This area includes several different types of jobs.

Environmental engineers specialize in solving—and preventing—pollution problems. Like traditional sanitary engineers, they design systems for handling wastes, so that these wastes will not contribute to pollution. They may also deal with the problems created by the disposal of toxic and hazardous wastes, such as toxic by-products of chemical production and other manufacturing processes. They may develop ways to monitor and limit various other kinds of industrial pollution. And before a new factory, power plant, or pipeline is built, environmental engineers may be called on to assess its environmental impact—what affect it will have on its surroundings, and whether it will be harmful. Because this field of work covers so much ground, many environmental engineers specialize in one or another aspect of it. For example, air-quality engineers focus mainly on the problem of analyzing and controlling pollution from vehicle exhausts, factory smokestacks, and the like.

Environmental engineering is considered a branch of civil engineering. This career requires a bachelor's degree and usually a master's degree. Some environmental engineers also study chemistry and related fields. Engineers generally must pass a registration exam to work on government or public projects. Many private businesses also prefer to hire registered engineers.

The **industrial hygienist** is also an important member of the environmental-protection team. An industrial hygienist combines knowledge from several fields— engineering, chemistry, biology—to identify and reduce hazards in the workplace. For example, the hygienist may develop policies to lessen the risks faced by those who must work with materials like asbestos or clean up toxic spills. People in this field generally have post-graduate degrees.

Hazardous materials ("hazmat") specialists are often in charge of carrying out the industrial hygiene policies and monitoring operations. Or they may be called on to respond to emergencies, such as chemical fires or oil spills, to advise on the safe handling of toxic materials. The level of training and education needed for these jobs varies depending on the exact type of work that the hazmat specialist is called on to perform.

Environmental health scientists are other important members of the environmental-protection team. They are experts on the effects pollution and other environmental problems have on people's health. Some materials, such as asbestos, are well known for their harmful effects; others are less well known. Environmental health scientists identify these problems and set standards for limiting or solving them. Most environmental health scientists work in government, and most hold undergraduate degrees in biology or chemistry along with a master's degree in public health or a related field.

A "hazmat" specialist hoses down a chemical leak. These professionals are often sought for their advice on the safe handling of toxic materials.

Other health professionals may also focus on environmental concerns. For example, **physicians** and **nurses** may specialize in environmental medicine, treating the diseases and other conditions caused by environmental problems. **Toxicologists,** who may hold medical degrees or advanced science degrees, are experts on the effects of harmful chemicals.

CONSERVATION

Some of the most serious environmental threats we face today involve ways in which natural resources—including forests, soil, lakes and rivers, and grasslands—are being used up, damaged, or destroyed by people.

Carelessness, greed, and the needs of the world's growing population have all played a role in creating these threats. And as people have become more aware of the risks to natural resources, career opportunities have grown in the field of conservation. Most of these careers require at least a bachelor's degree, and many call for some graduate study as well.

Foresters look for ways to balance the needs of natural forests with human needs for timber and recreation. They may control timber cutting, deciding how many trees may be cut in an area of forest and how cut areas should be replanted. They may direct recreational uses of forests, such as camping and hunting, deciding what activities will be permitted in what areas. They also work to protect forests from insects, diseases, and fires and to preserve water and air quality within forest lands. Forestry isn't a new career, but with the world's forests fast disappearing it is growing in importance. Most professional foresters work for government agencies or for paper and timber companies.

The job of a **range manager** is a lot like that of a forester. But a range manager works to protect grasslands and prairies, balancing the needs of grazing animals like cattle with the needs of wildlife and the ever-present need to con-

serve soil, plants, and water. Rangelands are extremely important in North America, especially in the West. The United States government owns vast areas of rangeland, but it allows ranchers to graze their cattle on much of the range. Range managers decide how many and what kinds of animals may graze in an area and what recreational uses will be allowed. They may also work to improve rangelands with seeding and other techniques. Like foresters, many range managers work for government agencies, although some livestock ranches also employ range managers.

Fertile soil is an essential resource. When it's lost through erosion, or when the vital nutrients in soil are depleted, farming and ranching suffer. **Soil conservationists** (or soil scientists) help farmers, ranchers, and others protect soil from loss or deterioration by designing windbreaks, advising on plowing methods and crop rotation, and so on. They also advise on how to rebuild eroded areas, control water runoff, and fix or prevent other

Top: Foresters supervise the replanting of natural forests to preserve them for future generations. Center: An agronomist informs an orchard manager about pest control. Bottom: A water-quality technologist measures the volume of water in a snowpack to forecast how much water will later be available for agriculture and other uses.

Volunteering

Is an environmental career right for you? A good way to test the waters is through programs run by school clubs, scout troops, and environmental organizations. These groups provide lots of opportunities for volunteer work, which is a great way to get started and gain experience in the field.

Nature centers, parks, zoos, and other facilities sometimes offer volunteer opportunities as well. Volunteer projects with an environmental focus might include:

- Cleaning up litter and trash at a beach, park, or stream, or on neighborhood streets.
- Planting a tree or a flower garden.
- Organizing a recycling drive to collect cans, bottles, plastic, and paper (*right*).

- Restoring or creating a small wildlife habitat area, to provide birds and other animals with food, water, shelter, and places to raise their young.

Kids have done a lot for the environment by volunteering. Some have even formed their own volunteer groups. The biggest and best known of these groups is Kids F.A.C.E., an international children's environmental organization. Kids F.A.C.E. was started in 1989 by Melissa Poe of Nashville, Tennessee, who was then just 9 years old. It now has 300,000 members worldwide.

You can find out more about the group and gather some more ideas for environmental projects at the Kids F.A.C.E. Web site: **http://www.kidsface.org**

---

problems, including the contamination of soil by toxic chemicals. Many soil conservationists work for various government agencies, for fertilizer companies, or as consultants.

The work of a soil conservationist is closely related to the work of an **agronomist**—a specialist in the raising of crops. Today people are increasingly aware of the damage that can be done to the environment by some farming methods. For example, intensive plowing can lead to the loss of fertile topsoil, and the use of chemical fertilizers and pesticides can contaminate soil and water. Concerns such as these have created new challenges for agronomists, who are helping to develop other, less-damaging methods of growing field crops, and for other agricultural scientists.

Water-quality technologists are experts in preserving another essential resource: the water supply. They may oversee water or wastewater treatment plants, making sure

that these plants run at top efficiency. Or they may advise government, industry, and agriculture on how to conserve water and prevent or clean up pollution.

LAND USE

Careers in the general area of land use are also closely involved with environmental concerns. Two of these careers are urban (or regional) planning and landscape architecture.

As their job titles suggest, **urban** and **regional planners** plot the ways in which towns and cities will grow. Their work covers a wide range—everything from traffic patterns to water supply to new parks and school buildings may be part of a city or regional plan. Besides having knowledge of many areas, planners must be able to work closely with environmental specialists and with leaders in government, industry, and the community, so that the needs of many different groups can be addressed in the plan. Most planners hold master's degrees in their field. They generally work for local, state, or national government agencies.

Landscape architects design the surroundings for buildings—lawns, trees, shrubs, gardens, walkways. They may also design parks and other public spaces, and they may be called on to help reclaim damaged or eroded areas. Concern about the environment has made landscape architecture an important field because a good landscape design can not only beautify an area, but also conserve soil

Urban and regional planners plot the ways in which towns and cities grow. They must balance the needs of people with the environment.

and water, provide homes for wildlife, and even reduce the energy used to heat or cool a building. The landscape architect's work involves drawing up plans, advising on the kinds of trees and shrubs to plant, estimating costs, and sometimes supervising the planting. Landscape architects generally hold bachelor's degrees. Most work for private firms, and many are self-employed.

WORKING WITH WILDLIFE

Many environmental careers focus on wild animals and their place in the environment. A **wildlife conservationist** (or wildlife manager) is concerned with maintaining animal populations. As people take over more and more wild areas for homes, farms, and businesses, wild animals are being pushed into ever smaller areas. This has made the work of wildlife conservationists more important than ever.

Wildlife conservation may mean protecting members of species whose numbers are dwindling or whose habitats are threatened. For this, wildlife conservationists may work to maintain habitat reserves, to prevent hunting, to fight diseases that affect the animals, and even develop captive-breeding programs or other programs to increase animal populations. Wildlife conservation may also mean regulating hunting and other activities so that the populations of certain animals don't grow out of control. For example, in some areas, if herds of deer grow too large, they can overgraze the land and damage the environment, making it more difficult for other animals to survive. Most wildlife conservationists have undergraduate degrees in wildlife biology or a related field, and some have advanced degrees. Most work for government agencies.

The job of a **fisheries conservationist** is similar to that of a wildlife conservationist. This work is growing in importance as water pollution, overfishing, and other problems threaten fisheries that are a major source of food for people and animals alike. Fisheries conservationists bring expert knowledge to these problems. Their work includes helping to control pollution and maintain habitat areas, manage fish hatcheries, and educate the public about fish and other aquatic creatures. Like wildlife managers, fisheries conservationists generally hold at least a bachelor's degree, and most work for government agencies.

The techniques and methods used by wildlife and fisheries conservationists often

Rachel Carson: Environmental Pioneer

Rachel Carson didn't set out to make a career in environmental science. In fact, this field didn't really exist when she was growing up. Carson was a writer and a marine biologist, a scientist who focused on the life of the ocean. But she became a pioneer of the environmental movement, and through her writing she alerted millions of people to the importance of protecting the environment. It's largely thanks to her that people became aware of the dangers of chemical insecticides.

Carson was born in Springdale, Pennsylvania, in 1907. As a girl, she had two great interests: She loved nature and spent many hours observing wildlife, and she loved to write. Those interests shaped her life. She went to Pennsylvania College for Women, planning to major in English. But in her junior year she switched her major to zoology, and she later earned a master's degree in that field at Johns Hopkins University.

As part of her studies, Carson spent the summer of 1929 at the Marine Biological Laboratories in Woods Hole, Massachusetts. This was the first time she had seen the ocean, and she was fascinated by it. From then on, her studies focused on the sea.

With her talents as a writer, Carson landed a part-time job writing radio scripts for the U.S. Bureau of Fisheries. That led to a full-time job as a scientist and editor with the U.S. Fish and Wildlife Service. Eventually she became editor-in-chief of all the agency's publications.

In her spare time, she wrote articles and books about the sea. Her writings often focused on ecology—the relationships between living things and their surroundings—and her 1951 book *The Sea Around Us* was a best seller. Its success allowed her to leave her job with the Fish and Wildlife Service to write full-time.

As a scientist, Carson became very concerned about the growing use of chemical pesticides. DDT and other toxic chemicals were being sprayed everywhere to control insect pests. Farmers and homeowners were thrilled to finally be winning the age-old war against insects, and no one seemed to notice or care that these pesticides were harmful to the environment. Carson decided to write about the great dangers of pesticides.

Her book *Silent Spring,* published in 1962, described in gripping words how pesticides were poisoning the land and water and entering the food chain, harming wildlife. She described a grim future in which "only silence lay over the fields and woods and marsh"—because pesticides had killed all the birds and other animals.

Silent Spring created an uproar. Chemical companies called Carson an alarmist—but science supported her claims. Thanks to her book, the use of DDT and other harmful chemicals was banned or restricted.

Rachel Carson died in 1964, just two years after *Silent Spring* was published. But she had succeeded in warning the world of the dangers of pesticides, and she had helped start the environmental movement.

Many environmental careers focus on wild animals and their place in the environment. Above: A wildlife conservationist holds a puffin while doing a bird count in Iceland. Right: Two fisheries conservationists examine oysters for signs of chemical contamination.

grow out of research done by other environmental specialists. **Environmental biologists** and **ecologists,** for example, study ways in which living things interact with their environment. They may conduct research into the effects of a change in water temperature on fish populations, or the role pesticide pollution plays in wildlife population levels. Most of these specialists hold master's or doctoral degrees in their fields. They may work for government or private agencies or for universities.

PUBLIC ACTION

While many of the careers covered so far rely on science to solve environmental problems, there are other ways to get involved.

The growth of laws and regulations to protect the environment has created a need for **environmental lawyers.** In fact, environmental law is one of the fastest growing legal specialties. Lawyers in this specialty are involved in drafting regulations, bringing or defending legal actions in court, and advising their clients on how best to comply with environmental laws. Like other legal careers, this one requires a graduate degree and state certification, by passing a bar examination. Environmental lawyers may work for government, for private industries or groups, or for law firms.

Environmental action groups also employ many people who aren't scientists. Although volunteers are the backbone of many of these

groups, especially the small ones, there are a number of career positions. For example, **fund-raisers** work to raise the money these groups need to keep going. Large organizations may use sophisticated marketing techniques to raise money and attract new members; they may employ professionals in the field of advertising or public relations. And **administrators** and **managers** coordinate the work of these groups at local and national levels. Although a college degree and knowledge of environmental problems are important for most of these careers, good communications skills and an ability to work well with other people are the essential requirements.

Lobbyists are also involved in the environmental field. A lobbyist tries to present a particular point of view to legislators and government officials, with the hope of affecting government policy. There are lobbyists who work for environmental groups, trying to get the environmentalists' point of view across. Others work for industry, presenting that point of view in environmental matters. It's important for a lobbyist to know about environmental law. Some are lawyers; others have backgrounds in planning or political sci-

Getting Started

Education is very important in this field. However, environmental careers cover a wide range, so no single course of study will prepare you. But science and math courses will help you gain the knowledge that you need, and language-arts courses will help you to develop communications skills.

Many colleges offer programs tailored to careers in environmental science, with courses in life, physical, and earth sciences; computer science; and math. People interested in policy also need to know something about economics and other social sciences. Generally, the more education you have, the more career paths will be open to you.

You may want to contact some of the many professional organizations involved in environmental fields. A partial listing follows. Check your local library for others.

American Academy of Environmental Engineers—130 Holiday Court, Annapolis, MD 21401 (*www.enviro-engrs.org*)

American Planning Association— 1776 Massachusetts Avenue, NW, Washington, D.C. 20036 (*www.planning.org*)

Canadian Institute of Planners— 116 Albert Street, Ottawa, Ontario K1P 5G3 (*www.cip-icu.ca/English/home.htm*)

American Society of Agronomy— 677 South Segoe Road, Madison, WI 53711 (*www.agronomy.org*)

American Society of Landscape Architects—636 Eye Street, NW, Washington, D.C. 20001 (*www.asla.org*)

An agricultural student pollinates wheatgrass.

American Water Resources Association— 4 West Federal Street, P.O. Box 1626, Middleburg, VA 20118 (*www.awra.org*)

Canadian Water Resources Association— P.O. Box 1329, Cambridge, Ontario, N1R 7G6 (*www.cwra.org*)

Ecological Society of America— 1707 H Street, NW, Washington, D.C. 20006 (*www.esa.org*)

Canadian Society of Environmental Biologists— P.O. Box 962, Station F, Toronto, Ontario M4Y 2N9 (*www.freenet.edmonton.ab.ca/cseb/english.htm*)

ence. Good communications skills are also important for this work.

Environmental education is another growing field. At the college level, more and more schools are offering degrees in environmental studies. At lower levels, the environment is becoming an important part of school studies.

Thus there is a growing need for teachers with knowledge of and concern about the world's environment.

These are just a few of the jobs to consider if you want to be involved in environmental work. And the number of "green-collar" jobs seems certain to grow in the future.

WWW.COOLSITES

Look through colorful photo albums created by kids in Africa. Discover what happens to the body when a person drinks alcohol. Help undercover agents nab rascally critters. Try to hit a fastball thrown by a major league baseball player. You can do all these things on the Internet's World Wide Web—one of the coolest places to be these days. If your computer is connected to an online service, visit the four Web sites described on these pages. Each site has an address that begins with the letters http. Type in the address exactly as shown, and in seconds you'll be at the site.

Africa for Kids
http://pbskids.org/africa/index.html

Visit the fabulous continent of Africa, with local kids as your guides. In My World albums, the kids describe their communities, their favorite sports, and what they study in school. Photos taken by the kids help you compare the houses, schools, playgrounds, and stores in their communities with those where you live. Next, listen to a story about Prince Sadaka, who needs your assistance to find his brothers. There are also instructions for making several kinds of African masks. And be sure to play some cool tunes on the thumb piano—an instrument that's popular with kids all over Africa.

Cyber Health and Emotions
http://www.cyke.com/land.swf

Explore the land of CYKE, where music, magic, and games teach important concepts of physical and emotional health. Meet Monkey, Piggy, and Sandy at the Adventure

Station and learn about emotions. At Mullet Point, join the cat, the camel, and the giraffe on a journey to discover the common bond they share. Enter Castle Fairhope to read jokes, discover how different kinds of music can make you feel certain ways, and view interactive movies on the heart and other body parts. Visit Densmore Forest to take a safari through a land of fantasy creatures. At Mount Spressmore there's a message board, a virtual coloring book, and a kids' gallery of art.

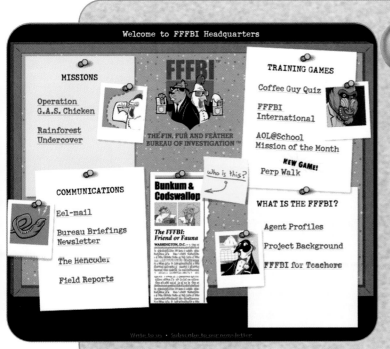

Use your investigative skills as you join the crime-fighting animals at the Fin, Fur and Feather Bureau of Investigation (FFFBI). Meet famous agents such as the hamster Harry Elbow and the weasel Mitch "The Itch" McGurk. Undergo training as you play the Coffee Guy Quiz and other games. Then work with your co-agents on missions Operation G.A.S. Chicken and Rainforest Undercover. Use Eel-Mail to publish your weird, funny, informative, and surprising Field Reports. If you've got a top-secret message for a friend, be sure to Hencode it so that your enemies can't read it!

Science of Baseball
http://www.exploratorium.edu/baseball

This is a must-see for baseball players and fans. It offers lots of pointers on how to improve your game: how to adjust the angle at which the ball leaves your bat, how to locate one of the "sweet spots" on a bat, how a pitcher's momentum is transferred to the ball, how to throw a slider or curveball. History buffs can discover how the baseball stats of legendary players such as Babe Ruth and Ty Cobb would change if they had played in different eras. And visit with Edith Houghton of the Philadelphia Bobbies and other female sluggers who played competitive baseball.

KID STUFF

A small rocket lifts off and streaks into the sky, carrying a precious cargo of. . .two raw eggs?? It happened all over the United States in 2003 as part of the **Team America Rocketry Challenge**—the first national high-school rocketry competition. Kids in this contest tried to design, build, and fly a model rocket that took two raw eggs as close as possible to 1,500 feet (457 meters). Of course, the rocket had to fly safely. And the eggs had to parachute back to the ground unbroken!

The National Association of Rocketry and the Aerospace Industries Association sponsored the contest to get kids interested in aerospace. More than 870 teams from high schools in all 50 states took part, building their multi-stage rockets from scratch. Qualifying flights narrowed the field. Then the top 100 teams gathered for a final fly-off on May 10 in The Plains, Virginia (above). The overall winner was the team from Boonsboro High School in Boonsboro, Maryland (inset). The top five teams shared a prize of about $50,000 in savings bonds.

Actor **Shia LaBeouf** had a big year in 2003—and not just because he turned 17. He starred in *Holes,* his first feature film (right). Then he appeared in two more movies—the comedy *Dumb and Dumberer: When Harry Met Lloyd* and the action movie *Charlie's Angels: Full Throttle.* And he was at work on a fourth film, *The Battle of Shaker Heights.* Shia has been acting in television shows since 1998. He started with guest roles on shows such as *Touched by an Angel* and *Freaks and Geeks,* and he made several television movies. But he's probably best known for the role of Louis Stevens on the Disney Channel series *Even Stevens.* Shia lives with his family in California, where he attended a magnet school for the performing arts.

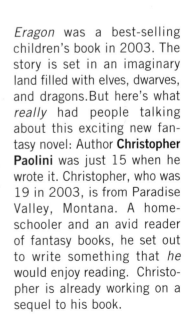

Eragon was a best-selling children's book in 2003. The story is set in an imaginary land filled with elves, dwarves, and dragons. But here's what *really* had people talking about this exciting new fantasy novel: Author **Christopher Paolini** was just 15 when he wrote it. Christopher, who was 19 in 2003, is from Paradise Valley, Montana. A home-schooler and an avid reader of fantasy books, he set out to write something that *he* would enjoy reading. Christopher is already working on a sequel to his book.

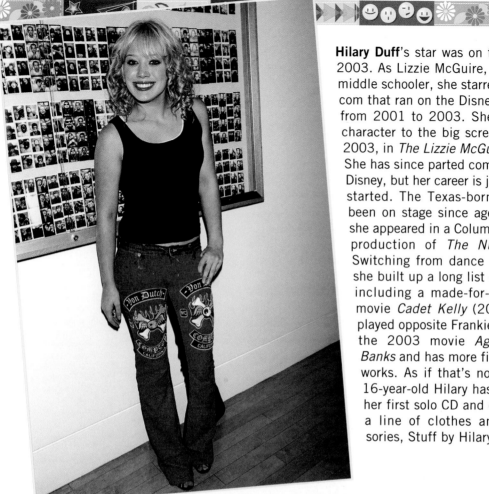

Hilary Duff's star was on the rise in 2003. As Lizzie McGuire, a madcap middle schooler, she starred in a sit-com that ran on the Disney Channel from 2001 to 2003. She took the character to the big screen in May 2003, in *The Lizzie McGuire Movie.* She has since parted company with Disney, but her career is just getting started. The Texas-born star has been on stage since age 6, when she appeared in a Columbus Ballet production of *The Nutcracker.* Switching from dance to acting, she built up a long list of credits, including a made-for-television movie *Cadet Kelly* (2002). She played opposite Frankie Muniz in the 2003 movie *Agent Cody Banks* and has more films in the works. As if that's not enough, 16-year-old Hilary has recorded her first solo CD and developed a line of clothes and acces-sories, Stuff by Hilary Duff.

If you watch cable television, you've probably watched **Amanda Bynes** grow up. At age 12 this teenage actress became the youngest person ever to host her own variety show—*The Amanda Show,* on Nickelodeon. In spring 2003, Amanda turned 17, and her second feature film, *What a Girl Wants* (right), opened in theaters. Amanda, who was born in Thousand Oaks, California, started acting at age 7. When she was 10, producers from Nickelodeon spotted her talent. That led to a part on the Nickelodeon show *All That* and, later, *The Amanda Show.* In 2002, Amanda starred in the hit film *Big Fat Liar,* and launched a new sitcom, *What I Like About You,* on the WB network.

Kids all across America were locked in duels in 2003. They were playing **Yu-Gi-Oh!,** the year's big game craze. Yu-Gi-Oh! is played with trading cards. In a match, two players face off in a series of three duels. Each player has a deck of 40 or more cards. There are hundreds of different cards, each with different powers. It takes skill and luck to use these cards well.

Yu-Gi-Oh! grew out of a popular comic strip and animated television show in Japan. The show, translated into English, was exported to U.S. television, followed by Yu-Gi-Oh! video games, board games, a Web site, and action figures. But the card game created the most excitement. Was it a fad, or would it last?

What country once ruled the tiny state of Goa, now part of India, as a colony? **James Williams** knew the answer— Portugal. And because he did, the 14-year-old home-schooler from Vancouver, Washington, won the 2003 National Geographic Bee on May 21, and a $25,000 scholarship. "I wasn't expecting this at all," James said. "It's really exciting!" The National Geographic Bee, sponsored by the National Geographic Society, is open to students in grades 4 to 8. The goal of the Bee is to promote interest in geography. More than 5 million students nationwide took part in 2003.

The adjective "pococurante" (poh-koh-kyoo-RAHN-tee) means careless. That's not a word many people use every day. But 13-year-old **Sai Gunturi** of Dallas, Texas, knew how to spell it. And that made him the winner of the 2003 Scripps Howard National Spelling Bee, held in Washington, D.C., at the end of May. Sai faced 250 other contestants at the Bee. All had qualified by winning regional spelling bees. One by one, contestants were eliminated as they stumbled over spellings. Sai clinched the win—and a $12,000 first prize—with pococurante.

Julia Socala of Tarzana, California, was just 15 in 2003. But she was already well on her way to a successful career as an artist. Her colorful, semi-abstract paintings were getting a lot of attention in the art world—and some of them were selling for as much as $15,000! "People have told me they see things in my paintings that I never intended them to see," Julia said. She gives half her profits to charity.

Jamie Rubin, 16, of Fort Myers, Florida, won the top award—a $100,000 college scholarship—in the 2003 Intel Science Talent Search (STS). STS is considered the top high-school science contest in the United States, and it's sometimes called the "junior Nobel Prize." The 2003 STS winners were announced in March in Washington, D.C.

Jamie's project grew out of her volunteer work at a hospice in her hometown. She saw that many hospice patients suffered from fungal infections, which can be very serious for people with weak immune systems, such as those with cancer or AIDS. For her STS project, Jamie figured out a new way to treat the infections. Working at the University of Florida's Biochemistry and Molecular Biology Lab, she identified small molecules that could be used to target treatment against the fungus.

At Canterbury School in Fort Meyers, Jamie was first in her class of 51 students. She also ran cross-country, played piano and handbells, and was active in theater. She planned to use her scholarship to study at Harvard University.

CREATIVITY

The artist Joseph Cornell selected various objects and uniquely arranged them in small wooden boxes. Each of his creations, such as A Pantry Ballet, *below, is a little dreamworld of delight and mystery.*

These flowers seem so real that you might be tempted to sniff them. But they're made of glass!

FLOWERS OF GLASS

You can almost see these graceful flowers nodding in the breeze and smell their delicious scents. They are as beautiful and as delicate as . . . glass.

In fact, the flowers *are* glass. These incredibly lifelike models are from a large collection of glass plants at Harvard University in Cambridge, Massachusetts. The collection is on display in a recently renovated gallery at Harvard's Museum of Natural History, along with a special exhibit that explains how the glass flowers were made.

The collection includes nearly 3,000 models, representing more than 840 different kinds of plants. For each type of plant, there's a scientifically accurate, life-size model, plus models that show the plant and flower parts enlarged, in great detail. There are also special models that show fruit diseases, the life cycle of mosses, and plant pollination by insects.

The collection was begun in the late 1880's by Harvard professors who were looking for a better way to teach plant sciences to their students. The university didn't have extensive greenhouses where living plants could be seen and studied. So Harvard founded a botanical museum, filled with specimens and models of plants.

But the museum's first director wasn't happy with the wax and papier-mâché models that were then available. They weren't very lifelike, and they didn't hold up well over time. Dried specimens, on the other hand, didn't convey the beauty of living plants. The director wanted something special for the museum—something that would not only teach people about plants but also enchant them with the beauty of the plant world.

The director found what he was looking for near Dresden, Germany, at the studio of two glass artisans, Leopold and Rudolf Blaschka. This father-and-son team belonged to a family that had been working with glass for centuries. They had previously made glass models of marine animals for Harvard's zoology museum, and they agreed to try their hands at plants.

Glass turned out to be the perfect material for portraying the fragile beauty of plants. The glass flowers and plants that the Blaschkas created over the next 50 years were so delicate and lifelike that many people thought a secret process had been used. But the glassmakers said they had no secret—any artisan could do what they had done. Their success, they said, was due to what they called "tact"—that is, skill.

The Blaschkas were dedicated to the project. They studied hundreds of plants. Among them were exotic specimens found in nearby greenhouses and specimens sent from America to be cultivated in the glassmakers' own garden. Rudolf even traveled to the Caribbean and to the United States to study plants and collect specimens.

They made their glass flowers piece by piece. First the corolla, the central tube of the flower, would be formed from hot glass. Then individual petals would be shaped with tweezers and joined to the corolla, by melting the glass at the joints. Needles were used to make the tiny surface lines and grooves on petals and leaves. Finally, the finished flowers and leaves were joined to the glass stem. Wires were used to strengthen some models, such as those with hanging fruits that might otherwise snap off under their own weight.

Early models were made of clear glass and then carefully painted. Over the years the paint has pulled away from the surfaces of some of these flowers. But after 1895, when Leopold Blaschka died, Rudolf Blaschka began to work with colored glass. For some models, he ground colored glass into a powder, applied it to the surface of a clear-glass model, and then heated it so that it welded into a permanent finish.

The Blaschkas found that glass was perfect for portraying flowers such as dahlias (*right*) and plants such as echeveria, or hens and chicks (*below*).

The Blaschkas worked to get every detail right. The plant models have all the color shadings of living plants. And they even have the flaws of living plants—missing petals, damaged leaves, and wilted blooms. It's this, as much as anything, that makes the models seem real.

Rudolf Blaschka continued to make models until he retired in 1936. At Harvard's Museum of Natural History, the glass plants he and his father made are still used as teaching tools. For that purpose, they are even better than real flowers—they bloom all year long.

The glass flowers are also a great attraction for the museum. They are world famous, and each year thousands of people visit the museum just to see them. Recently the

Harvard's glass flower collection includes 3,000 models of more than 840 different kinds of plants, each painstakingly shaped by hand. Among them are common garden flowers such as iris (*opposite page, top left*), coneflower (*opposite page, top right*), and poppy (*opposite page, bottom*). Less familiar are the exotic-looking flowers of eucalyptus (*above, left*) and a cactus (*above, right*). The leaves of red maple (*left*) are depicted in the fall. Details like wilted flowers and splotchy leaves make the models seem incredibly real.

museum acquired tools, glass samples, a workbench, and other items from the Blaschkas' studio near Dresden for an exhibition called "Modeling Nature: Slices of Glass History From the Collections." This special exhibition explains how the models were made, and it shows that the glassmakers' skill, patience, and love of their subject were the true secret techniques that allowed them to create these extraordinary flowers of glass.

Richard Gere and Catherine Zeta-Jones (best supporting actress) in *Chicago* (best motion picture).

ACADEMY

Awards

CATEGORY	WINNER
Motion Picture	*Chicago*
Actor	Adrien Brody (*The Pianist*)
Actress	Nicole Kidman (*The Hours*)
Supporting Actor	Chris Cooper (*Adaptation*)
Supporting Actress	Catherine Zeta-Jones (*Chicago*)
Director	Roman Polanski (*The Pianist*)
Cinematography	*Road to Perdition*
Visual Effects	*The Lord of the Rings: The Two Towers*
Song	"Lose Yourself" (*8 Mile*)
Animated Feature Film	*Spirited Away*
Foreign–Language Film	*Nowhere in Africa* (Germany)
Documentary Feature	*Bowling for Columbine*
Documentary Short	*Twin Towers*

2003

Left: Nicole Kidman (best actress) in *The Hours.* Above: Adrien Brody (best actor) in *The Pianist*. Below: *Spirited Away* (best animated feature film).

Johnny Depp (left; with Orlando Bloom) starred as a swashbuckling pirate in *Pirates of the Caribbean: The Curse of the Black Pearl*, one of 2003's most popular movies.

MOVIE TIME!

Swashbuckling pirates, comic-book heroes, romantic comedies, serious drama—there were movies for everyone in 2003. Fantasy reigned at the box office, especially during the summer months. But several of the year's biggest hits were based on true stories, showing that reality can be just as exciting as make-believe.

FANTASTIC FUN

One of the summer's most popular films was *Pirates of the Caribbean: The Curse of the Black Pearl*—a wild and comic fantasy that was inspired by the Disney theme park ride of that name. Johnny Depp starred as Captain Jack Sparrow, whose ship, the *Black Pearl*, is stolen by the pirate Barbossa (Geoffrey Rush). Barbossa and his ghostly crew also kidnap the beautiful Elizabeth Swann (Keira Knightley), planning to use

her magical gold medallion—and her blood—to break an ancient curse that haunts them. Sparrow and Elizabeth's true love, Will Turner (Orlando Bloom), race to catch up with the pirates before it's too late.

What if dogs were really aliens from outer space? That was the idea behind *Good Boy!*, a movie aimed at young audiences. A boy named Owen (Liam Aiken) adopts a dog named Hubble (voiced by Matthew Broderick) and discovers that his pet has just arrived from the Dog Star Sirius. Hubble's mission is to find out if dogs are in charge on Earth—and if they're not, he warns, they will all be recalled to their home planet.

In *The Lizzie McGuire Movie*, Lizzie (Hilary Duff) goes to Italy and meets handsome Paolo (Yani Gellman).

Role switching was the idea behind another fun fantasy, *Freaky Friday.* In this film, a remake of a 1977 movie, Jamie Lee Curtis played Tess, a widowed mom with a career as a psychotherapist, and Lindsay Lohan played Anna, her teenage daughter. Mom and daughter misunderstand each other completely—Tess thinks Anna is irresponsible, and Anna thinks Tess doesn't care about her problems. One Friday morning, through a little magic, they wake up to find that they have switched bodies. Now Tess, in Anna's body, must go to school and take Anna's tests (she flunks). And Anna, in Tess's body, has a whole new set of problems.

The main character in *Bruce Almighty* gets a surprising new role, too. After he complains about the state of the world, God grants him almighty powers and leaves him in charge—so he finds out how hard the job of running the world really is. Jim Carrey starred in this film.

Spy Kids 3-D: Game Over, the third Spy Kids movie, found Juni and Carmen Cortex (Daryl Sabara and Alexa Vega) trapped in a video game designed to steal children's minds. The kids battle menacing robots and other threats as they fight their way to freedom and defeat the game's inventor, the evil Toymaker (Sylvester Stallone). Audiences watched the film through special 3-D glasses that made objects seem to fly off the screen and into the theater.

Other fantasy-action sequels included *X2,* which carried on the X-Men story, and *Terminator 3.* Two sequels to the 1999 film *The Matrix* appeared in 2003. *The Matrix Reloaded* and *The Matrix Revolutions* brought to a close a complex, often violent story in which humans battled evil machines. And *The Hulk* brought a famous comic-book character to the screen—Bruce Banner (Eric Bana), who changes into a monstrous green giant when under stress.

TEENS ON SCREEN

In *The Lizzie McGuire Movie,* a popular television character made the move to a feature film. In the cable TV series *Lizzie McGuire,* Lizzie (Hillary Duff) is a slightly goofy junior-high student who's dealing with everything

Finding Nemo

The summer of 2003 brought many great movies to theaters. But the big splash was *Finding Nemo.* A colorful coral reef was the setting for this funny and suspenseful animated film. *Finding Nemo* was a fish story—that is, it was about fish. And since the story was a fantasy, the fish acted and talked just like people. The main characters were two clownfish, Marlin (voiced by Albert Brooks) and his son Nemo (Alexander Gould), who live in the waters of Australia's Great Barrier Reef.

Clownfish Marlin and blue tang Dory search for Nemo in the delightful animated film *Finding Nemo.*

At the start of the film, Marlin loses his wife and about 400 of their eggs to a barracuda. He's left with only Nemo. Not surprisingly, he's very protective of his son. But when Nemo sets off for his first day of school, he's "fishnapped." He ends up in an aquarium tank in a dentist's office in Sydney, Australia. As Nemo tries to figure out how to get back to the ocean, Marlin sets out to find his son. He's helped by a forgetful blue tang named Dory (Ellen DeGeneres). Together, they face some fin-raising adventures on their way to rescue Nemo.

Keira Knightley and Parminder Nagra are soccer-crazy London teens in the surprise hit, *Bend It Like Beckham.*

girls her age typically face. In the movie, 13-year-old Lizzie and her friends graduate from middle school and set off on a class trip to Italy—where she's mistaken for a missing pop star, Isabella, who looks exactly like her. Lizzie meets handsome Paolo, Isabella's former partner. And before you know it, she has ditched the class trip for a moment of stardom. Of course, reality intrudes on this fairy tale. But before it's over, Lizzie has gained confidence and learned some lessons about the meaning of friendship.

What a Girl Wants starred another young actress who made the jump from television to film. Amanda Bynes, 17, had the lead role in this story of an American girl who goes to Britain in search of her father, whom she has never met. Bynes had starred in her own show, *The Amanda Show,* on Nickelodeon when she was just 12.

In *Bend It Like Beckham,* the girls just want to play soccer—and their parents just can't understand it. One of 2003's surprise hits, this low-budget British film was the story of two London teens. Jess (Parminder Nagra) is the daughter of Sikhs from India, and her parents forbid her to play soccer. She does anyway, joining a team with her friend Jules (Keira Knightley). Jules has troubles of her own at home; her mother thinks she's a tomboy and wants her to be more feminine. There are misunderstandings all around, leading to lots of funny moments.

Young actor Haley Joel Osment starred with a pair of screen veterans in *Secondhand Lions.* Osment played Walter, a 14-year-old whose mother sends him to spend the summer with his two grouchy uncles, Garth (Michael Caine) and Hub (Robert Duvall). The uncles live like hermits in rural Texas, but they are full of tales about their 40 years in the French Foreign Legion—and rumors say they have a cache of treasure hidden on their ramshackle ranch. How much of this is true? The movie keeps the secret until the very end.

Hugh Grant (with Martine McCutcheon) was one of the stars of *Love Actually*—a romantic comedy that rolled nine love stories into one movie.

Holes

Holes, an award-winning novel by Louis Sachar, came to the screen in 2003. A fantastic setting, a fantastic plot, and some great young actors helped make the movie a hit.

The story is about a teenager named Stanley Yelnats (Shia LaBeouf). All the men in Stanley's family are cursed, going back four generations, and it seems that he is cursed, too. He's wrongly accused of a crime—stealing a pair of shoes—and packed off to Camp Green Lake, a work camp for kids who break the law. There's no lake at this camp, just a dry lakebed. It's a desert wasteland full of rattlesnakes and poisonous lizards, run by the evil Warden (Sigourney Weaver) and her assistants Mr. Sir (Jon Voight) and Dr. Pendanski (Tim Blake Nelson). They put Stanley and the other inmates to work digging holes all over the dry lakebed.

Why? To build character, the jailers say. But clearly, they are hoping the kids will find something. Stanley sets out to find out what it is. Along the way he unlocks the secrets of his

In the fantastic plot of *Holes*, teenagers Zero (Khleo Thomas, left) and Stanley Yelnats (Shia LaBeouf) become friends.

family's past and the reasons for the 100-year drought that has blighted this fictional corner of Texas. These secrets unfold in flashbacks. Meanwhile, Stanley befriends a boy named Zero (Khleo Thomas) and copes with the grim life at the work camp. Eventually the connections between the past and present become clear, and Stanley gets a chance to break the family curse.

LAUGHTER AND LOVE

The screen version of the hit Broadway musical *Chicago* offered a little of everything—singing, dancing, drama, romance, comedy. Set in Chicago during Prohibition, the story is about two showgirls, Roxie Hart (Renée Zellweger) and Velma Kelly (Catherine Zeta-Jones), who are both in jail for murder. They compete for fame and for the attentions of their suave lawyer (Richard Gere).

Intolerable Cruelty looked back to the "screwball" romantic comedies of the 1930's for inspiration. In this story, a fast-talking divorce lawyer (George Clooney) falls for the soon-to-be-ex-wife (Catherine Zeta-Jones) of a client. They are both cool, calculating characters—and made for each other.

Love Actually was more than a romantic comedy. It was nine romantic comedies rolled into one movie. The stories were set at Christmastime in places that ranged from Britain to Milwaukee, Wisconsin. Some of the stories were connected, but most were not. What tied them all together was the common theme of love—and the awkward, comical situations it leads people into. The star-studded cast included Hugh Grant, Emma Thompson, Liam Neeson, and Keira Knightley.

The main character of *Bringing Down the House* lands himself in a very awkward situation indeed. Peter Sanderson (Steve Martin) is a divorced lawyer who strikes up an Internet "chat" with a woman he thinks is a beautiful fellow attorney. But when she arrives at his door for their first meeting, she turns out to be Charlene (Queen Latifah), an escaped convict who wants him to help clear her name. When he refuses, she turns his life upside down.

Tobey McGuire played a jockey in *Seabiscuit*, the story of an underdog racehorse that becomes a champion.

Catch Me If You Can was also based on fact, although the story was amazing. During the 1960's a teenage impostor named Frank Abagnale, Jr., successfully posed as an airline pilot, a doctor, a lawyer, and more—meanwhile cashing millions of dollars in forged paychecks. Leonardo DiCaprio played Abagnale in the movie, and Tom Hanks played the FBI agent who finally tracks him down.

Rabbit-Proof Fence took a hard look at a dark chapter in Australian history. From 1905 to 1971, the government tore families of Australian aborigines apart by removing children of mixed race. The children were taken from their homes and placed in resettlement camps, where they were forbidden to speak their native language and were taught the customs of white society. The fact-based movie, set in 1931, was the story of three children who escaped from a camp and walked back to their home village, 1,200 miles (1,930 kilometers) away.

Winged Migration, a breathtaking movie first released in Europe, reached U.S. theaters in 2003. More than 450 people worked for three years to film this documentary about bird migration. The crews used remote-control glid-

In *Anger Management,* life is topsy-turvy for Dave Buznik (Adam Sandler). Dave, a mild-mannered New York businessman, is wrongly sentenced to an anger-management program. His instructor is the loud, obnoxious, and hot-tempered Dr. Buddy Ryddell (Jack Nicholson), who moves into his home and tries to steal his girlfriend. In short, the doctor is nuttier than the patient.

REALITY RULES

Pluck and determination win the day for humans and horses alike in *Seabiscuit.* This movie was based on Laura Hillenbrand's nonfiction best-seller about a racehorse that became a national hero during the Great Depression of the 1930's. Seabiscuit was an undersized underdog, but he outran the best horses of his day. In the film, his rider (played by Tobey McGuire), trainer (Chris Cooper), and owner (Jeff Bridges) each overcome great obstacles as they bring their champion to the winner's circle. The movie was praised for its depiction of the 1930's and its thrilling race scenes.

Leonardo DiCaprio portrayed a teenage impostor in the amazing fact-based drama *Catch Me If You Can.*

School of Rock

Guitarist Dewey Finn has been kicked out of his band. With no money, he's desperate for work, so he fakes his way into a job as a substitute teacher at an exclusive private school. There, under the suspicious eyes of the school's strict principal, he turns a group of high-achieving fifth graders into a high-voltage rock band for an upcoming Battle of the Bands.

That's the basic story of *School of Rock,* one of 2003's top comedies. Jack Black—an actor as well as the lead singer, songwriter, and guitarist of his own band, Tenacious D—played Dewey Finn. Joan Cusack was the school's principal. But the film's young rockers stole the show.

The kids all played their own instruments, and they were talented musicians. Many were new to the movies, and some were new to rock and roll. Robert Tsai, 12, had trained as a classical pianist but rocked as keyboard player Lawrence. Classical guitarist and cellist Rebecca Brown, 11, was bass player Katie.

Comedian Jack Black played an unlikely substitute teacher who turns a group of fifth graders into a groovin' rock band in *School of Rock.*

Joey Gaydos, Jr., a sixth grader who had his own band in Belleville, Michigan, made his film debut as Zack, the lead guitarist. Ten-year-old Maryam Hassan made her professional acting and singing debut as Tomika, a shy singer. She landed the role at an open audition in New York City.

Thanks to these talented kids and the others who made up the *School of Rock* band, the movie really rocked!

ers, ultralight aircraft, and other devices to bring cameras alongside flying geese, swans, and other birds, which in some cases cover thousands of miles in their migrations. Birds were filmed everywhere from the Arctic to the rain forests of the Amazon.

SERIOUS DRAMA

The year also had its share of serious dramas, including several films that won critical acclaim. *The Hours* wove together three stories, set in different times and places, about women who faced turning points in their lives. Each story covered one day in their lives. One was about the English novelist Virginia Woolf (Nicole Kidman); one focused on an unhappy housewife (Julianne Moore) in 1950's Los Angeles;

and the third was about a book editor (Meryl Streep) in contemporary New York City.

Mystic River was a dark story that traced the effects of a crime on three men (Tim Robbins, Kevin Bacon, and Sean Penn) who were boyhood friends. Set in Boston, this powerful movie was directed by Clint Eastwood and earned high praise from critics.

A warmhearted film set in beautiful New Zealand, *Whale Rider* reflected the contrasts between modern life and the traditions of the Maori, New Zealand's native people. It starred newcomer Keisha Castle-Hughes as Pai, a Maori teenager. Pai is destined to become the leader of her tribe, but she must first overcome the resistance of her grandfather and others in her village.

The deerstalker cap, the pipe, the magnifying glass—it can only be the famous fictional detective Sherlock Holmes, here portrayed by actor Basil Rathbone.

companion. And as always, Holmes's keen eye for detail and his superior powers of deduction solve the mystery.

Whether striding across a desolate moor in his deerstalker hat and cape-backed overcoat . . . or clattering through gaslit, fog-bound London streets in a horse-drawn cab . . . or in his lodgings at 221B Baker Street in London, pondering the facts through a haze of smoke from his pipe, Sherlock Holmes is without doubt the most famous detective in literature. He's the creation of the British writer Sir Arthur Conan Doyle (1859–1930), who wrote sixty tales—novels as well as short stories—featuring Holmes and Watson. The novels and stories have never gone out of print, and they have legions of fans.

THE DOCTOR AND THE DETECTIVE

Arthur Conan Doyle didn't set out to become the author of mystery stories. He was a doctor. In the 1880's, recently married, he was trying to make some extra money by writing. But he had little success until he tried his hand at writing a detective novel. He modeled the character of Holmes partly on one of his former teachers in medical school, Dr. Joseph Bell.

Bell was a tall, thin, wiry man with a prominent nose and a penetrating gaze. He told his students to develop their powers of observation to the utmost. Observe closely, he told them, and gather your facts. Then examine the facts carefully, even those that seem on the surface to be unimportant, to determine which ones are significant. Finally, put the facts together in a pattern to reach your conclusion.

SHERLOCK HOLMES: MASTER DETECTIVE

It was on a bitterly cold night and frosty morning, towards the end of the winter of '97, that I was awakened by a tugging at my shoulder. It was Holmes. The candle in his hand shone upon his eager, stooping face, and told me at a glance that something was amiss.

"Come, Watson, come!" he cried. "The game is afoot. Not a word! Into your clothes and come!"

And so readers plunge into another adventure with the man who has been called the world's greatest detective—Sherlock Holmes. Like all of Holmes's cases, this one, *The Adventure of the Abbey Grange*, is recounted by Dr. John Watson, his loyal

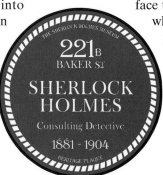

Holmes lived at 221B Baker Street, London, from 1881 to 1904, according to the stories by Arthur Conan

Bell would sit in his office, surrounded by his students, and ask for a patient to be sent in. When the patient entered, Bell would observe every detail of the person's appearance, from hair to shoes. Then he would quietly state what work the patient did, where the patient had been before coming to the office, and other startling facts. For example, Bell observed of one patient that he had served in the army and had recently been discharged. Then he turned to his astonished students and explained how he had reached his conclusions.

Sherlock Holmes displays the same amazing abilities. In *A Study in Scarlet,* the first book in which Holmes appears, Watson tells how he met Holmes for the first time:

> "Dr. Watson, Mr. Sherlock Holmes," said Stamford, introducing us.
>
> "How are you?" he said cordially, gripping my hand with a strength for which I should hardly have given him credit. "You have been in Afghanistan, I perceive."
>
> "How on earth did you know that?" I asked in astonishment.

A Study in Scarlet, which was published in 1887, wasn't a success. Doyle was discouraged and might have forgotten about Sherlock Holmes, but an American publisher asked him to write a second book with Holmes and Watson as the chief characters. That novel, *The Sign of Four,* launched the characters on the road to immortality. From the time it came out in 1890, Doyle could hardly keep up with the demand for stories about Sherlock Holmes. Many of the stories appeared first in the *Strand Magazine.*

Readers couldn't get enough of Sherlock Holmes—but it appeared that Doyle very quickly had enough. In 1893 he decided to do away with his famous detective, so he could turn his energies to more interesting projects. In the story called *The Final Problem,* he had Holmes and his arch-enemy Moriarty fall together from a cliff to their deaths. But the detective's fans wouldn't have it! They overwhelmed Doyle with letters from all over the world, begging him to bring Holmes back. Finally, he gave in.

The house at 221B Baker Street is the site of the Sherlock Holmes Museum. Inside, the study has been kept just as it would have been when the detective lived—if he had actually lived.

Sherlock Holmes returned in 1903 in *The Adventure of the Empty House,* explaining to a shocked Watson that he hadn't fallen off the cliff after all. Once again the famous detective was on the case, searching for evidence with his magnifying glass and carefully compiling the facts. "It is a capital mistake to theorize before one has data," Holmes tells Watson in *A Scandal in Bohemia.* "Insensibly one begins to twist facts to suit theories, instead of theories to suit facts."

Doyle kept turning out Sherlock Holmes stories until 1927, by which time the detective would have been well on in years. Doyle had Watson introduce the story collection *His Last Bow* by stating:

> "The friends of Mr. Sherlock Holmes will be glad to learn that he is still alive and well, though somewhat crippled by occasional attacks of rheumatism. He has, for many years, lived in a small farm upon the downs five miles from Eastbourne, where his time is divided between philosophy and agriculture."

HOLMES LIVES ON

To true fans, Sherlock Holmes is more than just a literary character. "Sherlockians"—as his fans are called—have written hundreds of essays and articles about the detective. They have even written biographies, recording every detail of his life. They discuss the brand of tobacco he smoked, the books he read, and the concerts he supposedly attended. Some people even think Holmes is a living person. Each week employees at the Sherlock Holmes Museum in London answer 40 to 100 letters that are addressed to him!

The museum is at 221B Baker Street—the site of Holmes's fictional lodgings. It's one of London's top tourist attractions. There, in a recreation of Holmes's study, visitors can sit in the detective's armchair and see his deerstalker hat, magnifying glass, pipe, violin, chemistry equipment, notebook, Persian slippers, and disguises.

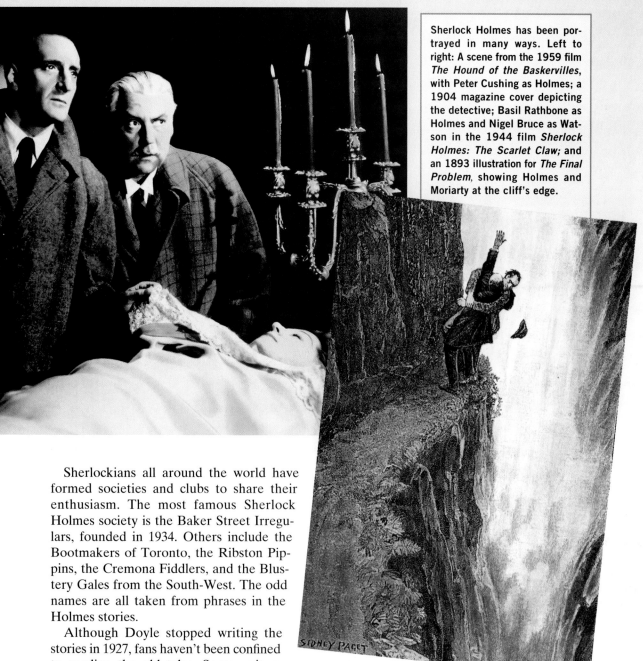

Sherlock Holmes has been portrayed in many ways. Left to right: A scene from the 1959 film *The Hound of the Baskervilles*, with Peter Cushing as Holmes; a 1904 magazine cover depicting the detective; Basil Rathbone as Holmes and Nigel Bruce as Watson in the 1944 film *Sherlock Holmes: The Scarlet Claw;* and an 1893 illustration for *The Final Problem*, showing Holmes and Moriarty at the cliff's edge.

SIDNEY PAGET

Sherlockians all around the world have formed societies and clubs to share their enthusiasm. The most famous Sherlock Holmes society is the Baker Street Irregulars, founded in 1934. Others include the Bootmakers of Toronto, the Ribston Pippins, the Cremona Fiddlers, and the Blustery Gales from the South-West. The odd names are all taken from phrases in the Holmes stories.

Although Doyle stopped writing the stories in 1927, fans haven't been confined to reading the old tales. Some writers have turned out their own stories featuring the famous detective. And Sherlock Holmes has been portrayed countless times on stage, film, and television—even in a ballet!

Some actors have been closely associated with the role. The American actor William Gillette practically made a career of it. He appeared in *Sherlock Holmes,* a play he co-wrote with Doyle, from 1899 to 1932. Basil Rathbone played Holmes in sixteen films in the 1930's and 1940's. In the 1980's and 1990's, Jeremy Brett took the part in a series that brought 41 of the Holmes stories to television. And in 2002, Richard Roxburgh appeared as Holmes in a new television version of one of the best-known stories, *The Hound of the Baskervilles.*

Brad Garrett (best supporting actor, comedy series), and Doris Roberts (best supporting actress, comedy series) in *Everybody Loves Raymond* (best comedy series.)

EMMY

Awards

CATEGORY	WINNER
Comedy Series	*Everybody Loves Raymond*
Actor—comedy series	Tony Shalhoub (*Monk*)
Actress—comedy series	Debra Messing (*Will & Grace*)
Supporting actor—comedy series	Brad Garrett (*Everybody Loves Raymond*)
Supporting actress—comedy series	Doris Roberts (*Everybody Loves Raymond*)
Drama Series	*The West Wing*
Actor—drama series	James Gandolfini (*The Sopranos*)
Actress—drama series	Edie Falco (*The Sopranos*)
Supporting actor—drama series	Joe Pantoliano (*The Sopranos*)
Supporting actress—drama series	Tyne Daly (*Judging Amy*)
Miniseries	*Steven Spielberg Presents Taken*
Variety, Music, or Comedy Series	*The Daily Show With Jon Stewart*

2003

Above: James Gandolfini (best actor, drama series), and Edie Falco (best actress, drama series) in *The Sopranos*. Right: Bitty Schram and Tony Shalhoub (best actor, comedy series) in *Monk*. Below: Eric McCormack and Debra Messing (best actress, comedy series) in *Will & Grace*.

Hip-hop duo OutKast (Andre 3000 and Big Boi) had a hit with their album *Speakerboxxx/The Love Below*.

THE MUSIC SCENE

New names joined pop stars of past years on the music charts in 2003. Musical artists continued to mix styles and break new ground, and fans welcomed new discs from a wide variety of performers.

HIP-HOP AND R&B

OutKast had one of the year's top albums with *Speakerboxxx/The Love Below*—a boxed set that was really two solo albums, packed side by side. Each disc featured one member of this hip-hop duo. *Speakerboxxx* showcased the smooth, funny rhymes of Big Boi (Antwan Patton), while *The Love Below* featured Andre 3000's distinctive falsetto voice. Critics gave the double album a big thumbs up, and fans made it a number-one seller. Two singles—"Hey Ya!," by Andre 3000, and "The Way you Move," by Big Boi—also moved up the charts.

The R&B boy band B2K had a number-one single—the catchy "Bump, Bump, Bump," off their album *Pandemonium!*. That disc also featured slow ballads like "One Kiss" that were favorites with fans of this young group. The Black Eyed Peas blended hip-hop with funk, soul, rock, and more on *Elephunk,* their fourth album. The group teamed with Justin Timberlake for "Where Is the Love?," a hit single off the album.

Destiny's Child lead singer Beyoncé Knowles, who turned 21 in 2003, showed she was ready to go it alone. In the summer, Beyoncé released her solo debut album, *Dangerously in Love*. The lead single was a bouncy hit called "Crazy in Love," featuring rapper Jay-Z. A second single, "Baby Boy," featuring Sean Paul, topped the charts. In the fall, Beyoncé's younger sister Solange, 16, released her own debut disc, titled simply *Solange*.

Some of the biggest female names in hip hop and R&B had new releases in 2003. Missy Elliott rapped with Jay-Z in "Back in the Day," a track from her new disc *Missy Elliott—*

Destiny's Child lead singer Beyoncé Knowles came out with her first solo album, *Dangerously in Love*. It featured the catchy hit singles "Crazy in Love" and "Baby Boy."

Under Construction. Mary J. Blige released her sixth studio album, *Love & Life,* for which she cowrote 17 of the 18 tracks. Lil' Kim's new album was *La Bella Mafia.*

Ashanti's *Chapter II,* the follow-up to her hit 2002 debut, included the hit single "Rain on Me." Mya's hit single "My Love Is Like...Wo," was featured on *Moodring,* her third disc. Macy Gray blended retro soul sounds with original twists on *The Trouble With Being Myself.* Monica's third disc, *After the Storm,* showcased her alto voice in a range of R&B tracks flavored with pop, hip-hop, soul, and gospel. And Ms. Dynamite, already a star in Britain, hit the United States with her debut album,

R&B star Missy Elliott returned to the limelight with the release of her new disc *Missy Elliott—Under Construction.*

A Little Deeper. In tracks that blended hip-hop, R&B, reggae, and pop, the 21-year-old singer took on issues such as drug abuse and violence.

The bouncy rhythms and rhymes on Chingy's first album, *Jackpot,* reminded many listeners of rapper Nelly. *Jackpot* included two hit singles, "Right Thurr" and the funky "Holidae In," which featured Snoop Dogg and Ludacris. Rapper 50 Cent (Curtis Jackson) was on the money with *Get Rich or Die Tryin',* a disc that highlighted his driving beats and streetwise rhymes. Chart-topping singles off this album included "In Da Club" and

Norah Jones: Sweeping the Grammys

Singer and pianist Norah Jones swept the 2003 Grammy Awards on February 23. She carried home five Grammys, including the award for best new artist. And her debut album, *Come Away With Me,* earned three more awards—for its producer, engineer, and the writer of the hit track "Don't Know Why."

Jones, 23, was surprised by her success. A year earlier, she had been playing for tips at New York City clubs. "I never, ever thought that the music I made would be considered popular music, so this is amazing," she said. *Come Away With Me* featured live performances of jazz-flavored ballads. It was a hit with music fans of all ages.

Norah Jones was raised in Texas, where she studied music in high school and college before heading to New York to start her career. She comes from a musical family. Her father is Ravi Shankar, a noted Indian musician who helped popularize Indian music in the West. He played with leading classical, jazz, and pop musicians, including Beatle George Harrison.

Shania Twain straddled the line between pop and country music with her album *Up!* One of its tracks was the hit single "Forever and For Always."

career got off to a late start, and her debut disc was ten years in the making. Finally released in 2003, *To Whom It May Concern* featured a blend of pop, country, and rock.

Pop diva Madonna mixed acoustic guitar and folk flavorings with electronic grooves in her ninth studio album, *American Life.* In *One Heart,* Celine Dion's eighth studio release, the Canadian star included bouncy dance tracks with the ballads for which she's best known. Jennifer Lopez was on the charts with *This Is Me...Then,* which included the hit single "All I Have," featuring LL Cool J.

Music critics have debated whether Shania Twain should be grouped with pop or country singers. Her album *Up!* gave the answer: both. This two-disc set had both country and pop mixes of 19 tracks. It included the hit single "Forever and For Always."

There were great second acts in 2003. John Mayer, who scooped up a Grammy Award early in the year for his single "Your Body Is a Wonderland," had a number-one album with his second studio release, *Heavier Things.* Singer-songwriter Dido's soaring vocals were featured on *Life for Rent,* her second album.

Dave Matthews thrilled fans with his first solo album, *Some Devil.* It offered more of the acoustic folk-pop made popular by the Dave Matthews Band.

"21 Questions," featuring Nate Dogg. Late-year arrivals on the R&B charts included Ja Rule's *Blood in My Eye* and Wyclef Jean's *The Preacher's Son.*

NONSTOP POP

The television reality show *American Idol* brought new faces to the pop music scene. Clay Aiken, the runner-up in the show's 2003 competition, topped the singles charts with "This Is the Night," edging out contest winner Ruben Studdard's "Flying Without Wings." Aiken's debut album, *Measure of a Man,* was released in October and sold 613,000 copies in its first week—the second highest first-week sales in history. Meanwhile, Kelly Clarkson, the show's 2002 winner, was on the charts with her first album, *Thankful.*

Some of 2003's new names were familiar from other contexts. Hilary Duff was already a star on television and in the movies. At age 16, she scored again with her first full-length album, *Metamorphosis,* which featured pop-rock tracks like "So Yesterday." As Elvis Presley's daughter, Lisa Marie Presley had one of the most famous names in music. But her

It combined catchy pop beats with Celtic-tinged folk in tunes like the hit single "White Flag." Stacie Orrico, who struck gold with her 2001 debut album, *Genuine,* was back with her second disc as well. Titled *Stacie Orrico,* it featured edgier R&B grooves from the 17-year-old singer-songwriter.

Dave Matthews, longtime leader of the Dave Matthews Band, came out with his first solo album, *Some Devil.* Fans weren't disappointed in the disc, which featured the sort of acoustic folk-pop that has made DMB popular. On their third album, *Welcome Interstate Managers,* the witty pop group Fountains Of Wayne tackled subjects that ranged from love to slow restaurant service. The disc included the hit single "Stacy's Mom."

Some other big names from the '90's were back in 2003. Sting added dance music to his smooth pop stylings on *Sacred Love.* The British singer Seal's third album, titled *Seal,* was a collection of richly textured ballads and upbeat dance numbers. The third disc from Hootie and the Blowfish, also self-titled, featured lots of the bouncy pop-rock that put this foursome on the charts in the past.

Jewel, a singer-songwriter who made her mark with acoustic folk ballads, branched out on *0304,* an album that included rhythmic electronic dance tracks. And Amy Grant featured straightforward arrangements that let her voice shine on *Simple Things.*

ROCK RULES

The British rock group Radiohead released its long-awaited sixth album, *Hail to the Thief,* in June. The complex and brooding tracks on this disc dealt with serious themes. But the music marked a turn away from the experimental sounds of the group's last release.

Music File Swapping— It's Illegal!

What's the easiest way to get your favorite tunes? Download music files to your home computer, over the Internet. Millions of people have been doing it—and that's causing problems for record companies.

File sharing is the biggest problem. Through file-sharing networks, people can download music files from other computers that also use the network—for free. But file sharing is a form of pirating, or stealing, and it violates copyright laws. When people copy songs and post them on the Internet, musical artists and recording companies don't make money.

In September 2003 the Recording Industry Association of America (RIAA) took action. The group, which represents recording companies, sued 261 file swappers who had opened big libraries of pirated music—1,000 songs or more—to Internet file-sharing networks. They ranged from a 12-year-old girl to a 71-year-old grandfather. Most had no idea that they were breaking the law by letting others download their music files. They quickly settled the lawsuits and promised to stop.

The RIAA said that its main goal in suing these people wasn't to punish them. Instead, the group wanted to alert others to the fact that file sharing is against the law. Record companies blame file sharing for falling sales of CD's. But some file swappers say they should be allowed to copy music files on the Internet. The record industry has made CD's too costly, they say—and it's much easier to download songs than to go to a store.

Online music stores, such as BuyMusic.com and iTunes, are one solution. These Web sites allow people to download songs for a fee, perhaps 99 cents per song. This way the musical artists can still earn a living. The recording companies can still make money. And as long as the music buyers don't give away copies of the song, they won't break the law.

These photos of the British rock group Radiohead appear on their hit album *Hail to the Thief.*

Instead, on tracks like "2+2=5," Radiohead featured live guitar jams and driving rock beats.

Out of the Vein was the first new album in more than three years from Third Eye Blind, the four-man band from San Francisco, California. The album's highlights included "Blinded (When I See You)" and "Crystal Baller," both released as singles. Fans of 3 Doors Down waited even longer for *Away From the Sun,* this group's second album and its first since 1996. Two top-ten singles from the album were "When I'm Gone" and "Here Without You."

Linkin Park was back on the charts with *Meteora,* a top-ten follow-up to the group's hugely successful 2001 debut rap-metal album, *Hybrid Theory.* Evanescence featured their own rap-metal sound on their debut disc, *Fallen,* which included the hit "Bring Me to Life." Godsmack's new release, *Faceless,* featured the blasting hit single "Straight Out of Line." Also on the rock charts was Limp Bizkit's fifth disc, *Results May Vary.*

Fans of garage and alternative rock had plenty of choices. The Strokes and the White Stripes, two bands whose fresh sounds helped spark a garage-rock wave in 2001, both released their second albums in 2003. The Strokes featured their trademark ragged vocals and driving guitars on *Room on Fire.* The White Stripes—made up of Meg and Jack White, from Detroit, Michigan—came out with *Elephant.* It was recorded entirely without the help of computers.

Zwan, a new group, featured two members of the disbanded alt-rock group Smashing Pumpkins—singer-guitarist Billy Corgan (also known as Billy Burke) and drummer Jimmy Chamberlain. Zwan's first album, *Mary Star of the Sea,* included tracks that veered toward pop and folk without losing the alt-rock edginess. David Bowie showed that rock has no age limits on his 26th album, *Reality.* In "Never Get Old" and other tracks, the 56-year-old British rocker was in top form.

One of the year's most interesting discs was *Let It Be. . .Naked,* a remix of the Beatles' last album, *Let It Be,* first released in 1970. The 2003 version stripped away the heavy orchestration that was added during the original production, letting the Beatles' voices and guitars shine through.

COUNTRY

Country music lost one of its biggest stars with the death of Johnny Cash on September 12 at age 71. Cash had tremendous influence on all forms of popular music, not just country, and he was honored at a memorial concert in Nashville, Tennessee, in November. Performers included rock songwriters such as Sheryl Crow and John Mellencamp, as well as top country stars like Willie Nelson, Hank Williams Jr., and George Jones. Cash's last album, *American IV: The Man Comes Around,* was named album of the year at the Country Music Association Awards. "Hurt," his version of a Nine Inch Nails song, was named single of the year.

Toby Keith ruled the country charts in 2003. His album *Unleashed* was still high on the charts when a new disc, *Shock'n Y'all,* debuted in the number-one spot. It featured the hit single "I Love This Bar."

Pat Green mixed country and bluesy rock on *Wave on Wave.* Chris Cagle's self-titled third album debuted at the top of the country chart. Jessica Andrews, 19, brought a youthful flair to the songs on her third album, *Now*. And at the other end of the age spectrum, country great Emmylou Harris, 56, released her 20th studio album, *Stumble into Grace*. It was a mix of traditional and new material, tied together by her elegant voice.

MUSIC NOTES

Three 1980's British punk and new wave bands—the Clash, the Police, and Elvis Costello and the Attractions—entered the Rock and Roll Hall of Fame in 2003. The Hall of Fame also inducted the Australian hard rock band AC/DC and the 1960's "blue-eyed soul" duo the Righteous Brothers.

On the concert scene, Avril Lavigne backed her debut CD, *Let Go,* with her first headlining tour, called "Try to Shut Me Up." Other hot tickets included Justin Timberlake and Christina Aguilera's "Justified and Stripped" tour and John Mayer, who teamed up to tour with Counting Crows.

The Dixie Chicks captured three Grammys in the Country category for their album *Home*.

2003 Grammy Awards

Record of the Year	"Don't Know Why"	Norah Jones, artist
Album of the Year	*Come Away With Me*	Norah Jones, artist
Song of the Year	"Don't Know Why"	Jesse Harris, songwriter
New Artist of the Year		Norah Jones
Pop Song, Female	"Don't Know Why"	Norah Jones, artist
Pop Song, Male	"Your Body Is a Wonderland"	John Mayer, artist
Pop Song, Group	"Hey Baby"	No Doubt, artists
Rock Song, Female	"Steve McQueen"	Sheryl Crow, artist
Rock Song, Male	"The Rising"	Bruce Springsteen, artist
Rock Song, Group	"In My Place"	Coldplay, artists
Rhythm and Blues Song, Female	"He Think I Don't Know"	Mary J. Blige, artist
Rhythm and Blues Song, Male	"U Don't Have to Call"	Usher, artist
Rhythm and Blues Song, Group	"Love's in Need of Love Today"	Stevie Wonder & Take 6, artists
Rap Song, Female	"Scream a.k.a. Itchin'"	Missy "Misdemeanor" Elliott, artist
Rap Song, Male	"Hot in Herre"	Nelly, artist
Rap Song, Group	"The Whole World"	OutKast featuring Killer Mike, artists
Music Video Performance	"Without Me"	Eminem, artist
Alternative Music Album	*A Rush of Blood to the Head*	Coldplay, artists
Score for a Motion Picture	*The Lord of the Rings: The Fellowship of the Ring*	Howard Shore, composer
Musical Show Album	*Hairspray*	Marc Shaiman, composer and lyricist; Scott Wittman, lyricist
Classical Album	*Vaughan Williams: A Sea Symphony*	Robert Spano, conductor

JOSEPH CORNELL'S MAGICAL BOXES

Joseph Cornell was an artist who lived in two worlds. One was the ordinary, everyday world in which we all live. The other was a magical world that existed only in his imagination. Through his art, he gave everyone a chance to see that magical world.

Cornell is best known for the hundreds of small wood shadow boxes that he created. He filled these boxes with familiar objects—seashells, marbles, twigs, paper cutouts of people and animals, clock springs, bird feathers. His magic lay in the way he arranged these objects. Each box became a window on a little dream, filled with delight and mystery.

The year 2003 marked the 100th anniversary of Cornell's birth, and his work was featured in a number of exhibits and other events. It was a good time to remember this unique artist, who led a quiet life but delighted millions of people with his creations.

CORNELL THE COLLECTOR

Cornell was born in Nyack, New York, but lived for most of his life in Flushing, an area of New York City. His family's fortunes took a turn for the worse in 1917, when his father died. Cornell was 13 at the time. From then on, he felt it was his job to look out for his mother and his brother, who was handicapped.

Cornell finished high school and then went to work as a textile salesman. In his spare time he roamed Manhattan, visiting museums and bookstalls and learning all he could about literature and the arts. He was especially fond of ballet, opera, theater, and movies. And he was fascinated by images from the past, especially from the Renaissance and Victorian eras. All these interests and passions came together in the art that he began to create.

Cornell's early works were paper collages in which pictures of unrelated objects were put together in surprising ways. By the mid-1930's he was creating shadow boxes and other three-dimensional constructions. In these early works, Cornell was influenced by surrealist artists, whose works he saw in New York galleries. The surrealists sought to portray the dream world of the unconscious mind in their paintings. But while Cornell admired

Medici Slot Machine

these artists, his art was unique. He never had formal art training, and he was in his late 30's before he decided to become a full-time artist.

A shy man, Cornell would spend hours looking for materials for his boxes. His thin, stooped figure haunted old bookshops, record stores, souvenir shops, second-hand stores, and five-and-dime stores in Manhattan. He collected all sorts of "loot," as he called it. Postage stamps, photographs, maps, ballet programs, magazines, driftwood, old clay pipes, sequins, toys, coins—he found and saved them all. In time, his house in Flushing became crowded with tens of thousands of objects and papers.

None of these items cost a lot of money. Cornell couldn't afford to buy expensive things. But although they were inexpensive, Cornell thought of them all as wonderful treasures. They became the raw materials of his work.

Paul and Virginia

265

pages from old books and magazines on the back of the box.

The most time-consuming part was arranging the treasures in the box. This could take months—sometimes even years. He added and removed items and moved them around until he felt what he called "a sense of rightness." By taking everyday objects out of their usual surroundings and putting them behind glass, Cornell made them seem to belong to the world of dreams.

CREATING DREAM WORLDS

Cornell's cluttered studio was in the basement of his home, and it was there that he created his boxes. It took him a long time to make each one. He wanted the box to seem old, so he polished the wood to give it the appearance of age. If the wood was painted, he might put it in the oven. The heat would make the paint peel and crack. Sometimes he would paste

Cornell didn't select objects only for the way they looked. Each of the objects in a box was a symbol—it carried a special meaning or was linked to an idea or feeling. A seashell was a reminder of the sea. A spiral watch spring represented the idea of time. A feather placed on the floor of a box suggested a bird that had flown away, and thus stood for the idea of loss.

Soap
Bubble
Set

like childhood. Cornell loved to show his work to children and talk to them about it.

Cornell's work was well received in the art world, and he was known and admired by other artists. He was only barely able to scrape out a living, though. He often did freelance design work on the side, to make ends meet.

When Cornell died, he left a house crammed with thousands of objects that he had collected over his lifetime. He had hoped that the house would become a sort of hands-on museum. His idea was that people could come, dig around in the collection, and use what they found to create their own shadow boxes.

That didn't happen. But a lot of the material he collected was saved. It is now at the Joseph Cornell Study Center, part of the National Museum of American Art in Washington, D.C. There are boxes, folders, and envelopes stuffed with maps clipped from old travel guides, pocket-watch faces, cutouts of birds, pressed butterflies, and countless other items.

Meanwhile, Joseph Cornell's work has gained a wider audience. His magical boxes have been exhibited all over the world, enchanting people everywhere.

When people looked at the box, they were reminded of these meanings and ideas—sometimes without even realizing it. Often, Cornell's works showed unexpected connections between very different objects. He showed the similarity between the rigging of a sailing ship and the threads of a spider's web. He showed connections between soap bubbles and planets and between butterflies and ballerinas. Many of Cornell's boxes include dolls and other toys. They seem to recall a sort of strange, dream-

Bébé Marie

267

WALT DISNEY'S

MICKEY MOUSE

IN STEAMBOAT WILLIE

movie scene, and Disney decided to add sound to his animated films. The result was *Steamboat Willie,* the world's first sound cartoon. It premiered at the Colony Theater in New York City on November 18, 1928.

Steamboat Willie was a huge success, so Disney added sound to *Plane Crazy* and a third Mickey cartoon, *Gallopin' Gaucho.* (Disney provided Mickey's voice in these cartoons and in all Mickey Mouse films through 1946.) Mickey's cartoons became so popular that people would ask if a theater was running a "Mickey" before they would buy a ticket. They loved the spunky little mouse who helped them laugh at life's ups and downs.

In 1929, Mickey's skyrocketing popularity led to the founding of the Mickey Mouse Club. Club chapters met every Saturday in local theaters for an afternoon of cartoons and games. The several million Mouse Clubbers had a secret handshake, a special greeting, a code of behavior, and even a special club song— "Minnie's Yoo Hoo."

HAPPY BIRTHDAY, MICKEY MOUSE

Who has the most famous ears in the world? Mickey Mouse, of course. And in 2003, Mickey Mouse celebrated his 75th birthday!

Mickey was a big hit when he first appeared in 1928, in the cartoon short *Steamboat Willie.* And today, this cartoon character has a special place in the hearts of people everywhere.

A STAR IS BORN

It all began with Walt Disney, who created his first animated cartoons in 1920. Mickey was born in Disney's imagination in 1928, on a train ride from New York to Los Angeles.

Disney first used the character in a silent cartoon, *Plane Crazy,* which appeared in a handful of theaters. Then sound burst onto the

California schoolchildren put together this computer-generated puzzle on a football field in 1996. It was the largest image of Mickey Mouse ever printed!

Mickey's popularity wasn't confined to the silver screen. By 1930 he was appearing on dozens of items, including wooden toys, drums, rubber balls, rattles, cups and plates, soap, candles, glass figurines, bookends, puppets, and clothing. The first Mickey Mouse comic strip appeared on January 13, 1930. The first Mickey Mouse wristwatch was made in 1933.

The high point of Mickey's early years came in 1940, with his starring role in the feature-length film *Fantasia.* A major artistic innovation, it interpreted music in colors, shapes, and story. The animation techniques were years ahead of their time. *Fantasia* also introduced stereophonic sound to theaters.

NEW ROLES

During World War II, the Disney studio turned its energies to aiding the war effort by making training films, posters, and insignia for the armed forces. Mickey played his part, appearing on insignia and on posters that urged national security and the purchase of war bonds. "Mickey Mouse" was even the password for D-Day, June 6, 1944, when Allied forces invaded Nazi-held France!

After the war, Mickey returned to cartoons. In 1947 he appeared in a second feature, *Fun and Fancy Free,* in which he costarred with Donald Duck and Goofy in a new version of "Jack and the Beanstalk." But by this time, Mickey was taking on a new role—as the symbol of the Disney studio.

In 1955, Mickey took on another new role. Disney created an afternoon television program, *The Mickey Mouse Club,* which became one of the most successful children's shows ever. The show was revived briefly in the 1970's as *The New Mickey Mouse Club.* A third version ran from 1989 through 1995 on Disney's cable television channel. Among the young stars who got their start on that show were pop performers Britney Spears, Christina Aguilera, and Justin Timberlake.

Mickey also became the symbol and chief greeter at Disneyland, the California theme park that opened in 1955, and at the many other Disney parks and resorts that followed. As his business expanded into these new areas, Walt Disney remarked, "I only hope that we never lose sight of one thing—that it was all started by a mouse."

Walt Disney died in 1966, but Mickey and the other characters he created are going strong. At 75, Mickey Mouse is still helping people laugh at life's ups and downs. His face—and ears—are known to people around the globe.

PEOPLE, PLACES, EVENTS

Where can you take the presidential oath of office and try on the robes of a Supreme Court Justice? At the **National Constitution Center (NCC)** in Philadelphia, Pennsylvania. The NCC, which opened in July 2003, brings the Constitution to life. It's in the Independence National Historical Park, along with Independence Hall—where the Constitution was signed.

Visitors to the NCC's permanent exhibit, "The Story of We the People," are asked to think of themselves as part of the Constitution story. Instead of tickets, they enter with delegates' passes. They stroll through a gallery full of the sights and sounds of Philadelphia in 1787, watch a multimedia production called *Freedom Rising,* and then enter the main exhibit space—a circular gallery enclosed by a glass wall that carries the full text of the Constitution. Within the wall, interactive exhibits tell the history of the Constitution, examine its role in America today, and ask visitors to ponder some big questions: What makes us Americans? Have we established equal justice? What makes us feel free?

Actress **Nicole Kidman** has come a long way since her first stage appearance—as a bleating sheep in a Christmas pageant at her elementary school. Kidman, 36, won the Academy Award for best actress in 2003, for her critically acclaimed portrayal of author Virginia Woolf in the 2002 movie *The Hours.* Kidman was born in Hawaii but raised in Australia, and she began her professional acting career as a teenager there. Her first movie role came in 1983 in an Australian holiday film, *Bush Christmas.* She made her U.S. debut in 1989, in the thriller *Dead Calm.* Since then, she has shown her acting talents in dramas like *The Hours,* comedies, action movies, even the 2001 musical *Moulin Rouge.* Kidman is divorced from actor Tom Cruise and has two adopted children. (She is shown here being honored with a star on the Hollywood Walk of Fame in January 2003.)

An **army of trash people** marched on the Matterhorn, a famous peak in the Swiss Alps, in August 2003. German artist HA Schult created the trashy army by pressing refuse onto plastic forms. His point? "We live in a trash time, we produce trash, and we become trash." He has also set up the figures on the Great Wall of China and in other famous spots.

U.S. television audiences continued their fascination with reality shows in 2003. And among the most popular of those shows was the Fox Network's **American Idol,** in which amateur performers competed to win a $1 million recording contract. More than 38 million people tuned in for the final episode of the show's second season in May 2003, in which soul singer Ruben Studdard (right) narrowly edged out Clay Aiken (left) to win the prize.

The show began its second season with nationwide auditions. Starting in January, wanna-be pop stars who made the cut had a chance to perform in the show's weekly episodes. Their performances were critiqued by a panel of judges, some famous for put-downs and cutting remarks. Then viewers voted by phone, gradually narrowing the field until only two remained: Aiken, 24, a college student from Raleigh, North Carolina, and Studdard, 25, a musician from Birmingham, Alabama.

Meanwhile, Kelly Clarkson, the winner in the show's 2002 season, came out with her first album, *Thankful.* It shot straight to the top of the pop charts. And Clarkson made a movie, *From Justin to Kelly,* in which she co-starred with Justin Guarini, the 2002 *American Idol* runner up.

The popularity of *American Idol* also gave rise to lots of similar talent-contest shows. Viewers could watch amateurs perform and compete on *Star Search, Nashville Star,* and *Born to Diva.* They could vote for America's *Next Top Model, Next Action Star,* and *Most Talented Senior.* Two shows focused on kids and teens—*America's Most Talented Kid* and *American Juniors.* There was even an animal talent show, *Pet Star!* But none of those shows topped the popularity of the original.

How old is Mickey Mouse? Walt Disney first sketched his mouse in 1928, so Mickey turned 75 in 2003. But a painting on a wall of a medieval church in Austria shows a figure that looks a lot like the famous mouse. And it was painted 700 years ago! Workers discovered the **medieval Mickey Mouse** while they were restoring a fresco on the outside of the church, which is in the village of Malta. The fresco (a painting made on a wet plaster wall) shows St. Christopher surrounded by animals and imaginary creatures. One faded figure has two big ears and a pointed nose. It might be a weasel, historians say. But it looks like Mickey Mouse.

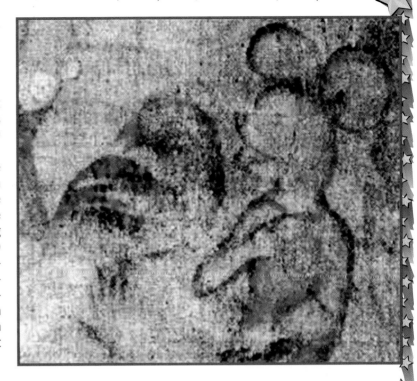

You can see right through the wearer of this **amazing coat.** Magic? No—a camera trick. A video camera records the scene behind the wearer, and the images are projected on the front of the coat. The coat is too bulky to be useful. But Susumu Tachi, its Japanese inventor, hopes to improve it and find other uses for the technology.

Is your McJob giving you agita? Did your compadres bogart the ball at the shootaround? Do you need some dead presidents? Oy!

If you don't understand that paragraph, just turn to the 11th edition of **Merriam-Webster's New Collegiate Dictionary,** published in July 2003. Among its 10,000 new words are McJob (low-paying, dead-end work), agita (a feeling of anxiety), compadre (buddy), bogart (use without sharing), shoot around (informal basketball practice), dead presidents (paper money), and oy (an exclamation of dismay).

Merriam-Webster's dictionaries are descended from the *American Dictionary of the English Language,* published by Noah Webster (inset) in 1828. The year 2003 also marked the 175th anniversary of that famous dictionary. Webster was among the first to see that U.S. and British English were different and that the United States needed its own dictionaries.

The *Merriam-Webster Collegiate Dictionary* first appeared in 1898. It has sold 55 million copies since then, and it's widely used in schools and offices today. Every ten years, the dictionary must be updated because English is always changing. English-speakers invent new words, change the meanings of old ones, and pick up words from other languages and from specialized fields such as science.

With their swirly petals and twisting stems, the sunflowers in this painting almost seem to be moving. They were painted by **Vincent van Gogh** (1853–1890), one of the greatest modern artists. In 2003, art lovers marked the 150th anniversary of his birth.

Van Gogh was a troubled and passionate artist. Born in the Netherlands, he dabbled in several careers—teacher, minister, missionary—before turning seriously to art in 1880. In 1886 he moved to France to join his brother Theo, who worked for an art dealer in Paris. There he met the Impressionists, a group of painters who sought to capture the effects of light in their works. They influenced him, but he developed a style all his own.

Strong colors, thick layers of paint, and bold brushstrokes are hallmarks of that style. Rather than simply painting what he saw, Van Gogh tried to portray emotions with his colors and designs. He once said that he deliberately exaggerated nature to "express . . . man's terrible passions." After suffering a nervous breakdown in 1888, he was overcome by despair. He died in 1890, a suicide. It was only after his death that the greatness of his art was recognized.

A one-legged sea captain, a little gray man, a delicate invalid attended by her nurse—these are some of the mysterious guests at the strange hotel in *The Last Resort*. The story tells of an artist who arrives at the lonely seaside hotel in search of his lost imagination. Each of the guests is searching for something, too. Who are these people? What do they seek? Roberto Innocenti's beautiful paintings illustrate this fascinating puzzle, which was written by J. Patrick Lewis.

Thumbelina

There was once a woman who wanted to have a tiny child. So she went to an old witch and asked her what to do.

"Oh, I think I can help you," said the witch. "Plant this magical barleycorn in a flowerpot and watch what happens!"

The woman went home and planted the barleycorn, and a large beautiful flower bud immediately appeared. "What a beautiful flower!" exclaimed the woman, and she kissed the red and yellow petals of the bud. As she kissed them, the flower burst open. And sitting in the middle of the velvety blossom was a tiny little girl. The lovely child was no bigger than a thumb, and so she was named Thumbelina.

Thumbelina was so tiny that she slept in a walnut shell. The blue petals of a violet were her mattress, and a rose petal was her blanket. During the day, the woman placed a bowl of water on a table. This miniature lake was ringed with white flowers, and in the middle was a large tulip petal. Thumbelina used this petal as a boat, and she would sit on it and sail from one side of the bowl to the other.

The years went by and Thumbelina grew into a lovely young woman. But she never grew bigger than a thumb.

One night, when Thumbelina was lying in her pretty walnut bed, an ugly toad crept in through a broken pane in the window. She hopped onto the table where Thumbelina was sleeping and gazed at the tiny girl.

"She would make a beautiful wife for my son," said the toad. And she took the walnut shell, with Thumbelina in it, and hopped out through the window into the garden.

Beyond the garden flowed a wide stream, with slippery and marshy banks. There the toad lived with her son. Ugh! He was as ugly and clammy as his mother. "Croak, croak, croak!" was all he could say when he saw the tiny girl in the walnut shell.

"Don't talk so loud or you will wake her," said the mother toad. "We must not allow her to escape. We will put her on a big water lily leaf in the stream. The leaf will be like an island, and she will never be able to reach shore." And that is where the toads left Thumbelina, still asleep in her walnut shell.

Morning came. Thumbelina woke up and looked around in great bewilderment and sadness. She saw water on every side of her and realized she could never escape.

Later that day, the old toad swam with her son to the leaf where Thumbelina was held captive. She said to Thumbelina in her low, rough voice: "Here is my son. You shall marry him tomorrow."

"Croak, croak, croak!" was all that the son could say. When the toads swam away, poor Thumbelina wept in despair.

The little fishes swimming in the water had heard the toad quite plainly, and they decided to help the tiny girl. They grouped together around the stalk that supported the leaf on which Thumbelina was sitting. And they nibbled away until the stalk was cut in two. Away floated the leaf down the stream, carrying Thumbelina far beyond the reach of the toads.

Thumbelina was delighted as she sailed past town after town. The sun shone on the water and made it sparkle like silver. Then a great insect came flying past. He caught sight of Thumbelina, lifted her off her lily leaf, and carried her to a tree. He placed the frightened girl on a large green leaf and gave her the honey from the flowers to eat. He told her that she was very pretty, although she was not in the least like an insect. Later on, all the other insects who lived in the same tree came to visit. They examined Thumbelina closely and remarked, "Why, she has only two legs! How very miserable!"

The little fishes swimming in the water heard the toad, and they decided to help the tiny girl.

"She has no feelers!" cried another.

"How ugly she is!" said the lady insects.

The insect who had stolen her thought that she was very pretty, but when he heard all the ladies saying she was ugly, he began to think so too. So he decided not to keep her. He flew down from the tree and placed Thumbelina on a daisy. There she sat and wept, because she was so ugly that the insects would have nothing to do with her—and yet she was really the most beautiful creature imaginable, like the loveliest rosebud.

The whole summer poor little Thumbelina lived alone in the woods. She wove a bed for herself of blades of grass and hung it up under a clover leaf so that she was protected from the rain. She gathered honey from the flowers for food, and drank the dew on the leaves every morning. Thus summer and autumn passed, but then came winter—the long, cold winter. All the birds who had sung so sweetly about her had flown away. The trees shed their leaves and the flowers died. The great clover leaf under which she had lived curled up and nothing remained of it but the withered stalk. She was terribly cold, for her clothes were ragged. It began to snow, and every snowflake that fell on her was like a whole shovelful because she was so tiny. Poor little Thumbelina.

Just outside the woods lay a great cornfield. But the corn had been gone a long time, and only the dry bare stubble was left standing in the frozen ground. This made a forest for Thumbelina to wander about in. One day she came upon the home of a field mouse, who had a little hole under a cornstalk. There the mouse lived warm and snug, with a store-room full of corn. The tiny girl begged the field mouse for a little piece of barley.

"Poor little creature," said the field mouse, for she was a kind-hearted thing. "Come into my warm room and have some dinner with me." The field mouse was so enchanted with Thumbelina that she told the girl she could spend the entire winter in her home.

Thumbelina was very happy, and she kept the field mouse's house clean and neat and told all kinds of tales about her experiences in the outside world.

"Now I am expecting a visitor," announced the field mouse. "My neighbor, the mole, comes to call on me once a week. He is quite rich and has great big rooms and wears a fine black velvet coat. If you could only marry him, you would be well provided for. But he is blind, and he dislikes the sun and birds and flowers. So you must tell him some of your prettiest tales to amuse him."

Thumbelina made the visitor feel welcome. She sang to him and told him wonderful stories. And the mole fell in love with her. But Thumbelina was not at all pleased, for she had no desire to marry a mole.

One day he asked Thumbelina to go for a walk with him through a long underground passage that connected the two houses. About halfway

through the passage, she saw a little swallow lying on its back. The mole told Thumbelina that the bird had probably died of the cold. The girl, who dearly loved all birds, was very troubled by the sight, for she wanted the swallow to lie warmly buried.

That night she wove a blanket of straw and carried it into the passage. She spread it over the dead bird and piled on top of it thistledown as soft as cotton-wool. But when the blanket began to warm the bird, Thumbelina heard the pit-pat of its heartbeat. The swallow was alive!

The bird was very weak. He could only open his eyes for a moment and gaze at Thumbelina. "Thank you, tiny girl," said the swallow. "I am so beautifully warm. Soon I shall regain my strength and be able to fly again into the warm sunshine."

"Oh," said Thumbelina, "it is very cold outside. It is snowing and freezing. Stay in your warm bed. I will take care of you."

The rest of the winter he remained in the passage, and Thumbelina nursed him tenderly. But she didn't tell the field mouse or the mole, for she feared that they did not like birds very much.

When spring came, the swallow said it was time for him to leave. Thumbelina helped him find his way out of the passage into the bright, warm sunshine. The swallow asked if she would go with him. Thumbelina wanted very much to fly far away into the green wood, but she knew that the old field mouse would be sad if she ran away. "No, I can't leave," she said sadly.

"Farewell, dear girl," said the swallow and flew away. Thumbelina gazed after him with tears in her eyes, for she had grown very fond of the swallow.

Thumbelina covered the bird with a blanket of straw and thistledown.

A few days later, the field mouse said to Thumbelina: "You are to be a bride! Our neighbor has proposed! What a piece of good fortune for a poor girl like you. Now you must prepare fine linens for your dowry."

Thumbelina had to spin all day long. Every evening the mole visited her and told her that when summer was over and the sun was not shining so brightly, they would marry.

The tiny girl was very unhappy. She had no desire to marry the mole and live underground and never again see the sun or birds or flowers.

Soon it was winter, and the wedding day arrived. Before the mole came to fetch Thumbelina, she stole outside to say good-bye to the beautiful sun. "Farewell, bright sun," she cried, stretching out her arms toward it. "Farewell," she repeated, "and give my love to the dear swallow when you see him."

"Tweet, tweet!" sounded in her ear all at once. She looked up and there was the swallow flying past! As soon as he saw Thumbelina, he was very glad. She told him that it was her wedding day but how unwilling she was to marry the mole.

The prince of the flowers placed a golden crown on Thumbelina's head and asked her to marry him.

"The cold winter is coming," said the swallow. "I must fly away to warmer lands. Will you come with me this time? You can sit on my back and we will fly far away from the mole, over the mountains, to the warm countries where it is always summer and there are always beautiful flowers. Do come with me, dear little Thumbelina, who saved my life when I lay frozen in the dark tunnel!"

"Yes, I will go with you," said Thumbelina, and she hopped on the swallow's back. Higher and higher into the air flew the swallow, far above lakes and woods, over oceans and forests, above mountains so lofty their peaks were crested with snow. The air grew warmer and warmer. The sun was brighter. Below were vines filled with the lushest green and purple grapes. On the trees grew oranges and lemons, and the air was scented with myrtle and mint.

But the swallow flew on, and the lands became even more beautiful. Soon they flew over the most splendid green trees, encircling a sparkling blue lake. Beside the lake stood a glittering white marble castle. Winding vines climbed up the graceful slender pillars, and nestled in the vines were hundreds of swallows' nests. In one of these nests lived Thumbelina's swallow.

"Here is my house," he said. "And you can live in one of the lovely flowers that grow alongside the castle."

"That will be wonderful," Thumbelina said, clapping her little hands in joy.

The swallow set Thumbelina down in a garden filled with the most beautiful flowers. There, to her great astonishment, she found a tiny young man sitting in the middle of one of the flowers. On top of his head was a golden crown, and on his shoulders were the most delicate wings. And he was just as small as Thumbelina.

He bowed to Thumbelina and told her he was the prince of the flowers, and he thought that she was the most beautiful maiden he had ever seen. He took his golden crown from his head and put it on hers and asked if she would be his wife and princess of all the flowers.

Thumbelina was happier than she had ever been. "Yes, little prince," she said. "I shall be happy to be your princess."

Then out of each flower stepped tiny fairylike creatures, the lords and ladies of the flowers. Each presented Thumbelina with a gift and bowed before her. The most beautiful gift of all was a pair of tiny white wings, as delicate as gossamer. The wings were fastened to Thumbelina's shoulders, so that now she too could fly from flower to flower whenever she wished.

And so Thumbelina and the little prince were married. At the wedding the bridal song was sung in the sweetest music, by the best friend of both the bride and the groom—the swallow who had brought the tiny couple together.

My Friend Rabbit

LOOKING AT BOOKS

Books filled with fantasy, including the long-awaited fifth entry in the *Harry Potter* series, kept young readers turning pages in 2003. And there were lots of other spellbinding choices as well—novels set in the present and the distant past, outstanding nonfiction, and colorful picture books.

AWARD-WINNING BOOKS

My Friend Rabbit, written and illustrated by Eric Rohmann, won the 2003 Caldecott Medal, given each year to the best American picture book for children. In this comical salute to friendship, Mouse shares his new toy airplane with his friend Rabbit. But Rabbit just can't help getting in trouble—and the results are both disastrous and hilarious. The airplane gets stuck in a tree, and Rabbit calls in everyone in the neighborhood to help. Elephant, Hippo, and

Alphabeasts

Crocodile are all pressed into service. The characters tumble across the pages in Rohmann's energetic illustrations, which feature strong outlines and bright colors.

Crispin: The Cross of Lead, by Avi, won the 2003 John Newbery Medal as the year's best American literary work for young readers. This story is set in 14th-century England. Crispin, a 13-year-old boy, has grown up in a small village, where he is known only as "Asta's son." His entire world falls apart when he suddenly becomes orphaned. He loses his home and all his possessions—and, on top of that, he's accused of murder! Fleeing his village, Crispin falls in with a juggler named Bear, who becomes his protector. Together, they try to escape from Crispin's enemies and solve the mystery of the boy's true identity. It's an exciting story, and the book's detailed descriptions bring to life the sights, sounds, smells, and tastes of the Middle Ages.

The illustrations in Wallace Edwards' *Alphabeasts* create a magical world. In this book, the alphabet is presented in a strange house filled with animals. All the animals are doing surprising, human things—from an alligator sprawled across a big stuffed chair, to a pig tucked into bed, to a zebra taking a bath. This book won Canada's 2003 Governor General's Award for best illustration in an English-language children's book.

True Confessions of a Heartless Girl, by Martha Brooks, won the Canadian Governor

PICTURE BOOKS

The beautiful countryside around the Li River in China is the setting for *Daisy Comes Home,* written and illustrated by Jan Brett. Mei Mei, who lives beside the river, keeps "the six happiest hens in China." But one rainy night the river rises over its banks. It carries away the smallest hen, Daisy, who is sleeping in a market basket. The rich illustrations in this book follow two story lines—Daisy's adventures on the river, and Mei Mei's search for her.

Daisy Comes Home

General's Award for English-language text for children. The "heartless girl" of the title, Noreen, is a teenage runaway who arrives in a small Canadian town driving a stolen pickup truck. She soon displays a talent for trouble, and through flashbacks the book explores the factors that helped bring her to this state. As other people in the small town try to help her, they confront their own problems.

In *Henry Builds a Cabin,* written and illustrated by D. B. Johnson, Henry the bear builds a cabin in the woods. His friends offer help and advice, but Henry does it his way—keeping the building small, and using old boards, windows, and doors. This picture book was inspired by *Walden,* by the 19th-century writer Henry David Thoreau. Thoreau believed that people were happiest when they lived simply, and he

Henry Builds a Cabin

built a cabin at Walden Pond in Massachusetts to show how simply people could live.

For very young readers, the author-illustrator team of Leo and Diane Dillon presented the story of Bill "Bojangles" Robinson, perhaps the greatest tap dancer of all time. The famous dancer leaps through the pages of their *Rap a Tap Tap: Here's Bojangles—Think of That!*, while the clever rhyming text tells the story.

Rap a Tap Tap

Another famous African-American was featured in *Talkin' About Bessie: The Story of Aviator Elizabeth Coleman.* Coleman was the first African-American female pilot. In this book, author Nikki Grimes presents Coleman's story through the eyes of people who knew her, from her parents to the young fans who watched her perform at air shows in the 1920's.

The Boy Who Drew Cats is based on an old Japanese legend about a boy whose talents as an artist are so great that his pictures come to life. At first, the boy gets in trouble because he draws cats everywhere, all the time—even during study hours at the temple where he's training to become a priest. But when the boy is threatened by a goblin, the cats he has drawn come alive and save his life. The legend was adapted by Margaret Hodges and illustrated by Aki Sogabe in a style that mimics classical Japanese art.

Harry Potter and the Order of the Phoenix broke publishing records when it was released in June. Fans snapped up more than 5 million copies on the first day. They had waited three years for the fifth book in J. K. Rowling's series about a young wizard-in-training, and they eagerly whipped through its 800-plus pages. In *Phoenix,* Harry is a teenager in his fifth year at sorcery school, and he faces growing dangers from his archenemy, Lord Voldemort.

Talkin' About Bessie

Artemis Fowl: The Eternity Code was a new entry in another popular fantasy series, this one by Eoin Colfer. In this book, a magical device called the C Cube gives Artemis Fowl, the world's youngest criminal mastermind, a new plan to make money. But the plan backfires. Artemis loses the cube and nearly loses his life. What price will he pay to regain the device?

The city of Venice, Italy, provides a magical setting for *The Thief Lord,* by Cornelia Funke. Two orphaned boys, 12-year-old Prosper and 5-year-old Bo, run away when their aunt and uncle decide to split them up. They head for Venice, where they become involved with a gang of street children. The gang's leader is the secretive Thief Lord, a boy named Scipio who steals from the homes of wealthy Venetians to buy clothes for the street children. As a detective hunts for Prosper and Bo, they join Scipio in a hunt for a missing part that will bring a magic merry-go-round to life.

Readers turned to books set in the here and now, too. In Stephanie S. Tolan's *Surviving the Applewhites,* Jake, a teenage delinquent with spiked hair and multiple body piercings, turns up at Wit's End farm, home of the Applewhite family. He's there to attend the Creative Academy, where the Applewhite kids are home-schooled, and it's his last chance to turn around. Jake tries to stay tough, but he's soon drawn into the hilarious doings of the wacky Applewhites.

Among the outstanding nonfiction books of 2003 was Jim Murphy's *Inside the Alamo,* which tells the story of Anglo settlement in Texas and separates facts from myths about the famous Alamo siege. And Patrick O'Brien brought a bit of Civil War history to life in *Duel of the Ironclads: The Monitor vs. the Virginia.* These exciting books proved that even true stories can cast spells.

The Boy Who Drew Cats

In fourteen hundred and ninety-two
Columbus sailed the ocean blue.

For generations, children have chanted this rhyme. And for generations it was accepted as fact that the navigator Christopher Columbus (known in his native Italy as Cristoforo Colombo) discovered the New World—North and South America. But historians now say that others may have reached the New World before Columbus.

There are claims that some Africans sailed to the Americas in simple boats in 1500 B.C. Others cite evidence that Phoenicians in 600 B.C. and Romans in A.D. 64 were among the first to reach the Americas. Chinese people will tell you that a man named Hoei-shin made his way across the Pacific to Mexico around A.D. 499. And Poles say that the seaman Jan of Kolno made a round-trip voyage to North America in 1476—sixteen years before Columbus set sail from Spain.

We know that around A.D. 1000, Norwegian Vikings led by Leif Ericson landed in Newfoundland in what is now Canada and set up a short-lived colony called Vinland. And certainly English and Portuguese fishermen fished in American waters, around Nova Scotia and Labrador, in the 1480's. There may have been other seafarers who visited but left no records.

So what makes Columbus so special? Simply because the other "discoverers" were merely tourists. They came, they saw, and they went home. But Columbus's 1492 voy-

Christopher Columbus and his crew land at San Salvador (Guanahani) in the Bahamas, on October 12, 1492.

age and the three that followed were fully reported. Believing that he had discovered a short sea route to Asia, he reported that he had reached the Indies—the fabled Spice Islands. He described the "Indians" of the islands as "gentle and peaceful" people who would make good Christians—and good slaves. Gold and precious gems were in abundance, he told his backers, King Ferdinand and Queen Isabella of Spain—a report that was more fantasy than fact.

Actually, Columbus hadn't reached Asia. He had accidentally reached the Bahamas, islands off the coast of North America. But his "discovery" did begin an era of exploration and settlement of lands that would become the United States, Canada, Mexico, and the nations of South America.

But we should remember, too, that October 12, 1492, was also a day of discovery for the Taino people (part of the Arawak Indian group). When Columbus and his men landed on the island called Guanahani by its people, the Tainos discovered strange-looking people in strange-looking ships who came from an unknown land across the sea. So that October day was indeed a day of mutual discovery.

The story that follows is a fictionalized account of Columbus's first voyage to America, as seen through the eyes of a young Taino Indian boy and his fellow Native Americans. The characters are mainly imaginary, but the descriptions and drama of the discovery are true to life.

THE DISCOVERY

A gentle breeze drifted lazily across coral reefs and over the sun-bleached sands of the small island. It softly stroked the swaying palm trees, creating a low whooshing sound. Overhead, the sun was full in the sky, its strong rays skipping playfully across the sea.

Under the cool shade of a clump of trees, three Taino children were busily mixing brightly colored paint in small clay pots. The oldest was a wiry 14-year-old boy named Tami with a broad face and high forehead, dark eyes and jet black hair. Like most Taino people, he wore his straight, coarse hair so that its bangs covered his forehead. In back, it hung in a long, knotted ponytail.

Seated next to him were his sister Mara and a younger boy named Garo. Earlier in the day, Tami and Garo had gone out fishing with their fathers, paddling their dugout canoe beyond the reef-enclosed bay into the heaving waters of the great ocean. Mara, like the other girls and women in their little village, had spent the morning working in the fields where corn, yams, and other vegetables were grown.

Now it was time to play. Nearby, several Taino children were playing a game in which they kicked around a rubber ball. Tami watched the game out of the corner of his eye as he dabbed streaks of white and black paint on his sun-bronzed face. Garo was busily putting gobs of bright red paint on his face and chest. Noticing this Mara became angry. She rose and stamped her bare foot.

"It is not fair, Garo," she snapped. "You are using up all the pretty red paint. You know that red is my favorite color."

Garo frowned. "Oh, stop fussing. Use the white for a change."

"No, I won't—I want the red," shouted Mara, grabbing at Garo's ponytail and pulling him down. Soon they were engaged in a good-natured wrestling match in the sand, until Tami jumped in and pulled them apart.

"Why don't you just give her some red paint, Garo," Tami said with annoyance. "You know how girls are—she will just keep squawking if you don't let her have her way."

Garo gave in with a shrug. Mara made a face, grabbed the pot of red paint, and walked away. Standing off to one side, the 10-year-old girl dabbed her nose with splotches of red paint. Turning away from the boys, she continued painting herself while staring out at the sea.

Suddenly the girl gasped. She dropped the pot of paint and began frantically gesturing out toward where foamy waves crashed against the distant reefs.

"Look—look!" she shouted. "Sea monsters—three of them—and they are coming right at us."

Tami and Garo jumped up quickly. Shielding his eyes from the sun, Tami peered out toward the entrance of the bay. Three large, hulking objects with what looked like white wings were bobbing up and down as they headed toward the island. At first, Tami also thought them to be strange sea creatures. But then, as he looked them over more closely, he saw that the "bodies" were wooden hulls. And the "wings" were actually some sort of material—like the cotton his mother spun and wove into clothes and hammocks.

No, these weren't sea monsters that were frightening his sister. They were just boats. Big boats, to be sure, far bigger than even the largest *kanawas*—dugout canoes—the Tainos had.

"They aren't monsters! They are just big canoes," Tami said with authority.

"But who is on them?" asked Mara, clutching herself and trembling slightly.

Garo chimed in, "Maybe they are carrying Caribs"—a reference to a more warlike people who sometimes raided the smaller islands to get slaves and booty.

Tami scowled. He ran a hand over his *zemi*—a charm many Tainos wore around their necks to protect against danger. *Caribs,* he thought, as he stroked his charm. *May the gods protect us.*

Then the older boy blurted, "If they are Caribs, we had better warn the village. Come on, let's run quickly."

He grabbed his sister by the hand and pulled her along. They raced wildly through the trees and down a narrow path that led through the dense foliage. Other children on the beach had seen the big, menacing-looking boats and they, too, were running away.

Tami ran as fast as his strong, muscular legs could carry him. His sister had trouble keeping up. At one point, she stumbled and fell. But her brother quickly pulled her to her feet, held on to her protectively, and dragged her with him.

At last, they arrived at the village, with its cluster of thatch-roofed huts. When Tami and Mara arrived at their house, they were so winded they collapsed at the door. Guyami, their father, swung himself out of the hammock in which he had been dozing, saw the look of fright on his children's faces, and asked, "What is wrong—why do you look so afraid?"

A breathless Tami managed to gasp out: "Big boats—three of them, heading toward our island. Mara and I saw them . . ."

Mara tugged at her brother's arm. "I saw them first. I am the one who discovered them. And I still think they are sea monsters!"

Guyami frowned. "Big boats, you say. Are there Caribs on them?"

Tami shrugged. "We ran off to warn the village before they came ashore."

"You did well," the older man said. "If they are enemies, we must be ready for them." He turned to Tami's mother, who had come out of the wooden hut, and told her to take the younger children to a hiding place in the woods.

By now the others had arrived from the beach and the whole village was alerted. At first, there was some panic and confusion. But then the village chief appeared and ordered the men and older boys to get their weapons and gather in the village square, which was ringed by a low stone wall. Then he led his warriors through the forest toward the beach.

Guyami and Tami tightly gripped their small spears tipped with sharp fish teeth. Some of the other village men carried similar spears with wooden tips that had been sharpened with stones. Moving cautiously, the Tainos filtered through the trees in a ragged line. Near the edge of the tree line that fringed the beach, they dropped to their hands and knees and crawled to where they could see the beach without being seen themselves.

Quietly parting the thick leaves in front of them, Tami and his father observed the strangest sight they had ever seen. The three enormous boats, bigger even than whales, bobbed lazily off shore. The white winglike cloth pieces that Tami had seen earlier were now tucked under wooden poles. These horizontal poles were attached to larger and thicker vertical poles that jutted out of the hulls of the boats.

A small group of strange-looking men with odd garments and headgear were gathered in the middle of the beach. Some of them carried long, silvery objects that came to a point and glittered in the sunlight. In the center of the group stood a tall man who was more elaborately dressed than the others. With all his fine plumage, he reminded Tami of a big parrot. In one hand, the man held a wooden pole from which fluttered a white cloth with some sort of complicated design.

Tami assumed the tall man must be the chief of these odd-looking people. But he couldn't understand why on such a hot day they were all covered from head to foot in heavy garments. It seemed silly to him, and he thought that they must be very uncomfortable.

Suddenly, the chief of the newcomers waved his silvery rod in the air and shouted something. He spoke loud enough so that his words could be heard by the Tainos as they lay concealed in the underbrush.

But his words were strange. He certainly wasn't speaking Arawak, the language of the Tainos and the peoples of the neighboring islands.

As Tami and the others watched wide-eyed, the tall man took the pole with the cloth and stuck it deep into the sand. Then he said something to the others and they all dropped to their knees. The strangers removed their head coverings, bowed their heads, and began to chant in unison. *This must be some sort of ceremony,* Tami thought. *Perhaps they are giving thanks to the god of the sea for giving them a safe passage from their island to Guanahani.*

Glancing to his left, Tami saw that his father and several of the village elders were conferring with the chief. He crept closer and heard the old chief say, "They are not Caribs, and they do not look like they have come to attack us. A few of you come with me and we will greet them. The rest will remain in hiding."

Tami's father, the chief, and five other men rose and walked slowly onto the beach. Tami tagged along until his father spotted him, frowned, and said, "Go back—there may be danger here."

"It is all right, father," Tami responded. "I have good strong legs. If there's trouble, I will run very fast."

By now the strangers had spotted them. They began gesturing and waving. The tall man who had planted the pole with the cloth got up and moved toward them, holding his hand up in a sign of friendly greeting. The Tainos pointed their spears toward the sand to show they meant no harm, and the chief raised his hand high, palm open, to show he had no weapon.

When they were quite close, they all stopped and looked with equal amazement at each other. Tami had never seen such strange people. Their garments were of all possible colors, and some wore one color cloth on one leg and another color on the other. How pretty, Tami thought. Some had a spicy scent, as if they had rubbed flowers on their bodies. And most amazing of all—they had thick tufts of hair on their faces, covering everything but the mouth, nose, and eyes. Tami had never seen people with hair on their faces, and it seemed quite wonderful to him.

The tall man who appeared to be their chief stepped forward with another man who was holding some sort of paper. This man spoke in a language different from the other strangers. He kept pointing to the sky and used the word "Allah" many times. (The man was Luis de Torres, who spoke Arabic. Columbus, believing he was in Cathay—China—thought that the people would understand this language because of the overland trade between China and the Arab countries.)

When the Tainos didn't respond, the man shrugged and said something to his chief. Tami now had a good view of the chief, who was quite tall, with a deep reddish

skin color. His eyes were bold and seemed to take in everything. Although he didn't seem very old, his hair was as white as the clouds in the sky.

The Taino village chief approached the leader of the newcomers. As a sign of friendship, he handed him a yellow metal trinket he wore around his neck. The tall man seemed quite pleased with the gift. He held it high to show his followers, and there were excited shouts. Tami heard the word "gold!" repeated over and over.

The tall man then pointed all around at the island and said the words "San Salvador" several times. The Tainos understood that the man believed their island was called "San Salvador."

The Taino chief shook his head and politely corrected him. "This island is called Gua-nahani," he said, putting emphasis on the last syllable. Then he repeated it slowly— "Gwa-na-ha NEE."

But the chief of the strangers paid no attention and just babbled on about "San Salvador" and "gold."

By now, other Tainos were approaching the strangers. They came in twos and threes, timidly at first. But when the strangers gave no sign of doing them harm, they came as close as they could to look them over.

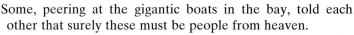

Some, peering at the gigantic boats in the bay, told each other that surely these must be people from heaven.

Being a generous people, the Tainos gave gifts to the strangers. They handed them trinkets and charms, clay pots and jugs of water.

One of the strangers approached Tami and pointed to the yellow metal pendant he wore around his neck next to his *zemi*. The stranger made a sign indicating he wanted it. Tami pulled it from his neck and handed it to the man. The man fondled it and broke into a broad smile. "Gold" he said, repeating the word over and over as if it were some holy chant.

The stranger pulled a dirty piece of colored cloth he wore around his neck and handed it to the Taino boy. Tami didn't really care for the gift, but he politely accepted it.

Suddenly the chief of the strangers came over and spoke harshly to the man, shaking a finger in his face. Tami could tell that he was scolding the man because he looked and sounded just like Tami's father when he was bawling him out for doing something wrong. The chief put a friendly hand on Tami's shoulder and made a sign for him to wait.

Then he called to a young boy—no older than Tami—and told him something. The boy scampered off to an open basket the strangers had brought with them. He pulled some items out of the basket and came trotting back. He was a pale-faced boy with a friendly smile and lively blue eyes. He handed Tami some glass beads, a small tinkling bell, and a red cloth head covering. The newcomer placed the last item on Tami's head, pointed to it, and said "cap."

Tami was quite thrilled. All these wonderful gifts for one piece of yellow metal, which he didn't really care much for anyway. He thought these strangers were quite generous to give so much for so little. He would give the red "cap" to his sister Mara—since she was so fond of that color—and the beads to his mother. But he would keep the bell for himself. Tami took a piece of string, twisted and knotted it, and placed the bell around his neck. He liked the sound it made when he moved.

The other boy now pointed to himself, smiled, and said "Pedro!" He said it several times, and Tami understood that that must be his name.

"Pay-dro," Tami repeated, then tapped a finger on his own chest and said "Tah-mee." They clapped each other on the shoulder with a laugh and went off together to explore each other's worlds.

* * * * * * * * * *

That first day after Columbus and his men landed was a day of discovery for Tainos and Europeans alike. At one point, Tami, his father, and a dozen men piled into one of their larger dugout canoes and paddled swiftly out to where the big boats were anchored. Tami's new friend, Pedro, went with them. The warm spray lashed at their faces, making the boys giggle. When they got to the boats, Pedro pointed to the biggest of the three and said "*Santa María.*" He made them understand that the others were called *Niña* and *Pinta*.

More gifts were exchanged. The newcomers marveled at the net-like hammocks strung between tree trunks. At first they had difficulty learning to use them. Tami and the other children laughed as the strangers tried

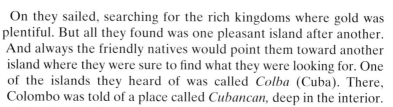

On they sailed, searching for the rich kingdoms where gold was plentiful. But all they found was one pleasant island after another. And always the friendly natives would point them toward another island where they were sure to find what they were looking for. One of the islands they heard of was called *Colba* (Cuba). There, Colombo was told of a place called *Cubancan,* deep in the interior.

Hearing what he wanted to hear, Colombo thought the Cubans had said *El Gran Can*—the Great Khan of Cathay. Tami's father tried to correct the chief of the strangers. "No, they speak of Cubancan—a great valley where you may find gold," Guyami told Colombo. But it was no use. The strangers pressed on, only to find more friendly people like the Tainos. Their *cacique* (chieftain) feasted the strange men from heaven, but there was no gold. However, the Spaniards did see people rolling sweetly scented leaves into *tobacos* (cigars). To the amazement of the newcomers, the natives set the leaves on fire and inhaled the smoke.

Some of the Spanish sailors tried the *tobacos,* but Tami warned his friend Pedro to stay away from the burning leaves. "I tried it once and it burned my lungs," said the Taino boy. "It tastes awful, too."

Hearing of gold in a place called *Babeque,* the captain of the Pinta took off without warning—leaving an angry Colombo with only two ships. Continuing, he came to a great and beautiful island which reminded Colombo of Spain. So he called it *La Isla Española* (or Hispaniola)—the Spanish Island.

The ships made their way up a wide river through a lush, forested valley. The local chief arrived with a large party of followers. Tami noticed that all the islanders who came on board the big ship were covered in ornaments made of gold. And he noticed the look of pleasure on the faces of the Spanish seamen when they saw this. Colombo had the ship's cannon fire a salute. Pedro had told Tami about these thunder sticks. The first time he had heard one fired it hurt his ears, so now he remembered to cover them.

A big celebration was held on board the ship, and many hundreds of local people came out to the Santa María in canoes. One of the local chiefs sent Colombo a beautiful belt with a buckle in the form of a face made of solid gold. Colombo was told that the great gold mines were at a nearby place called *Cibao*—which sounded to Colombo like *Cipangu* (Japan).

So once again they set sail, with an excited Colombo telling his Taino guides that soon they would meet the Emperor of Japan! Pedro told Tami that Colombo was absolutely certain they were near Japan—although neither Tami nor his father had heard of such a place.

But before they could reach Cibao, the winds fell silent and the sails drooped; and that evening the two ships drifted through calm waters. Pedro told Tami that the following day they would celebrate the birth of Christ. Because the sea was so calm, and everyone was so tired, the crew and captain went to sleep. Only Pedro and Tami stayed up to hold onto the tiller, which was used to steer the ship.

As it grew darker, even Tami began to drift off to sleep. Then, suddenly, with no warning at all, the hull of the ship struck a concealed reef. The jagged rocks tore great holes in the bottom of the ship. Water

leader of the strangers. Gradually, Tami and his friend Pedro learned to speak a little of each other's language. Pedro learned some Arawak words, and Tami learned a little Spanish.

Using these words and sign language, Pedro taught Tami about ship life and explained where the newcomers came from. "We sailed here from a big land called Spain. Our leader is from another land called Italy. His name is Cristoforo Colombo, and he is a great sailor. He is the captain general of our fleet." Pedro further explained that the ships had been sent by the king and queen of Spain to find two great lands called Cipangu (Japan) and Cathay (China). They hoped to find great amounts of gold and jewels. Tami couldn't really understand why such things were so important—and why people would travel so far from their homeland to find them.

The best part of the voyage was learning about the big boat. Tami was shown the wooden firebox on the deck where food was cooked. But the young Taino didn't care much for the tough, salty meat, hard bread, and dried green peas that the sailors ate. Also the water they took out of big barrels was often stale and sour, not fresh and clean like on his island. But he did like the red liquid—Pedro called it wine—he was given. It made him feel dizzy and a little silly. The sailors laughed when he walked and danced crazily after drinking the wine; but his father scolded him and made him promise not to drink it again.

From Pedro, Tami learned how the great white wings—or sails—caught the wind, and that this made the boat move. Tami had fun scampering up the rigging with the sailors and watching how they unfolded or folded the sails, depending on how fast they wanted the boat to go. When Tami asked about the white cloth with a symbol of one green stick crossed over another, Pedro explained that this was a flag—the special banner of their fleet. The green emblem was a cross, the symbol of the Christian faith.

"The cross is the sign of Jesus Christ, who is the savior of all mankind," Pedro told him.

"Is he like our god *Baibrama?*" asked Tami. "Can he make crops grow and winds blow?"

"Yes, of course," said Pedro. "Our God is all powerful. You and your father should become Christians so your souls can go to heaven."

Tami said he would think about this, but to himself he thought that he would stay with the gods he knew and to whom all Tainos prayed.

But Tami loved the little ceremony at the end of the day when the sailors gave thanks to their God and sang songs. Although their singing wasn't that good, Tami liked the music, and Pedro taught him some of the words of one song called *Salve Regina*.

One of Pedro's jobs was to turn over the time glass, with its narrow neck through which sand flowed from one glass container to another. Pedro explained that this was used to measure the parts of the day. Each time Pedro or one of the other boys turned the glass a song would be sung. One of them went like this:

> *"Five is past and six floweth,*
> *More shall flow if God willeth,*
> *Count and Pass make voyage fast."*

to hoist themselves into the hammocks and got all tangled up in the nets. Then the Tainos showed their guests how to use the hammocks and some of them began snoozing.

At one point Tami noticed Pedro using a small, silver object to jab holes in the sand. The bright metal attracted the Taino boy, and he reached out and stroked the edges. He quickly recoiled as the object cut his hand.

"Ouch," he yelped, "that hurts."

Pedro laughed. He pointed to the object and said "knife" several times. He explained that the long knives carried by the older men were called "swords" and were used for fighting.

Tami was awed by these wonderful objects that could cut. *How wonderful it would be to have one,* he thought to himself. Then he showed Pedro the simple rod with a fish tooth at the end that he and other Tainos used to spear fish and to fight off enemies.

The newcomers spent the next two days exploring the island they insisted on calling "San Salvador." The strangers kept asking about places in the area where they might find the yellow metal called "gold" that excited them so much. All the Tainos could do was tell them about the many islands to the west and south of Guanahani. Perhaps they would find what they were looking for there.

On the second day, Tami saw his father pack some things in a small sack and announce, "I must go with the strangers to guide them to the other islands."

Tami's mother was unhappy when she heard this and said fearfully, "But why must you go? I am afraid you may get hurt."

Guyami shrugged. "Our chief says they need someone who knows the seas, which I do. Besides, the strangers are very insistent, and he thinks there will be trouble if we do not help them. They have many powerful weapons and it is better to keep them as friends."

When Tami heard all this, he became excited. "A trip to the other islands! Please father, take me with you."

At first Guyami was reluctant, and there was much wrangling. There were to be two Tainos on each of the three ships, and Tami argued that it would be better for his father to have him as companion than one of the other villagers. "You know you can count on me if there is trouble," he argued, and Guyami finally agreed.

That afternoon, the three big boats left Guanahani, propelled by a brisk wind that puffed out their white wings. For Tami it was the beginning of a great adventure.

The big ships headed southward, stopping at many islands on the way. At each island they were greeted by friendly people who brought them water, gold ornaments, parrots, and other gifts. And always they asked the local islanders where they had gotten the gold that was used to make their bracelets and nose rings. Out of ignorance or in order to please the strange "men from heaven," the islanders would point south and west. Someplace over there—that is where you will find the yellow metal you seek, they would say.

For Tami, the weeks that followed the departure from Guanahani were the happiest and most exciting of his life. Everything he saw on the big boat was new and wonderful. He and his father were on board the boat that was called *Santa María,* which carried the began to seep into the lower deck. Panicky crewmen quickly lowered the ship's small boat. Some jumped over the side onto the rocky ledge.

Guyami hoisted himself over the rail and beckoned to his son. "Come quickly, before this boat sinks."

Tami was about to jump when he heard a shout for help. It was Pedro screaming that he couldn't swim, and when Tami looked back he could see Pedro floundering in the water filling the lower deck.

"Over here!" Tami shouted to his friend. But in the darkness Pedro couldn't see him. Then Tami had a thought. He jingled the hawk's bell given to him by Pedro many weeks before.

"Listen to the bell—come toward it!" he shouted.

Pedro splashed around and Tami was finally able to clutch him. Together they went over the side into the water. A strong swimmer himself, Tami draped an arm under Pedro's chin and swam with him to the safety of the surf-splashed reef. Soon a small boat from the *Niña* came to pick up the crew of the *Santa María*. Miraculously, not one member of the *Santa María*'s crew had been lost.

* * * * * * * * * * * * * *

The wreck of the *Santa María* brought an end to Colombo's voyage. Believing that he had found the Indies—and calling the people of the islands "Indians"—he determined to set sail for Spain to report the discovery. A small group of Spanish seamen was left behind to build a fort to continue the search for gold.

A few days after what the strangers called New Year's Day, Tami and his father, Guyami, watched the *Niña* hoist its sails and set a course eastward. Tami fingered the gift Pedro had given him after he saved his life. It was the Spanish boy's knife, in a cover made of some soft material like the skin of an animal. Tami was thrilled to have it, and he thought of all the different ways he could use it.

Suddenly the sound of the ship's thunder sticks boomed across the bay. Tami covered his ears and watched as the *Niña* fired its cannon into what remained of the *Santa María*, sending chunks of wood hurtling in the air.

Tami was impressed by the power of the cannon. "These men from heaven have such strong weapons," he remarked to his father.

"Yes, but the problem is we do not," said Guyami with a troubled tone in his voice. "It might be better for us if they stay home—on their own island—and look for this gold they hunger for somewhere else. I fear that things may not be so good for us if they come back."

Tami was puzzled by his father's remarks. But he just shrugged and thought about his great adventure. It would be something he would be able to talk about for all of his life.

Father and son waited until the *Niña* had slipped over the eastern horizon. Then Guyami placed an arm around his son's shoulder, and they turned toward the village—where they would get a canoe to carry them back to Guanahani. Ahead of them, in the western sky, the sun was now a bright red ball. They watched as it dropped from the sky to its resting place beyond the edge of the great sea.

HENRY I. KURTZ
Author, *John and Sebastian Cabot*

POETRY

THE PYTHON

A Python I should not advise,—
It needs a doctor for its eyes,
And has the measles yearly.
However, if you feel inclined
To get one (to improve your mind,
And not from fashion merely),
Allow no music near its cage;
And when it flies into a rage
Chastise it, most severely.

I had an Aunt in Yucatan
Who bought a Python from a man
And kept it for a pet.
She died, because she never knew
These simple little rules and few;—
The snake is living yet.

HILAIRE BELLOC (1870–1953)

THE SNOW MAN

We built a great big man of snow,
  With eyes of coal and a wooden nose,
And pebbles for buttons down his coat,
  A dozen pebbles in double rows.

We stuck a soap-bubble pipe in his mouth,
  And on his head put an old straw hat,
And gave him a cane to hold him up,
  For our Snow Man was very fat!

He was a wonderful sight to see
  When we got him made of hard-packed snow,
And he was tough as a forest tree,
  I slapped him once—and I ought to know!

For a week he stood by the garden gate,
  For a week the weather was cold and dry,
And then all the ice began to melt,
  And the sun shone out in a warmer sky.

And the Snow Man dripped and dripped and
    dripped,
  Melted away in the soft spring air,
Till only the pebbles and pipe and hat,
  The wood and the pieces of coal were there.

RUPERT SARGENT HOLLAND (1878–1952)

NEEDLE AND THREAD

Old Mother Twitchett had but one eye,
And a long tail which she let fly;
And every time she went through a gap,
A bit of her tail she left in a trap.

UNKNOWN

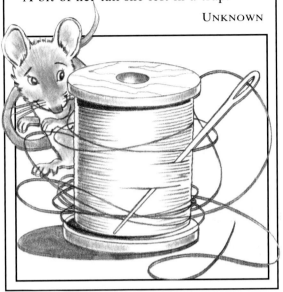

MIDSUMMER VIGIL

Dawn already, after the shortest night,
Has dimmed the harbour lanterns, still alight.

SHIKI (1866–1902)

TWILIGHT AT SEA

The twilight hours, like birds, flew by,
　As lightly and as free,
Ten thousand stars were in the sky,
　Ten thousand on the sea;
For every wave, with dimpled face,
　That leaped upon the air,
Had caught a star in its embrace,
　And held it trembling there.

AMELIA COPPUCK WELBY (dates unknown)

THE BODHISATTVA'S NECKLACE

When from the moor the autumn mists have fled,
A spider's web has dew on every thread.

HAKUYÛ (dates unknown)

THE BALD CAVALIER

When periwigs came first in wear,
　Their use was to supply
And cover the bald pate with hair,
　To keep it warm and dry.

For this good end, our Cavalier
　Determined one to buy,
Which did so natural appear
　That it deceived the eye.

But riding out one windy day,
　Behold! a sudden squall
Soon blew his feathered hat away,
　And periwig and all.

He joined the laugh with noddle bare,
　And sang in concert tone,
"How should I save another's hair,
　Who could not save my own?"

UNKNOWN

Little Women, *by Louisa May Alcott, is one of the most famous children's classics. Parts of the book may seem old-fashioned today, but this story of four sisters growing up in a small New England town has been a favorite for 135 years. The book's main characters—Meg, Jo, Beth, and Amy March—have much in common with Louisa May Alcott and her sisters, who grew up in Concord, Massachusetts. Louisa's father was a respected educator, but the family seldom had much money. Louisa wrote from the time she was young—a diary, poems, stories, and plays that she and her three sisters put on. She became a professional writer as a way of earning money.* Her first book, Flower Fables, *was a collection of fairy stories.* Hospital Sketches *told of her experiences as a nurse during the Civil War. When an editor suggested that she write a book for children, she began* Little Women, *which was published in two parts (1868 and 1869). Other children's books followed.*

Many incidents in Little Women, *including Meg's marriage and Beth's death, were taken from the Alcotts' lives. And Jo is in many ways a self-portrait of Louisa May Alcott. Jo, like her creator, became a writer. And both struggled with a strong temper, as Jo does in this excerpt.*

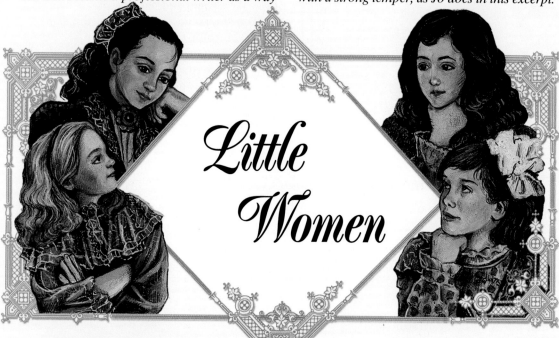

Little Women

"Girls, where are you going?" asked Amy, coming into their room one Saturday afternoon and finding them getting ready to go out with an air of secrecy which excited her curiosity.

"Never mind. Little girls shouldn't ask questions," returned Jo sharply.

Now if there is anything mortifying to our feelings when we are young, it is to be told that; and to be bidden to "run away, dear," is still more trying to us. Amy bridled up at this insult, and determined to find out the secret if she teased for an hour. Turning to Meg, who never refused her anything very long, she said coaxingly: "Do tell me! I should think you might let me go too; for Beth is fussing over her piano, and I haven't got anything to do, and am *so* lonely."

"I can't, dear, because you aren't invited," began Meg, but Jo broke in impatiently: "Now, Meg, be quiet, or you will spoil it all. You can't go, Amy, so don't be a baby and whine about it."

"You are going somewhere with Laurie, I know you are. You were whispering and laughing together on the sofa last night, and you stopped when I came in. Aren't you going with him?"

"Yes, we are. Now do be still, and stop bothering."

Amy held her tongue, but used her eyes, and saw Meg slip a fan into her pocket.

"I know I know! You're going to the theater to see *The Seven Castles*!" she cried, adding resolutely, "and I *shall* go, for Mother said I might see it, and I've got my rag money, and it was mean not to tell me in time."

"Just listen to me a minute, and be a good child," said Meg soothingly. "Mother doesn't wish you to go this week, because your eyes are not well enough yet to bear the light of this fairy piece. Next week you can go with Beth and Hannah, and have a nice time."

"I don't like that half as well as going with you and Laurie. Please let me. I've been sick with this cold so long, and shut up, I'm dying for some fun. Do, Meg! I'll be ever so good," pleaded Amy, looking as pathetic as she could.

"Suppose we take her. I don't believe Mother would mind, if we bundle her up well," began Meg.

"If she goes I shan't! And if I don't, Laurie won't like it, and it will be very rude, after he invited only us, to go and drag in Amy. I should think she'd hate to poke herself where she isn't wanted," said Jo crossly, for she disliked the trouble of overseeing a fidgety child, when she wanted to enjoy herself.

Her tone and manner angered Amy, who began to put her boots on, saying in her most aggravating way: "I *shall* go. Meg says I may, and if I pay for myself, Laurie hasn't anything to do with it."

"You can't sit with us, for our seats are reserved, and you mustn't sit alone; so Laurie will give you his place, and that will spoil our pleasure, or he'll get another seat for you, and that isn't proper, when you weren't asked. You shan't stir a step, so you may just stay where you are," scolded Jo, crosser than ever, having just pricked her finger in her hurry.

Sitting on the floor, with one boot on, Amy began to cry and Meg to reason with her, when Laurie called from below, and the two girls hurried down, leaving their sister wailing. For now and then she forgot her grown-up ways, and acted like a spoilt child. Just as the party was setting out, Amy called over the banisters in a threatening tone: "You'll be sorry for this, Jo March, see if you ain't."

"Fiddlesticks," returned Jo, slamming the door.

They had a charming time, for *The Seven Castles of the Diamond Lake* were as brilliant and wonderful as heart could wish. But in spite of the comical red imps, sparkling elves, and gorgeous princes and princesses, Jo's pleasure had a drop of bitterness in it; the fairy queen's yellow curls

reminded her of Amy, and between the acts she amused herself with wondering what her sister would do to make her "sorry for it." She and Amy had had many lively skirmishes in the course of their lives, for both had quick tempers and were apt to be violent when fairly roused. Amy teased Jo, and Jo irritated Amy, and semi-occasional explosions occurred of which both were much ashamed afterward. Although the older, Jo had the least self-control, and had hard times trying to curb the fiery spirit which was continually getting her into trouble. Her anger never lasted long, and having humbly confessed her fault, she sincerely repented, and tried to do better. Her sisters used to say that they rather liked to get Jo into a fury, because she was such an angel afterward. Poor Jo tried desperately to be good, but her bosom enemy was always ready to flame up and defeat her, and it took years of patient effort to subdue it.

When they got home, they found Amy reading in the parlor. She assumed an injured air as they came in, never lifted her eyes from her book, or asked a single question. Perhaps curiosity might have conquered resentment if Beth had not been there to inquire and receive a glowing description of the play. On going up to put away her best hat, Jo's first look was toward the bureau, for in their last quarrel Amy had soothed her feelings by turning Jo's top drawer upside down on the floor. Everything was in its place, however, and after a hasty glance into her various closets, bags, and boxes, Jo decided that Amy had forgiven and forgotten her wrongs.

There Jo was mistaken, for next day she made a discovery which produced a tempest. Meg, Beth, and Amy were sitting together, late in the afternoon, when Jo burst into the room looking excited, and demanding breathlessly: "Has anyone taken my book?"

Meg and Beth said "No," at once, and looked surprised. Amy poked the fire, and said nothing. Jo saw her color rise, and was down upon her in a minute.

"Amy, you've got it!"

"No I haven't."

"You know where it is, then!"

"No I don't."

"That's a fib!" cried Jo, taking her by the shoulders, and looking fierce enough to frighten a much braver child than Amy.

"It isn't. I haven't got it, don't know where it is now, and don't care."

"You know something about it, and you'd better tell at once or I'll make you." And Jo gave her a slight shake.

"Scold as much as you like, you'll never see your silly old book again," cried Amy, getting excited in her turn.

"Why not?"

"I burned it up."

"What! My little book I was so fond of, and worked over, and meant to finish before Father got home? Have you really burned it?" said Jo, turning very pale, while her eyes kindled and her hands clutched Amy nervously.

"Yes, I did! I told you I'd make you pay for being so cross yesterday, and I have, so—"

Amy got no farther, for Jo's hot temper mastered her, and she shook Amy till her teeth chattered in her head, crying in a passion of grief and anger: "You wicked, wicked girl! I never can write it again, and I'll never forgive you as long as I live."

Meg flew to rescue Amy, and Beth to pacify Jo, but Jo was quite beside herself; and with a parting box on her sister's ear, she rushed out of the room up to the old sofa in the garret, and finished her fight alone.

The storm cleared up below, for Mrs. March came home, and having heard the story, soon brought Amy to a sense of the wrong she had done her sister. Jo's book was the pride of her heart, and was regarded by her family as a literary sprout of great promise. It was only half a dozen little fairy tales, but Jo had worked over them patiently, putting her whole heart into her work, hoping to make something good enough to print. She had just copied them with great care, and had destroyed the old manuscript, so that Amy's bonfire had consumed the loving work of several years. It seemed a small loss to others, but to Jo it was a dreadful calamity, and she felt that it never could be made up to her. Beth mourned as for a departed kitten, and Meg refused to defend her pet. Mrs. March looked grave and grieved, and Amy felt that no one would love her till she had asked pardon for the act which she now regretted more than any of them.

When the tea bell rang, Jo appeared looking so grim and unapproachable that it took all Amy's courage to say meekly: "Please forgive me, Jo. I'm very, very sorry."

"I never shall forgive you," was Jo's stern answer, and from that moment she ignored Amy entirely.

No one spoke of the great trouble—not even Mrs. March—for all had learned by experience that when Jo was in that mood words were wasted, and the wisest course was to wait till some little accident, or her own generous nature, softened Jo's resentment and healed the breach. It was not a happy evening; for though they sewed as usual while their mother read aloud from Bremer, Scott, or Edgeworth, something was wanting, and the sweet home peace was disturbed. They felt this most when singing time came; for Beth could only play, Jo stood dumb as a stone, and Amy broke down, so Meg and Mother sang alone. But, in spite of their efforts to be as cheery as larks, the flute-like voices did not seem to chord as usual, and all felt out of tune. As Jo received her goodnight kiss, Mrs. March whispered gently: "My dear, don't let the sun go down upon your anger. Forgive each other, help each other, and begin again tomorrow."

Jo wanted to lay her head down on that motherly bosom and cry her grief and anger all away; but tears were an unmanly weakness, and she felt so deeply injured that she really *couldn't* quite forgive yet. So she winked hard, shook her head, and said, gruffly because Amy was listening: "It was an abominable thing, and she don't deserve to be forgiven." With that she marched off to bed, and there was no merry or confidential gossip that night.

Amy was much offended that her overtures of peace had been repulsed, and began to wish she had not humbled herself, to feel more injured than ever, and to plume herself on her superior virtue in a way which was particularly exasperating. Jo still looked like a thundercloud, and nothing went well all day. It was bitter cold in the morning; she dropped her precious turnover in the gutter; Aunt March had an attack of fidgets; Meg was pensive; Beth *would* look grieved and wist-

ful when she got home; and Amy kept making remarks about people who were always talking about being good, and yet wouldn't try when other people set them a virtuous example.

"Everybody is so hateful I'll ask Laurie to go skating. He is always kind and jolly, and will put me to rights, I know," said Jo to herself, and off she went.

Amy heard the clash of skates, and looked out with an impatient exclamation: "There! She promised I should go next time, for this is the last ice we shall have. But it's no use to ask such a crosspatch to take me."

"Don't say that. You *were* very naughty, and it *is* hard to forgive the loss of her precious little book; but I think she might do it now, and I guess she will, if you try her at the right minute," said Meg. "Go after them. Don't say anything till Jo has got good-natured with Laurie, then take a quiet minute and just kiss her, or do some kind thing, and I'm sure she'll be friends again, with all her heart."

"I'll try," said Amy, for the advice suited her, and after a flurry to get ready, she ran after the friends, who were just disappearing over the hill.

It was not far to the river, but both were ready before Amy reached them. Jo saw her coming and turned her back. Laurie did not see, for he was carefully skating along the shore, sounding the ice, for a warm spell had preceded the cold snap.

"I'll go on to the first bend, and see if it's all right, before we begin to race," Amy heard him say as he shot away, looking like a young Russian in his fur-trimmed coat and cap.

Jo heard Amy panting after her run, stamping her feet and blowing her fingers as she tried to put her skates on; but Jo never turned, and went slowly zigzagging down the river, taking a bitter, unhappy sort of satisfaction in her sister's troubles. She had cherished her anger

till it grew strong, and took possession of her. . . . As Laurie turned the bend, he shouted back: "Keep near the shore. It is not safe in the middle."

Jo heard, but Amy was just struggling to her feet and did not catch a word. Jo glanced over her shoulder, and the little demon she was harboring said in her ear: "No matter whether she heard or not. Let her take care of herself."

Laurie had vanished round the bend, Jo was just at the turn, and Amy far behind, striking out toward the smoother ice in the middle of the river. For a minute Jo stood still, with a strange feeling at her heart; then she resolved to go on, but something held her and turned her round just in time to see Amy throw up her hands and go down, with the sudden crash of rotten ice, the splash of water, and a cry that made Jo's heart stand still with fear. She tried to call Laurie, but her voice was gone; she tried to rush forward, but her feet seemed to have no strength in them; and for a second she could only stand motionless, staring with a terror-stricken face at the little blue hood above the black water. Something rushed swiftly by her, and Laurie's voice cried out: "Bring a rail—quick, quick!"

How she did it she never knew; but for the next few minutes she worked as if possessed, blindly obeying Laurie, who was quite self-possessed and, lying flat, held Amy up by his arm till Jo dragged a rail from the fence, and together they got the child out, more frightened than hurt.

"Now then, we must walk her home as fast as we can. Pile our things on her while I get off these confounded skates," cried Laurie, wrapping his coat round Amy and tugging away at the straps, which never seemed so intricate before.

Shivering, dripping, and crying, they got Amy home; and, after an exciting time of it, she fell asleep, rolled in blankets, before a hot fire. During the bustle Jo had scarcely spoken, but flown about looking pale and wild, with her things half off, her dress torn, and her hands cut and bruised by ice and rails and refractory buckles. When Amy was comfortably asleep, the house quiet, and Mrs. March sitting by the bed, she called Jo to her and began to bind up the hurt hands.

"Are you sure she is safe?" whispered Jo, looking remorsefully at the golden head which might have been swept away from her sight forever under the treacherous ice.

"Quite safe, dear. She is not hurt, and won't even take cold, I think, you were so sensible in covering her and getting her home quickly," replied her mother cheerfully.

"Laurie did it all, I only let her go. Mother, if she *should* die, it would be my fault." And Jo dropped down beside the bed in a passion of penitent tears, telling all that had happened, bitterly condemning her hardness of heart, and sobbing out her gratitude for being spared the heavy punishment which might have come upon her. "It's my dreadful temper! I try to cure it. I think I have, and then it breaks out worse than ever. O Mother, what shall I do? What shall I do?" cried poor Jo in despair.

"Watch and pray, dear, never get tired of trying, and never think it is impossible to conquer your fault," said Mrs. March, drawing the blowzy head to her shoulder and kissing the wet cheek so tenderly that Jo cried harder than ever.

"You don't know, you can't guess how bad it is! It seems as if I could do anything when I'm in a passion. I get so savage. I could hurt anyone and enjoy it. I'm afraid I *shall* do something dreadful some day, and spoil my life, and make everybody hate me. O Mother, help me, do help me!"

"I will, my child, I will. Don't cry so bitterly, but remember this day, and resolve with all your soul that you will never know another like it. Jo dear, we all have our temptations, some far greater than yours, and it often takes us all our lives to conquer them. You think your temper is the worst in the world, but mine used to be just like it."

"Yours, Mother? Why, you are never angry!" And for the moment Jo forgot remorse in surprise.

"I've been trying to cure it for forty years, and have only succeeded in controlling it. I am angry nearly every day of my life, Jo; but I have learned not to show it, and I still hope to learn not to feel it, though it may take me another forty years to do so."

The patience and the humility of the face she loved so well was a better lesson to Jo than the wisest lecture, the sharpest reproof. She felt comforted at once by the sympathy and confidence given her. The knowledge that her mother had a fault like hers, and tried to mend it, made her own easier to bear and strengthened her resolution to cure it—though forty years seemed rather a long time to watch and pray, to a girl of fifteen.

"Mother, are you angry when you fold your lips tight together and go out of the room sometimes, when Aunt March scolds or people worry you?" asked Jo, feeling nearer and dearer to her mother than ever before.

"Yes, I've learned to check the hasty words that rise to my lips; and when I feel that they mean to break out against my will, I just go away a minute, and give myself a little shake for being so weak and wicked," answered Mrs. March with a sigh and a smile, as she smoothed and fastened up Jo's disheveled hair.

"How did you learn to keep still? That is what troubles me—for the sharp words fly out before I know what I'm about. And the more I say, the worse I get, till it's a pleasure to hurt people's feelings, and say dreadful things. Tell me how you do it, Marmee dear."

"My good mother used to help me—"

"As you do us," interrupted Jo, with a grateful kiss.

"But I lost her when I was a little older than you are, and for years had to struggle on alone, for I was too proud to confess my weakness to anyone else. I had a hard time, Jo, and shed a good many bitter tears over my failures; for in spite of my efforts, I never seemed to get on. Then your father came, and I was so happy that I found it easy to be good. But by and by, when I had four little daughters round me, and we were poor, the old trouble began again; for I am not patient by nature, and it tried me very much to see my children wanting anything."

"Poor Mother! What helped you then?"

"Your father, Jo. He never loses patience—never doubts or complains, but always hopes, and works and waits so cheerfully that one is ashamed to do otherwise before him. He helped and comforted me, and showed me that I must try to practice all the virtues I would have my little girls possess, for I was their example. It was easier to try for your sakes than for my own; a startled or surprised look from one of you when I spoke sharply rebuked me more than any words could have done; and the love, respect, and confidence of my children was the sweetest reward I could receive for my efforts to be the woman I would have them copy."

"O Mother, if I'm ever half as good as you, I shall be satisfied," cried Jo, much touched.

"I hope you will be a great deal better, dear; but you must keep watch over your 'bosom enemy,' as Father calls it, or it may sadden if not spoil your life. You have had a warning. Remember it, and try with heart and soul to master this quick temper before it brings you greater sorrow and regret than you have known today."

"I will try, Mother, I truly will. But you must help me, remind me, and keep me from flying out. I used to see Father sometimes put his finger

on his lips and look at you with a very kind but sober face, and you always folded your lips tight or went away. Was he reminding you then?" asked Jo softly.

"Yes. I asked him to help me so, and he never forgot it, but saved me from many a sharp word by that little gesture and kind look."

Jo saw that her mother's eyes filled and her lips trembled as she spoke; and fearing that she had said too much, she whispered anxiously: "Was it wrong to watch you, and to speak of it? I didn't mean to be rude, but it's so comfortable to say all I think to you, and feel so safe and happy here."

"My Jo, you may say anything to your mother, for it is my greatest happiness and pride to feel that my girls confide in me, and know how much I love them."

"I thought I'd grieved you."

"No, my dear. But speaking of Father reminded me how much I miss him, how much I owe him, and how faithfully I should watch and work to keep his little daughters safe and good for him."

"Yet you told him to go, Mother, and didn't cry when he went, and never complain now, or seem as if you needed any help," said Jo, wondering.

"I gave my best to the country I love, and kept my tears till he was gone. Why should I complain when we both have merely done our duty and will surely be the happier for it in the end? If I don't seem to need help, it is because I have a better Friend even than Father to comfort and sustain me. My child, the troubles and temptations of your life are beginning, and may be many; but you can overcome and outlive them all if you learn to feel the strength and tenderness of your Heavenly Father as you do that of your earthly one. . . . .His love and care never tire or change, can never be taken from you, but may become the source of life-long peace, happiness, and strength. Believe this heartily, and go to God with all your little cares, and hopes, and sins, and sorrows as freely and confidingly as you come to your mother."

Jo's only answer was to hold her mother close, and in the silence which followed, the sincerest prayer she had ever prayed left her heart without words; for in that sad yet happy hour she had learned not only the bitterness of remorse and despair, but the sweetness of self-denial and self-control; and, led by her mother's hand, she had drawn nearer to the Friend who welcomes every child with a love stronger than that of any father, tenderer than that of any mother.

Amy stirred, and sighed in her sleep, and as if eager to begin at once to mend her fault, Jo looked up with an expression on her face which it had never worn before. "I let the sun go down on my anger. I wouldn't forgive her, and today, if it hadn't been for Laurie, it might have been too late! How could I be so wicked?" said Jo half aloud as she leaned over her sister, softly stroking the wet hair scattered on the pillow.

As if she heard, Amy opened her eyes and held out her arms, with a smile that went straight to Jo's heart. Neither said a word, but they hugged one another close, in spite of the blankets, and everything was forgiven and forgotten in one hearty kiss.

THE NEW BOOK OF KNOWLEDGE
2004

The following articles are from the 2004 edition of *The New Book of Knowledge*. They are included here to help you keep your encyclopedia up to date.

HOMELAND SECURITY, UNITED STATES DEPARTMENT OF

 The Department of Homeland Security (DHS) began operating on March 1, 2003, making it the newest of the 15 executive departments of the United States government. Its chief purpose is to find and arrest terrorists, stop their efforts to acquire weapons of mass destruction, and lend assistance to the American public in the event of an attack. The department is headed by a secretary, who is a member of the president's cabinet.

The need for a comprehensive homeland security plan became urgent after September 11, 2001, when the United States was attacked by terrorists, resulting in the deaths of more than 3,000 people. A few weeks later, a series of letters contaminated with anthrax, a deadly biological agent, were mailed to news organizations and members of Congress. These acts of bioterrorism killed six people, made more than a dozen others ill, and forced the temporary closure of several government buildings.

These events demonstrated not only that the United States was vulnerable to attack but also that the nation was unprepared to deal with the variety of ways in which a domestic attack might be launched. Restrictions on the activities of U.S. intelligence and law enforcement agencies prevented them from sharing information or from aggressively investigating possible terrorist activities within the United States. Some states and cities did not have plans for dealing with terrorist attacks. Police, firefighters, and emergency medical personnel, the so-called "first responders," were not well equipped or trained to deal with terror-related emergencies. The country had thousands of miles of open borders, and many critical facilities, including airports and seaports, power plants, and factories, were not well protected. The nation's hospitals did not have sufficient space to take care of large numbers of injured or sick people. Doctors often were not aware of the symptoms of diseases caused by biological or chemical weapons.

To improve homeland security, many changes were instituted in the way the federal government was empowered and organized to deal with terrorism. New laws were passed, most notably the controversial Patriot Act, which made it easier for law enforcement agencies to investigate suspected terrorists. A Terrorist Threat Intelligence Center was created so that all the government's information on possible terrorist activities could be shared at federal, state, and local levels. A daily Homeland Security Advisory System was set up to alert the public about the level of potential terrorist activities—low (green), guarded (blue), elevated (yellow), high (orange), and severe (red). And funding was provided to states and communities to improve their homeland security efforts and support the development of medical treatments for biological threats.

Organization. The Department of Homeland Security has four operating divisions. Many agencies within these divisions were formerly part of other U.S. executive departments.

Border and Transportation Security includes the U.S. Customs Service; the Immigration and Naturalization Service and Border Patrol; the Transportation Security Administration; the Federal Protective Service; the U.S. Coast Guard; and the port operations of the Animal and Plant Health Inspection Service. **Emergency Preparedness and Response** has taken on the duties of the Federal Emergency Management Agency (FEMA), formerly an independent agency. **Chemical, Biological, Radiological, and Nuclear Countermeasures** focuses on protection in the fields of science and technology. **Information Analysis and Infrastructure Protection** identifies and evaluates current threats to the homeland. The Departent of Homeland Security also administers U.S. Secret Service activities. It enlists the cooperation of agenices that gather foreign and domestic intelligence, namely the Central Intelligence Agency (CIA) and the Federal Bureau of Investigation (FBI).

DANIEL GOURÉ
Vice President, The Lexington Institute

Secretaries of Homeland Security		
Name	Took Office	Under President
Tom Ridge	2003	G. W. Bush

ANTHROPOLOGY

Anthropology is the study of humans and their ways of life. The word "anthropology" comes from two Greek words: *anthropos* ("human being") and *logos* ("study"). The people who work in this field are called anthropologists.

Anthropology emerged as a science in the mid-1800's as Western scholars became interested in the peoples encountered by explorers and missionaries. At that time most anthropologists studied isolated, non-Western cultures. Today anthropologists study people

all over the world, in many different settings.

Other fields, such as economics, sociology, and psychology, also involve the study of humans. What makes anthropology different is its goals and approaches. Anthropology's goal is to develop a broad and comprehensive understanding of what it means to be human. To gain this understanding, anthropologists use a holistic approach, which means they study all aspects of human beings—biological and social. It also means they focus on human societies as whole systems composed of interacting parts. An economist might be interested in how societies produce and exchange goods; a sociologist in how humans interact with others in their society; a psychologist in how humans think and feel. Anthropologists study all these aspects of social life and their interrelationship.

To discover what it means to be human, anthropologists look for what makes all humans similar as well as what makes them unique. To do so, they use a comparative approach, studying all societies, past and present. Some anthropologists compare humans to their close animal relatives to reveal what is uniquely human. One significant difference between humans and other animals is that humans develop complex systems of meaning known as culture. Culture is the entire way of life that a group of people learns—everything it has, makes, thinks, believes, and passes on to children. Culture includes knowledge, beliefs, art, morals, law, custom, and all other habits and abilities that members of the group acquire.

Anthropologists also compare human groups to determine what makes them different, both biologically and culturally. Understanding why humans differ is essential for developing an appreciation of human diversity. It helps overcome prejudices that many people may have about those who look and behave differently than they do.

Anthropologists study the similarities and differences between peoples and groups, including methods of obtaining food. *Top:* An Indonesian farmer cultivates rice. *Center:* Inuit hunters capture a ring seal. *Right:* An American woman buys produce in a supermarket.

Because anthropology seeks to understand humans fully, it is divided into four main subfields: biological anthropology, cultural anthropology, archaeology, and linguistic anthropology. Most anthropologists have broad training in each of these areas but specialize in one.

Many anthropologists, regardless of subfield, use their knowledge to develop practical solutions to social problems. They are called applied anthropologists. They often work for governments or private agencies, helping officials understand the impact of proposed programs or development projects on a culture. They may also analyze how to best introduce a program into a particular cultural setting. For instance, applied anthropologists have advised physicians on the most effective ways to introduce new AIDS medications in Africa. Others have helped governments identify their country's prehistoric sites so they can be preserved before development projects begin.

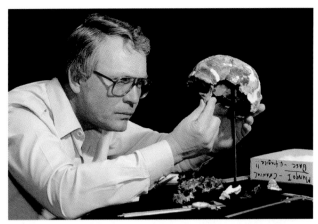

A biological anthropologist reconstructs an ancient human skull. Biological anthropology focuses on humans as physical creatures.

▶ BIOLOGICAL ANTHROPOLOGY

Biological, or physical, anthropologists focus on humans as physical creatures. They study human biological evolution and variation, past and present.

Paleoanthropologists are one type of biological anthropologist. They study the fossil remains of ancient peoples to learn about human beginnings. They study the bones, teeth, and sometimes the DNA of human ancestors as old as several millions of years. They also reconstruct the environments of early humans to understand why humans evolved and why they look the way they do.

Because humans are closely related to animals known as primates, a group including monkeys and apes, some biological anthropologists study them for clues about the origins and evolution of early humans. These anthropologists are called primatologists.

Most biological anthropologists investigate how and why populations of living people differ in their biological makeup. They carry out human variation studies, measuring and comparing physical characteristics such as skin color, blood type, and genetic composition to understand how human populations have adapted to a range of environments. They study how the forces of evolution act on human populations to change them over time. Today, studies of human biological differences help answer questions such as why certain diseases afflict some populations more than others or how urban noise levels can impair children's development.

▶ CULTURAL ANTHROPOLOGY

Cultural anthropologists study how people live throughout the world, focusing on their culture. This area of anthropology has two main goals: (1) to describe all cultures and (2) to explain their similarities and differences.

Cultural anthropologists learn about a culture by immersing themselves in it. This is called doing fieldwork. They learn the language of the people they study. They observe, and participate in, all aspects of a group's cultural life to get firsthand knowledge of it. They return from their fieldwork to write an **ethnography**, a description and explanation of a culture.

Traditionally, cultural anthropologists traveled alone to distant places to study a group's way of life. Today many anthropologists work in teams, studying people living in urban centers and in complex societies.

Because cultural anthropologists are interested in broad and holistic knowledge about humans, they concentrate on many different aspects of people's lives, including how they make a living and spend their earnings, how they educate their children, how they choose marriage partners and organize themselves

A cultural anthropologist takes notes as she watches a tribal woman weaving cloth. Cultural anthropologists study the different cultures of people throughout the world.

an artifact. (A spectrometer is a device that measures radiation wavelength emissions from an object.) Archaeologists want to understand how early humans adapted to their environments and how they organized their societies to survive.

Archaeologists also help us understand how cultures have changed over centuries. By studying the past, they discover long-range trends. For example, they have traced the development of Mexico's political systems from those based on small family groups to powerful states. They have discovered how writing systems developed in the Middle East from earlier uses of pictures to communicate ideas.

into families, how they protect themselves and make decisions about leadership, what they think about their environment, what they believe about God and other supernatural beings, and what kind of music and art they produce.

Since it is very difficult to know everything about a culture, especially the complex ones anthropologists tend to study today, cultural anthropologists often specialize in particular areas of interest. A medical anthropologist might focus on how different ideas about the body affect people's responses to illness. An urban anthropologist might study why some people are drawn to cities and how this movement affects their religious beliefs or the size of their families.

▶ ARCHAEOLOGY

Archaeologists are anthropologists who focus on ancient human societies. By digging up and examining the remains of extinct societies, they help shed light on the human cultural past. Like cultural anthropologists, archaeologists add to our understanding of what it means to be human and of cultural similarities and differences.

Archaeologists use tools as simple as dental picks and shovels to carefully uncover the skeletal remains of ancient people, the objects they made, and the remains of their environment. They also use sophisticated technology to do their work: for example, they might rely on radar to locate ancient sites and spectrometers to analyze the age of

▶ LINGUISTIC ANTHROPOLOGY

Linguistics is the study of language. Linguistic anthropology focuses on the relationship of language to culture. Although it was once believed that humans were the only ani-

Archaeologists dig up and examine remains of ancient societies. By shedding light on our cultural past, they add to our understanding of what it means to be human.

316

mals with language, this idea has recently been challenged. Some studies show that chimpanzees and gorillas can learn words and can be taught to communicate with them, even if they do not actually speak these words but convey them with symbols. Regardless of whether humans are unique in their capacity for language, there is no doubt that language has been important to the development of human societies. Language is the primary means by which culture is transmitted.

Linguistic anthropology developed in the 1800's because the languages of the people many anthropologists studied were dying out. Anthropologists developed an international system of symbols (International Phonetic Alphabet) to represent the sounds of these languages, thereby preserving them.

Linguistic anthropologists study the characteristics and structure—or grammar—of existing languages. They compare the sounds, words, sentence structures, and meanings of languages to understand how different people think and view the world. For example, some languages have no past, present, or future tenses, which reflects and affects a people's understanding of time. One important finding of linguistic anthropology is that all languages are complex and allow for complicated meanings to be conveyed.

Historical linguists study the relationships among different languages to determine how languages have changed over time. By comparing different languages, they can trace how today's languages branched off from earlier languages. This splitting occurred at different times as groups of people moved away from one another and developed other habits. By looking at the similarities and differences among languages like these, historical linguists can uncover relationships that may have once existed between various groups.

▶ HISTORY OF ANTHROPOLOGY

Anthropology took shape in the late 1800's in Europe and the United States. Until then, few individuals had made a serious study of different peoples. European explorers had long brought back stories about the people of Africa, Asia, and the Pacific islands, who differed in many ways from people in the Western world. Many Westerners considered these people primitive and inferior and thought they should become more like Westerners. By the late 1800's, some people began to hold different ideas. They thought it was important

Renowned anthropologist Margaret Mead did much of her fieldwork in the early 1900's. Her ethnographies of Pacific Islanders are still read today.

to understand other ways of life, not to condemn them. From such ideas grew the field of anthropology.

Early anthropologists wanted to compare all known societies to understand their differences; they were particularly interested in learning why some societies were relatively simple and others complex. They thought that perhaps societies adapt and evolve to survive just as animals do. Their way of thinking came to be known as **social evolutionism**.

These anthropologists also thought they could learn about different cultures from the reports brought back by missionaries and colonizers. Soon, however, it became clear that such reports were biased. The social evolutionists were criticized for using faulty information. One flaw in their thinking was the belief that the culture and the race of a people were linked. They thought that darker skinned people developed simple cultures because they were incapable of developing complex ones. When it became apparent that this was not the case, the ideas of social evolutionists were widely viewed as invalid.

Franz Boas was one of the most important critics of social evolutionism. He was a German-born scholar who traveled to the United States in the early 1900's to study Native Americans. Boas established almost all of anthropology's goals and approaches. He showed the importance of gaining firsthand knowledge of a culture through extensive fieldwork. He was also the first to define the four subfields of anthropology.

Boas was among the leading anthropologists to show that culture and race are not linked. Native Americans, he argued, did not develop inferior cultures. They were only thought inferior by many Europeans because of ethnocentrism (judging others according to one's own cultural ideas and values). Boas emphasized the importance of understanding another culture on its own terms, rather than simply judging it as inferior because it is different. This approach came to be known as **cultural relativism**.

Boas was concerned that Native American cultures were quickly vanishing. He urged other anthropologists to collect information about them so that their customs and languages could become part of the record of human diversity. Out of this desire to preserve the fast-disappearing languages of Native Americans emerged the subfield of linguistic anthropology.

Boas trained many students in his methods of anthropology. One, Margaret Mead, became one of the best-known anthropologists in history. Although Mead did much of her fieldwork in the early 1900's, her ethnographies of Pacific Islanders are still widely read today.

Some anthropologists living in Europe during the early 1900's also questioned social evolutionary views. One of these, Bronislaw Malinowski, believed as Boas did in the need to conduct long-term fieldwork to understand a culture. The Polish-born Malinowski spent

years studying the people of the Trobriand Islands in the South Pacific. He was interested in how the various parts of Trobriand society—its economic, political, and social systems—functioned together to help these people survive. This approach is called **functionalism**. Malinowski inspired many other anthropologists to use this approach to study how cultures work.

Since anthropology's beginnings, many new approaches to understanding human diversity have developed. Some anthropologists have focused on how societies are structured, while others have focused on how humans use symbols to create meaning. Still others are interested in how humans adapt to their physical surroundings. Regardless of the particular emphasis, anthropologists continue to seek ways to understand the full range of human societies. Today they propose new concepts and approaches to keep pace with an ever-changing world.

▶ **ANTHROPOLOGY TODAY**

The world is a very different place today than it was when anthropology first developed more than 100 years ago. Today's world is an interdependent one—few human groups remain isolated. Decisions about oil production in the Middle East, for example, can have a major impact on people living in Australia, Asia, or the United States. We live in a truly global community—people everywhere are connected through travel and vast communications networks.

Some scholars think such connections will make humans more and more alike in their

As communities become more culturally diverse, the work of anthropologists to help us understand and appreciate cultural differences has become ever more important.

Kurdish refugees carry their belongings across the Iran-Iraq border. The study of such population movements is a growing area of interest for anthropologists.

ideas and behavior. But anthropologists have shown that people make very different uses of the products and information that circulate globally, interpreting them within the beliefs and values of their own traditions.

The work of anthropologists has become especially important in today's changing world. Understanding and appreciating human diversity is essential for developing ideas and policies that can help human groups coexist peacefully.

One important change that has occurred due to globalization is that cultural ideas and practices may no longer be tied to specific places or shared by all people in those places. This weakening of the tie between culture and place is called **deterritorialization**. It has required many anthropologists to rethink traditional approaches, including where and how they do their research. Until recently, most anthropologists traveled to one place to study a people's culture, but now it might be necessary for them to do fieldwork in several locations. For example, an anthropologist studying the Hmong would have once just traveled to Laos in Southeast Asia. Today, to understand Hmong culture fully, an anthropologist would also have to travel to California and Minnesota, where more than 100,000 contemporary Hmong live.

The separation of ideas and people from traditional locations has led many anthropologists to study **hybridity**, new forms of culture that develop along borders between groups (for example, the boundary between ethnic neighborhoods in urban centers).

The movement of populations is another growing area of interest. Many recent studies focus on immigrants, exiles, and refugees as they travel across traditional boundaries and come to live in new places.

A number of new issues are raised by today's population movements. People and groups are less likely than those in the past to settle in the first place to which they move. This can make it difficult to develop the shared group identity associated with culture. But this situation also produces opportunities for the creation of new cultural ideas and practices, providing anthropologists with many new places to undertake their study of what it means to be human.

▶ CAREERS IN ANTHROPOLOGY

Although most anthropologists work at colleges and universities, where they teach and conduct research, anthropologists today may also be employed in almost any area where knowledge of human behavior can help institutions accomplish their goals. Archaeologists and cultural anthropologists work for museums and government agencies. Biological and cultural anthropologists have found employment in medical settings and mental health facilities, and with population councils and urban planning groups. Some anthropologists work as researchers for marketing firms and other companies doing business worldwide.

FRANCES E. MASCIA-LEES
Sarah Lawrence College

319

PHOTOGRAPHY

When most people think of photography, they think of using a camera to "take a picture." People around the world will take more than 10,000 pictures in the time it takes you to read this sentence, and several hundred million on this day alone. Photography is so much a part of daily life that we can forget how much it has changed the world.

The book you are now reading would have been impossible without photography—and

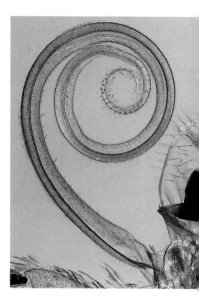

not just because of the photos used in the articles. Books, magazines, and just about everything in print today—words as well as pictures—are printed by photographic processes. If you are reading articles online, the same holds true. The microchips that make your computer work have their tiny circuits imprinted by a kind of photography.

Photography enables us to record our lives, as well as the events that shape history. It lets us see things we cannot normally see, freezing a baseball in midair or revealing tiny molecules that can be viewed only through a microscope. Special types of photography let physicians detect disease and injuries sooner and treat them better. Cameras carried by spacecraft have photographed all the planets, and some of these are now going beyond our solar system.

Skilled and imaginative photographers have made photography an art form. The beautiful pictures they take increase our appreciation and understanding of the world. Photographs documenting social problems and human suffering have moved people to take action and governments to change laws.

Today photography can be done almost in real time—people using digital cameras can see their pictures about as fast as they can take them. News photographers can instantly transmit photos from the scene of breaking

film or a digital imager, though, the cameras are otherwise very similar.

When you take a picture, light reflected from your subject enters the camera through the lens, which focuses it on the film or on the digital imager. If you use film, the light rays form a latent (not visible) image of the subject on the film. The film has now been **exposed**, but to make the latent image visible, the film must be **developed**, or treated with chemicals. In digital recording, the focused light strikes a grid of tiny picture elements, or

Ever since the first photograph was taken more than 150 years ago, photography has changed the way we see the world. *From far left:* Photographs taken by the Hubble Space Telescope provide glimpses of the universe, such as these star-forming towers of gas in the Eagle Nebula. This picture of a photojournalist is famous for its artful composition. Photomicrography combines a camera with a microscope to take pictures of objects—such as this butterfly proboscis—too small to be seen with the naked eye. Digital photographs can be enhanced using light painting and other techniques. Stop-motion photography is especially useful for sports photography.

news. A person sitting at a home computer can send a digital image halfway around the world in seconds.

▶ HOW PHOTOGRAPHS ARE MADE

The word "photography" comes from two Greek words meaning "writing" and "light," and photography is much like making a painting or drawing with light. To take a photograph, you need only three things: light, a camera, and a recording medium. For the first 150 years of photography, the recording medium was film—transparent plastic coated with crystals of a light-sensitive silver compound. In more and more cameras today, the recording medium is an electronic sensor or "imager" that converts the light that strikes it into digital information that can be stored in computer memory. Whether a camera uses

pixels. Each pixel records the brightness and color of the light that strikes it. Circuits in the camera then process the information into a bundle of organized information (an **image file**) that can later be read by a computer and reassembled into a picture.

▶ PHOTOGRAPHIC EQUIPMENT

The camera and the recording medium are the basic tools of photography. Other important equipment includes interchangeable lenses, lights, flash units, and filters.

The Camera

All cameras, whether simple or complex, have five basic parts—the body, lens, shutter, film holder (in a digital camera, this is the imager), and viewfinder. More complex cameras may have special features as well.

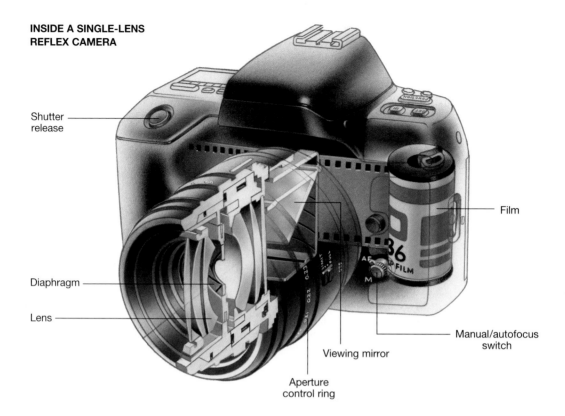

Shutter release

Diaphragm

Lens

Aperture control ring

Viewing mirror

Film

Manual/autofocus switch

The **body** of a camera is a lightproof framework, or box. It keeps out all light except what passes through the lens.

The **lens**—one or more pieces of glass or plastic with curved surfaces—is somewhat like a small magnifying glass. The lens concentrates the light entering the camera to make a sharp image of the photographed object on the film. All lenses must be **focused** so that the subject is as clear as possible.

The simplest cameras have a **fixed-focus** lens. This means the focus was set at one distance when the camera was made and cannot be changed. They are set to focus on objects beyond about 5 feet (1.5 meters).

With a more complex camera, the focus can be changed. Cameras that let you do this yourself—usually by turning a ring on the lens—are called **manual-focus** cameras. Those that change the focus automatically are called **autofocus** cameras. Some cameras are a combination of both.

The **shutter** is a mechanical device behind the lens that opens and closes to admit light. The photographer operates the shutter by pressing the shutter release, a button on the camera. In many cameras you can change the shutter speed. In dim light, a slower speed is preferable. This keeps the shutter open longer so that more light enters the camera. In bright sunlight, the shutter can be set at a faster speed, since there is plenty of light to produce an image on the film. A fast shutter speed lets you take pictures of subjects without blurring, even if they are moving.

When you press the shutter release on some digital cameras, the camera turns the

Profiles: *A Dozen Great Photographers*

There are many photographers who, over the past 150 years, have raised photography to an art form. The following pages feature twelve of them. If you are interested in seeing the works of more great photographers, there are countless books and Web sites available, and many museums have photo collections.

digital imager on and off. This works much like the shutter on a film camera. Some digital cameras use mechanical shutters, however.

Very simple cameras have only one shutter speed. More complex and expensive cameras have many shutter speeds, ranging from 30 seconds to 1/8,000 of a second or even faster. Some cameras also have a setting that keeps the shutter open for long exposures.

Most cameras have a diaphragm, which is used to make the **aperture**, or lens opening, larger or smaller to admit more or less light. Apertures are measured in f-numbers. The lower f-numbers, such as f/1.4 and f/2, are wide openings. These transmit more light to the film. The higher f-numbers, such as f/11 and f/16, are small lens openings. They transmit less light to the film.

The diaphragm also controls a photograph's depth of field. This is the amount of space in front of and behind the subject that is in focus. Higher f-stops increase the depth of field, and lower f-stops decrease it.

Film cameras include **film holders** to keep the film flat so that the image can be accurately focused. With small cameras, the film holder is built into the back of the camera. You load the film into the holder and close the camera. After taking a photograph, you advance the film so that the next blank spot on the roll (called a frame) is in place for the next picture. Most popular film cameras use cartridges of film that produce from 12 to 36 pictures and have frame counters to keep track of exposed pictures.

In digital cameras, the imager takes the place of the film holder. You do not have to load or advance film. But you will still have to store and keep track of the pictures you have taken, just as with a film camera. When you take a digital picture, the camera must move the image file to another place in the camera so you can take another picture. Some cameras have built-in memory, but that limits the number of pictures you can take—if you use all the memory, you have to either download the pictures to a computer or erase some of them. So most digital cameras instead store images on a memory card, which uses the same kind of memory chips a computer uses. These are about the size of postage stamps and are inserted into a side of the camera. The camera will indicate how many photos are stored on the card and how many more photos you can take before the card is filled up.

Every camera has a **viewfinder**—usually a small plastic or glass window—that shows the scene you are focusing on. Viewfinders in better cameras may also include lenses or reflecting prisms to provide a more accurate view of the picture being taken.

GREAT PHOTOGRAPHERS

A Pioneer of the Art:
Julia Margaret Cameron
(1815–79)

When Julia Margaret Cameron was 48 years old, her two daughters gave her a camera. That may not sound unusual, but the year was 1863, when few people knew how to take photos. Cameron, born in Calcutta, India, learned the difficult wet plate process then used to make photographs and went on to become one of the greatest portrait photographers. Even today, photographers admire her dramatic use of lighting, which was considered ahead of its time, and her use of selective focus—a way of making only part of a picture sharp.

Julia Margaret Cameron, self-portrait.

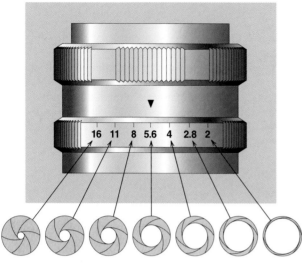

The aperture, or lens opening, is measured in f-numbers. The lower the f-number, the larger the aperture. Larger apertures transmit more light to the film.

All but the simplest cameras include electronic circuits that measure the amount of light coming from the subject. In many cameras the proper exposure settings are shown in the viewfinder as the user adjusts the shutter speed and f-stop. This is called manual exposure setting. Some cameras set the exposure automatically, which is called autoexposure.

Film Cameras. Film cameras range from tiny pocket-sized units to very large cameras used primarily in professional studios.

The simplest cameras are called **one-time-use cameras**, or OTUC's. Also known as disposable cameras, these are the small cardboard and plastic cameras that are taken back to a store to get developed. An OTUC has a fixed-focus lens and a single exposure setting. You can get OTUC's with or without built-in flash. Some are designed for specific uses, such as taking black-and-white or underwater photography.

The **point-and-shoot** camera is more complex but is very popular because of its ease of use. It has an autofocus lens and different shutter speeds and lens openings that are set automatically, although some allow the user to make small changes in the exposure. This camera has a built-in flash that will fire when needed, unless it is turned off. It automatically loads the film, advances it to the next frame, and rewinds it when you finish the roll. Because you cannot change the lens, many point-and-shoot cameras have zoom lenses, which let you change the view from wide-angle to telephoto. Most point-and-shoot cameras use 35mm film, but some types use Advanced Photo System (APS) film, which comes in a small cartridge that is easier to load.

Instant cameras produce a fully developed print shortly after the picture is snapped. This is possible because the film includes the developing chemicals. After an image is exposed, the film comes in contact with the developers and is automatically processed. Instant cameras are less popular now that digital cameras allow pictures to be viewed right away.

Cameras that can be focused and use different lens openings and shutter speeds are called **adjustable** cameras. Most of these measure the light and indicate the correct lens opening and shutter speed or set them automatically. Today the most widely used adjustable camera is the single-lens reflex.

The **single-lens reflex** (SLR) is the most popular type of camera for serious photography, whether for film or digital capture. In the SLR camera, a mirror behind the lens reflects the image upward through a prism and onto a viewing screen. You can then see your picture and focus it. When you shoot the picture, the mirror automatically swings up out of the light path. The image strikes the film or imager as the shutter opens, and the exposure is made.

Most SLR's now use both autoexposure and autofocus, but better models also allow you to focus manually and make your own exposure settings. Many use interchangeable lenses, have built-in electronic flash, and take pictures on 35mm (millimeter) film.

Some SLR's use a type of roll film known as 120/220. This is larger than 35mm film, and the photos taken with it can show finer detail. These cameras are usually larger than 35mm SLR's, so they are often used with tripods. (A tripod is a three-legged stand that holds the camera steady and prevents blurring of the image.)

View cameras are another type of adjustable camera. They are most common in professional studios, but they are also used outdoors for photographing landscapes and architecture. They are much larger than SLR's and use individual sheets of film (usually 4 by 5 inches, but sometimes larger). They are used mostly by photographers who make pictures of products for advertising or other types of photography that require precise control of the image.

Many roll-film SLR's, as well as view cameras, have interchangeable film backs that can be switched with digital backs. This way, a photographer can shoot both film and digital versions of a subject.

Digital Cameras. Most digital cameras for amateurs are the point-and-shoot type. They focus automatically, set the lens opening and shutter speed automatically, and fire the flash when needed. Digital cameras have various other kinds of adjustments, but a digital point-and-shoot can set these automatically, too.

A digital point-and-shoot camera usually has an LCD monitor screen, which is like a small computer screen on the back of the camera. You can compose a picture using this screen—for this reason some digital cameras have no viewfinder—as well as view pictures you have already taken. Digital point-and-shoot cameras use memory cards to store pictures. The most popular are the Compact Flash (CF) and the Secure Digital (SD) types. Because digital pictures are electronic files, memory cards are not measured in frames but in megabytes, as in computer memory (1 megabyte equals about 1 million bytes). Memory cards come in sizes from 8 megabytes to 1 gigabyte (1 gigabyte equals 1,000 megabytes), and even larger ones are becoming available.

Most digital cameras for professional use are based on 35mm SLR's. These cameras use interchangeable lenses and allow a wide range of adjustments. They can take pictures that are sharper and clearer than digital point-and-shoot cameras and can often take pictures in a fast burst—several in less than a second. Digital SLR's are now widely used by news and nature photographers, among many others.

A new type of digital camera, the Electronic Viewfinder (EVF), works much like a SLR. However, the viewfinder eyepiece is really a tiny monitor. This eliminates the need for expensive and complex optical parts such as the mirror and prism.

GREAT PHOTOGRAPHERS

Photography for Art's Sake:
Alfred Stieglitz
(1864–1946)

If Alfred Stieglitz had never taken a single photograph, he would still be one of the most important figures in photography. He founded the magazine *Camera Work*, which was one of the first dedicated to photography, and had a gallery called 291 that showed photographs as art—something that had never been done before. But Stieglitz, born in Hoboken, New Jersey, was also a superb photographer. His 1907 picture called *The Steerage*, of European immigrants aboard a ship, is considered one of the greatest photographs ever taken. He was married to the artist Georgia O'Keeffe, who is the subject of many of his photographs.

The Steerage, **taken in 1907 by Alfred Stieglitz, shows immigrants on the lower decks of an ocean liner.**

Recording Media

Film. There are three main types of photographic film for general use: Black-and-white negative film for black-and-white photographs (usually prints), color negative film for color prints, and color reversal film (usually called color slide film) for color slides or transparencies.

All film has a plastic base thinly coated with crystals of a silver-bromide compound. The crystals are mixed in a transparent gelatin called an emulsion. Black-and-white film usually has just one layer of emulsion. Color film has three (or more) layers. Each is sensitive to, or records, one of the three primary colors of light—blue, green, and red.

When choosing general-use film, three factors must be considered—speed, graininess, and contrast. Film speed refers to a film's sensitivity to light, which can vary. Graininess is the degree of visibility of the silver crystals, or grains, in the photographic image. Graininess is especially noticeable when a photograph is enlarged. Contrast is the degree of difference between the light and dark areas of the subject. Generally, the faster the film, the grainier the photograph will be and the less contrast it will have. Photographs with too much contrast or too much grain lack fine detail.

Film speed is measured on a scale called the ISO film-speed index (for International Organization for Standards). Each film is given an ISO number that indicates its speed. Fast films have high numbers, and slow films have low numbers. The faster the film is, the more sensitive it is to light. Films for general purposes range from ISO 25 to ISO 3200. Films between ISO 200 and ISO 400 are the most commonly used all-purpose and outdoor films, but there are slower and faster special-purpose films.

RECORDING MEDIA: FILM AND DIGITAL

In film photography, the light entering the camera forms a latent image of the subject on the film. This image becomes visible after the film is developed. In digital photography, the light entering the camera strikes a grid containing many tiny picture elements (pixels). Each pixel records the brightness and color of the light that strikes it. The camera then turns this information into an image file that can be read by a computer and reassembled into a picture.

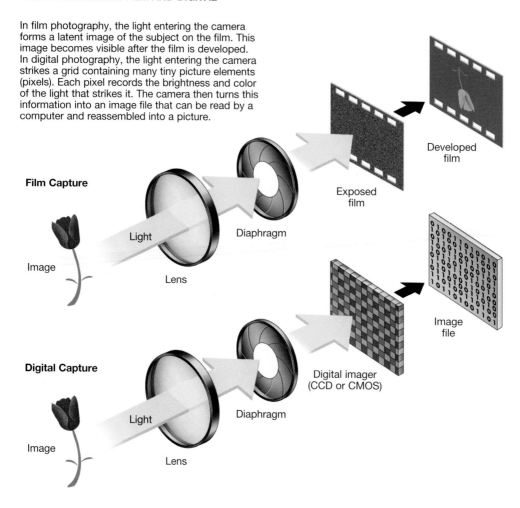

Most digital cameras include LCD monitor screens, which are like tiny computer screens. These are used to compose pictures or to view those already taken.

Digital Imagers. Digital cameras do not use film but a digital imager—either a charge-coupled device (CCD) or a complementary metal-oxide semiconductor (CMOS). Both devices have a chip containing millions of tiny receptors (pixels) that record the color and intensity of the light falling on them. The more pixels an imager contains, the sharper and finer grained the resulting picture will be. (That is, it has a higher resolution.) Digital camera imagers are rated by the maximum number of pixels they can use. If a camera can take a picture made up of 1,600 by 1,200 pixels, for example, that means it has a resolution of 1,920,000 pixels (just multiply 1,600 by 1,200). This would be called a 1.9 megapixel camera. A 2,560 by 1,920 imager works out to 4,915,200 pixels, or about 4.9 megapixels.

A digital camera can take pictures at different quality levels, not just the highest available. For instance, a typical 3.2 megapixel camera can take pictures at the full 3.2 megapixels or at 2 megapixels, 1 megapixel, or at 640 by 480 pixels. What resolution should you use? A simple rule is to divide the resolution measurements by 200. This will tell you how big a print you can make, in inches, with full photographic quality. For example, if you take a picture at 1,600 by 1,200 pixels, you should be able to make an inkjet print of about 8 by 6 inches that looks as good as one you took with film. (Going a little bigger might give prints some grain and duller colors.) If you are just making a picture to e-mail, 640 by 480 is fine.

GREAT PHOTOGRAPHERS

New Art in the Jazz Age:
Man Ray
(1890–1976)

Emmanuel Radnitsky was born in Philadelphia, Pennsylvania, and became known as Man Ray, a member of the avant-garde in Paris during the 1920's and 1930's ("avant-garde" refers to artists who are experimenting with new forms). Man Ray produced a type of shadow photograph, without a camera, by placing various objects on photo printing paper and exposing it to light. He also used many ideas from modern art movements in his photography, films, paintings, and sculpture.

Man Ray retouches a fashion photograph.

Wide-Angle Lens

Using different lenses, photographers can change focus and picture composition. *Left:* A wide-angle lens shows a large area and gives a sense of depth. *Below:* A normal lens shows a scene the way the eye sees it. *Below left:* A telephoto lens focuses on a particular part of the scene and enlarges it. *Bottom:* A macro lens allows close focusing to show tiny details.

Normal Lens

Telephoto Lens

Macro Lens

Another setting on digital cameras is compression. This is a method of squeezing the information in a digital file so it takes up less memory. When the computer opens the picture, it uncompresses it, but some information may be lost. For the very best pictures, you should use as little compression as possible. But if you only want to e-mail pictures or make small prints, you can use more compression.

Lenses

For SLR and view cameras, additional lenses are important accessories. These can be used to create images of different sizes and to take pictures of subjects that are far away or very close up.

Lenses come in a number of different focal lengths: normal, short, and long. With 35mm cameras, a normal-length lens—about 50mm—shows what the eye sees when looking at a scene.

Lenses with very short focal lengths are called wide-angle lenses. They take in a very large area but produce a small image of any object in a scene. One of the most interesting wide-angle lenses is the fish-eye lens. An 8mm fish-eye has a 180-degree angle (half circle) of view.

Telephoto lenses—those with long focal lengths—show less of the scene from a given spot. But they focus on a particular part of the scene and enlarge it, the way binoculars or telescopes do. Telephoto lenses are usually used for wildlife and sports photos.

Lenses with focal lengths that can be changed are called zoom lenses. You can get zoom lenses that stay in the telephoto range, such as 70-200mm, or zooms that stay in the wide-angle range, such as 17-28mm. The most popular zooms let you range from wide-angle to telephoto.

Lenses designed to focus very close up are called macro lenses. With these, you can photograph tiny details and small objects. You can also use simple, inexpensive lenses attached to the front of your normal or zoom lens to allow close focusing. These are called close-up lenses.

Lighting, Flashes, and Filters

How can you tell whether the light is bright enough to take a picture? You use an **exposure meter**. This measures the light and provides the proper exposure settings for the type of film you are using. Most cameras have exposure meters built into them. You can also buy a separate, handheld meter.

With an **electronic flash**, you can take pictures even when the other light is not bright enough. Most point-and-shoot cameras, and many OTUC's, have flash units built in. These automatically provide the correct exposure for subjects up to about 20 feet (6 meters) away.

Better cameras such as SLR's can use bigger add-on flash units. These are more powerful and provide more light. Some photographers use several flash units at once for a picture. They may also use continuous lighting (called hot lights), which are like powerful lightbulbs.

Filters are transparent pieces of glass or plastic that are placed over the lens. They change the light that hits the film. When used with black-and-white film, they change the tones of gray. When used with color film, they usually change the actual colors. In some cases, filters improve the light reaching the camera. For example, a polarizing filter gets rid of reflections, so that pictures can be taken through windows. Polarizers can also make a blue sky darker without altering

GREAT PHOTOGRAPHERS

Reverence for the Natural World:
Eliot Porter
(1901–1990)

Eliot Porter was one of the first great nature photographers to use color, and he remains one of the most influential of all time. Born in Winnetka, Illinois, he earned an M.D. from Harvard Medical School in 1929 and spent the next decade teaching science at Harvard and Radcliffe. Porter began taking photographs in his spare time, then quit teaching to become a full-time photographer. He soon became known for his unique style: pictures of plants and animals that focused on rich textures and fine detail, as well as the subject's surroundings. Like Ansel Adams, Porter was also an activist for wilderness preservation.

Fall leaves and pine needles, photographed by Eliot Porter in 1956, form a study in contrast and texture. Porter was a nature photographer for more than 40 years.

Using continuous lighting (hot lights) and a light meter, a photographer and his assistant photograph a vase of flowers in a studio.

other colors. Other filters are used for special effects, such as mist or soft focus.

▶ STORING IMAGES AND MAKING PRINTS

When you finish a roll of film, the next step is developing and printing. If you take the film to the photofinishing counter in the supermarket or drugstore, it is usually sent to a large processing lab, especially if it is black-and-white or slide film. However, some places (minilabs) process color negative film at their own on-site labs, often within an hour.

Photofinishers can also make digital files from your negatives or slides and put them on a CD. This lets you view the images on a

SPECIAL USES OF PHOTOGRAPHY

With special cameras, films, and other equipment, photography has been adapted to many uses in science and industry.

Aerial photography is photography from the air. Aerial photos are useful to mapmakers and surveyors. Archaeologists also use them to locate the boundary lines of ancient fields and long-forgotten cities.

Astrophotography is the photography of objects in space—such as the stars and planets—through a telescope. The space age saw the launching of telescopes aboard exploratory spacecraft. The Hubble Space Telescope, launched in 1990, gathers its images with a digital camera.

Diagnostic imaging is widely used in medicine and science. It includes X-ray photography, which uses invisible electromagnetic waves that can pass through objects that visible light cannot penetrate. X rays are used to indicate where bones are broken and to examine internal organs. They are also used in industry to test and inspect materials and parts. Since the introduction of digital photography, many other types of medical imaging have been developed. These include computerized axial tomography (or CAT scan) and magnetic resonance imaging (MRI). A CAT scan consists of a series of X rays that are interpreted by a computer and shown as cross-sectional slices of the body. An MRI provides a detailed picture of internal tissue and organs via digitally recorded electromagnetic impulses sent through the body.

There is now even a digital camera inside a pill that transmits pictures of a person's intestinal tract to an external digital recorder.

Holography is three-dimensional photography. To create a hologram, part of a laser beam is directed at a subject, and is then reflected to a sensitized photographic plate. The other part of the beam is focused directly on the photographic plate. Together, the two parts of the beam record all the information needed to reproduce a three-dimensional image. Holography may be most familiar as the process used to make 3-D pictures on credit cards.

Infrared photography uses special film that is sensitive to infrared radiation. Infrared rays, which are invisible, have a longer wavelength than visible light, and can penetrate haze that scatters the waves of

Night-vision photograph of a U.S. Army training range

computer or television screen, then e-mail them, post them on your Web site, or use them for greeting cards, school reports, and other printed material. Photofinishers can also send these pictures to a Web site where your family and friends can view them.

If you take pictures with a digital camera, you can download them to a computer and see them almost immediately. To download, you can use a cable supplied with most cameras that connects the camera to the computer; a dock (a little cradle that holds the camera); or a card reader. The card reader is like a small disk drive that can read your camera's memory card. After downloading, you can look at the pictures on the screen and e-mail them.

If you want prints or enlargements of your digital pictures, you can bring your memory card to a photofinisher or you can make them yourself. Fairly inexpensive color inkjet printers can make very good color prints and enlargements.

Using software for desktop publishing, you can put your photos into greeting cards, calendars, and announcements. You may also want to enhance these photos with image-editing software. This process is often called the digital darkroom. (For more information, see the feature on page 338.)

visible light. For this reason, infrared photographs are often much clearer than ordinary photographs. Infrared photography combined with aerial photography can provide detailed information on the type of vegetation growing below. Infrared photography is also used in medicine to inspect damage to veins and healing beneath scabs.

Night-vision photography is a special form of digital photography. A very weak image taken at night or in a dark area is amplified by electronic circuitry so more detail can be seen. This type of photography is used in surveillance, police work, and military operations.

Photomicrography combines a camera with a microscope to take pictures of things too small to be seen with the naked eye. These pictures, called photomicrographs, are very useful to scientists and engineers. They enable them to study the cells of living tissue, or the crystal structure of a piece of metal, or parts of ancient plants discovered in a thin slice of coal.

Satellite photography is photography from satellites. This is used for mapping, weather forecasting, and military intelligence. Military specialists study these to learn about airfields, fortifications, missile bases, and other military installations.

Spectrography combines a camera with a spectroscope, an instrument that breaks up light into its different wavelengths. Using spectrography, scientists can analyze the light emitted by the stars and the sun. Spectrographs of the planets reveal which gases are present in their atmospheres. Spectrographs can be used to analyze materials such as metal alloys.

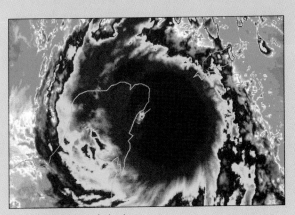
Satellite image of a hurricane

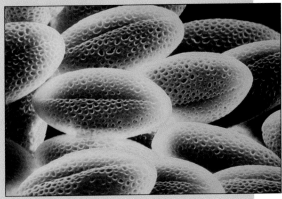
Photomicrograph of pollen

An American Classic:
Ansel Adams
(1902–84)

Ask nearly any American to name a famous photographer and the answer is likely to be Ansel Adams. Adams, born in San Francisco, California, was noted for his stunning black-and-white landscapes of the American West (especially the national parks), as well as his work for environmental protection of these areas. While his pictures are considered fairly traditional, they also show the influence of modern art, such as the use of abstraction (reducing a picture to basic forms). He was also a scientific thinker, and devised the Zone System, a method for exposing and developing film to get the best tonal range (areas from very light to very dark) in photos.

Ansel Adams' spectacular images of the American West are familiar to millions. This famous photo of the Snake River was taken in 1942 at Grand Teton National Park in Wyoming.

▶ **CAREERS IN PHOTOGRAPHY**

At one time, most professional photographers were either self-taught or learned the trade as apprentices. Today, studying photography at a college or university is the best way to learn the profession. Those who just want to learn some of the basics—or perhaps concentrate on a specific topic in photography—can take individual courses in many colleges, universities, and some high schools. Taking one or two of these courses can also be a good way to decide if you want to pursue photography as a career.

Competition is strong for jobs in this field. Most professional photographers specialize in one or two kinds of pictures, such as advertising work, weddings and portraits, medical photography, nature photography, photomicrography, or photojournalism.

Stock photographers provide pictures to agencies, called stock agencies, which provide pictures to magazines and advertisers on a fee basis. The photographer usually shares a percentage of the fee. Stock photographers often specialize in specific areas.

▶ **HISTORY OF PHOTOGRAPHY**

A forerunner of the camera, the **camera obscura**, was invented hundreds of years before photography. It was actually a dark room with a tiny hole in one wall. Light came through the hole, producing an image on the opposite wall of the subject outside the hole.

For about 500 years, the camera obscura was used primarily for watching solar eclipses. Then artists and mapmakers realized it could be useful to them. As a result, portable versions were developed.

In time, the camera obscura was reduced to a small box much like a modern camera. A lens was placed in the hole where the light entered to help concentrate the light rays. There was also a diaphragm to control the amount of light coming in. The back of the box was a translucent screen. (Something translucent lets light pass through, but we cannot see detail through it.) A sheet of paper could be placed over the screen and the image traced on the paper. Artists such as Jan Vermeer used the camera obscura to make more realistic paintings.

In 1727, a German doctor, Johann Schulze, made the discovery that finally led to film. Schulze found that sunlight would blacken chalk that had been treated with a solution of silver nitrate. Modern photography is based on Schulze's discovery that light affects certain silver compounds.

The first successful photograph was made by a French inventor, Joseph Nicéphore Niepce, in 1826. He succeeded in capturing an image that did not immediately fade when light struck it. He placed the exposed metal plate (coated with an asphalt compound) in a solution that brought out the picture. The solution also washed away all the compound that had not yet been exposed to light. In other words, he fixed the picture. In 1829, Niepce became a partner of Louis Daguerre, a French theatrical designer. Before they had finished improving a developing process, Niepce died. Daguerre continued work on the process. In 1839, he revealed what became the first widely successful system of photography. His pictures were called daguerreotypes. Each was unique. There was no negative, and no prints could be made.

At about the same time, in England, William Henry Fox Talbot invented the first practical process that produced a negative from which prints could be made. This process, called calotype, began with a negative image on paper. It was then printed on another sensitized piece of paper to make a positive print.

Paper negatives had a drawback, however. The natural grain of the paper made the details of the picture somewhat unclear. To avoid this, people began experimenting with glass plates. Unfortunately, photographic chemicals would not stay on the glass. In 1847, Abel Niepce de Saint-Victor, the nephew of Joseph Niepce, tried something new. He coated a glass plate with albumen (the white of an egg). This sticky coating held the chemical fast.

In 1851, Frederick Scott Archer, an English chemist, introduced the wet collodion process. This process uses a syrupy, transparent liquid called collodion to hold the silver compounds on glass. The response of collodion plates to light was much faster than in other processes. But the photographer still had to coat the glass plate

This grainy view from an upstairs window is the world's first successful photograph. It was taken in 1826 by French inventor Joseph Nicéphore Niepce.

GREAT PHOTOGRAPHERS

The Photojournalist:
Margaret Bourke-White
(1904–71)

Margaret Bourke-White, a pioneer in photojournalism, documented many important events.

Margaret Bourke-White, born in New York City, was a pioneer in photojournalism. The first photographer for *Fortune* magazine and a staff photographer for *Life* magazine, she was also the first Western photojournalist allowed into the Soviet Union. Bourke-White documented the crushing poverty of rural America during the Great Depression of the 1930's in her book *You Have Seen Their Faces.* During World War II she became one of the first female photojournalists allowed in combat zones and one of the first to photograph the Nazi death camps.

TAKING GOOD PHOTOGRAPHS

Photography is a favorite pastime because nearly everyone knows how to take a picture. But following some simple rules can greatly improve your photographs.

The most important thing to remember is that no camera can "take" a picture. Only you can. And you can take excellent pictures with the simplest equipment. The key to good photographs is *seeing*.

Using Simple Cameras

One of the easiest ways to learn the basics of photography is to use a disposable one-time-use camera, or OTUC. Since an OTUC has no settings to figure out, you can concentrate completely on composing your picture. Choose an OTUC with a built-in flash.

Taking outdoor pictures on bright days is a good starting point. Look through the viewfinder and see what happens to the picture in the frame if you aim the camera a little differently. Move closer to or farther from your subject. (Do not get too close or the picture will not be sharp.) Try crouching down to take a picture looking up. Or stand on a chair to take a picture looking down. The idea is to frame a picture, not just aim the camera. When you see a picture you want to take, hold the camera steady and press the shutter button. To take another picture, advance the film to bring another frame into position.

Using Point-and-Shoot Cameras (Film or Digital)

Point-and-shoot cameras let you take pictures in more kinds of light than an OTUC and at many different distances. Autofocus point-and-shoot cameras let you shoot close to your subject—a couple of feet or less. Move close enough so that you see your subject from the waist or shoulders up. Try closing in on just the face. If your point-and-shoot has a zoom lens, you can get a closer view of your subject without actually moving closer. Try framing and taking pictures at different zoom settings.

Most point-and-shoot cameras let you choose different flash modes. The "flash on" or "fill flash" setting makes the flash fire in any picture you take. This is a good setting to use outdoors when there are shadows covering people's faces. The "flash off" setting will keep the flash from firing, whether it is light or dark, and keep the shutter open longer. This works well when you are shooting a sunset or a distant scene that is dim. For this you must hold the camera very steady, so try resting it on something.

Light

Always consider your light source when taking pictures. Light from different directions—from above, below, behind, in front of, or to the side of the subject— produces entirely different shadow effects.

Light from behind, no flash   Light from behind, fill flash

Outside, the sun is your light source. The direction of the sun and the shadows it makes change throughout the day, and this can completely change the look of a scene.

Direct sunlight should be avoided for pictures of people, as it can make harsh shadows on your subject's face. You can lessen these by turning your camera's flash on, or by facing the subject away from the light. Do not let a cloudy, overcast day keep you from taking pictures. The soft, even light on such days is excellent for portraits and close-ups of flowers and other subjects.

Focusing

To produce a sharp image, the camera must be properly focused. With OTUC's, the focus cannot be changed, so you will need to take the picture from the correct distance, usually at least 5 feet (1.5 meters) from the subject.

With an autofocus point-and-shoot camera, you will see a small set of brackets or a circle in the middle of the frame when you look through the viewfinder. This shows where the camera will focus. When you press very lightly on the shutter, the camera tries to focus on whatever is in that focusing point. Once the camera focuses, a small lamp next to the viewfinder will light up steadily. If the camera has trouble focusing, the small lamp will blink. Move back a bit, or aim the focusing point at a sharp detail, and try again.

You need not leave your subject in the middle of the frame. A point-and-shoot will let you lock the focus, then re-aim the camera so that your subject is off to the side. You should keep gentle but steady pressure on the shutter button to do this. (Try practicing with an empty camera.)

Most SLR's have both autofocus and manual-focus modes. In manual-focus, you turn a ring on the lens while looking through the viewfinder, until the subject looks sharp.

Aperture of f/2 decreases depth of field

Aperture of f/22 increases depth of field

Exposure

Exposure is the amount of light that falls on the film or the imager. If the light is too weak, the picture will be underexposed and there will be no detail in the shadows. If the light is too strong, it will be overexposed and there will be no detail in the bright parts.

A simple camera, such as an OTUC, will have only one exposure setting. For this reason OTUC's are always loaded with film that has good exposure latitude. That is, it still results in fairly good prints even if the film has not been properly exposed.

Point-and-shoot and adjustable cameras have many shutter speeds and lens openings, so you can take pictures under many lighting conditions. (Many SLR's also have an autoexposure setting.) With film cameras, try using fast film, like ISO 800 or 1600 color-negative film, to take pictures indoors without flash. With digital cameras, you can increase the setting for "ISO equivalent" and try the same thing.

Composition

Composition refers to the arrangement of the elements in a picture. The simplest pictures are often the best. They present one main subject, with no clutter in the background. As a rule, it is better not to have a person or other subject exactly in the center of a picture. The subject should be slightly away from the center, and other objects in the picture should guide the eye toward the subject. Avoid a cluttered background if possible. If you are using an adjustable camera, you can open the lens wide (that is, use a smaller aperture, such as f/1.4, f/2, f/2.8) to decrease the depth of field and blur out the background.

In a close-up shot, the subject will fill most of the picture, and less of the background will be seen. If you are taking pictures of lakes, parks, or other scenic spots, put people in the foreground. Doing so increases the feeling of depth and size in the picture.

Many subjects can be photographed either horizontally or vertically. Before pressing the shutter button, hold the camera in both positions. See which position provides a better picture.

Try to have each picture tell a story. A good way to do this is to show the subject doing something. For example, if you are taking a picture of a small child, show the child playing with a toy. When you take pictures, ask your subjects not to look at you. These pictures look more natural than posed pictures and are called candid photos.

The Decisive Moment:
Henri Cartier-Bresson
(1908–)

Like many photographs by Henri Cartier-Bresson, this image captures a pivotal moment in a sequence of events, as well as the relationship between subject and environment.

At first glance, a photograph by Henri Cartier-Bresson might look like a snapshot. But if you keep looking, you will see how perfectly he captured an expression or a gesture that reveals something about the subject. Cartier-Bresson calls the timing required for this "the decisive moment," and his work has been a tremendous influence on photojournalists right up to today. Born in Chanteloup, France, Cartier-Bresson began his photographic career in 1930. Over a period of several decades, he took photographs in many locales, including China, India, the USSR, the United States, Canada, and Japan. He was also a pioneer in available-light photography (photos taken without flash or studio light).

and load it into the camera. Then the plate had to be exposed, and the image developed, before the collodion dried. By the 1870's, gelatin-based dry emulsion began to replace the wet collodion plates.

Advances

In the 1880's, two developments changed photography. First, flexible, roll-up film was introduced by George Eastman, founder of the Eastman Kodak Company in Rochester, New York. A few years later, Eastman brought out a hand-held roll-film camera. This camera was easy to carry and use. Eastman's company even processed the film, so amateur photographers no longer had to do their own developing. This marked the beginning of photography's popularity as a hobby.

Along with its increasing popularity, photography began to be recognized as an art. Some photographers of the early 1900's experimented with new printing techniques to make their photographs look more like paintings. Later photographers produced abstract compositions through various darkroom techniques and multiple exposures. Others continued to use the shapes and textures of the natural world to create beautiful photographs.

In the 1920's and 1930's, more technical advances affected amateur and professional photographers alike. In 1924, the Leica camera was introduced in Germany. This miniature 35mm camera came with a wide range of accessories and attachments. The Leica gave photographers new flexibility, allowing them to take sharp, detailed pictures under many conditions. It was the forerunner of today's 35mm cameras. The range of photography was further extended with the development of convenient flash equipment in the late 1920's and early 1930's.

Many photographers used this new flexibility to dramatize social issues, such as poverty, with moving candid shots. This became known as documentary photography. Other photographers concentrated on recording news events. With advances in printing, newspapers and magazines were demanding more and more photographs for illustration.

Meanwhile, color photography had been developing since the early 1900's. In 1935, Kodachrome slide film was introduced. It became the first popular, affordable color film and is still used today. Early in the 1940's color-negative film appeared. This captured images on a negative, and so it could be readily printed on color printing paper. Color-negative film quickly became the most popular type of film in the world and remains so today.

Instant film, which develops within seconds, appeared in 1947. It was invented by the American scientist Edwin H. Land for use in his Polaroid Land Camera.

One of the most important developments in photography was the electronic flash, invented in the 1930's by Dr. Harold Edgerton of the Massachusetts Institute of Technology (MIT). This consisted of a burst of electricity shot through a tube to create a short but brilliant light. Unlike the single-use flash bulbs that had come before, a flash could be fired many times. It could also be made one-millionth of a second or shorter. This enabled photographers to freeze motion.

GREAT PHOTOGRAPHERS

The Eye of the Portraitist:
Arnold Newman
(1918–)

Arnold Newman has probably photographed more famous people than any other photographer—world leaders, musicians, artists, actors. Born in New York City, where he has worked most of his life, Newman specializes in the environmental portrait—photos of people posed with objects associated with their work or personal interests.

Arnold Newman, self-portrait.

GREAT PHOTOGRAPHERS

Portraits from the Dark Side:
Diane Arbus (1923–1971)

Diane Arbus, born in New York City, took photographs that many consider disturbing. She began her career as a fashion photographer, working closely with her husband, but soon began taking documentary photographs of people in their homes, in stores, or on the street. She often photographed people who were physically different—midgets and giants for example—but even her portraits of "ordinary" people make them appear strange. Part of this was due to her technique. Arbus photographed people at odd angles, usually with direct flash, so that they were harshly lit. Her techniques, considered radical at the time, influenced many later photographers.

Diane Arbus photographing a man and his dogs. Arbus often photographed people she met on the street.

THE DIGITAL DARKROOM

At one time, all photographs were processed with chemicals in a darkroom. Today this process is becoming obsolete, and the computer is the new "darkroom."

There are four basic steps to producing photos in the digital darkroom: capture, downloading, image editing, and printing.

Capture means getting an electronic **image file** that your computer can read. If you use a digital camera to take a picture, you already have one. To convert a negative, a slide, or a print to an image file, you will need to scan it with a scanner (or have it scanned at a photo lab). A scanner is basically a digital camera that takes a picture of a picture. A flatbed scanner has a glass plate like a photocopier's. You place the print face down on the glass plate, close the cover, and start the scan. To scan a negative or slide, you will need a film scanner, which has a special holder for film.

Once you have a digital file of your picture, the next step is **downloading** it, or getting it into your computer. If you have your own scanner, the scanner software has already done this. If you are transferring the image from a digital camera into your computer, you can use a cable, a dock, or a card reader. (For more information, see Storing Images and Making Prints on pages 330-31.)

The process of modifying your picture is called **image editing**. This is done with image-editing software. This software is often included when you purchase a digital camera, printer, or scanner.

Image-editing programs let you modify your photos in many ways. You can lighten and darken them (entirely or in specific areas), adjust the contrast (for more or less), adjust the color, sharpen fuzzy images, and eliminate red-eye, which sometimes appears when people are photographed with flash. You can also use the program's cropping

A girl adds whimsical details to a digital image of herself. With image-editing software, photos can be modified in countless ways.

From the 1950's on, many of the advances in photography were for systems that automated various camera adjustments. In recent years remarkable improvements have been made in film, especially high-speed color-negative films.

History of Electronic Photography

Discoveries about electricity and magnetism in the early 1800's led to the invention of the electric telegraph. Inventors soon began seeking ways to transmit pictures over telegraph wires by electrical signals and to record them as electronic impulses, without the use of film or chemicals. The first facsimile (fax) machine was patented in 1843. By the end of the 1800's, facsimile machines that could send pictures were being developed, and in 1920 a photograph was transmitted across the Atlantic via the underwater telegraph cable. This was one of the first digital transmissions of photography. From then on, the development of electronic photography was closely tied to the development of television and the technology that could send images via electromagnetic waves.

By the late 1950's the United States and the former Soviet Union were engaged in a space race. The U.S. government now became a major force in designing electronic cameras that could transmit images from manned and unmanned spacecraft. Some of these were used for spying. In 1964 the world saw the first electronic photos of Mars, taken by the *Mariner 6* and *Mariner 7* spacecraft. Five years later, people around the globe marveled at the first pictures taken on the moon's surface, made by an RCA television camera attached to a leg of the *Apollo 11* lunar lander.

tool to cut off unwanted portions of your picture and enlarge the rest. Before making any changes, however, you should make a separate copy of the original image so you can go back to it if needed.

Some image-editing programs let you make a picture look like stained glass, liquid, or metal or distort things or faces. (Just make sure your friends have a good sense of humor before you do this to pictures of them!)

Many people use image-editing programs to fix old photos that are faded and damaged. This is done by scanning the original photo, then using various tools to restore tone and color. One of these tools, called a clone tool, can cover up rips and tears. It does this by "memorizing" the tone and texture of an undamaged part of the picture, then lets you "paint" over the damaged areas.

Once you have made changes to your picture, it is time to print it. Inexpensive color inkjet printers can make very good color prints if you use photo paper. This paper is available in different surface textures and shows far more color and detail than regular printer paper. It is also important to use the printer profiles that come with the image-editing software. This lets you tailor the printing to a specific printer (which you can select from a list), which results in better prints.

GREAT PHOTOGRAPHERS

Social Commentary Through the Lens:
Robert Frank
(1924–)

Robert Frank, photographed in his studio.

When Robert Frank set out in the mid-1950's to photograph America, he was not intending to take postcard images. Instead, he photographed on the streets and in diners, post offices, stores, and bus stations, taking unposed pictures of ordinary people. These photographs, published in the book *The Americans*, show a country that is lonely, disconnected, and divided by race and class. Many people have criticized the book, saying that it deliberately shows the United States in a bad light. But the book is a powerful document for many, influencing a generation of "street shooter" photographers. Frank was born in Zurich, Switzerland.

GREAT PHOTOGRAPHERS

Spokesman for Humanity:
Sebastião Salgado
(1944–)

Many people consider Sebastião Salgado one of the greatest living photographers. Born in Aimores, Minas Gerais, Brazil, Salgado has dedicated himself to photographing the poor and displaced peoples of the world, such as families forced to flee their homelands. A good example is the series of portraits called *The Children*, pictures of small children who have been left homeless by war or poverty. Proceeds from his exhibitions often go to help refugee organizations.

A visitor to a London gallery views photos by Sebastião Salgado. Salgado is one of the world's leading contemporary photographers.

The Colors of Nature:
Frans Lanting
(1951–)

Frans Lanting is one of the most respected contemporary nature photographers. Born in Rotterdam, the Netherlands, Lanting is known for thoroughly researching his subjects before photographing them. He has often worked for *National Geographic* magazine on unusual assignments, such as searching for the last white rhinos in central Africa. His photos emphasize the need to preserve complete ecosystems, not just single species. Lanting's work, which includes seldom-seen aspects of nature, has encouraged governments to be more protective of endangered areas.

Two albatross groom each other during a courting ritual. Photographer Frans Lanting took this photo on the sub-Antarctic island of South Georgia.

Just a few months later, two men, Willard Boyle and George Smith, began work on a device that would revolutionize photography. This was the charge-coupled device (CCD), which could record images electronically. Within a few years, the first working CCD camera was made. By the late 1970's, CCD cameras were being made for industrial uses and were quickly adapted for astronomy and space exploration.

In the early 1980's, the Sony Corporation of Japan introduced a consumer electronic camera, the Mavica (for *magnetic video camera*). It recorded images on two-inch floppy disks and played them back on a television set or video monitor. Other electronic cameras soon followed, and news organizations began to use electronic cameras. Although these cameras recorded without film or chemicals, however, they were not digital cameras: They stored visual information as analog signals rather than as binary code.

Fully digital cameras began to appear in the early 1980's. In 1990, Kodak unveiled the DCS-100, a digital camera housed in a modified Nikon SLR body. This was the first digital camera designed as a full professional system. It was very expensive and had to be attached to an external hard drive, but the race was on. Within a few years, professional digital cameras became self-contained, with much greater resolving power (pixel count). Digital backs were also devised for existing professional cameras and for studio view cameras. A less expensive alternative to the CCD, the complementary metal-oxide semiconductor (CMOS), emerged in the 1990's.

In the late 1990's digital point-and-shoot cameras exploded in popularity. People liked seeing their pictures right away and having the ability to e-mail them. By the early 2000's digital cameras had greatly improved—their image quality was equal to or even better than that of film. As a result, digital cameras began to outsell film cameras in the United States.

Digital cameras are now being combined with other electronic devices, such as cell phones, laptop computers, and digital organizers. Cameras themselves are becoming more connected—several manufacturers already make cameras that can store e-mail addresses so you can send photos faster. We can expect more wireless transmission of photographs, as well as a camera that can transmit high-quality photos directly, without any other attachments.

As the cost of digital cameras continues to drop, more people will be able to afford them. And more picture "fixes" such as red-eye removal will likely become automated within the camera. All these factors will make it even easier to take good photos. But no piece of equipment can replace the value of a sensitive photographic eye.

DAN RICHARDS
Popular Photography and Imaging

SHELLS

Many kinds of animals grow hard external covers, or shells, to protect their bodies from predators and the environment. Turtles, crustaceans (such as crabs, lobsters, and shrimps), and even some microscopic organisms all have very distinct kinds of shells. However, when most people think of shells, they think of the shells of mollusks. Mollusks are a group of invertebrates (animals without a backbone) that includes snails, clams, oysters, mussels, and nautiluses. This article discusses the shells of mollusks.

▶ MOLLUSK SHELLS

There are five primary kinds, or classes, of mollusks: gastropods, bivalves, cephalopods, chitons, and scaphopods. Most of these animals have shells. The main exceptions are land and sea slugs, octopuses, and squids. While crustaceans and some kinds of insects continually shed and replace their shells as they grow, in a process called molting, a mollusk has only one shell during its lifetime.

Shelled mollusks are born with shells, and as they grow, their shells grow with them. Specialized tissue along the mantle, the skin-like envelope covering the animal's soft body, continuously adds thin layers to the edge of the shell's opening. This gradual buildup of new shell material is called **accretion**.

The shell material consists of several layers of calcium carbonate crystals and protein, which makes the shell strong as well as slightly flexible. The outer layer of a shell, called the **periostracum**, protects the rest of the shell. In the **prismatic layer**, the crystals of calcium carbonate are shaped like prisms. Some shells have an inner **nacreous layer**, in which the calcium carbonate and protein form a lustrous material called nacre, or mother-of-pearl. Mother-of-pearl is the substance that builds up inside oysters to form pearls.

Mollusk shells are found in a variety of colors, including white, gray, pink, silver, or brown. Some shells have vivid spots, bands, or stripes of black, red, yellow, and sometimes green. A shell's coloration often serves as camouflage, helping the animal blend into its surroundings. Coloration may also serve to attract mates or as a warning to predators.

The largest mollusk shells belong to giant white clams, whose shells can grow more

The shells of snails are formed by a series of coils or whorls that typically produce a tapered, spiral shape. *Clockwise from top left:* Cone shells are popular with collectors, but the snails living in them often inflict venomous stings. Limpet shells stop coiling early in the snail's life and form into a flat disc. Lister's conch is found in the Indian Ocean. Trumpet triton shells have been used as horns by native peoples living on islands in the Pacific Ocean. The spikes on the shells of the arthritic spider conch and the thorny whelk may help protect the animals from predators. Cowry shells are usually smooth and oval.

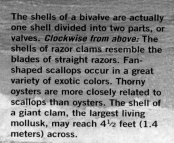

The shells of a bivalve are actually one shell divided into two parts, or valves. *Clockwise from above:* The shells of razor clams resemble the blades of straight razors. Fan-shaped scallops occur in a great variety of exotic colors. Thorny oysters are more closely related to scallops than oysters. The shell of a giant clam, the largest living mollusk, may reach 4½ feet (1.4 meters) across.

than 4½ feet (1.4 meters) wide. The smallest shell is that of the snail *Ammon-icera japonica*, whose shell has a diameter of only about 0.014 inch (0.35 millimeter).

Gastropods. Gastropods (from the Greek words meaning "stomach-foot") are the largest group of mollusks. They include snails and slugs (which have no shells) that live on land and in fresh and salt water. Snail shells grow in a process called **coiling**, in which a spiral is formed by a succession of coils or **whorls**. The whorls of the shell become larger and wider as the animal grows, and the animal lives in the last or last few whorls. Limpets are a kind of snail in which coiling stops at an early stage of growth, resulting in a flat, saucer-shaped shell.

The surface of snail shells may be smooth or have ribs, knobs, spines, or a combination of these. These features may strengthen the shell and may also protect it from predators that would try to swallow or bore into it.

Bivalves. Bivalves are mollusks with shells divided into two parts, or valves, and they include ani-

mals such as clams, oysters, mussels, and scallops. The two parts of a bivalve shell are connected by a flexible ligament, which acts like a hinge. When a set of muscles is contracted, the two valves close against each other. When these muscles relax, the valves separate.

Some bivalves are wedge-shaped, which helps them burrow into the sand or mud. The shells of mussels and some oysters are streamlined to help protect the animal from pounding waves. The fan-shaped shell of a scallop helps the animal travel short distances when it squirts water out of its shell.

Cephalopods. Most cephalopods (from the Greek words meaning "head-foot"), such as squids and octopuses, do not have shells. However, fossil records indicate that many different kinds of shelled cephalopods lived in the oceans millions of years ago. Fossils of one such

As its name suggests, the shell of the chambered nautilus is made up of a series of chambers. As the animal grows, it creates a new chamber to accommodate its larger size.

How to Start a Shell Collection

Shell collecting is a hobby enjoyed by many people. If you would like to collect shells, look through various books on shells or explore a museum's invertebrate collection to help you decide what kind of shell interests you the most. Some people collect only one kind of shell—scallops or cone-shells, for example—while others collect shells from a particular habitat or geographic location. Some people even specialize in collecting shells of just one color.

Among the best places to look for shells are beaches, mudflats, and breakwaters. As you gather each shell, make sure it is not still inhabited; if it is, carefully put it back where you found it.

After you bring your shells home, wash them thoroughly to remove any sand or remains of the mollusks that lived in them. To make the shells shine,

gently polish them with a soft cloth or apply a thin coat of mineral oil. Record the common and scientific names of your shells, as well as when and where you found them, and then store them in a dry place out of direct sunlight.

group of animals, called ammonites, have been found that measure up to 6 feet (2 meters) in diameter.

The best-known shelled cephalopod living today is the chambered, or pearly, nautilus. It resembles the extinct ammonites and lives in the Indian and Pacific oceans. This animal grows a shell with internal chambers that can be filled with or emptied of water, allowing the animal to move up or down in the ocean. The animal lives in the last and largest chamber of the shell.

Chitons. Chitons are flat, oval-shaped mollusks found in most oceans of the world, usu-

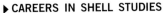

Chitons have flat, oval shells formed by a series of overlapping plates. Some species can grow to 1 foot (0.3 meter) in length.

ally in shallow coastal areas. Their shells are composed of eight (or sometimes seven) overlapping plates that are hinged to-gether, which makes it easy for the animals' bodies to conform to the rocky surfaces on which they live.

Scaphopods. Scaphopods (from the Greek words meaning "shovel-foot") are often called tusk shells because their long, narrow shells resemble teeth or tusks. The shapes of these shells help the animals burrow into the sand.

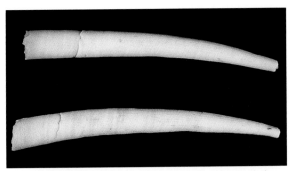

Scaphopods are also called tusk shells because their long and narrow shape resembles a tusk, or tooth. This shape helps the animal burrow into the sand.

▶ **CAREERS IN SHELL STUDIES**

The scientific study of mollusk shells is called conchology, and it is always linked with the study of mollusks, which is called malacology. Although there are no academic programs in the United States devoted solely to conchology or malacology, there are many institutions (such as universities, research centers, and natural history museums) that emphasize the study of mollusks through programs in zoology, marine biology, ecology, genetics, and other related subjects.

JOSÉ H. LEAL
Director, The Bailey-Matthews Shell Museum

343

EUROPE

On a world map or globe most of the continents can be seen plainly as masses of land set in the vast expanse of the oceans. Australia, Antarctica, and Africa are well defined, although Africa is attached to Asia by the Isthmus of Suez. North and South America, although joined at the Isthmus of Panama, also stand out as large individual landmasses. Europe, however, seems to be an extension of Asia. In fact, geographically, Europe and Asia are sometimes regarded as a single great continent called Eurasia, with Europe as an enormous peninsula. But because Europe has a distinctive history and culture, it is usually considered a separate continent.

The idea that Europe is a separate continent is a very old one. It is believed by some authorities that many centuries before the birth of Christ, the people of the Middle East divided the world they knew into three parts: One part was their own familiar region. They called the land to the east Asu—the Land of the Rising Sun. They named the land to the west Ereb—the Land of the Setting Sun. It may be from these ancient names that we get the modern names Asia and Europe.

Geographers do not always agree on the boundary between Europe and Asia. But most consider it to run from the Atlantic Ocean westward to the Ural Mountains and the north shore of the Caspian Sea, then along the

Caucasus Mountains to the Black Sea, and southward through the Bosporus and Dardanelles straits. The Urals also divide the giant nation of Russia into European and Asian areas.

Europe, with just 8 percent of the world's land area, ranks as the second smallest continent after Australia. But its placement at the crossroads of the trade routes between Asia, Africa, and the Americas—and its impact on world history—has given the continent a global importance far greater than its small size would suggest.

Europe was the birthplace of ideas that helped shape the modern world. From ancient Greece came the idea of democracy and the spirit of scientific inquiry. From Rome came the idea of just laws and the first attempts to unite Europe. In the northern European lowlands people learned to rotate the crops they planted from year to year. This helped keep the soil fertile and made it possible to establish permanent settlements. Europeans were also the first to make use of machines to replace human labor on a large scale. The Industrial Revolution in the 1700's and early 1800's made Europe the world's workshop. From the late 1400's, European ships roamed the seas, dominating world trade and exploration for the next four centuries. Enormous colonial empires were carved out in North America, South America, Africa, Asia, and Australia. European settlers carried their traditions and languages to all parts of the globe.

Clockwise from opposite page, top left: **The Eiffel Tower in Paris, France, Europe's largest city; a Latvian girl wearing a traditional bow; Polish farmers driving a horse-drawn hay wagon; cyclists competing in the annual Tour de France bicycle race; green pastures along the Atlantic coast in Galway, Ireland; the Parthenon in Athens, Greece; a chamois standing before Mont Blanc, the highest peak in the Alps.**

THE NATIONS OF EUROPE

Country	Capital
Albania	Tiranë
Andorra	Andorra la Vella
Austria	Vienna
Belarus	Minsk
Belgium	Brussels
Bosnia and Herzegovina	Sarajevo
Bulgaria	Sofia
Croatia	Zagreb
Cyprus[1]	Nicosia
Czech Republic	Prague
Denmark	Copenhagen
Estonia	Tallinn
Finland	Helsinki
France	Paris
Germany	Berlin
Greece	Athens
Hungary	Budapest
Iceland	Reykjavík
Ireland	Dublin
Italy	Rome
Latvia	Riga
Liechtenstein	Vaduz
Lithuania	Vilnius
Luxembourg	Luxembourg
Macedonia	Skopje
Malta	Valletta
Moldova	Chişinău
Monaco	Monaco-Ville
Netherlands	Amsterdam
Norway	Oslo
Poland	Warsaw
Portugal	Lisbon
Romania	Bucharest
Russia[2]	Moscow
San Marino	San Marino
Serbia and Montenegro	Belgrade
Slovakia	Bratislava
Slovenia	Ljubljana
Spain	Madrid
Sweden	Stockholm
Switzerland	Bern
Ukraine	Kiev
United Kingdom	London
Vatican City	Vatican City

[1] Cyprus is geographically part of Asia, but it belongs to the European Union.
[2] Russia includes land in Europe and Asia. Small areas of Turkey, Azerbaijan, Georgia, and Kazakhstan also lie in Europe.

FACTS and figures

LOCATION AND SIZE: Europe extends from: **Latitude**—71° 10′ N to 36° 10′ N. **Longitude**—66° E to 9° 30′ W. **Area**—(including Russia in Europe and adjacent islands)—approximately 4,000,000 sq mi (10,360,000 km²). **Highest Point**—Mt. Elbrus, 18,510 ft (5,642 m). **Lowest Point**—Caspian Sea, 92 ft (28 m) below sea level.

POPULATION: 729,000,000 (estimate includes Asian Russia but none of Turkey).

PRINCIPAL LAKES: Caspian Sea (between Europe and Asia), Ladoga, Onega, Vänern, Vättern, Saimaa, Balaton, Constance.

PRINCIPAL RIVERS: Volga, Danube, Dnieper, Don, Pechora, Dniester, Rhine, Elbe, Vistula, Loire, Tagus, Neman, Ebro, Oder, Rhône.

PRINCIPAL MOUNTAIN RANGES: Caucasus—Mt. Elbrus, Dykh Tau, Mt. Kazbek; **Alps**—Mont Blanc, Dufourspitze, Monte Leone, Barre des Écrins, Matterhorn; **Pyrenees**—Pico de Aneto; **Sierra Nevada**—Mulhacén.

following World War II, Europe was roughly divided into two political camps. Most of the Eastern European nations became satellites of the Soviet Union, the world's first Communist state. Much of Western Europe allied itself with the democratic United States. This division of the continent came to an end between 1989 and 1991, when the Eastern European Communist countries replaced their governments with democratically elected ones, and the Soviet Union itself collapsed.

By the turn of the century, the 15 member nations of the European Union (EU) had made great strides toward forming an economic bloc large enough to rival that of the United States. Unity was also furthered by expanding European Union membership to include several nations that had formerly belonged to the Soviet Union.

▶ **THE NATIONS OF EUROPE**

Europe is made up of all or part of 48 countries. The nations of northern Europe include Norway, Sweden, Denmark (known as the Scandinavian countries), Finland, and the distant island of Iceland. The United Kingdom and Ireland are a part of western Europe. (The United Kingdom includes the island of Great Britain and a small area in northern Ireland.)

France, the largest nation in western Europe, is ringed on three sides by eight other

But in the 1900's, two world wars (1914–18 and 1939–45) almost destroyed Europe and its rich heritage. Many cities were completely devastated. Out of the ashes and rubble, Europeans had to rebuild their nations. In the years

At the end of the last Ice Age, melting glaciers carved narrow channels called fjords through the towering cliffs of the Northwest Mountains region in Norway.

nations. On the low-lying plains of northwestern Europe lie Belgium, the Netherlands, and Luxembourg. Spain and Portugal both occupy the Iberian Peninsula of southwestern Europe, with Portugal being the most westerly country on the European mainland. Italy lies in southern Europe. Switzerland, Germany, and Austria are situated roughly in central Europe, while Poland, Hungary, the Czech Republic, and Slovakia lie in east central Europe. Serbia and Montenegro, Croatia, Slovenia, Bosnia and Herzegovina, Macedonia, Romania, Bulgaria, Greece, and Albania occupy the Balkan Peninsula in southeastern Europe. The Baltic States—Latvia, Lithuania, and Estonia—are so called because of their location on the Baltic Sea in northeastern Europe. Moldova, Ukraine, and Belarus lie at the eastern edge of the continent.

Europe also has several tiny countries: Andorra, nestled in the Pyrenees mountains; Liechtenstein, between Switzerland and Austria; Monaco, an enclave on the southern coast of France; the island of Malta in the Mediterranean Sea; mountainous San Marino in Italy; and Vatican City, realm of the pope, situated within the city of Rome.

Several countries lie in both Europe and Asia. They include Russia (Europe's largest country) and small parts of Azerbaijan, Georgia, Kazakhstan, and Turkey. Geographically, the island nation of Cyprus in the eastern Mediterranean Sea belongs to Asia, but it is linked politically and economically to Europe.

▶ LAND

Europe stretches from the Atlantic Ocean in the west to the Ural Mountains in the east. The northernmost point on the European mainland is Cape Nordkyn in Norway. The most southerly point on the mainland of Europe is Point Tarifa in Spain.

Land Regions

There are four major geographical regions of Europe: the Northwest Mountains, the Great European Plain, the Central Uplands, and the Alpine Mountain System.

The Northwest Mountains, made up of high plateaus, rugged mountains, and deep valleys,

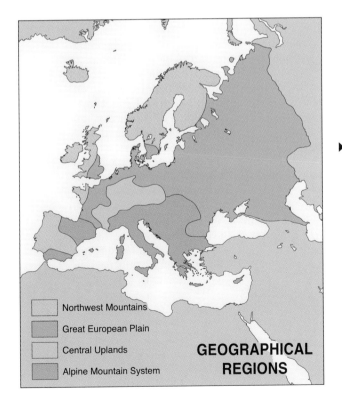

Northwest Mountains

Great European Plain

Central Uplands

Alpine Mountain System

GEOGRAPHICAL REGIONS

347

The Great European Plain extends from the Atlantic Ocean to the Ural Mountains. Poppies bloom on the plain in the Burgundy region of northern France.

extend from western France through parts of the United Kingdom and the Scandinavian Peninsula, then sweep to the northeast along the Arctic coast all the way to Russia. In Scandinavia the land rises steeply along the Atlantic coast but slopes rather gently down to the Gulf of Bothnia and the Baltic Sea. During the Ice Age, glaciers deepened the short valleys near the coast. After the ice retreated, the ocean water flowed in. These narrow arms of the sea are called fjords. Although the Northwest Mountains receive ample precipitation, the rugged terrain makes farming difficult.

The Great European Plain, the largest of the European land regions, is the most densely settled part of the continent. Its fine harbors, vast network of railroads, and many rivers and canal systems have made it a leading center of transportation and industry.

The Great European Plain is shaped like a funnel. The narrow end lies at the foot of the Pyrenees in southwestern France and grows wider as it extends northeast. It includes a large part of western and northern France, most of Belgium, the Netherlands, northern Germany, Denmark, and nearly all of Poland and Russia. The plain is widest in western Russia, where it stretches from the Arctic Ocean to the Black Sea. Its eastern boundary is formed by the Ural Mountains.

The Central Uplands lie between the Great European Plain and the Alpine mountains to the south. They reach from the Atlantic coast of Spain through France and Germany to central Europe. As in the Northwest Mountains, farming in this region is limited due to the rugged landscape. Major sections of the highlands include the Massif Central, the Vosges mountains, and the Ardennes.

The Alpine Mountain System stretches from the Franco-Italian border through central Europe and the Balkan Peninsula. The

Wheat, corn, and other grains thrive in the vast grasslands of Ukraine. This part of the Great European Plain has been called the Breadbasket of Europe.

Sierra Nevada range in Spain parallels the Mediterranean coast. The Pyrenees form the border between Spain and France. Many of the islands in the western Mediterranean, such as Corsica, Sardinia, and the Balearics, are also mountainous. The backbone of the Italian peninsula is formed by the mountains of the Apennines.

The mountains north of the Po River are called the Alps. The Alps form a mountain barrier between southern Europe and western and central Europe. However, there are natural passes through the Alps. It is through these passes that Roman legions marched northward in their conquest of Europe. Later it was through the same passes that the conquerors of the Roman Empire entered the Italian peninsula.

One branch of the Alps, called the Jura Mountains, borders the Swiss plateau on which most of the Swiss cities are built. Two branches of the Alps circle the Great Danube Plain and part of the Balkan Peninsula. The Carpathian Mountains form the northern branch of the Alps. The southern branch is known as the Dinaric Alps.

The towering Caucasus Mountains, between the Black and Caspian seas, are often considered part of the Alpine Mountain System. The Caucasus form a high wall that shuts Europe off from the Middle East. Both the highest and the lowest points in Europe are in the Caucasus. They are Mt. Elbrus, which is 18,510 feet (5,642 meters) above sea level; and the Caspian Sea, part of which lies about 92 feet (28 meters) below sea level.

Rivers, Lakes, and Coastal Waters

Several arms of the Atlantic Ocean penetrate deeply into the continent. No point in the western part of Europe is more than 500 miles (800 kilometers) from a seacoast. Only the plains of the eastern European steppe are far from the sea.

The deepest penetration by the Atlantic Ocean is the Mediterranean Sea in the south. The peninsulas of Italy and the Balkans divide the Mediterranean into separate parts, such as the Ligurian, Tyrrhenian, Adriatic, Ionian, and Aegean seas.

The Mediterranean Sea extends to the east to form the Black Sea and the Sea of Azov. The seas form part of Europe's southern border. They provide a link between the landlocked heart of Eurasia and the ancient trade routes of the Mediterranean. The Caspian Sea is all that remains of an arm of the Mediterranean that once stretched east to the Aral Sea.

The northern branch of the Atlantic is the Baltic Sea. It may be entered from the North Sea by way of the Danish straits.

For centuries transportation in Europe has moved along a network of rivers and canals. The Volga, Europe's longest river, rises in the hills near Moscow, capital of Russia, and flows through the Russian heartland, before emptying into the Caspian Sea. Two other rivers—the Dnieper, which flows through Russia and

The Caucasus Mountains mark Europe's southeastern boundary. Mount Elbrus, Europe's tallest mountain, is located there.

349

Ukraine, and the Dniester, forming part of the border of Moldova—empty into the Black Sea. The Don, another important Russian river, flows into the Sea of Azov. The famed Danube, Europe's second longest river, is the major waterway of central Europe.

Several broad rivers wind across northern and western Europe and end in the North Sea or the Baltic. They include the Rhine, the Weser, the Elbe, and the Vistula. These rivers are navigable (deep enough and wide enough for ships) for most of their length and carry traffic from the coast to the interior. Six major rivers flow to the Atlantic—three Spanish (the Tagus, Douro, and Guadalquivir) and three French (the Seine, Loire, and Garonne). The Ebro in Spain and the Rhône in France empty into the Mediterranean. The most important river in northern Italy, the Po, flows into the Adriatic Sea.

The Caspian Sea, which is actually a lake, lies on the border between Europe and Asia. It is the world's largest inland body of water. The largest lake entirely within Europe is Ladoga, in Russia. Three other large European lakes are in Scandinavia: Saimaa in Finland

INDEX TO
EUROPE PHYSICAL MAP

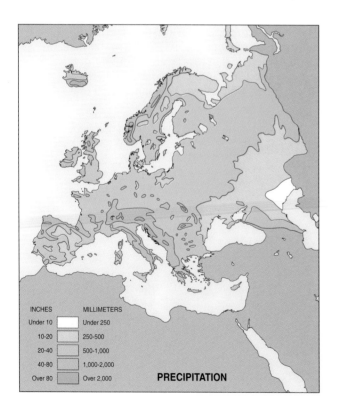

INCHES	MILLIMETERS
Under 10	Under 250
10-20	250-500
20-40	500-1,000
40-80	1,000-2,000
Over 80	Over 2,000

PRECIPITATION

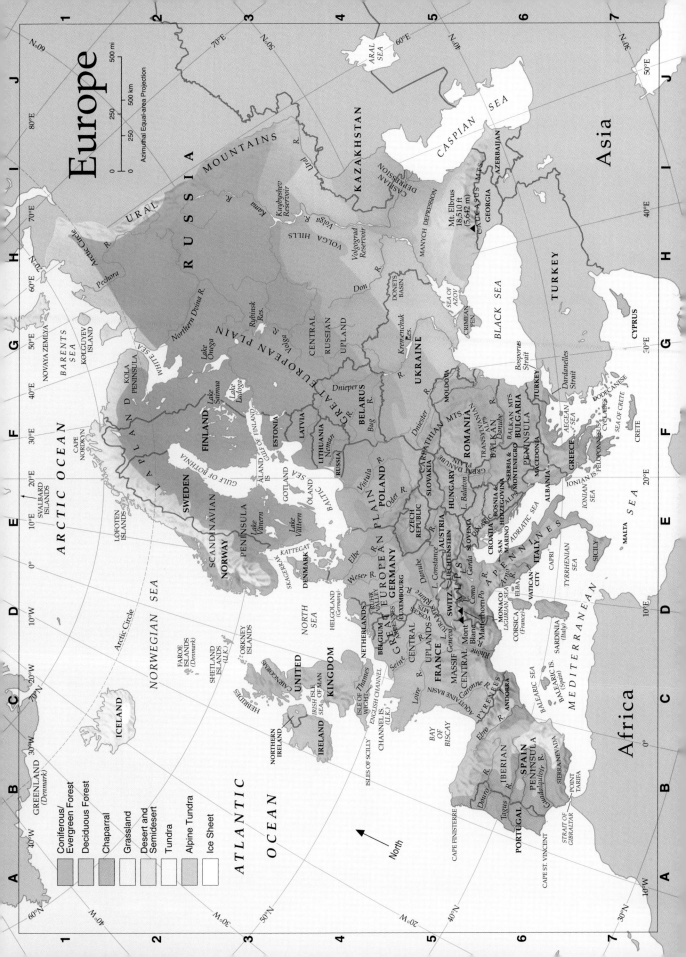

Europe

500 mi

500 km

250

250

0

0

Azimuthal Equal-area Projection

Legend:
- Coniferous/Evergreen Forest
- Deciduous Forest
- Chaparral
- Grassland
- Desert and Semidesert
- Tundra
- Alpine Tundra
- Ice Sheet

North

ARCTIC OCEAN

ATLANTIC OCEAN

NORWEGIAN SEA

BARENTS SEA

NOVAYA ZEMLYA

KOLGUYEV ISLAND

SVALBARD ISLANDS

GREENLAND (Denmark)

ICELAND

FAROE ISLANDS (Denmark)

SHETLAND ISLANDS (U.K.)

ORKNEY ISLANDS

HEBRIDES

CAIRNGORMS

ISLE OF MAN

IRISH SEA

ISLE OF MAN

NORTHERN IRELAND

IRELAND

UNITED KINGDOM

ISLE OF WIGHT

ISLES OF SCILLY

ENGLISH CHANNEL

CHANNEL IS. (U.K.)

Thames R.

NORTH SEA

HELGOLAND (Germany)

NETHERLANDS

BELGIUM

LUXEMBOURG

GERMANY

GREAT EUROPEAN PLAIN

Rhine R.

Elbe

Weser R.

Oder R.

Danube

RUHR VALLEY

VOSGES MTS.

JURA MTS.

ARDENNES

CENTRAL UPLANDS

FRANCE

MASSIF CENTRAL

BAY OF BISCAY

CAPE FINISTERRE

CAPE ST. VINCENT

PORTUGAL

SPAIN

IBERIAN PENINSULA

Duero R.

Tagus R.

Guadalquivir R.

Ebro R.

Douro R.

SIERRA NEVADA

POINT TARIFA

STRAIT OF GIBRALTAR

Africa

PYRENEES

ANDORRA

AQUITAINE BASIN

Garonne R.

Loire R.

Seine R.

Rhône R.

Mont Blanc

Matterhorn

General

ALPS

SWITZ.

LIECHTENSTEIN

MONACO (France)

CORSICA (France)

SARDINIA (Italy)

LIGURIAN SEA

VATICAN CITY

SAN MARINO

APENNINES

ITALY

Po R.

L. Como

L. Garda

L. Maggiore

L. Constance

Danube

BALEARIC SEA

BALEARIC IS. (Spain)

MEDITERRANEAN SEA

TYRRHENIAN SEA

CAPRI

SICILY

MALTA

AUSTRIA

SLOVENIA

CROATIA

BOSNIA & HERZEGOVINA

SERBIA & MONTENEGRO

DINARIC ALPS

ADRIATIC SEA

ALBANIA

MACEDONIA

GREECE

IONIAN SEA

IONIAN IS.

PELOPONNESUS

AEGEAN SEA

CYCLADES

SEA OF CRETE

CRETE

DODECANESE

TURKEY

Dardanelles Strait

Bosporus Strait

BLACK SEA

BULGARIA

Danube

ROMANIA

GREAT HUNGARIAN PLAIN

CARPATHIAN MTS.

TRANSYLVANIAN ALPS

Balkan Mts.

BALKAN PENINSULA

HUNGARY

SLOVAKIA

CZECH REPUBLIC

POLAND

Vistula R.

L. Balaton

MOLDOVA

UKRAINE

CRIMEAN PEN.

SEA OF AZOV

Dniester R.

Bug R.

Dnieper R.

Don

DONETS BASIN

Kremenchuk Res.

CENTRAL RUSSIAN UPLAND

CAUCASUS MTS.

Mt. Elbrus 18,510 ft (5,642 m)

GEORGIA

AZERBAIJAN

CASPIAN DEPRESSION

CASPIAN SEA

ARAL SEA

KAZAKHSTAN

Asia

CYPRUS

RUSSIA

BELARUS

LITHUANIA

Neman R.

LATVIA

ESTONIA

GULF OF FINLAND

BALTIC SEA

GOTLAND

ÖLAND

ÅLAND IS.

KATTEGAT

SKAGERRAK

DENMARK

Lake Vänern

Lake Vättern

SWEDEN

NORWAY

SCANDINAVIAN PENINSULA

LOFOTEN ISLANDS

CAPE NORDKYN

FINLAND

Lake Saimaa

Lake Ladoga

Lake Onega

KOLA PENINSULA

WHITE SEA

LAPLAND

Arctic Circle

GREAT EUROPEAN PLAIN

Northern Dvina R.

Volga R.

Kama

R.

Rybinsk Res.

Kuybyshev Reservoir

Volgograd Reservoir

VOLGA HILLS

Ural

R.

Pechora

R.

URAL MOUNTAINS

Manych Depression

VATICAN CITY

60°N

70°N

50°N

40°N

30°N

Arctic Circle

40°W

30°W

20°W

10°W

0°

10°E

20°E

30°E

40°E

50°E

60°E

70°E

80°E

30°E

The Danube, Europe's second longest river, rises in the Black Forest region of Germany and flows 1,771 miles (2,850 kilometers) through central Europe to the Black Sea.

and Vättern and Vänern in Sweden. Lake Balaton in Hungary is that country's most popular vacation spot. Lake Constance on the border of Switzerland, Austria, and Germany is another famous tourist attraction, as are the lakes in northern Italy—Como and Garda. Italy and Switzerland share lakes Lugano and Maggiore. Important Swiss cities are built on the banks of lakes Zürich, Geneva, and Lucerne.

The gleaming domes of a Greek Orthodox church decorate the landscape of Thíra (also known as Santorini), one of the many islands in the Cyclades chain in the south Aegean Sea.

Islands

Europe encompasses thousands of islands. Five of them—Iceland, the United Kingdom, Ireland, Malta, and Cyprus—are nations unto themselves.

Among the most important island groups are the Faeroe Islands (Denmark); the Lofoten and Svalbard (Norway); the Åland (Finland); the Hebrides, Orkneys, Shetland, Isles of Scilly, and Channel Islands (United Kingdom); the Azores (Portugal); the Balearic and Canary Islands (Spain); and the Cyclades, Dodecanese, and Ionian Islands (Greece). Notable individual islands include Capri, Elba, Sardinia, and Sicily (Italy); Corsica (France); Crete (Greece); Greenland (Denmark); Helgoland (Germany); Madeira (Portugal); and the Isle of Man and Isle of Wight (United Kingdom).

Climate

Western Europe's climate is influenced by the North Atlantic Drift, an ocean current that brings mild sea air from the west and accounts for the generally moderate temperatures, both in winter and summer. Precipitation (including rain and snow) is heaviest in mountainous areas, such as the west coast of Norway and in many parts of the Alps.

Southern Europe has a Mediterranean climate, with mild, wet winters and warm, dry summers. Because of the warming influence of the Mediterranean Sea, winter temperatures rarely fall below 48°F (9°C). Storms are infrequent and days are usually sunny.

The greatest extremes of climate, with the coldest winters and hottest summers, are found in the inland regions of the continent. The lowest winter temperatures occur in northern Russia and in interior areas of the Scandinavian Peninsula.

Although most of Europe receives enough rainfall for crops to grow, some regions receive very little rain. The land in the southern part of Russia and the interior plateau of Spain is too dry for farming and is used for grazing livestock. In other areas, crops can be grown only with irrigation.

Plant Life

The most northerly zone of vegetation in Europe is the tundra. In the tundra zone of Lapland and northern Russia, reindeer graze on mosses, lichens, and low scrub growth during the summer. But animals must move south in search of food during the winter months. Below the tundra is a vast area known as the boreal forest, or taiga. It forms a wide belt all around the world and includes parts of Sweden, Finland, and Russia. The taiga is Europe's chief source of softwoods, such as pine, spruce, hemlock, and fir.

South of the taiga, running through much of central Europe, are temperate deciduous forests of larch, ash, beech, birch, elm, maple, and oak. Grasslands cover much of Ukraine and southwest Russia. Chaparral covers the dry, southernmost regions of Europe. In the Mediterranean region laurel, cypress, cedar, evergreen oak, cork oak, and olive trees are common. A typical form of Mediterranean

Windmill on the River Zaan, the Netherlands

WONDER QUESTION

Where and what are the Low Countries?

The Low Countries are a region in northwestern Europe lying between France and Germany. Historically, they include the modern nations of Belgium, the Netherlands, and Luxembourg—sometimes called the Benelux countries. Geographically, the region takes its name from the low-lying plains of the Netherlands and northern Belgium along the North Sea coast. At one time the entire region was known as the Netherlands (meaning "low countries"), but that name now applies just to the one country. The Netherlands are sometimes mistakenly called Holland. Holland is actually the largest province of the Netherlands.

Combined, the Low Countries are smaller in area than the state of South Carolina. But their importance is far greater than their small size would suggest. They form one of the most densely populated regions of Europe and one of its major manufacturing centers.

The Low Countries were united by the dukes of Burgundy in the late 1300's and 1400's. By marriage, they passed to the Habsburg rulers of Austria and Spain. The great wealth of the region was then based in large part on cloth weaving. The Netherlands was the first to win full independence, from Spain in the 1600's. In 1815, the Netherlands and Belgium were united in a single kingdom. The Belgians, unhappy with the union, declared their independence after a revolt in 1830. The tiny Grand Duchy of Luxembourg dates its modern era of independence from 1839.

Left: The cork oak, a tree native to the Mediterranean region, is cultivated in Spain and Portugal. Its bark tissue is used in many products, from bottle stoppers to baseballs. *Below:* Tulips and other flowers are commercially grown in Holland, a province of the Netherlands.

vegetation is the maquis—a mixture of scrub plants that look lifeless in the summer but blossom during the rainy season.

Wildflowers are a part of the landscape everywhere in Europe. They are most beautiful in the mountains, especially in the Alpine pastures. Even the semi-arid steppes of southern Russia have a carpeting of colorful wildflowers in the early spring.

Animal Life

Many animals that once roamed throughout Europe are now found only in zoos. Some, however, are still found in fairly large numbers in the wild. Rabbits and hares are caught everywhere. Deer are hunted during the hunting season. Mink, ermine, sable, and some varieties of fox are trapped in the forests of northern Russia for their fur. Fox hunting with dogs, once a popular sport in Britain, has been outlawed.

Birds have survived better, although game birds, such as grouse, partridge, and wild duck, are diminishing in number. Among the more familiar European birds are skylarks, nightingales, finches, and starlings. Storks, which used to be numerous, are now rare.

Fish have suffered from the pollution of many lakes and rivers, although fishing is still popular. Probably the best-known freshwater fish is the trout. The sturgeon of the Caspian Sea is caught for its roe (eggs), known as caviar.

Natural Resources

Forests. Northern Europe and other mountainous regions of the continent are densely forested. Southern Europe once had many forests, but long ago the land was cleared to provide lumber for building and other wood products. These old forests were replaced with cultivated fields and grasslands. Today, however, due to strict conservation measures, Europe's forests are expanding by more than 1.25 million acres (500,000 hectares) every year. Many forestlands are further protected to minimize the destruction caused by pollution and other environmental hazards.

Soils. Only parts of eastern, central, and southern Europe have fertile soils. But European agriculture has a high level of productivity because fertilizers are used to enrich the soil where it is poor.

Minerals. Russia and Ukraine have deposits of many of the most important minerals needed in industry. Outside of these countries, however, Europe is not rich in minerals, aside from coal. Iron ore is produced mainly in Sweden and France. There are also relatively small deposits of copper, lead, zinc, bauxite (aluminum ore), silver, and chrome in various parts of Europe. Nearly all European countries must import the minerals they need for their economies.

Environmental Issues. As a heavily populated continent with generally high living standards and limited natural resources, Europe is especially concerned about environmental problems. Europe's vulnerability was demonstrated in 1986 when a nuclear accident at Chernobyl in Ukraine (then part of the Soviet Union) spread nuclear contamination for thousands of miles around. In addition, acid rain, one of the many results of industrial pollution, has affected the forests and lakes of Scandinavia and Germany. In Germany a small but active environmental and political group, the "Greens," has members elected to the legislature. Efforts are being made to clean up the Mediterranean Sea, which suffers not only from industrial pollution, but also from recreational pollution caused by the many tourists who come to the region each year.

▶ **PEOPLE**

Although it is the second smallest continent in area, Europe (including European Russia) is the third largest in population, after Asia and Africa. Europe is the most densely popu-

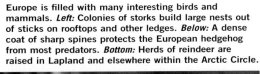

Europe is filled with many interesting birds and mammals. *Left:* Colonies of storks build large nests out of sticks on rooftops and other ledges. *Below:* A dense coat of sharp spines protects the European hedgehog from most predators. *Bottom:* Herds of reindeer are raised in Lapland and elsewhere within the Arctic Circle.

lated of the continents. Its people make up more than 12 percent of the world's total population. The population in most European countries has remained stable, with little or no increase in the rate of growth. However, immigration is swelling the population figures in western Europe.

Europe's population density varies greatly from region to region. Few people live in the northern part of Scandinavia and in some of Europe's more mountainous regions. Industrial areas, however, are heavily populated. There are also dense populations in some rural areas where farming depends on a great deal of human labor, as in parts of the Mediterranean region. A zone of high density runs from the United Kingdom and northern France well into the interior of Europe. A second area of high population density is found in the Po River basin and Arno River valley in northern Italy.

Ethnic Groups

For such a relatively small region, Europe has many different ethnic groups. Ethnic divisions exist even within a single country. Some examples include the English, Welsh, Scots, and Irish in the United Kingdom; the German-, French-, Italian-, and Romansch-speaking peoples of Switzerland; the Flemings and Walloons in Belgium; the Bretons in France; and the Basques in Spain. The arrival of peoples from former European colonies has added to Europe's cultural mix. These include Indonesians in the Netherlands; Algerians in France; and Jamaicans, Pakistanis, and Indians in the United Kingdom.

Many ethnic groups have lived together in peace for centuries, as in Switzerland. But ethnic identity has sometimes led to violence, as in the case of the Basques in Spain who demand their own homeland. Religion has sometimes contributed to ethnic unrest, as in Northern Ireland, where Protestants and Roman Catholics have clashed.

Languages

Europe has three major

language groups, all branches of the Indo-European language family—Germanic, Romance, and Slavic. Each group consists of a number of different but related languages.

The Germanic languages are German, English, Dutch, Danish, Swedish, Norwegian, and Icelandic. The Romance languages, which are derived from Latin, are Italian, French, Spanish, Portuguese, Romanian, Catalan (spoken in the Spanish province of Catalonia), and the Romansch of Switzerland. Slavic languages are Russian, Ukrainian, Belarusian, Polish, Serbo-Croatian, Czech, Slovak, Bulgarian, Slovene, and Macedonian. The languages of Latvia and Lithuania are considered part of a larger Balto-Slavic group.

Separate European language groups include

Greek and Albanian. Celtic languages, once spoken widely in Europe, are now used by a relatively few people in Ireland, Wales, and Scotland and by the Bretons in the French province of Brittany.

Several languages of Europe do not belong to the Indo-European family. They include Finnish and Estonian, which are closely related; Hungarian (Magyar), which is more distantly related to Finnish and Estonian; and Basque, which is spoken in the Pyrenees mountain region of Spain and France.

European languages contributed to the spread of European customs, manners, and values to much of the world. English, French, Spanish, and Portuguese are today spoken by millions of non-European people, and English has become the preferred second language in many countries.

Faces of Europe (*clockwise from opposite page, far left*): A Muslim woman and her baby in Germany; a dogsled musher in Finland; a palace guard in Sweden; a woman in Greece in traditional dress; a fisherman in Portugal; a Basque man and his cow in Spain; a "bobby" (policeman) in the United Kingdom; a farm woman in Sweden; a Ukrainian at a midsummer celebration.

INDEX TO
EUROPE POLITICAL MAP

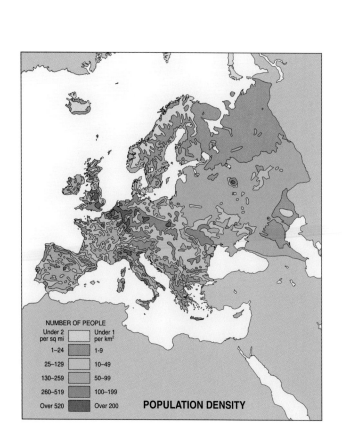

NUMBER OF PEOPLE

Under 2 per sq mi	Under 1 per km²
1–24	1–9
25–129	10–49
130–259	50–99
260–519	100–199
Over 520	Over 200

POPULATION DENSITY

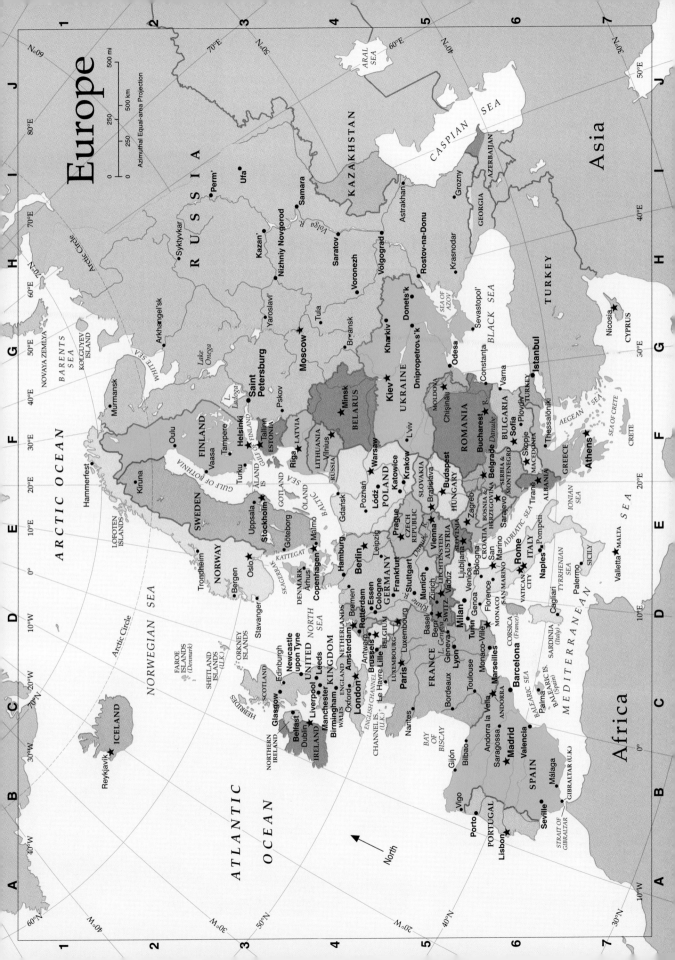

Crowds gather in St. Peter's Square in Vatican City to worship in the presence of the pope, the supreme head of the Roman Catholic Church.

Religion

Most Europeans are Christians. There are three chief religious groups—Roman Catholic, Eastern Orthodox, and Protestant. The break between the Roman Catholic and Orthodox churches came about as a result of the rivalry between Rome and Constantinople, after the fall of the Roman Empire in the A.D. 400's. The Protestant Church emerged during the religious Reformation of the 1500's, when many Christians split from the Roman Catholic Church.

Ireland, France, Belgium, Italy, Spain, Portugal, Austria, the Czech Republic, Slovakia, Poland, Croatia, Slovenia, and southern Germany are chiefly Roman Catholic. The Scandinavian countries, Finland, the

Public school attendance is required in Belarus and elsewhere throughout Europe. Most European countries have an extremely high literacy rate.

United Kingdom, Iceland, northern Germany, Estonia, and Latvia are largely Protestant. Switzerland and the Netherlands are about equally divided between Roman Catholics and Protestants, and many other countries also have mixed religious populations. The Eastern Orthodox faith is found chiefly in eastern and southeastern European countries—Russia, Ukraine, Belarus, Bulgaria, Romania, Greece, and Serbia and Montenegro. Albania is unique in being the only nation in Europe with a Muslim majority. Bosnia and Herzegovina also has a considerable Muslim population.

Education

Almost all Europeans are literate (able to read and write). Only a few countries have a literacy rate below 97 percent.

In most countries, children attend school from the age of 5 or 6. At about 11, they take tests that determine further schooling. Most qualify to study at a comprehensive or technical school. Those with highest marks attend an academic secondary school that prepares them for study at a university.

Some European universities are very old and have distinguished histories. Among the oldest are the University of Bologna (founded in 1088) in Italy, the University of Oxford (1249) in England, and the Sorbonne (1253) in France. They set standards of excellence that made them models for later universities everywhere.

Family Life

In the rich fabric of European traditions there are some common threads of behavior.

A favorite pastime of many Europeans is to relax at an outdoor café and have a drink or a meal while watching other people stroll by.

Skiing is a popular sport as well as a regular form of transportation for Europeans living in small villages in mountainous regions.

The family is the basic social unit, and many activities revolve around the home and family events. In many parts of Europe, especially in the southern and eastern regions, it is still the custom for several generations of a family to live together. Children are trained to be polite and quiet in the presence of adults, but their upbringing is not as strict as it was before World War II. The father of a family has traditionally been the main wage earner, but more and more European women are seeking jobs outside the home.

Living standards vary throughout Europe. They are highest in western and northern European countries, both in the cities and in rural (country) areas. In eastern and southern Europe, city dwellers are more likely to have modern conveniences than country dwellers.

Food and Drink

Although the French style of cooking is the best known, each nation of Europe has its own food specialties. These include the roast beef and Yorkshire pudding of England, the *smörgåsbord* (buffet of cold and hot appetizers) of Sweden, the numerous varieties of pasta of Italy, the goulash (paprika-flavored beef stew) of Hungary, and the *mousáká* (ground lamb and eggplant) of Greece, to name just a few. Wines from France, Germany, Italy, and Hungary; cheeses from the Netherlands, France, and Switzerland; chocolates from Belgium and Switzerland; and caviar from Russia are world famous.

Dress

While each European nation or region has its own distinctive dress, such traditional clothes are usually worn only on special occasions, and most Europeans wear modern dress. European teenagers, like those the world over, are fond of blue jeans.

Sports and Recreation

Soccer is the most popular sport throughout Europe, although basketball has grown in popularity in recent years. Cricket is played in the United Kingdom. Skiing is a traditional sport in Norway and in the Alpine regions of Switzerland, France, and Austria. Bicycling is both a popular sport and a common form of transportation.

Vacationers come from all over the world to enjoy the Riviera and other sparkling beachfronts along the Mediterranean coast. Tourism is one of Europe's most profitable industries.

▶ ECONOMY

Europe's economy suffered tremendously after World War II, but it recovered with the help of the Marshall Plan, an economic aid package offered by the United States. The creation of the European Economic Community (EEC, or Common Market) in 1957 further strengthened economic conditions.

Services

In recent years, heavy industry has declined, while such service industries as government and banking have gained strength. Shopping has increasingly become a leisure activity, and many stores have begun lengthening their hours of operation to attract buyers. Also of growing importance are the so-called knowledge industries, involving research and the use of advanced computers and other modern technologies.

Tourism is one of Europe's largest and most varied service industries. Most non-Europeans who vacation there come from the United States and Japan. Mountainous regions, particularly the Alps, the Pyrenees, and the Cairngorms in Scotland, attract skiers. The beaches of the Mediterranean draw sun-seekers, with the Riviera being a particularly fashionable destination. Dozens of cities such as London, Paris, Rome, and Vienna, are magnets for those interested in the arts.

Manufacturing

The chief manufacturing regions of Europe lie in a belt extending from the United Kingdom through northern France, Belgium, and the Netherlands into Germany, Poland, the Czech Republic, the Donets Basin area in Ukraine, and the Urals region of Russia. Concentrations of heavy industry are also found in Italy's Po Valley, parts of Switzerland, and central Sweden.

Europe's manufactured products include steel, textiles, machinery, and processed foods; motor vehicles and transportation equipment; and petrochemicals. Western Europe has long been

The manufacture of automobiles and other motor vehicles and transportation equipment is an important industry throughout Europe.

Wine grapes are grown in most southern European countries. *Above:* The vineyards of the Bordeaux region of France produce some of the world's finest wines.

industrialized, but industry developed in eastern Europe only after World War II.

Agriculture and Fishing

Although Europe is a small continent, it is one of the most important agricultural areas of the world. It produces substantial amounts of the world's wheat, oats, rye, potatoes, dairy products, and meat. The land is intensively farmed and yields are generally high.

In western Europe, farms are usually small and under private ownership. In some countries, such as France, the government has encouraged farmers to combine their lands into larger plots so that they can be more productive. The cooperative movement, where farmers share in the cultivation and sale of crops, is strong in Scandinavia.

Land use varies, depending on the characteristics of a particular region—its type of land and climate. The region just south of the taiga consists largely of pastureland, where dairy cattle and other livestock are raised. Here the main crops grown are fodder (food) for livestock. Milk, butter, and cheese are the main products, but chickens are also raised for their meat and eggs. The Netherlands and Denmark are among Europe's leading producers of dairy products. Some kinds of vegetables can also be grown here. In addition, greenhouses are used to grow crops such as tomatoes and grapes, which otherwise would not ripen.

Farther south is a region where grains, especially wheat and rye, are the most important crops. Sugar beets and potatoes are also of great economic importance in this region. Some cattle are raised as well. Grapes are grown in vineyards, and apples, pears, and cherries are cultivated in orchards. One of Europe's largest grain-growing regions is Ukraine, a land of vast plains and rich black soils.

In the southern part of this region, where summers are warmer, corn competes with wheat for importance. Europe's corn-growing area extends from northern Portugal through southern France and northern Italy into the Danube River basin and then eastward to the borders of the Caspian Sea. Vegetables and fruits are grown in truck gardens near the large cities and are sold in local markets. In the mild climate of the Black Sea region, citrus fruits, tea, and grapes can be grown.

Land use changes dramatically in the Mediterranean region. Much of the land here is too rugged to be productive, and summers are too dry for summer crops to be grown without irrigation. If water is available for irrigation, fruits and vegetables grow abundantly. Many areas are famous for their wine grapes. Oranges are a typical crop, and large yields of rice can be obtained. Olives and figs grow well on the hilly slopes. Sheep and goats are more plentiful than dairy cattle.

Since the days of the Vikings the people of the region have turned to the sea for a living. The North Atlantic is one of the world's leading fishing grounds. The shallow seas bordering northwestern Europe have long provided substantial harvests of cod and herring. Commercial fishing traditionally was an important part of the economies of coastal areas of the United Kingdom, Norway, Denmark, France, the Netherlands, Germany, and

Some of Europe's largest coal deposits are found in the Donets Basin in Ukraine. Poland is also one of the chief coal-producing countries in eastern Europe. Russia has large deposits of coal and oil. Romania produces oil both from its Ploesti fields and from offshore deposits in the Black Sea.

The chief petroleum and natural gas fields in western Europe are located in the North Sea. These especially benefit the United Kingdom and Norway, and to a lesser extent Denmark, the Netherlands, and Germany. Much of western Europe's oil, however, must still be imported.

Sweden, Switzerland, Austria, and France have abundant sources of hydroelectric power (energy produced from rushing or falling water), which partly offsets their lack of coal and oil. Russia also produces enormous amounts of hydroelectric power, with two of the world's largest hydroelectric power stations located on the Volga River.

Nuclear power is especially important in western Europe because of its limited deposits of petroleum. France, Germany, the United Kingdom, and

Vast petroleum and natural gas deposits were discovered beneath the North Sea in 1959. The North Sea has since become a major source of oil and gas production.

Portugal. Iceland depends on fishing for most of its income. The Mediterranean Sea, historically, has also been a major fishing region. Although fishing is still carried out in both regions, it is now of less importance.

Energy

Petroleum has surpassed coal as the leading source of energy in Europe, but coal remains important. Western Europe's chief coal mining area extends from Britain into northern France and through Belgium into Germany. The major concentrations of bituminous (soft) coal are in Britain and Germany's Ruhr Valley. Eastern Germany has large deposits of lignite (brown coal).

Sweden are among the chief producers of nuclear energy. However, several western European nations, including Sweden and Germany, are reconsidering their nuclear power programs because of the safety factor. Sweden and the United Kingdom are expected to phase out their nuclear power plants.

Trade

Trade is essential to Europe's prosperity. In spite of extensive agriculture, most western European nations cannot grow enough food to feed their relatively large populations. Because of their limited natural resources, most countries must also import raw materials for their industries. The United Kingdom, for

Left: Eurostar trains provide passenger service between Britain and France by way of the Chunnel, an underwater tunnel in the English Channel. *Above:* Rotterdam-Europoort, the world's busiest port, provides a gateway to the industrial centers of northern Europe.

example, must import about half its food and industrial raw materials.

Today's European Union (EU), an extension of the Common Market, was founded to remove trade restrictions among the member countries. It is now the largest single trading bloc in the world.

Transportation

Railways. Europe has more railroads per square mile than anywhere else in the world. Much freight is still carried by trains that link key industrial regions. Modern passenger trains moving at high speeds are a comfortable way to travel. In 1994, for the first time in history, Britain and the European mainland were connected by rail with the opening of the underwater Channel Tunnel (popularly known as the Chunnel).

Roadways. The number of private automobiles has increased tremendously as the people of western Europe have improved their standard of living. There are far fewer cars in eastern Europe. European roads vary in quality. Although there are modern highways, such as the Autobahn in Germany and the Autostrada in Italy, many of the smaller, narrower roads cannot handle the growing traffic.

Airways. All of Europe's major cities have international airports. Air France, British Airways, Aer Lingus (Ireland), Alitalia (Italy), Lufthansa (Germany), and KLM (the Netherlands) are just a few of the continent's major airlines.

Ports and Waterways. Europoort, which serves Rotterdam and the interior of the Netherlands, is Europe's largest port. Other leading European ports include Le Havre and Marseilles in France; Antwerp in Belgium; the British port of London; Hamburg and Bremen in northern Germany; Naples in Italy; and Odesa on the Black Sea in Ukraine.

Canals were being built in Europe long before there were railroads. They connect the navigable rivers and are used to transport freight.

Among the many navigable rivers in Europe, the most important are the Rhine, the Danube, and the Volga. The Rhine is one of the world's most traveled rivers. It is usable by ships from its outlet, the city of Rotterdam in the Netherlands, to the town of Basel in Switzerland. The Rhine is connected by canal with the Danube. The Volga and its many tributaries are Russia's most important waterways.

▶ MAJOR CITIES

Europe has more than 30 urban centers with populations of more than 1 million people. The two largest, with more than 9 million each, are **Paris**, the capital of France, and **Moscow**, the capital of Russia. **Istanbul**, a city that lies in both Europe and Asia, also has more than 9 million residents. Europe's next largest city, with more than 7 million people, is **London**, the capital of the United Kingdom.

Other interesting capital cities in western Europe are **Amsterdam** (the Netherlands), **Copenhagen** (Denmark), **Stockholm** (Sweden), **Oslo** (Norway), **Rome** (Italy), **Madrid** (Spain), **Lisbon** (Portugal), and **Vienna** (Austria). The largest capitals in central, eastern, and southeastern Europe include **Prague** (Czech Republic), **Belgrade** (Serbia and Montenegro), **Budapest** (Hungary), **Bucharest** (Romania), **Warsaw** (Poland), and **Athens** (Greece).

Most of Europe's capitals and other major cities have an Old World charm dating back at least one thousand years. *Clockwise from right:* Trolley cars pass through the main square of Zagreb, the capital of Croatia; gondolas ply the Grand Canal in Venice, Italy; pedestrians rest beside shaded tree-lined boulevards in Madrid, the capital of Spain.

▶ CULTURAL HERITAGE

Among the most striking reminders of the long European artistic tradition are the ruins of ancient temples in Greece, where Western civilization began more than 2,500 years ago. Later the Romans, who studied the ancient Greeks, represented European culture.

During the Middle Ages, Christianity was the most influential force in European art and architecture. In the West, its greatest examples are still found in the religious paintings and soaring Gothic churches of the period. In the East, in the Byzantine Empire centered in Constantinople, a distinctive form of art developed that still remains a part of the Eastern Orthodox church.

The classical tradition of ancient Greece was given new life during the Renaissance, which began in Italy in the 1300's and later spread to the rest of western Europe. The works of the great European painters of this and later periods can be seen in museums throughout the world.

Western music began in Europe centuries ago. The opera, symphony, concerto, ballet, and other familiar musical forms are all European in origin.

As in music, many forms of literature were perfected in Europe, including the novel, essay, and such types of poetry as the ode, epic, and sonnet. Western science, art, and philosophy originated in Greece and, literally, had a "rebirth" in Italy during the period known as the Renaissance. A list of the great thinkers and scientific discoverers would include names from many European countries. Later, new European ideas about science, society, government, and economics began to influence other parts of the world

▶ HISTORY

Prehistoric Times. Modern humans were already living in Europe during the last Ice Age. After the ice retreated and the climate warmed, about 15,000 years ago, populations began to move. The early Europeans lived by hunting and fishing and only slowly became animal herders and farmers. Stone was first

367

IMPORTANT DATES

1600?–1400? B.C.	Period of Minoan civilization.
753 B.C.	Traditional date of the founding of Rome.
500? B.C.	Beginning of the Golden Age of Greece; Athens became the center of Greek civilization.
431–404 B.C.	Peloponnesian War between Athens and Sparta led to the decline of Athens.
218–201 B.C.	Second Punic War; Roman armies defeated Hannibal and Carthaginian army; marked rise of Roman power.
31 B.C.	Roman Empire established.
A.D. 324	Emperor Constantine, first Christian Roman emperor, made Constantinople his capital.
395	Roman Empire divided into eastern and western halves.
476	Traditional date for fall of Western Roman Empire.
711	Muslims invaded Spain.
800	Charlemagne crowned "emperor of the Romans."
800?–1000	Period of greatest Viking power; about 1000, Vikings reached North America.
1054	Eastern Orthodox Church cut ties with Rome.
1066	Normans invaded England.
1096	First Crusade to Holy Land began.
1215	King John signed Magna Carta, cornerstone of English liberties.
1270	Last Crusade to Holy Land began.
1300?	Renaissance began in Italy.
1387?	Chaucer began writing *The Canterbury Tales*.
1453	Constantinople (now Istanbul) fell to the Ottoman Turks, ending the Byzantine Empire.
1453?–55?	Johann Gutenberg issued first Bible printed in movable type.
1492	Christopher Columbus made his first voyage to the Americas.
1497–98	Vasco da Gama found sea route to India.
1513	Vasco Núñez de Balboa became first European to see Pacific Ocean.
1517	Martin Luther posted 95 theses on church door in Wittenberg, beginning Protestant Reformation.
1519	Ferdinand Magellan began first round-the-world voyage.
1536	John Calvin published *Institutes of the Christian Religion*.
1543	Nicolaus Copernicus published *On the Revolutions of the Heavenly Bodies*, a description of solar system.
1545	Council of Trent opened, with aim of reforming Roman Catholic Church.
1571	Turks defeated at Battle of Lepanto; Turkish naval power declines in the Mediterranean.
1588	English fleet crushed the Spanish Armada; beginning of England's importance as a world power.
1601?	William Shakespeare's *Hamlet* first produced.
1607	First English colony in America founded at Jamestown (Virginia).
1609	Johannes Kepler published his *New Astronomy*, describing laws of planetary movement.
1618–48	Thirty Years' War involved most of Europe.
1620	Pilgrims landed at Plymouth Rock.
1687	Sir Isaac Newton published his *Mathematical Principles of Natural Philosophy* (*Principia*), describing laws of motion and gravitation.
1689	Parliamentary government established in England; Bill of Rights proclaimed.
Mid-1700's	Industrial Revolution began in Britain.
1775	Britain's American colonies started War for Independence.
1789	French Revolution began.
1804	Napoleon became emperor of the French.
1815	Napoleon I defeated at the Battle of Waterloo.
1859	*On the Origin of Species by Means of Natural Selection* published by Charles Darwin.
1861	Victor Emmanuel II became first king of Italy.
1867	Karl Marx finished the first volume of *Das Kapital*, his revolutionary work on Communist theory.
1870–71	France defeated in Franco-Prussian War.
1871	German Empire founded.
1914–18	World War I.
1917	Revolution in Russia overthrew the czar.
1922	Union of Soviet Socialist Republics established.
1933	Adolf Hitler became chancellor of Germany.
1939–45	World War II.
1945	United Nations founded.
1949	North Atlantic Treaty Organization (NATO) formed.
1956	Hungarian rebellion against Communist rule suppressed.
1958	European Economic Community (Common Market) founded.
1961	Soviet Union's *Vostok 1* became first manned space capsule to orbit the Earth.
1962	Twenty-first Ecumenical Council opened.
1968	Czechoslovakia's attempt to liberalize Communist rule ended by Soviet troops.
1973	United Kingdom, Ireland, and Denmark were formally admitted to the European Economic Community (EEC).
1974	Government coup in Portugal led to independence for Portuguese territories in Africa.
1981	Greece was formally admitted to the European Economic Community.
1986	Spain and Portugal officially became members of the European Economic Community.
1989	Soviet Union began political and economic reforms; popular governments elected in former Communist nations of eastern Europe.
1990	Germany was reunited as a single nation.
1991	Soviet Union recognized the independence of Latvia, Lithuania, and Estonia; Russia, Ukraine, Belarus, and Moldova became independent nations.
1991–92	Slovenia, Croatia, Macedonia, and Bosnia and Herzegovina declared their independence from Yugoslavia, leaving a smaller Yugoslav state made up of Serbia and Montenegro. Civil war erupted, mainly in Bosnia.
1993	Czechoslovakia split into two separate nations: the Czech Republic and Slovakia.
2002	The euro replaced the national currencies in 12 of the 15 member nations of the European Union; major flooding along the Danube and other rivers in Central Europe caused billions of dollars in damages.
2003	The two remaining republics of Yugoslavia renamed the country Serbia and Montenegro.

used for tools and weapons, followed by copper and bronze and later iron. Europe was very backward in comparison with the highly developed civilizations of Egypt and Babylon. But those ancient Europeans had an artistic sense, as indicated by the wall paintings that can still be seen in caves in southern France and Spain.

Ancient Greece and Rome. Civilization came to Europe by way of the eastern Mediterranean. The island of Crete was known for its great culture as early as 2000 B.C. Somewhat later the Greek city-states developed. The most important of

Europe was the birthplace of Western civilization. *Above:* Cave paintings discovered in southwestern France date back 17,000 years. *Left:* In Roman times, the forum was the center of business and government administration.

these was Athens. Greek art, science, poetry, drama, and philosophy formed the cornerstone of European civilization. It was also in Greece that the idea of democracy was born. Greek merchants as well as those from Phoenicia (in what is now Lebanon) established colonies along the European coasts of the Mediterranean.

During the last centuries before Christ, Rome gradually extended its power from its central location on the Italian peninsula. At its height, during the first centuries A.D., the Roman Empire ruled most of the island of Great Britain, western and southern Europe, and nearby regions of Africa and Asia. On the continent the Roman boundary roughly followed the Danube River. Beyond that lay a Europe inhabited largely by Germanic peoples but influenced by Roman ideas. Roman roads and settlements had opened the European continent and made it part of the civilized world. The Latin language and the Christian religion, which spread through western Europe in the later centuries of the Roman Empire, helped unite Europe.

The Roman Empire in the West gradually weakened under attacks from Germanic tribes on its borders and eventually fell to them in the A.D. 400's. However, the eastern half of the Roman Empire, located at Constantinople (modern Istanbul) and known as Byzantium or the Byzantine Empire, flourished for a thousand years more.

The Middle Ages and the Renaissance. The period following the end of the Western Roman Empire is known as the Middle Ages. Familiar to us as a time of warring nobles, knights in armor, and fortified castles, it was also a period in which western Europe was split into many small kingdoms and principalities. Western Europe was briefly united, from 800 to 814, under Charlemagne. A little more than a century later, Otto I, in imitation of the Roman Empire, established the Holy Roman Empire in what is now Germany and parts of Italy and eastern Europe. Although it lasted in name until the early 1800's, the Holy Roman Empire became little more than a federation of many small states.

Beginning in the 1300's, Europe underwent a rebirth of interest in ancient Greek and Roman art and literature. This rebirth of classical learning, called the Renaissance, led to one of the greatest periods of artistic creativity in European history. It originated in Italy and, over the next 300 years, spread through western and northern Europe.

Empire Building and the Reformation. In 1453, Constantinople, the capital of the Byzantine Empire, fell to the Ottoman Turks, who began their long rule of southeastern and parts of central Europe. Christopher Columbus' first voyage of discovery to the Caribbean Sea in 1492 began the great age of exploration and settlement of the Americas, as Spain, Portugal, England, France, and the Netherlands established colonies in the New World.

The religious disputes between Catholics and Protestants that had begun with the Reformation reached a head in the Thirty Years' War (1618–48). Starting as a religious war, it eventually became a political one.

France emerged from the war as a leading power in Europe, a role it kept for nearly 300 years. England and the Netherlands built empires based on sea power and trade. Spain's great wealth was drawn from the gold and silver of its colonies in America. Habsburg emperors ruled Austria, parts of Italy, and the states of the Holy Roman Empire.

Two Revolutions. The Industrial Revolution began in Britain in the mid-1700's and transformed Europe. Goods once made by hand were now made by machines. The steam engine was the first of many inventions that would forever change methods of transportation. Cities expanded as people moved from the countryside to work in the growing factories. Britain's head start in becoming an industrialized nation helped make it a world power.

The French Revolution (1789–99), which overthrew the French king, stressed liberty and equality, radical ideas in Europe at the time. But France had a republican government only briefly. In 1804, Napoleon, whose armies had conquered much of western Europe, made himself emperor of the French. Napoleon was finally defeated by an alliance of European nations led by Britain in 1814 and again in 1815, and the French monarch was restored to the throne.

In the early 1800's, the French emperor Napoleon I nearly succeeded in conquering all of Europe. He was defeated in 1815 by an alliance of nations led by Britain.

Vladimir Ilich Lenin, a Communist revolutionary and founder of the Soviet Union, was among the most influential leaders of the 1900's.

Nationalism and Imperialism. The 1800's was a period of growing nationalism. European peoples still under foreign domination struggled to win independence, while others sought unification as nations. Belgium gained independence from the Netherlands in 1830. Greece freed itself from Ottoman Turkish rule that year, and other southeastern European countries were eventually to do the same. Although Hungary failed in its attempt to win independence from Austria in 1848, it became a partner in the Austro-Hungarian Empire. Italy was united as an independent nation in the second half of the 1800's, and Germany was created out of the states of the former Holy Roman Empire in 1871.

During the middle and late 1800's, European powers carved out new colonial empires in Africa and Asia. Britain—whose empire included Canada, India, and Australia and rivaled that of ancient Rome—and France were the chief imperial powers. But Belgium and Germany also joined the race to acquire African colonies.

Two World Wars. The map of Europe took most of its present shape as a result of World War I (1914–18). The new countries of Austria, Hungary, Czechoslovakia, and Yugoslavia emerged from the ruins of the

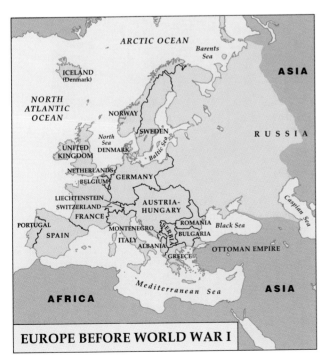

EUROPE BEFORE WORLD WAR I

EUROPE AFTER WORLD WAR I

Austro-Hungarian Empire. Poland, which for more than a century had been partitioned among its neighbors, was again made an independent nation. In Russia, revolutions in 1917 overthrew the czar and led to the creation of the Soviet Union, the world's first Communist state. Finland won independence, along with Latvia, Lithuania, and Estonia, but the latter three were later absorbed into the Soviet Union.

World War II (1939–45) was equally far-reaching in its political impact. It left Britain and France weaker than they once were, while the Soviet Union emerged from the war, along with the United States, as a major world superpower. The Soviet Union came

the gradual independence of former European colonies, mostly throughout Africa and Asia.

Between 1989 and 1992, democratic movements spread rapidly across eastern Europe, and free elections brought popular governments to power. Germany, divided into a Communist East and a non-Communist West, was reunited in 1990. In 1991, Yugoslavia broke into various independent republics, which resulted in numerous civil wars throughout the Balkans. The Soviet Union also broke apart at the end of 1991, and from it emerged seven additional independent nations in Europe—Russia, Ukraine, Belarus, Moldova, Latvia, Lithuania, and Estonia.

The European Parliament is an elected body of the European Union (EU), an organization that promotes political and economic unity among its member nations.

to dominate eastern Europe, whose countries were under the rule of Communist governments.

Modern Europe. Western Europe recovered rapidly from the war's destruction, with economic aid from the United States through the Marshall Plan. In eastern Europe, recovery was much slower, as countries that were once mainly agricultural sought to industrialize quickly. The years following World War II were also marked by

Europe's map changed again in 1993, when Czechoslovakia peacefully split into two separate nations, the Czech Republic and Slovakia. And in 2003, the two remaining republics of Yugoslavia renamed the country Serbia and Montenegro.

DALE R. LOTT
SAMUEL VAN VALKENBURG
Author, *Elements of Political Geography*

Reviewed by JEREMY BLACK
University of Exeter

A Vietnamese American family gathers for a group portrait. Most Asian American families are close knit, and several generations may live within one household.

ASIAN AMERICANS

Asian Americans are U.S. citizens who were born in Asia or whose ancestors emigrated from Asia. They are one of the country's fastest-growing minority groups. According to the U.S. Census, some 12 million Americans—approximately 4 percent of the total population—claim Asian ancestry. This percentage was expected to grow to 10 percent by 2050.

The majority of Asian Americans—more than 20 percent—are of Chinese origin. Americans of Filipino ancestry form the next largest group, followed by Asian Indian, Vietnamese, Korean, and Japanese Americans. Increasingly, the term **Asian Pacific Americans** is used, to encompass people from the Pacific Islands (including native Hawaiians).

About half of all Asian Americans live in three states: California, New York, and Hawaii. Influential cities with large Asian populations include New York City, Los Angeles, San Francisco, and Honolulu.

▶ WAY OF LIFE

The traditional Asian American way of life emphasizes family values, a reverence for education, a strong work ethic, religious observance, and participation in community events.

Family Life. Most Asian American families are close knit, with several generations sometimes living within one household. Respect for elders and the importance of study and hard work are among the values passed along to younger family members. Traditional val-ues sometimes conflict with the American ideal of individual freedom. For example, Asian American women have sought to gain greater equality in the home and workplace while remaining respectful of traditional roles.

Religion. Asian Americans practice a number of different religions, depending on their ethnic origins. Buddhism, Confucianism, Hinduism, Islam, and Taoism are among the leading faiths. Christianity is also widely practiced—many U.S. Christian denominations have been reinvigorated by the presence of active Korean and Chinese churches.

Holidays and Cultural Celebrations. For Chinese and Vietnamese Americans, the lunar New Year holiday is an occasion for celebration and renewal. The Korean Harvest Festival and the Chinese Moon Festival, both celebrated in September, are times to give thanks for the gifts and abundance of the year.

Several Asian American groups celebrate Children's Day on May 5 to honor future generations. In summer, Japanese Americans celebrate Nisei Week, a cultural festival first held in 1934. Many Asian Indian Americans celebrate two national holidays of India: Independence Day, on August 15, and Republic Day, on January 26. In May of each year, Asian American Heritage Month commemorates the Asian American experience.

▶ INFLUENCES ON AMERICAN CULTURE

Asian influences can be found in many areas of American culture. For example, the English language has been enriched by words with Asian origins, including tycoon (a powerful businessperson), guru (a spiritual guide or teacher), and yen (a strong desire or craving).

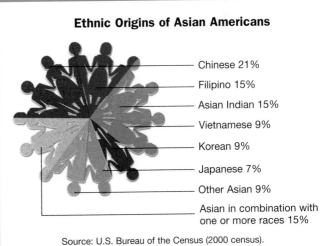

Ethnic Origins of Asian Americans

Chinese 21%
Filipino 15%
Asian Indian 15%
Vietnamese 9%
Korean 9%
Japanese 7%
Other Asian 9%
Asian in combination with one or more races 15%

Source: U.S. Bureau of the Census (2000 census).

Right: Asian Indian women in traditional dress take a lunch break in Pasadena, California. Many women of Asian descent have blended successfully into American society while maintaining their cultural identity. *Below:* Business associates review design plans. Asian American business professionals work in many different fields.

Most Americans are familiar with Chinese foods such as dim sum (assorted appetizers) and Japanese sushi (raw fish with rice). Indian curries and tandoori dishes (meats and breads cooked in a clay oven) are increasingly popular. Other well-known Asian dishes include kimchi (spicy pickled cabbage) from Korea; pad thai, a noodle dish from Thailand; and pho bo, Vietnamese noodle soup. Many chefs have adapted Asian seasonings and cooking techniques to create a cuisine known as Asian fusion.

Most of the best-known martial arts originated in Asia—judo, karate, and aikido in Japan; kung fu in China; and tae kwon do in Korea. Yoga, an ancient Indian discipline, is widely practiced today as a form of exercise and relaxation. Many Americans practice tai chi chuan, an ancient Chinese system of exercises.

Chinese Americans introduced holistic healing—an approach to health care that considers the whole person—to American medicine, as well as alternative therapies such as acupuncture. Western design has been influenced by the Chinese concept of feng shui, which aims to achieve balance and harmony in one's environment. And many Americans have embraced Zen Buddhism, a form of the Buddhist faith that stresses the practice of meditation as a means of enlightenment.

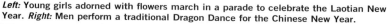

Left: Young girls adorned with flowers march in a parade to celebrate the Laotian New Year. *Right:* Men perform a traditional Dragon Dance for the Chinese New Year.

▶ NOTABLE ASIAN AMERICANS

Asian Americans have made important contributions to nearly every aspect of American life. In politics, Dalip Singh Saund became the first Asian American to serve in the U.S. Congress, in 1956. In 2000, Norman Yoshio Mineta became the first Asian American member of a U.S. presidential cabinet. In science, Tsung Dao Lee and Chen Ning Yang were the first Asian Americans to receive the Nobel Prize, for their work in physics in 1957. Entrepreneurs Charles Wang and Jerry Yang are leaders in technology.

Many Asian Americans have had distinguished careers in the arts, including orchestra conductors Seiji Ozawa (the first Asian American to direct a major American symphony orchestra) and Zubin Mehta, cellist Yo-Yo Ma, and violinists Sarah Chang and Midori. The elegant and functional designs of I. M. Pei are landmarks of modern architecture. Authors Maxine Hong Kingston, Amy Tan, Jhumpa Lahiri, and Bharati Mukherjee have told of the Asian immigrant experience in their work, as have filmmakers Ang Lee and Wayne Wang.

Asian American athletes have excelled in a variety of sports. Divers Sammy Lee and Vicki Manalo Draves won gold medals at the 1948 Olympic Games. Kristi Yamaguchi, the first Asian American to win an Olympic gold medal in figure skating (1992), and Michelle Kwan are leading figure skaters. Other important Asian American athletes include tennis player Michael Chang and golfer Tiger Woods (who is of both African American and Asian American heritage).

▶ HISTORY

Early Asian Immigration. The first Chinese immigrants went to the United States in 1849, attracted by the discovery of gold in California. Thousands more immigrated to the state in 1865 to help build the transcontinental railroad. The Chinese were paid very low wages. Many other workers regarded cheap Chinese labor as a threat. This led to outbreaks of violence and, in 1882, the Chinese Exclusion Act, which barred all Chinese laborers from immigrating to the United States.

Above: A Korean grocer welcomes a customer to his market in Los Angeles. The city has one of the country's largest populations of Asian Americans. **Left:** An acupuncturist works with a patient. Acupuncture, a traditional form of Chinese medicine, is one of many Asian influences on American culture.

Meanwhile, Japanese immigrants arrived in Hawaii to work on the sugar plantations and in California to work on farms. After the United States acquired the Philippines from Spain in 1898, many Filipinos went to work in agriculture and in the cannery industries along the Pacific Coast. In 1903, the Pensionado Act gave Filipino students the opportunity to study in the United States. (The students were called pensionados because they were supported by government stipends.)

Asian Exclusion. Although Asian immigrants were establishing themselves in the United States, they were excluded from full participation in American society. For example, California and other western states passed alien land laws that prohibited Asians from owning land. At various times, the U.S. government restricted or prohibited immigration from certain Asian countries.

Despite the obstacles they faced, Asian Americans created vibrant communities. In the 1880's, Chinese residents of San Francisco established laundries that became bustling places of business, and the area soon evolved into the city's famous Chinatown. Other Chinatowns flourished, as did Koreatowns, Little Tokyos, and Manilatowns.

World War II. Japan's surprise attack on the U.S. naval base at Pearl Harbor in 1941 caused the United States to enter World War II (1939–45). In 1942 a combination of hysteria and mistrust of the Japanese led to the forced impris-

375

Japanese Americans line up at a relocation center in Manzanar, California, in 1942. During World War II, thousands of persons of Japanese ancestry were forced into detention camps.

Asia—India, Thailand, Taiwan, Malaysia, and Burma. They came for both economic and educational opportunities.

The aftermath of the Vietnam War (1957–75) brought more immigrants from Southeast Asia, including Vietnamese, Lao, and Cambodians. They have added diversity to a number of cities. Vietnamese, for example, have established an important center in Orange County, California, known as Little Saigon.

Modern-Day Issues. As the Asian American population has grown, new challenges have arisen. The perception of the Asian American as a high-achieving "model minority" has sometimes caused those in need of social services to be overlooked.

In the late 1960's an Asian American movement arose. Inspired by the African American civil rights movement, it sought equality, social justice, and political empowerment for Asian Americans. Departments of Asian American studies were established at major universities. Japanese Americans, after years of silence about the detention camps of World War II, fought to redress the wrongs that had been done. Under the 1988 federal Civil Liberties Act, the government apologized and paid reparations to survivors.

Asian Americans continue to work toward a better America through numerous organizations. Advocacy groups such as Asian Immigrant Women Advocates and the Asian Law Caucus work for immigrant rights and other reforms. The Committee Against Anti-Asian Violence fights racial hatred.

Institutions such as the Wing Luke Asian Museum in Seattle, Washington, and the Asia Society in New York City promote awareness of Asian culture. Newspapers such as *The Rafu Shimpo* and *AsianWeek* help educate and inform Asian Americans as well as the wider community.

JUDY SOO HOO
UCLA Asian American Studies Center

onment of more than 110,000 Japanese Americans in relocation camps in desolate regions of the country. Even U.S.-born citizens of Japanese ancestry were forced to abandon homes, schools, and businesses. To show their patriotism, many Japanese Americans from the camps volunteered to serve in the U.S. Army. The all-Japanese American unit, the 442nd, was the most highly decorated of the war.

However, conditions for other Asian groups improved during wartime. Chinese and Filipinos were employed in the booming war industry or joined the army to fight. Their contributions were recognized, and the U.S. government changed a number of laws that had prevented Asians from exercising their rights. The Chinese Exclusion Act was repealed in 1943, allowing Chinese to become citizens. With the passage of the Luce-Cellar Act in 1946, citizenship rights were granted to Filipinos and Asian Indians.

After World War II, Congress passed the War Brides Act, which allowed women—including Asian women—to immigrate to America as brides of U.S. servicemen. Other legislative changes resulted in the granting of citizenship rights to Japanese and Koreans and the repeal of the alien land laws in 1956.

A New Wave of Immigration. In 1965, amendments to the Immigration and Nationality Act removed the national origins quota system that had limited Asian immigration to the United States. As a result, the Asian American population grew dramatically. Asians immigrated to the United States not only from China, Japan, and the Philippines but from elsewhere in

ASTHMA

Asthma is a long-term disease affecting the airways to the lungs. It causes breathing difficulties that may be mild, moderate, or severe. Asthma often begins in childhood, but a person can develop it at any time of life. In the United States, more than 10 million adults and nearly 5 million children have asthma.

In many people with asthma, the airways to the lungs become inflamed and more likely to be irritated when exposed to certain physical and environmental triggers. This can start breathing difficulties that result in an asthma attack. An attack can come on suddenly or slowly and can last from a few minutes to several days.

Asthma is a disease that causes breathing difficulties. It is often treated with medication that is inhaled directly into the lungs.

During an asthma attack, bands of muscles surrounding the airways tighten, the lining of the airways swells, and glands inside the airways produce excess mucus. These three things reduce the opening of the airways and make it difficult to breathe. Symptoms of an attack include coughing, shortness of breath, tightness in the chest, and wheezing.

Most mild or moderate asthma attacks can be controlled with medicine. Sometimes, however, an attack can be severe and even life threatening. Symptoms such as extreme difficulty breathing or talking and blue lips or fingertips indicate an emergency, and 911 or the local emergency number should be called immediately.

Causes. Asthma has no single cause. Instead, attacks are brought on by a variety of triggers, acting alone or in combination. In many people, attacks are brought on by allergic reactions to pollen, dust, grass, mold, animal dander, foods, and other allergens. Other triggers include tobacco smoke, air pollution, viral infections such as colds, and strenuous physical exercise. Asthma is known to run in families.

Between 1980 and 1994, the number of reported cases of asthma in the United States rose by 75 percent. Possible causes for this increase include greater exposure to air pollutants and to indoor triggers such as dust mites and cigarette smoke. Another theory suggests that modern advances such as vaccinations and antibiotics may prevent childhood infections that actually keep the immune system from developing the changes that lead to asthma. Much research is being done in these areas.

Treatment. Although there is no cure for asthma, it can be controlled with medication. It is important to have a doctor diagnose and treat asthma. Once a diagnosis is made, a doctor can prepare a personalized asthma action plan. This tells the patient how to use asthma medicines and what to do if symptoms appear. Fast-acting medicines can stop an attack by relaxing the muscles around the airways. Long-term treatment includes the use of steroids to control inflammation and swelling, thus preventing attacks. Most asthma medication is breathed directly into the lungs with an inhaler. All asthma medicines are safe and cause few or no side effects when used according to a doctor's instructions.

Asthma can also be controlled by avoiding the triggers that cause airway irritation. (People with asthma should not avoid exercise, however; instead, they should use medicine to control the reaction.) If the trigger is an allergen, special skin or blood tests can identify the substance so that it can be avoided or the allergy treated.

Part of an asthma action plan may include self monitoring with a small handheld device called a peak flow meter. By blowing forcefully into the meter, patients can measure how well their lungs are working and thus better manage their asthma.

ADRIAN M. CASILLAS, M.D.
UCLA School of Medicine

OBESITY

Obesity—excessive body fat—is a fast-growing epidemic and one of the largest public health problems in the industrialized world. It increases the risk of many diseases, as well as of early death, and may lead to social and emotional problems.

In the United States, two out of three adults are overweight. Within this group, one in three is obese. An adult is considered overweight when a measurement called the Body Mass Index (BMI) is 25 or more. Obesity is defined as a BMI of 30 or more. (For more information about the BMI, see the feature accompanying this article.)

Although many children have excess body fat, the medical community does not term them obese. Instead, they are said to be "at risk" of being overweight or simply "overweight," based on the BMI. Recent figures indicate that nearly one in three American children is at risk and one in six is overweight. Studies show that those who remain overweight throughout their school years are more likely to be obese adults.

Obesity is sometimes linked to certain medical disorders, such as diabetes, and to genetic (inherited) traits, such as a greater tendency to store excess calories as body fat. In most cases, however, lifestyle plays a major role. In the United States and elsewhere, people are snacking more often, eating larger portions, and consuming more fattening foods, such as fast foods and sugary soft drinks. And they are less active than in the past, spending more of their leisure time watching television or sitting at the computer. When the food energy, or calories, taken in each day exceeds the energy spent in physical activity, body fat rises.

Obesity is considered a significant public health issue because overweight and obese people have many more health problems than people of normal weight. They are at much greater risk for cardiovascular disease, type II diabetes, high blood pressure, certain types of cancer, and lung and bone problems. Many overweight children suffer from adjustment problems and depression, which can be severe and may not disappear with age. Because of the health problems associated with it, obesity is expensive. In the United States, health care costs related to obesity are estimated to exceed $120 billion each year. For all these reasons, the risk of obesity should be identified early in life and controlled.

A doctor or other health professional is the best person to determine whether a person's weight is healthy. For an adult, this is done by calculating the BMI. For a child, it is done by calculating the BMI during each checkup and plotting it on a graph, then observing how it changes as the child grows. A child is considered at risk when the BMI reaches the graph's 85th percentile and overweight when the BMI reaches the 95th percentile.

If a weight problem is identified, a doctor will first rule out any medical condition as the cause, then may recommend a weight-control program of diet and exercise. As part of this program, people are taught how to select the right foods and portion sizes. They are advised to limit sugary drinks and fruit juices, to eat meals at home whenever possible (for more control over food choices), and to be more physically active.

For adults with health problems caused by excess weight, other treatments may include drugs that suppress the appetite and surgery to reduce the size of the stomach so that less food is needed to feel full. These treatments are not used for overweight children except in extreme cases. Instead, doctors prefer to control the rate of weight gain and allow a child to grow into the weight gradually.

To contain the obesity epidemic, many experts say prevention is also necessary, including large-scale public health measures. For example, school systems can help fight obesity by providing healthy lunch programs, physical education classes, and after-school activity programs. Communities can also play a role by creating more places for physical activities, such as parks and playgrounds.

ROBERT MURRAY, M.D.
Columbus Children's Hospital
The Ohio State University

Did you know that...

body fat can be calculated according to the relationship between height and weight? This measurement, called the Body Mass Index (BMI), can be determined by dividing weight in kilograms by height in meters, then dividing that number by height in meters again. To calculate the BMI using pounds and inches, use the same formula, then multiply the final figure by 703.

SUPPLEMENT

Deaths

Independent Nations of the World

The United States

    Senate

    House of Representatives

    Cabinet

    Supreme Court

    State Governors

Canada and Its Provinces and Territories

DEATHS

Atkins, Robert C. American cardiologist and diet-book author; died on April 17, at the age of 72. He created the controversial Atkins Diet, which advised people to eat mostly fats and proteins and cut down on carbohydrates to lose weight. Though rejected by most nutrition experts, the Atkins Diet became one of the most popular weight-loss programs ever.

Brinkley, David. American television newscaster and commentator; died on June 11, at the age of 82. With Chet Huntley, he cohosted the evening *Huntley-Brinkley Report* from 1956 to 1970 and, after Huntley's retirement, he hosted *This Week With David Brinkley.* He was the recipient of ten Emmy Awards.

Bronson, Charles. American actor; died on August 30, at the age of 81. The tough-looking Bronson often played menacing characters on screen. He was best known for his role as a vigilante in *Death Wish* (1974) and its four sequels.

Carney, Art. American actor; died on November 9, at the age of 85. Carney played the role of the not-too-bright sewer worker Ed Norton

Art Carney (with Jackie Gleason)

on the classic 1950's television show *The Honeymooners.* He won an Academy Award for his performance in the film comedy *Harry and Tonto* (1974).

Johnny Cash

Cash, Johnny. American country music singer; died on September 12, at the age of 71. Known as The Man in Black, Cash was a country music legend and a pioneer of rock 'n' roll. Among the more than 1,500 songs he recorded were "Folsom Prison Blues" (1956), "I Walk the Line" (1956), and "A Boy Named Sue" (1969). Cash was inducted into both the Country Music Hall of Fame and the Rock and Roll Hall of Fame.

Crenna, Richard. American actor; died on January 17, at the age of 76. During his long career, he starred in radio, film, and television. His best-known role was as the seasoned Army colonel in the *Rambo* action movies of the 1980's.

Cronyn, Hume. Canadian-born actor; died on June 15, at the age of 91. A compelling character actor, Cronyn starred on stage and screen for more than 60 years. On stage, he often appeared opposite his wife, Jessica Tandy. His most notable performance in recent years was in the movie *Cocoon* (1985) and its sequel.

Ebsen, Buddy. American actor; died on July 6, at the age of 95. The personable Ebsen began his career as a song-and-dance man in the 1920's. He was best known for his TV roles in *The Beverly Hillbillies* (1962–71) and *Barnaby Jones* (1973–80).

Gibson, Althea. American tennis player; died on September 28, at the age of 76. With her long reach and powerful serve, Gibson was a dominant figure in women's tennis in the 1950's. She was the first African American player to win the singles titles at the French Open (1956), Wimbledon (1957, 1958), and the U.S. nationals (1957, 1958), the forerunner of the U.S. Open.

Althea Gibson

Hackett, Buddy. American comedian; died on June 30, at the age of 78. The cherubic Hackett began his career as a stand-up comic, and became an audience favorite in nightclubs, in films, on television, and on stage.

Katharine Hepburn

Hepburn, Katharine. American actress; died on June 29, at the age of 96. Hepburn's fiery spirit and distinctive speaking manner helped make her one of the foremost actresses of the 20th century. During her seven-decade-long career, she won the Academy Award as best actress four times, for *Morning Glory* (1933), *Guess Who's Coming to Dinner* (1967), *The Lion in Winter* (1968), and *On Golden Pond* (1981).

Hines, Gregory. American tap dancer and actor; died on August 9, at the age of 57. A master of improvisation, Hines electrified stage and screen audiences with his exuberant tap dancing. His

Bob Hope

way and Hollywood history. He won Academy Awards as best director for *Gentleman's Agreement* (1947) and *On the Waterfront* (1954).

Moynihan, Daniel Patrick. Former U.S. Senator from New York; died on March 26, at the age of 76. Moynihan, a Democrat, served four terms in the Senate from 1977–2001. A distinguished scholar, he was known for his ability to identify social problems and propose novel solutions.

O'Connor, Donald. American dancer, singer, and actor; died on September 27, at the age of 78. O'Connor's jaunty and acrobatic dancing was featured in many Hollywood musicals. The high point of his career was his solo "Make 'Em Laugh" in *Singing in the Rain* (1952)—still considered one of the finest dance routines in movie history.

Peck, Gregory. American actor; died on June 12, at the age of 87. Widely admired for his courteous and dignified demeanor, Peck often

films included *The Cotton Club* (1984) and *White Nights* (1985). In 1992, he won a Tony Award for his performance in the Broadway show *Jelly's Last Jam*.

Hirschfeld, Al. American caricaturist; died on January 20, at the age of 99. For more than 75 years, Hirschfeld's witty line drawings of theatrical celebrities appeared on the pages of *The New York Times*. After the birth of his daughter Nina in 1945, Hirschfeld hid her name in each of his sketches. Spotting the hidden name was a favorite game of Hirschfeld fans.

Hope, Bob. British-born comedian; died on July 27, at the age of 100. Hope was one of the key entertainment figures of the twentieth century. Famed for his breezy, rapid-fire delivery of one-liners, he was a star of stage, film, and television. Over five decades, beginning in World War II, he traveled millions of miles to entertain U.S. troops stationed overseas.

Kazan, Elia. Turkish-born director; died on September 28, at the age of 94. Kazan was one of the most influential directors in Broad-

Gregory Peck

John Ritter

portrayed characters of great moral courage. He won an Academy Award in 1962 for his role as lawyer Atticus Finch in *To Kill a Mockingbird.* In 2003, the American Film Institute named Peck's Finch the greatest hero in motion-picture history.

Ritter, John. American actor; died on September 11, at the age of 54. The genial Ritter gained fame as Jack Tripper, the male roommate in the hit television comedy series *Three's Company* (1977–84). At the time of his death, he was starring in the comedy series *8 Simple Rules for Dating My Teenage Daughter.*

Rogers, Fred. American creator and host of the Public Broadcasting System TV show *Mister Rogers' Neighborhood;* died on February 27, at the age of 74. Some 1,700 episodes of the hugely popular children's show were aired between 1968 and 2001, and reruns are still on TV. Each show began with Mr. Rogers singing "Won't You Be My Neighbor?" as he put on a pair of sneakers and his favorite sweater.

Stack, Robert. American actor; died on May 14, at the age of 84. Stack made his name portraying real-life crime-fighter Eliot Ness in the television series *The Untouchables* (1959–63). In recent years, he hosted the reality series *Unsolved Mysteries.*

Steig, William. American cartoonist and author; died on October 3, at the age of 95. Steig's lighthearted and symbolic cartoons appeared in *The New Yorker* magazine for more than six decades. He also wrote more than 25 children's books. The most popular was *Shrek!,* which was turned into a movie that won the Academy Award for best animated feature film in 2002.

Thurmond, Strom. Former U.S. Senator from South Carolina; died on June 26, at the age of 100. Thurmond was the longest-serving senator in U.S. history—retiring from the Senate in January 2003 after nearly 48 years in office. Elected in 1954, Thurmond was a Democrat who opposed civil rights. He switched parties in 1964 and was a key figure in changing the once solidly Democratic South into a Republican stronghold.

Fred Rogers

INDEPENDENT NATIONS OF THE WORLD

NATION	CAPITAL	AREA (in sq mi)	POPULATION (estimate)	GOVERNMENT
Afghanistan	Kabul	250,000	28,700,000	Hamid Karzai—president
Albania	Tirana	11,100	3,100,000	Alfred Moisiu—president Fatos Nano—premier
Algeria	Algiers	919,595	31,700,000	Abdelaziz Bouteflika—president
Andorra	Andorra la Vella	175	100,000	Marc Forne Molne—premier
Angola	Luanda	481,354	13,100,000	José Eduardo dos Santos—president
Antigua and Barbuda	St. John's	171	100,000	Lester Bird—prime minister
Argentina	Buenos Aires	1,068,297	36,900,000	Nestor Carlos Kirchner—president
Armenia	Yerevan	11,500	3,200,000	Robert Kocharyan—president
Australia	Canberra	2,967,895	19,900,000	John Howard—prime minister
Austria	Vienna	32,374	8,200,000	Thomas Klestil—president Wolfgang Schüssel—chancellor
Azerbaijan	Baku	33,500	8,200,000	Ilham Aliyev—president
Bahamas	Nassau	5,380	300,000	Perry Christie—prime minister
Bahrain	Manama	240	700,000	Hamad bin Isa al-Khalifa—head of state
Bangladesh	Dhaka	55,598	146,700,000	Iajuddin Ahmed—president Khaleda Zia—prime minister
Barbados	Bridgetown	168	300,000	Owen Arthur—prime minister
Belarus	Minsk	80,154	9,900,000	Aleksandr Lukashenko—president
Belgium	Brussels	11,781	10,400,000	Albert II—king Guy Verhofstadt—premier
Belize	Belmopan	8,867	300,000	Said Musa—prime minister
Benin	Porto-Novo	43,484	7,000,000	Mathieu Kerekou—president
Bhutan	Thimbu	18,147	900,000	Jigme Singye Wangchuck—king
Bolivia	La Paz Sucre	424,165	8,600,000	Carlos Mesa—president
Bosnia and Herzegovina	Sarajevo	19,800	3,900,000	3-member presidency
Botswana	Gaborone	231,804	1,600,000	Festus Mogae—president
Brazil	Brasília	3,286,478	176,500,000	Luiz Ignácio Lula da Silva—president
Brunei Darussalam	Bandar Seri Begawan	2,226	400,000	Hassanal Bolkiah—head of state
Bulgaria	Sofia	42,823	7,500,000	Georgi Parvanov—president Simeon Saxe-Coburg—premier
Burkina Faso	Ouagadougou	105,869	13,200,000	Blaise Compaoré—president
Burma (Myanmar)	Rangoon (Yangon)	261,218	49,500,000	Than Shwe—head of government
Burundi	Bujumbura	10,747	6,100,000	Domitien Ndayizeye—president

NATION	CAPITAL	AREA (in sq mi)	POPULATION (estimate)	GOVERNMENT
Cambodia	Phnom Penh	69,898	12,600,000	Norodom Sihanouk—king Hun Sen—prime minister
Cameroon	Yaoundé	183,569	15,700,000	Paul Biya—president
Canada	Ottawa	3,851,809	31,600,000	Paul Martin—prime minister
Cape Verde	Praia	1,557	500,000	Pedro Pires—president
Central African Republic	Bangui	240,535	3,700,000	François Bozizé—president
Chad	N'Djamena	495,754	9,300,000	Idriss Deby—president
Chile	Santiago	292,257	15,800,000	Ricardo Lagos Escobar—president
China	Beijing	3,705,390	1,288,700,000	Hu Jintao—communist party secretary Wen Jiabao—premier
Colombia	Bogotá	439,736	44,200,000	Alvaro Uribe Vélez—president
Comoros	Moroni	838	600,000	Azaly Assoumani—president
Congo (Zaire)	Kinshasa	905,565	56,600,000	Joseph Kabila—president
Congo Republic	Brazzaville	132,047	3,700,000	Denis Sassou-Nguesso—president
Costa Rica	San José	19,575	4,200,000	Abel Pacheco—president
Croatia	Zagreb	21,829	4,300,000	Stipe Mesic—president
Cuba	Havana	44,218	11,300,000	Fidel Castro—president
Cyprus	Nicosia	3,572	900,000	Tassos Papadopoulos—president
Czech Republic	Prague	30,469	10,200,000	Vaclav Klaus—president Vladimir Spidla—premier
Denmark	Copenhagen	16,629	5,400,000	Margrethe II—queen Anders Fogh Rasmussen—premier
Djibouti	Djibouti	8,494	700,000	Ismail Omar Guelleh—president
Dominica	Roseau	290	100,000	Pierre Charles—prime minister
Dominican Republic	Santo Domingo	18,816	8,700,000	Hipólito Mejía Dominguez—president
East Timor	Dili	5,743	800,000	José Alexandre Gusmao—president
Ecuador	Quito	109,483	12,600,000	Lucio Gutiérrez Borbua—president
Egypt	Cairo	386,660	72,100,000	Mohammed Hosni Mubarak—president Atef Mohamed Ebeid—premier
El Salvador	San Salvador	8,124	6,600,000	Francisco Flores Pérez—president
Equatorial Guinea	Malabo	10,831	500,000	Teodoro Obiang Nguema Mbasogo—president
Eritrea	Asmara	45,405	4,400,000	Isaias Afeworki—president
Estonia	Tallinn	17,413	1,400,000	Arnold Ruutel—president
Ethiopia	Addis Ababa	426,372	70,700,000	Girma Woldegiorgis—president
Fiji	Suva	7,055	900,000	Ratu Josefa Iloilo—president
Finland	Helsinki	130,120	5,200,000	Tarja Halonen—president Matti Vanhanen—premier
France	Paris	213,000	59,800,000	Jacques Chirac—president Jean-Pierre Raffarin—premier
Gabon	Libreville	103,346	1,300,000	Omar Bongo—president
Gambia	Banjul	4,361	1,500,000	Yahya Jammeh—head of state

NATION	CAPITAL	AREA (in sq mi)	POPULATION (estimate)	GOVERNMENT
Georgia	Tbilisi	27,000	4,700,000	Nino Burdzhanadze—acting president
Germany	Berlin	137,744	82,600,000	Johannes Rau—president Gerhard Schröder—chancellor
Ghana	Accra	92,099	20,500,000	John Kufuor—president
Greece	Athens	50,944	11,000,000	Costis Stefanopoulos—president Costas Simitis—premier
Grenada	St. George's	133	100,000	Keith Mitchell—prime minister
Guatemala	Guatemala City	42,042	12,400,000	Oscar Berger Perdomo—president
Guinea	Conakry	94,926	9,000,000	Lansana Conté—president
Guinea-Bissau	Bissau	13,948	1,300,000	Henrique Rosa—president
Guyana	Georgetown	83,000	800,000	Bharrat Jagdeo—president
Haiti	Port-au-Prince	10,714	7,500,000	Jean-Bertrand Aristide—president
Honduras	Tegucigalpa	43,277	6,900,000	Ricardo Maduro Joest—president
Hungary	Budapest	35,919	10,100,000	Ferenc Madl—president Peter Medgyessy—premier
Iceland	Reykjavik	39,768	300,000	Olafur Grimsson—president David Oddsson—premier
India	New Delhi	1,269,340	1,068,600,000	A.P.J. Abdul Kalam—president Atal Bihari Vajpayee—prime minister
Indonesia	Jakarta	735,358	220,500,000	Megawati Sukarnoputri—president
Iran	Tehran	636,293	66,600,000	Ayatollah Ali Khamenei—religious leader Mohammed Khatami—president
Iraq	Baghdad	167,925	24,200,000	25-member governing council
Ireland	Dublin	27,136	4,000,000	Mary McAleese—president Bertie Ahern—prime minister
Israel	Jerusalem	8,019	6,700,000	Moshe Katsav—president Ariel Sharon—prime minister
Italy	Rome	116,303	57,200,000	Carlo Azeglio Ciampi—president Silvio Berlusconi—premier
Ivory Coast	Yamoussoukro	124,503	17,000,000	Laurent Gbagbo—president
Jamaica	Kingston	4,244	2,600,000	Percival J. Patterson—prime minister
Japan	Tokyo	143,751	127,500,000	Akihito—emperor Junichiro Koizumi—premier
Jordan	Amman	35,475	5,500,000	Abdullah II—king Faisal al-Fayez—prime minister
Kazakhstan	Almaty	1,049,000	14,800,000	Nursultan A. Nazarbayev—president
Kenya	Nairobi	224,959	31,600,000	Mwai Kibaki—president
Kiribati	Tarawa	264	100,000	Anote Tong—president
Korea (North)	Pyongyang	46,540	22,700,000	Kim Jong II—president Pak Pong Chu—premier
Korea (South)	Seoul	38,025	47,900,000	Roh Moo Hyun—president Goh Kun—premier
Kuwait	Kuwait	6,880	2,400,000	Jabir al-Ahmad al-Sabah—head of state
Kyrgyzstan	Bishkek	76,641	5,000,000	Askar Akayev—president
Laos	Vientiane	91,429	5,600,000	Khamtai Siphandon—president Boungnang Volachit—premier

NATION	CAPITAL	AREA (in sq mi)	POPULATION (estimate)	GOVERNMENT
Latvia	Riga	24,600	2,300,000	Vaira Vike-Freiberga—president
Lebanon	Beirut	4,015	4,200,000	Emile Lahoud—president Rafik al-Hariri—premier
Lesotho	Maseru	11,720	1,800,000	Letsie III—king Bethuel Pakalitha Mosisili—premier
Liberia	Monrovia	43,000	3,300,000	Gyude Bryant—president
Libya	Tripoli	679,362	5,500,000	Muammar el-Qaddafi—head of government
Liechtenstein	Vaduz	61	40,000	Hans Adam II—prince
Lithuania	Vilnius	25,174	3,500,000	Rolandas Paksas—president
Luxembourg	Luxembourg	998	500,000	Henri—grand duke Jean-Claude Juncker—premier
Macedonia	Skopje	9,928	2,100,000	Boris Trajkovski—president
Madagascar	Antananarivo	226,657	17,000,000	Marc Ravalomanana—president
Malawi	Lilongwe	45,747	11,700,000	Bakili Muluzi—president
Malaysia	Kuala Lumpur	127,317	25,100,000	Tuanku Syed Sirajuddin ibni Almarhum Tuanku Syed Putra Jamalullail—king Abdullah Badawi—prime minister
Maldives	Male	115	300,000	Maumoon Abdul Gayoom—president
Mali	Bamako	478,765	11,600,000	Amadou Toumani Touré—president
Malta	Valletta	122	400,000	Guido De Marco—president Eddie Fenech Adami—prime minister
Marshall Islands	Majuro	70	100,000	Kessai Note—president
Mauritania	Nouakchott	397,954	2,900,000	Maaouya Ould Sid Ahmed Taya—president
Mauritius	Port Louis	790	1,200,000	Anerood Jugnauth—president Paul R. Berenger—premier
Mexico	Mexico City	761,602	104,900,000	Vicente Fox Quesada—president
Micronesia	Colonia	271	100,000	Joseph J. Urusemal—president
Moldova	Kishiniev	13,000	4,300,000	Vladimir Voronin—president
Monaco	Monaco-Ville	0.6	30,000	Rainier III—prince
Mongolia	Ulan Bator	604,248	2,500,000	Natsagiin Bagabandi—president
Morocco	Rabat	172,413	30,400,000	Mohammed VI—king Driss Jettou—premier
Mozambique	Maputo	309,494	17,500,000	Joaquím A. Chissano—president
Namibia	Windhoek	318,260	1,900,000	Sam Nujoma—president
Nauru	Yaren District	8	10,000	Rene Harris—president
Nepal	Katmandu	54,362	25,200,000	Gyanendra Bir Bikram Shah—king Surya Bahadur Thapa—premier
Netherlands	Amsterdam	15,770	16,200,000	Beatrix—queen Jan Peter Balkenende—premier
New Zealand	Wellington	103,736	4,000,000	Helen Clark—prime minister
Nicaragua	Managua	50,193	5,500,000	Enrique Bolaños—president
Niger	Niamey	489,190	12,100,000	Mamadou Tandja—president
Nigeria	Abuja	356,667	133,900,000	Olusegun Obasanjo—president

NATION	CAPITAL	AREA (in sq mi)	POPULATION (estimate)	GOVERNMENT
Norway	Oslo	125,056	4,600,000	Harold V—king Kjell Magne Bondevik—premier
Oman	Muscat	82,030	2,600,000	Qaboos bin Said Al Said—sultan
Pakistan	Islamabad	310,404	149,100,000	Pervez Musharraf—president
Palau	Koror	192	20,000	Tommy Remengesau—president
Panama	Panama City	29,761	3,000,000	Mireya Moscoso Rodriguez—president
Papua New Guinea	Port Moresby	178,260	5,500,000	Michael Somare—prime minister
Paraguay	Asunción	157,047	6,200,000	Nicanor Duarte Frutos—president
Peru	Lima	496,222	27,100,000	Alejandro Toledo—president
Philippines	Manila	115,830	81,600,000	Gloria Macapagal-Arroyo—president Teofisto Guingona—vice-president
Poland	Warsaw	120,725	38,600,000	Aleksander Kwasniewski—president Leszek Miller—premier
Portugal	Lisbon	35,553	10,400,000	Jorge Sampaio—president José Manuel Durao Barroso—premier
Qatar	Doha	4,247	600,000	Hamad bin Khalifa al-Thani—head of state
Romania	Bucharest	91,700	21,600,000	Ion Iliescu—president Adrian Nastase—premier
Russia	Moscow	6,600,000	145,500,000	Vladimir V. Putin—president
Rwanda	Kigali	10,169	8,300,000	Paul Kagame—president
St. Kitts and Nevis	Basseterre	105	50,000	Denzil Douglas—prime minister
St. Lucia	Castries	238	200,000	Kenny Anthony—prime minister
St. Vincent and the Grenadines	Kingstown	150	100,000	Ralph Gonsalves—prime minister
Samoa	Apia	1,097	200,000	Malietoa Tanumafili II—head of state
San Marino	San Marino	24	30,000	Fiorenzo Stolfi—head of state
São Tomé and Príncipe	São Tomé	372	200,000	Fradique De Menezes—president
Saudi Arabia	Riyadh	830,000	24,100,000	Fahd bin Abdul-Aziz al-Saud—king
Senegal	Dakar	75,750	10,600,000	Abdoulaye Wade—president
Serbia and Montenegro	Belgrade	39,390	10,700,000	Tomislav Nikolic—president-elect Zoran Zivkovic—premier
Seychelles	Victoria	107	100,000	France Albert René—president
Sierra Leone	Freetown	27,700	5,700,000	Ahmad Tejan Kabbah—president
Singapore	Singapore	224	4,200,000	S. R. Nathan—president Goh Chok Tong—prime minister
Slovakia	Bratislava	18,933	5,400,000	Rudolf Schuster—president
Slovenia	Ljubljana	7,819	2,000,000	Janez Drnovsek—president
Solomon Islands	Honiara	10,983	500,000	Allan Kemakeza—prime minister
Somalia	Mogadishu	246,200	8,000,000	Abdikassim Salad Hassan—president
South Africa	Pretoria Cape Town Bloemfontein	471,444	44,000,000	Thabo Mbeki—president
Spain	Madrid	194,896	41,300,000	Juan Carlos I—king José María Aznar—premier

NATION	CAPITAL	AREA (in sq mi)	POPULATION (estimate)	GOVERNMENT
Sri Lanka	Colombo	25,332	19,300,000	C. Bandaranaike Kumaratunga—president
Sudan	Khartoum	967,500	38,100,000	O. Hassan Ahmed al-Bashir—president
Suriname	Paramaribo	63,037	400,000	Runaldo Ronald Venetiaan—president
Swaziland	Mbabane	6,704	1,200,000	Mswati III—king
Sweden	Stockholm	173,731	9,000,000	Carl XVI Gustaf—king Göran Persson—premier
Switzerland	Bern	15,941	7,300,000	Ruth Metzler-Arnold—president
Syria	Damascus	71,498	17,500,000	Bashar al-Assad—president Naji Otari—premier
Taiwan	Taipei	13,885	22,600,000	Chen Shui-bian—president Yu Shyi-kin —premier
Tajikistan	Dushanbe	55,250	6,600,000	Oqil Oqilov—premier
Tanzania	Dar es Salaam	364,898	35,400,000	Benjamin William Mkapa—president
Thailand	Bangkok	198,457	63,100,000	Bhumibol Adulyadej—king Thaksin Shinawatra—premier
Togo	Lomé	21,622	5,400,000	Gnassingbe Eyadema—president
Tonga	Nuku'alofa	270	100,000	Taufa'ahau Tupou IV—king Lavaka ata Ulukalala—premier
Trinidad & Tobago	Port of Spain	1,980	1,300,000	George Maxwell Richards—president Patrick Manning—prime minister
Tunisia	Tunis	63,170	9,900,000	Zine el-Abidine Ben Ali—president
Turkey	Ankara	301,381	71,200,000	Ahmet Necdet Sezer—president Recep Tayyip Erdogan—prime minister
Turkmenistan	Ashkhabad	188,455	5,700,000	Saparmurad Niyazov—president
Tuvalu	Funafuti	10	10,000	Koloa Talake—prime minister
Uganda	Kampala	91,134	25,300,000	Yoweri Museveni—president
Ukraine	Kiev	231,990	47,800,000	Leonid M. Kuchma—president
United Arab Emirates	Abu Dhabi	32,278	3,900,000	Zayed bin Sultan al-Nuhayyan—president
United Kingdom	London	94,226	59,200,000	Elizabeth II—queen Tony Blair—prime minister
United States	Washington, D.C.	3,618,467	291,500,000	George W. Bush—president Richard Cheney—vice-president
Uruguay	Montevideo	68,037	3,400,000	Jorge Batlle—president
Uzbekistan	Tashkent	172,750	25,700,000	Islam A. Karimov—president
Vanuatu	Vila	5,700	200,000	John Bani—president
Vatican City	Vatican City	0.17	900	John Paul II—pope
Venezuela	Caracas	352,143	25,700,000	Hugo Chávez—president
Vietnam	Hanoi	128,402	80,800,000	Nong Duc Manh—communist party secretary Phan Van Khai—premier
Yemen	Sana	203,849	19,400,000	Ali Abdullah Saleh—president Abd al-Qadir al-Ba Jamel—premier
Zambia	Lusaka	290,585	10,900,000	Levy Mwanawasa—president
Zimbabwe	Harare	150,333	12,600,000	Robert Mugabe—president

THE CONGRESS OF THE UNITED STATES

UNITED STATES SENATE
(51 Republicans, 48 Democrats, 1 Independent)

Alabama
Richard C. Shelby (R)
Jeff Sessions (R)

Alaska
Ted Stevens (R)
Lisa Murkowski (R)

Arizona
John S. McCain III (R)
Jon Kyl (R)

Arkansas
Blanche L. Lincoln (D)
Mark Pryor (D)

California
Barbara Boxer (D)
Dianne Feinstein (D)

Colorado
Ben Nighthorse Campbell (R)
Wayne Allard (R)

Connecticut
Christopher J. Dodd (D)
Joseph I. Lieberman (D)

Delaware
Joseph R. Biden, Jr. (D)
Thomas Carper (D)

Florida
Bob Graham (D)
Bill Nelson (D)

Georgia
Zell Miller (D)
Saxby Chambliss (R)

Hawaii
Daniel K. Inouye (D)
Daniel K. Akaka (D)

Idaho
Larry Craig (R)
Mike Crapo (R)

Illinois
Richard J. Durbin (D)
Peter Fitzgerald (R)

Indiana
Richard G. Lugar (R)
Evan Bayh (D)

Iowa
Chuck Grassley (R)
Tom Harkin (D)

Kansas
Sam Brownback (R)
Pat Roberts (R)

Kentucky
Mitch McConnell (R)
Jim Bunning (R)

Louisiana
John Breaux (D)
Mary Landrieu (D)

Maine
Olympia J. Snowe (R)
Susan Collins (R)

Maryland
Paul S. Sarbanes (D)
Barbara A. Mikulski (D)

Massachusetts
Edward M. Kennedy (D)
John Kerry (D)

Michigan
Carl Levin (D)
Debbie Stabenow (D)

Minnesota
Mark Dayton (D)
Norm Coleman (R)

Mississippi
Thad Cochran (R)
Trent Lott (R)

Missouri
Christopher S. Bond (R)
James Talent (R)

Montana
Max Baucus (D)
Conrad Burns (R)

Nebraska
Chuck Hagel (R)
Ben Nelson (D)

Nevada
Harry Reid (D)
John Ensign (R)

New Hampshire
Judd Gregg (R)
John E. Sununu (R)

New Jersey
Jon S. Corzine (D)
Frank Lautenberg (D)

New Mexico
Pete V. Domenici (R)
Jeff Bingaman (D)

New York
Charles E. Schumer (D)
Hillary Rodham Clinton (D)

North Carolina
John Edwards (D)
Elizabeth Dole (R)

North Dakota
Kent Conrad (D)
Byron L. Dorgan (D)

Ohio
Mike DeWine (R)
George Voinovich (R)

Oklahoma
Don Nickles (R)
James M. Inhofe (R)

Oregon
Gordon Smith(R)
Ron Wyden (D)

Pennsylvania
Arlen Specter (R)
Rick Santorum (R)

Rhode Island
Lincoln D. Chafee (R)
Jack Reed (D)

South Carolina
Ernest E. Hollings (D)
Lindsey Graham (R)

South Dakota
Thomas A. Daschle (D)
Tim Johnson (D)

Tennessee
Bill Frist (R)
Lamar Alexander (R)

Texas
Kay Bailey Hutchison (R)
John Cornyn (R)

Utah
Orrin G. Hatch (R)
Robert F. Bennett (R)

Vermont
Patrick J. Leahy (D)
James M. Jeffords (I)

Virginia
John W. Warner (R)
George Allen (R)

Washington
Patty Murray (D)
Maria Cantwell (D)

West Virginia
Robert C. Byrd (D)
John D. Rockefeller IV (D)

Wisconsin
Herb Kohl (D)
Russell D Feingold (D)

Wyoming
Craig Thomas (R)
Michael Enzi (R)

(D) Democrat
(R) Republican
(I) Independent

UNITED STATES HOUSE OF REPRESENTATIVES
(228 Republicans, 205 Democrats, 1 Independent, 1 Vacancy)

Alabama
1. J. Bonner (R)
2. T. Everett (R)
3. M. Rogers (R)
4. R. B. Aderholt (R)
5. R.E. Cramer, Jr. (D)
6. S. Bachus (R)
7. A. Davis (D)

Alaska
   D. Young (R)

Arizona
1. R. Renzi (R)
2. T. Franks (R)
3. J. B. Shadegg (R)
4. E. Pastor (D)
5. J. D. Hayworth (R)
6. J. Flake (R)
7. R. M. Grijalva (D)
8. J. Kolbe (R)

Arkansas
1. M. Berry (D)
2. V. Snyder (D)
3. J. Boozman (R)
4. M. Ross (D)

California
1. M. Thompson (D)
2. W. Herger (R)
3. D. Ose (R)
4. J. T. Doolittle (R)
5. R. T. Matsui (D)
6. L. C. Woolsey (D)
7. G. Miller (D)
8. N. Pelosi (D)
9. B. Lee (D)
10. E. O. Tauscher (D)
11. R. W. Pombo (R)
12. T. Lantos (D)
13. F. P. Stark (D)
14. A. G. Eshoo (D)
15. M. M. Honda (D)
16. Z. Lofgren (D)
17. S. Farr (D)
18. D. A. Cardoza (D)
19. G. Radanovich (R)
20. C. M. Dooley (D)
21. D. Nunes (R)
22. W. M. Thomas (R)
23. L. Capps (D)
24. E. Gallegly (R)
25. H. P. McKeon (R)
26. D. Dreier (R)
27. B. Sherman (D)
28. H. L. Berman (D)
29. A. B. Schiff (D)
30. H. A.Waxman (D)
31. X. Becerra (D)
32. H. L. Solis (D)
33. D. E. Watson (D)
34. L. Roybal-Allard (D)
35. M. Waters (D)
36. J. Harman (D)
37. J. Millender-McDonald (D)
38. G. F. Napolitano (D)
39. L. T. Sanchez (D)
40. E. A. Royce (R)
41. J. Lewis (R)
42. G. G. Miller (R)
43. J. Baca (D)
44. K. Calvert (R)
45. M. Bono (R)
46. D. Rohrabacher (R)
47. L. Sanchez (D)
48. C. Cox (R)
49. D. E. Issa (R)
50. R. Cunningham (R)
51. B. Filner (D)
52. D. Hunter (R)
53 S. A. Davis (D)

Colorado
1. D. DeGette (D)
2. M. Udall (D)
3. S. McInnis (R)
4. M. N. Musgrave (R)
5. J. Hefley (R)
6. T. G. Tancredo (R)
7. B. Beauprez (R)

Connecticut
1. J. B. Larson (D)
2. R. Simmons (R)
3. R. L. DeLauro (D)
4. C. Shays (R)
5. N. L. Johnson (R)

Delaware
   M. N. Castle (R)

Florida
1. J. Miller (R)
2. A. Boyd (D)
3. C. Brown (D)
4. A. Crenshaw (R)
5. G. Brown-Waite (R)
6. C. Stearns (R)
7. J. L. Mica (R)
8. R. Keller (R)
9. M. Bilirakis (R)
10. C. W. Young (R)
11. J. Davis (D)
12. A. H. Putnam (R)
13. K. Harris (R)
14. P. J. Goss (R)
15. D. Weldon (R)
16. M. Foley (R)
17. K. B. Meek (D)
18. I. Ros-Lehtinen (R)
19. R. Wexler (D)
20. P. Deutsch (D)
21. L. Diaz-Balart (R)
22. E. C. Shaw, Jr. (R)
23. A. L. Hastings (D)
24 T. Feeney (R)
25 M. Diaz-Balart (R)

Georgia
1. J. Kingston (R)
2. S. D. Bishop, Jr. (D)
3. J. Marshall (D)
4. D. L. Majette (D)
5. J. Lewis (D)
6. J. Isakson (R)
7. J. Linder (R)
8. M. Collins (R)
9. C. Norwood (R)
10. N. Deal (R)
11 P. Gingrey (R)
12 M. Burns (R)
13 D. Scott (D)

Hawaii
1. N. Abercrombie (D)
2. E. Case (D)*

Idaho
1. C. L. Otter (R)
2. M. K. Simpson (R)

Illinois
1. B. L. Rush (D)
2. J. L. Jackson, Jr. (D)
3. W. O. Lipinski (D)
4. L. V. Gutierrez (D)
5. R. Emanuel (D)
6. H. J. Hyde (R)
7. D. K. Davis (D)
8. P. M. Crane (R)
9. J. D. Schakowsky (D)
10. M. S. Kirk (R)
11. J. Weller (R)
12. J. F. Costello (D)
13. J. Biggert (R)
14. J. D. Hastert (R)
15. T. V. Johnson (R)
16. D. A. Manzullo (R)
17. L. Evans (D)
18. R. LaHood (R)
19 J. Shimkus (R)

Indiana
1. P. J. Visclosky (D)
2. C. Chocola (R)
3. M. E. Souder (R)
4. S. Buyer (R)
5. D. Burton (R)
6. M. Pence (R)
7. J. Carson (D)
8. J. N. Hostettler (R)
9 B. P. Hill (D)

Iowa
1. J. Nussle (R)
2. J. A. Leach (R)
3. L. L. Boswell (D)
4. T. Latham (R)
5. S. King (R)

Kansas
1. J. Moran (R)
2. J. Ryun (R)
3. D. Moore (D)
4. T. Tiahrt (R)

Kentucky
1. E. Whitfield (R)
2. R. Lewis (R)
3. A. M. Northup (R)
4. K. Lucas (D)
5. H. Rogers (R)
6. Vacant

Louisiana
1. D. Vitter (R)
2. W. J. Jefferson (D)
3. W. J. Tauzin (R)
4. J. McCrery (R)
5. R. Alexander (D)
6. R. H. Baker (R)
7. C. John (D)

Maine
1. T. H. Allen (D)
2. M. H. Michaud (D)

Maryland
1. W. T. Gilchrest (R)
2. C.A. Ruppersberger (D)
3. B. L. Cardin (D)
4. A. R. Wynn (D)
5. S. H. Hoyer (D)
6. R. G. Bartlett (R)
7. E. E. Cummings (D)
8. C. Van Hollen (D)

Massachusetts
1. J. W. Olver (D)
2. R. E. Neal (D)
3. J. P. McGovern (D)
4. B. Frank (D)
5. M. T. Meehan (D)
6. J. F. Tierney (D)
7. E. J. Markey (D)
8. M. E. Capuano (D)
9. S. F. Lynch (D)
10. W. D. Delahunt (D)

Michigan
1. B. Stupak (D)
2. P. Hoekstra (R)
3. V. J. Ehlers (R)
4 D. Camp (R)
5. D. E. Kildee (D)
6. F. Upton (R)
7. N. Smith (R)
8. M. Rogers (R)
9. J. Knollenberg (R)
10. C. S. Miller (R)
11. T. G. McCotter (R)
12. S. M. Levin (D)
13. C. C. Kilpatrick (D)
14 J. Conyers, Jr. (D)
15 J. D. Dingell (D)

Minnesota
1. G. Gutknecht (R)
2. J. Kline (R)
3. J. Ramstad (R)
4. B. McCollum (D)

5. M. O. Sabo (D)
6. M. R. Kennedy (R)
7. C. C. Peterson (D)
8. J. L. Oberstar (D)

Mississippi
1. R. F. Wicker (R)
2. B. G. Thompson (D)
3. C. W. Pickering (R)
4. G. Taylor (D)

Missouri
1. W. L. Clay (D)
2. W. T. Akin (R)
3. R. A. Gephardt (D)
4. I. Skelton (D)
5. K. McCarthy (D)
6. S. Graves (R)
7. R. Blunt (R)
8. J. A. Emerson (R)
9. K. C. Hulshof (R)

Montana
D. R. Rehberg (R)

Nebraska
1. D. Bereuter (R)
2. L. Terry (R)
3. T. Osborne (R)

Nevada
1. S. Berkley (D)
2. J. Gibbons (R)
3. J. C. Porter (R)

New Hampshire
1. J. Bradley (R)
2. C. F. Bass (R)

New Jersey
1. R. E. Andrews (D)
2. F. A. LoBiondo (R)
3. J. Saxton (R)
4. C. H. Smith (R)
5. S. Garrett (R)
6. F. Pallone, Jr. (D)
7. M. Ferguson (R)
8. B. Pascrell, Jr. (D)
9. S. R. Rothman (D)
10. D. M. Payne (D)
11. R. P. Frelinghuysen (R)
12. R. D. Holt (D)
13. R. Menendez (D)

New Mexico
1. H. Wilson (R)
2. S. Pearce (R)
3. T. Udall (D)

New York
1. T. H. Bishop (D)
2. S. Israel (D)
3. P. T. King (R)
4. C. McCarthy (D)
5. G. L. Ackerman (D)
6. G. W. Meeks (D)

7. J. Crowley (D)
8. J. Nadler (D)
9. A. D. Weiner (D)
10. E. Towns (D)
11. M. R. Owens (D)
12. N. M. Velázquez (D)
13. V. Fossella (R)
14. C. B. Maloney (D)
15. C. B. Rangel (D)
16. J. E. Serrano (D)
17. E. L. Engel (D)
18. N. M. Lowey (D)
19. S. W. Kelly (R)
20. J. E. Sweeney (R)
21. M. R. McNulty (D)
22. M. D. Hinchey (D)
23. J. M. McHugh (R)
24. S. Boehlert (R)
25. J. T. Walsh (R)
26. T. M. Reynolds (R)
27. J. Quinn (R)
28. L. M. Slaughter (D)
29. A. Houghton (R)

North Carolina
1. F. W. Ballance, Jr. (D)
2. B. Etheridge (D)
3. W. B. Jones (R)
4. D. E. Price (D)
5. R. Burr (R)
6. H. Coble (R)
7. M. McIntyre (D)
8. R. Hayes (R)
9. S. W. Myrick (R)
10. C. Ballenger (R)
11. C. H. Taylor (R)
12. M. L. Watt (D)
13. B. Miller (D)

North Dakota
E. Pomeroy (D)

Ohio
1. S. Chabot (R)
2. R. Portman (R)
3. M. R. Turner (R)
4. M. G. Oxley (R)
5. P. E. Gillmor (R)
6. T. Strickland (D)
7. D. L. Hobson (R)
8. J. A. Boehner (R)
9. M. Kaptur (D)
10. D. J. Kucinich (D)
11. S. T. Jones (D)
12. P. J. Tiberi (R)
13. S. Brown (D)
14. S. C. LaTourette (R)
15. D. Pryce (R)
16. R. Regula (R)
17. T. Ryan (D)
18. R. W. Ney (R)

Oklahoma
1. J. Sullivan (R)
2. B. Carson (D)
3. F. D. Lucas (R)
4. T. Cole (R)
5. E. J. Istook, Jr. (R)

Oregon
1. D. Wu (D)
2. G. Walden (R)
3. E. Blumenauer (D)

4. P. A. DeFazio (D)
5. D. Hooley (D)

Pennsylvania
1. R. A. Brady (D)
2. C. Fattah (D)
3. P. English (R)
4. M. A. Hart (R)
5. J. E. Peterson (R)
6. J. Gerlach (R)
7. C. Weldon (R)
8. J. C. Greenwood (R)
9. B. Shuster (R)
10. D. Sherwood (R)
11. P. E. Kanjorski (D)
12. J. P. Murtha (D)
13. J. M. Hoeffel (D)
14. M. F. Doyle (D)
15. P. J. Toomey (R)
16. J. R. Pitts (R)
17. T. Holden (D)
18. T. Murphy (R)
19. T. R. Platts (R)

Rhode Island
1. P. J. Kennedy (D)
2. J. R. Langevin (D)

South Carolina
1. H. E. Brown, Jr. (R)
2. J. Wilson (R)
3. J. G. Barrett (R)
4. J. DeMint (R)
5. J. M. Spratt, Jr. (D)
6. J. E. Clyburn (D)

South Dakota
W. J. Janklow (R)**

Tennessee
1. W. L. Jenkins (R)
2. J. J. Duncan, Jr. (R)
3. Z. Wamp (R)
4. L. Davis (D)
5. J. Cooper (D)
6. B. Gordon (D)
7. M. Blackburn (R)
8. J. S. Tanner (D)
9. H. E. Ford, Jr. (D)

Texas
1. M. Sandlin (D)
2. J. Turner (D)
3. S. Johnson (R)
4. R. M. Hall (D)
5. J. Hensarling (R)
6. J. Barton (R)
7. J. A. Culberson (R)
8. K. Brady (R)
9. N. Lampson (D)
10. L. Doggett (D)
11. C. Edwards (D)
12. K. Granger (R)
13. M. Thornberry (R)
14. R. Paul (R)
15. R. Hinojosa (D)
16. S. Reyes (D)
17. C. W. Stenholm (D)
18. S. Jackson-Lee (D)
19. R. Neugebauer (R)*

20. C. A. Gonzalez (D)
21. L. S. Smith (R)
22. T. DeLay (R)
23. H. Bonilla (R)
24. M. Frost (D)
25. C. Bell (D)
26. M. C. Burgess (R)
27. S. P. Ortiz (D)
28. C. D. Rodriguez (D)
29. G. Green (D)
30. E. B. Johnson (D)
31. J. R. Carter (R)
32. P. Sessions (R)

Utah
1. R. Bishop (R)
2. J. Matheson (D)
3. C. Cannon (R)

Vermont
B. Sanders (I)

Virginia
1. J. A. Davis (R)
2. E. L. Schrock (R)
3. R. C. Scott (D)
4. J. R. Forbes (R)
5. V. H. Goode, Jr. (R)
6. B. Goodlatte (R)
7. E. Cantor (R)
8. J. P. Moran (D)
9. R. Boucher (D)
10. F. R. Wolf (R)
11. T. Davis (R)

Washington
1. J. Inslee (D)
2. R. Larsen (D)
3. B. Baird (D)
4. D. Hastings (R)
5. G. R. Nethercutt, Jr. (R)
6. N. D. Dicks (D)
7. J. McDermott (D)
8. J. Dunn (R)
9. A. Smith (D)

West Virginia
1. A. B. Mollohan (D)
2. S. M. Capito (R)
3. N. J. Rahall II (D)

Wisconsin
1. P. Ryan (R)
2. T. Baldwin (D)
3. R. Kind (D)
4. G. D. Kleczka (D)
5. F. J. Sensenbrenner, Jr. (R)
6. T. E. Petri (R)
7. D. R. Obey (D)
8. M. Green (R)

Wyoming
B. Cubin (R)

(D) Democrat
(R) Republican
(I) Independent

*elected in special election in 2003
**announced resignation, effective January 20, 2004

UNITED STATES SUPREME COURT

Chief Justice: William H. Rehnquist (1986)
Associate Justices:
John Paul Stevens (1975)
Sandra Day O'Connor (1981)
Antonin Scalia (1986)
Anthony M. Kennedy (1988)
David H. Souter (1990)
Clarence Thomas (1991)
Ruth Bader Ginsburg (1993)
Stephen G. Breyer (1994)

UNITED STATES CABINET

Secretary of Agriculture: Ann M. Veneman
Attorney General: John Ashcroft
Secretary of Commerce: Donald L. Evans
Secretary of Defense: Donald H. Rumsfeld
Secretary of Education: Rod Paige
Secretary of Energy: Spencer Abraham
Secretary of Health and Human Services: Tommy G. Thompson
Secretary of Homeland Security: Tom Ridge
Secretary of Housing and Urban Development: Alphonso Jackson (nominated December 12, 2003)
Secretary of the Interior: Gale A. Norton
Secretary of Labor: Elaine Chao
Secretary of State: Colin Powell
Secretary of Transportation: Norman Y. Mineta
Secretary of the Treasury: John W. Snow
Secretary of Veteran Affairs: Anthony J. Principi

Democrat Kathleen B. Blanco was elected Louisiana's first woman governor in 2003.

STATE GOVERNORS

Alabama	Bob Riley (R)
Alaska	Frank Murkowski (R)
Arizona	Janet Napolitano (D)
Arkansas	Mike Huckabee (R)
California	Arnold Schwarzenegger (R)*
Colorado	Bill Owens (R)
Connecticut	John Rowland (R)
Delaware	Ruth Ann Minner (D)
Florida	Jeb Bush (R)
Georgia	Sonny Perdue (R)
Hawaii	Linda Lingle (R)
Idaho	Dirk Kempthorne (R)
Illinois	Rod Blagojevich (D)
Indiana	Joseph E. Kernan (D)**
Iowa	Tom Vilsack (D)
Kansas	Kathleen Sebelius (D)
Kentucky	Ernie Fletcher (R)***
Louisiana	Kathleen B. Blanco (D)***
Maine	John Baldacci (D)
Maryland	Robert Ehrlich, Jr. (R)
Massachusetts	Mitt Romney (R)
Michigan	Jennifer Granholm (D)
Minnesota	Tim Pawlenty (R)
Mississippi	Haley Barbour (R)***
Missouri	Bob Holden (D)
Montana	Judy Martz (R)
Nebraska	Mike Johanns (R)
Nevada	Kenny Guinn (R)
New Hampshire	Craig Benson (R)
New Jersey	James E. McGreevey (D)
New Mexico	Bill Richardson (D)
New York	George Pataki (R)
North Carolina	Michael F. Easley (D)
North Dakota	John Hoeven (R)
Ohio	Bob Taft (R)
Oklahoma	Brad Henry (D)
Oregon	Ted Kulongoski (D)
Pennsylvania	Edward G. Rendell (D)
Rhode Island	Don Carcieri (R)
South Carolina	Mark Sanford (R)
South Dakota	Mike Rounds (R)
Tennessee	Phil Bredesen (D)
Texas	Rick Perry (R)
Utah	Olene S. Walker (R)**
Vermont	Jim Douglas (R)
Virginia	Mark Warner (D)
Washington	Gary Locke (D)
West Virginia	Bob Wise (D)
Wisconsin	Jim Doyle (D)
Wyoming	Dave Freudenthal (D)

*elected in recall election in 2003   **filled vacancy in 2003   ***elected in 2003   (D) Democrat (R) Republican

CANADA

Capital: Ottawa
Head of State: Queen Elizabeth II
Governor General: Adrienne Clarkson
Prime Minister: Paul Martin (Liberal)
Leader of the Opposition: Stephen Harper (Canadian Alliance)
Population: 31,630,000
Area: 3,851,809 sq mi (9,976,185 km²)

PROVINCES AND TERRITORIES

Alberta
Capital: Edmonton
Lieutenant Governor: Lois E. Hole
Premier: Ralph Klein (Progressive Conservative)
Leader of the Opposition: Ken Nicol (Liberal)
Entered Confederation: Sept. 1, 1905
Population: 3,153,000
Area: 255,285 sq mi (661,188 km²)

British Columbia
Capital: Victoria
Lieutenant Governor: Iona Campagnolo
Premier: Gordon Campbell (Liberal)
Leader of the Opposition: Joy MacPhail
    (New Democratic Party)
Entered Confederation: July 20, 1871
Population: 4,150,000
Area: 366,255 sq mi (948,600 km²)

Manitoba
Capital: Winnipeg
Lieutenant Governor: Peter M. Liba
Premier: Gary Albert Doer (New Democratic Party)
Leader of the Opposition: Stuart Murray
    (Progressive Conservative)
Entered Confederation: July 15, 1870
Population: 1,165,000
Area: 251,000 sq mi (650,090 km²)

New Brunswick
Capital: Fredericton
Lieutenant Governor: Herménégilde Chiasson
Premier: Bernard Lord (Progressive Conservative)
Leader of the Opposition: Shawn L. Graham (Liberal)
Entered Confederation: July 1, 1867
Population: 751,000
Area: 28,354 sq mi (73,436 km²)

Newfoundland and Labrador
Capital: St. John's
Lieutenant Governor: Edward M. Roberts
Premier: Danny Williams (Progressive Conservative)
Leader of the Opposition: Roger Grimes (Liberal)
Entered Confederation: March 31, 1949
Population: 520,000
Area: 156,185 sq mi (404,517 km²)

Nova Scotia
Capital: Halifax
Lieutenant Governor: Myra A. Freeman
Premier: John F. Hamm (Progressive Conservative)
Leader of the Opposition: Darrell Dexter (New
    Democratic Party)
Entered Confederation: July 1, 1867
Population: 937,000
Area: 21,425 sq mi (55,491 km²)

Ontario
Capital: Toronto
Lieutenant Governor: James K. Bartleman
Premier: Dalton McGuinty (Liberal)
Leader of the Opposition: Ernie Eves (Progressive
    Conservative)
Entered Confederation: July 1, 1867
Population: 12,240,000
Area: 412,582 sq mi (1,068,582 km²)

Prince Edward Island
Capital: Charlottetown
Lieutenant Governor: J. Léonce Bernard
Premier: Patrick Binns (Progressive Conservative)
Leader of the Opposition: Robert Ghiz (Liberal)
Entered Confederation: July 1, 1873
Population: 138,000
Area: 2,184 sq mi (5,657 km²)

Quebec
Capital: Quebec City
Lieutenant Governor: Lise Thibault
Premier: Jean Charest (Liberal)
Leader of the Opposition: Bernard Landry (Parti Québécois)
Entered Confederation: July 1, 1867
Population: 7,490,000
Area: 594,860 sq mi (1,540,700 km^2)

Saskatchewan
Capital: Regina
Lieutenant Governor: Lynda M. Haverstock
Premier: Lorne Calvert (New Democratic Party)
Leader of the Opposition: Elwin Hermanson
  (Saskatchewan Party)
Entered Confederation: Sept. 1, 1905
Population: 995,000
Area: 251,700 sq mi (651,900 km^2)

Yukon
Capital: Whitehorse
Premier: Dennis Fentie (Yukon Party)

Leader of the Opposition: Todd Hardy (New
  Democratic Party)
Commissioner: Jack Cable
Organized as a Territory: June 13, 1898
Population: 31,100
Area: 186,299 sq mi (482,515 km^2)

Northwest Territories
Capital: Yellowknife
Commissioner: Glenna F. Hansen
Premier: Joseph Handley
Reconstituted as a Territory: Sept. 1, 1905
Population: 41,900
Area: 468,000 sq mi (1,170,000 km^2)

Nunavut
Capital: Iqaluit
Commissioner: Peter Irniq
Government Leader: Paul Okalik
Organized as a Territory: April 1, 1999
Population: 29,400
Area: 797,600 sq mi (1,994,000 km^2)

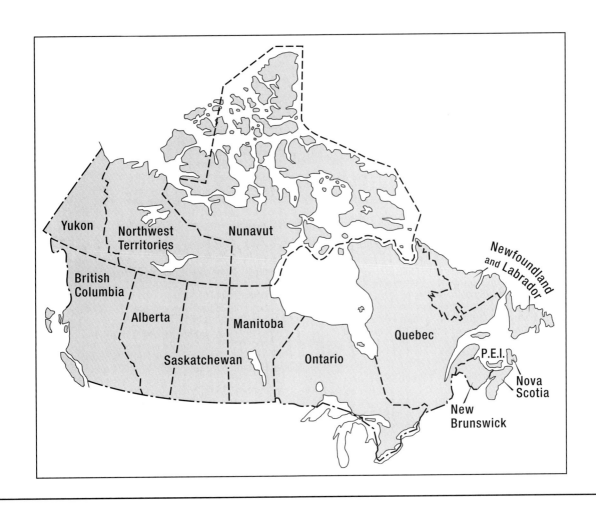

INDEX

A

D

E

Eagles 87
Earth (planet) 130–33
Earthquakes 27, 41
East Timor 385
Ebadi, Shirin (Iranian lawyer) 37, 60, *picture* 37
Ebsen, Buddy (American actor) 381
Echolocation (using echoes to locate things) 48, 79
Ecologists 228
Ecology *see* Environment
Economics
    budget deficit, United States 50–51
    European Union 62–63
    Nobel Prizes 37
Ecosystems (plants and animals living together in a habitat) 133
Ecuador 385
Education
    environmental education 229
    race as college admission factor 28
Edwards, Wallace (Canadian author)
    Alphabeasts (book) 285
Egypt 215, 385
Eiffel Tower (Paris, France), *picture* 28
Elderly *see* Old age
Elections *see also* Presidents (of the United States)
    California's recall election 51, 64
    general elections in the United States 38
Electricity
    blackout (North America) 33
    hurricane Isabel, loss of power caused by 34
Elizabeth II (queen of the United Kingdom) 38, 165
Elliott, Missy (American singer) 258–59
El Salvador 385
Embedded reporters 45
Emmy Awards 256–57, *pictures* 256, 257
Emotions, Web site on 230
Endangered species
    climate and global warming 132–33
    frogs 77
    National Wildlife Refuge System 114–19
    pygmy owls, *picture* 98
Engineers, environmental 222–23
England *see* United Kingdom
Engle, Robert F. (American economist) 37
English language 200, 201, 202, 203, 274
Environment
    Arizona deserts 98
    environmental careers 222–29
    freshwater supply 130
    frogs in danger 76, 77
    littering on Mount Everest 112
Environmental health scientists 223
Environmental Protection Agency (United States) 38
Equatorial Guinea 385
Eragon (book by Christopher Paolini) 233
Erdogan, Recep Tayyip (prime minister of Turkey) 23
Eritrea 385
Erosion 132

Eskimos *see* Inuit
Estivation (summer sleep) 82
Estonia 24, 63, 385
Ethiopia 28, 385
Euro (European currency) 63
Europa stamps 155
Europe 344–72
    dragon legends 216–17
    European Union 24, 62–63
    heat wave 32
    hedgehogs 80
European Atomic Energy Community 62
European Coal and Steel Community 62
European Economic Community 62
European Space Agency 138, 139
European Union (EU) 24, 62–63
Evanescence (music group) 262
Everest, Mount 110–13
Everybody Loves Raymond (television program), *picture* 256
Exploration and discovery
    Discovery, The (story) 288–99
    Lewis and Clark Expedition 192–99, *picture* 190–91
    SS *Republic* shipwreck site 39
    word puzzles 158–59
Eyes 106, 108

F

Fafnir (dragon in Norse mythology) 217
Falco, Edie (American actress), *picture* 257
Fantasia (movie) 269, *picture* 268
Farallon National Wildlife Refuge (California) 115
Fayez, Faisal al- (prime minister of Jordan) 37
Federer, Roger (Swiss athlete) 185
Ferrero, Juan Carlos (Spanish athlete) 185
Ferrets 115, *picture* 115
50 Cent (American rapper) 259–60
Fiji 385
File sharing 261
Finding Nemo (movie) 247, *picture* 247
Finland 28, 62, 385
Fire
    nightclub fire (Rhode Island) 20
    wildfires (California) 36
Firefighters 153, *pictures* 49, 220–21
Fish 88, 133
Fisheries conservationists 226, *picture* 228
Flag, American, stamps commemorating 152
Fletcher, Ernie (governor of Kentucky) 38
Floods 26
Florida
    Astronauts Memorial, *picture* 20
    large eagle's nest 87
    National Wildlife Refuges 114, 119, 153
Florida Marlins (baseball team) 168–69
Flowers
    glass flowers at Harvard University 240–43
    seen in ultraviolet light, *pictures* 107
    stamps commemorating 155
Flyer (Wright brothers' airplane) 164, 212, 213, *pictures* 210, 213
Foale, Michael (American astronaut) 36, *picture* 136

ILLUSTRATION CREDITS AND ACKNOWLEDGMENTS

The following list credits or acknowledges, by page, the source of illustrations and text excerpts used in this work. Illustration credits are listed illustration by illustration—left to right, top to bottom. When two or more illustrations appear on one page, their credits are separated by semicolons. When both the photographer or artist and an agency or other source are given for an illustration, they are usually separated by a slash. Excerpts from previously published works are listed by inclusive page numbers.

6   © Gail Shumway; Artist, Gary Torrisi; © Matt Gentry/*The Roanoke Times*

7   © Cary Wolinsky/Stock, Boston, Inc./PictureQuest; © Bill Brooks/Masterfile; © Walt Disney/Courtesy, The Everett Collection

12– © Jerome Delay/AP/Wide World Photos
13

14   © Josh Reynolds/AP/Wide World Photos; © Nasser Ishtayeh/AP/Wide World Photos

15   © Yun Jai-hyoung/AP/Wide World Photos; © Dennis Cook/AP/Wide World Photos

16   © Mark J. Terrill/AP/Wide World Photos; NASA

17   © Reuters/Landov; © Kevork Kjansezian/AP/Wide World Photos

18   Drawing by Portia Sloan for IVPP

19   © Dick Luria/Taxi/Getty Images

20   © Greg Fight/*The Tampa Tribune*/AP/Wide World Photos

21   © Lower Manhattan Development Corporation/AP/Wide World Photos; © Lower Manhattan Development Corporation; © Studio Daniel Libeskind/AP/Wide World Photos

22   © Josh Reynolds/AP/Wide World Photos

23   © Mikica Petrovic/AP/Wide World Photos

24   © Digital Art/Corbis

25   © Winfried Rothermel/AP/Wide World Photos

26   © Charles Rex Arborgast/AP/Wide World Photos

27   © Jim Cole/AP/Wide World Photos

28   © Francois Mori/AP/Wide World Photos

29   © Scott Olson/Getty Images

30   © Charles Dharapak/AP/Wide World Photos

31   © Hayden Roger Celestin/EPA/AP/Wide World Photos; © Bob Handelman/Stone/Getty Images

32   © Giovanna Lazzara/AP/Wide World Photos

33   © Chad Rachman/Polaris; © Paul Sancya/AP/Wide World Photos

34   © Alex Wong/Getty Images

35   Courtesy, Bureau of Engraving and Printing/U.S. Department of the Treasury

36   © Jerome Favre/AP/Wide World Photos

37   © Abedin Taherkenareh/AP/Wide World Photos

38   © Anja Niedringhaus/Pool/EPA/AP/Wide World Photos

39   Courtesy of the Peabody Essex Museum; © Copyright 2003 Odyssey Marine Exploration

40   U.S. Army/AP/Wide World Photos

42   © Paul Grover/AP/Wide World Photos

43   © Virginia Mayo/AP/Wide World Photos; © Lawrence Jackson/AP/Wide World Photos; © Richard Lewis/AP/Wide World Photos; AP/Wide World Photos

44   © Jerome Delay/AP/Wide World Photos; © Kevork Djansezian/AP/Wide World Photos

45   © Laurent Rebours/AP/Wide World Photos

46   Courtesy, U.S. Central Command

47   Department of Defense/AP/Wide World Photos

48   © Brien Aho, U.S. Navy/AP/Wide World Photos

49   © Marco Di Lauro/Getty Images; © Gursel Eser/Anatolia/AP/Wide World Photos; © Hadi Mizban/AP/Wide World Photos

50   © Dennis Cook/AP/Wide World Photos

52   © Vincent Yu/AP/Wide World Photos; © Reuters/Landov

52– © Kevin Frayer/AP/Wide World Photos
53

54   © Reuters

55   © Moshe Milner/GPO via Getty Images; © Getty Images

56   © Suzanne Plunkett/AP/Wide World Photos

57   © Nasser Ishtayeh/AP/Wide World Photos; © Abid Katib/Getty Images

58   © Abedin Taherkenareh/AP/Wide World Photos

59   © Schalk van Zuydam/AP/Wide World Photos; © Chris Hondros/Getty Images

60   © Jean-Marc Bouju/AP/Wide World Photos; © Seth Rossman/AP/Wide World Photos

61   © Yun Jai-hyoung/AP/Wide World Photos

62   © Sean Gallup/Getty Images

63   © Joerg Sarbach/AP/Wide World Photos

64   © Mark J. Terrill/AP/Wide World Photos

65   © Joe Marquette/AP/Wide World Photos; © Phil Noble/WPA Pool/EPA/AP/Wide World Photos

66   North Wind Picture Archives; Library of Congress/AP/Wide World Photos

67   UPI/Landov

68– © Gail Shumway/Taxi/Getty Images
69

70   © Gail Shumway; © Zig Leszczynski/Animals Animals

71   © Zig Leszczynski/Animals Animals; © Breck P.Kent; © Jany Sauvanet/Photo Researchers, Inc.

72   © D. Biju/Reprinted with permission of *Nature* © 2003 Macmillan Magazines Unlimited; © Jane Burton/Bruce Coleman Inc.

73   © Gail Shumway; © Kim Taylor/Bruce Coleman Inc.

75   © Michael Fogden/DRK Photo; © Michael Fogden/Bruce Coleman Inc.; © Michael Fogden/DRK Photo

76   Galen Rathbun, U.S. Geological Survey

77   © Tom McHugh/Photo Researchers, Inc.

78   SOLUTION: copterbird

78– Artist, Steve Delmonte
79

80   © Dwight Kuhn

81   © Dwight Kuhn; © Dwight Kuhn; © Jane Burton/Bruce Coleman Inc.

82   © Dietmar Nill/Nature Picture Library; © Jim Tuten/Animals Animals; © Mark Moffett/Minden Pictures

83   © Richard Nowitz

84   © Ken Highfill/Photo Researchers, Inc.

85   © Erwin & Peggy Bauer/Bruce Coleman Inc.; © Victoria McCormick/Animals Animals/Earth Scenes

86   © Nigel J. Dennis/NHPA; © Nigel J. Dennis/NHPA; © Brian Rogers/Natural Visions

87   © Michael Fogden/Animals Animals; © Robert P. Carr/Bruce Coleman Inc.; © Michael Wickes/Bruce Coleman Inc.

88   © Hans Pfletschinger/Peter Arnold, Inc.

89   © D. K. & Dennie Cody/Masterfile; © Heather Angel/Natural Visions; © Brian Rogers/Natural Visions

90   © Scott Camazine/Photo Researchers, Inc.; © Patti Murray/Animals Animals

91   © Rex Features

92   © Gerard Lacz/Animals Animals; © F. J. Hiersche/Okapia/Photo Researchers, Inc.

92– © Sid Bahrt/Photo Researchers, Inc.
93

93   © C. K. Lorenz/Photo Researchers, Inc.; © Tui De Roy/Bruce Coleman Inc.

94   Copyright Science/Illustration Carin L. Cain

95   © Marcio Jose Sanchez/AP/Wide World Photos; © William Meyer/*Milwaukee Journal Sentinel* Inc.

96   © Mario Tama/Newsmakers/Getty Images; © Katsumi Kasahara/AP/Wide World Photos

97   Courtesy, St. Clair Kennels

98   © John Miller/AP/Wide World Photos

99   © Mark Mitchell/*New Zealand Herald*

100– JPL/NASA
101

102   © Dr. Scott Lieberman/*Tyler Morning Telegraph*/AP/Wide World Photos; © Tim Sharp/AP/Wide World Photos

103   NASA

104   © Peter Cosgrove/AP/Wide World Photos

105   NASA/Getty Images; © Alex Wong/Getty Images; © Ric Feld/AP/Wide World Photos

106   Ned Shaw

107   © Thomas Eisner

108   Illustration by Gary W. Meyer, University of Oregon, and Donald P. Greenberg/Cornell University Program of Computer Graphics

109   Ned Shaw; Illustration by Gary W. Meyer, University of Oregon, and Donald P. Greenberg/Cornell Universtiy Program of Computer Graphics

110   © J.A. Kraulis/Masterfile; AP/Wide World Photos

111   © Binod Joshi/AP/Wide World Photos; © Gurinder Osan/AP/Wide World Photos; © Binod Joshi/AP/Wide World Photos; AP Wide World Photos

112   © Gurinder Osan/AP/Wide World Photos; © Binod Joshi/AP/Wide World Photos

113   © Gurinder Osan/AP/Wide World Photos; © Binod Joshi/AP/Wide World Photos

114   Courtesy, U.S. Fish and Wildlife Service; Photo by John and Karen Hollingsworth/Courtesy, U.S. Fish and Wildlife Service

115 © Tom & Pat Leeson

116 © Dominique Braud/Animals Animals; © E.R. Degginger/Animals Animals

117 © Peter Ward/Bruce Coleman Inc.; © Tom & Pat Leeson

118 © Jeremy Woodhouse/Masterfile; © Jeff Foott/Bruce Coleman Inc.

119 © William H. Mullins/Photo Researchers, Inc.; © Wardene Weisser/Bruce Coleman Inc.

120 © Matt Gentry/*The Roanoke Times*; Jericho Historical Society, VT

121 Jericho Historical Society, VT

122 Snowflakes: Jericho Historical Society, VT; © Gerban Oppermans/Stone/Getty Images

123 Artist, Natasha Lessnik Tibbott

124 © Scott Tysick/Masterfile

125 *Newsweek*-Kevin Hand. © 2002, Newsweek, Inc. All rights reserved. Reprinted by permission.

126– © 2003 Time, Inc. Reprinted by permission
128 © Darren McCollester/Getty Images; Courtesy, Valmont Communications; Courtesy, Valmont Communications

129 Courtesy, Valmont Communications; Photo courtesy of STEALTH Concealment Solutions, formerly known as Stealth Network Technologies, Inc.; Courtesy Valmont Communications

130 © Manish Swarup/AP/Wide World Photos; © U. Kaiser/Zefa Collection

131 © Ken Domangue/AP/Wide World Photos; © Cheryl Gerber/AP/Wide World Photos; © Jeff Foott/Discovery Images/PictureQuest

132 © David Madison/Bruce Coleman Inc.; © Philip Roullard/San Diego Natural History Museum/AP/Wide World Photos; © Mike Macri/Masterfile

133 © Bill Eschmeyer and John E. Randall/Census of Marine Life/AP/Wide World Photos; © Dale Sanders/Masterfile

134 © Wu Xiang/Imaginechina

135 © Dale Wilson/Masterfile

136 NASA; © James Nielson/Getty Images

137 © Zhao Jianwei/Xinhua/AP/Wide World Photos; NASA; NASA

138 NASA/JPL-Caltech

139 JPL/NASA; NASA/AP/Wide World Photos

140– Artist, Natasha Lessnik Tibbott
141

142 © David Young-Wolff/PhotoEdit

148– Artist, Natasha Lessnik Tibbott
149

150 SOLUTION: Dayton, Ohio

156– From *Many Friends Cooking: An International*
157 *Cookbook for Boys and Girls,* by Terry Touff Cooper and Marilyn Ratner. Illustrations by Tony Chen. Reprinted by permission of Philomel Books, a division of the Putnam Publishing Group

158 Artist, Leslie Dunlap

160– Courtesy, *Crafts 'n Things magazine*
163

164– Courtesy, Krause Publications, Inc.
165

166– © Andreas Rentz/BONGARTS/SportsChrome Inc.
167

168 © Bill Kostroun/AP/Wide World Photos

169 © Eliot J. Schechter/Getty Images

171 © Carolyn Kaster/AP/Wide World Photos

172 © David J. Phillip/AP/Wide World Photos

174 © Bob Child/AP/Wide World Photos

175 © Nick Wass/AP/Wide World Photos

176 © Luis M. Alvarez/AP/Wide World Photos

177 © Kathy Willens/AP/Wide World Photos

178 © Elise Amendola/AP/Wide World Photos

179 © Rusty Kennedy/AP/Wide World Photos

180 © Paul Chaisson/AP/Wide World Photos; © Silvia Pecota/NHLI/Getty Images

182 © Roberto Borea/AP/ Wide World Photos

183 © Dusan Vranic/AP/Wide World Photos

184 © Alex Livsey/Getty Images

185 © Al Bello/Getty Images

186 © Paul Buck/EPA/AP/Wide World Photos; © Steve Miler/AP/Wide World Photos

187 © Brian Branch-Price/AP/Wide World Photos

188 © Pascale Rondeau/AP/Wide World Photos; © Al Grillo/AP/Wide World Photos; © Colin James/AP/Wide World Photos

189 © Jesse D. Garrabant/NBAE/Getty Images

190– © Bettman/Corbis
191

192 American Philosophical Society; The Granger Collection; The Granger Collection; American Philosophical Society; © 2003 Painted Pony Press, Inc. All Rights reserved. Illustration by Kathleen McKeehen

193 The Granger Collection; Artist, Gary Torrisi

194 © 2003 Painted Pony Press, Inc. All rights reserved. Illustration by Kathleen McKeehen; American Philosophical Society; American Philosophical Society

195– www.lewisandclarktrail.com; © 2003 Painted Pony
198 Press, Inc. All rights reserved. Illustration by Kathleen McKeehen

199 The Granger Collection; The Granger Collection; The Granger Collection; The Granger Collection; © Joseph Sohm/ChromoSohm Media Inc./Photo Researchers, Inc.

200– Artist, Charles Varner
203

204 The Newark Museum/Art Resource, NY; © Steven Clevenger, *Farmington Daily Times*/AP/Wide World Photos; © David Young-Wolff/PhotoEdit

205 The Newark Museum/Art Resource, NY; © Bonnie Kamin/PhotoEdit; © Cary Wolinsky/Stock, Boston, Inc./PictureQuest

206 The Newark Museum/Art Resource, NY; The Granger Collection

207 © Dan McCoy/Rainbow/PictureQuest

208 The Bridgeman Art Library; The Bridgeman Art Library; © Jeff Greenberg/PhotoEdit

209 © Jamie Martin/AP/Wide World Photos

210 © Mary Evans Photo Library/Photo Researchers, Inc.; Hulton/Archive by Getty Images; New York Times Co./Hulton/Archive by Getty Images

211 The Granger Collection; Hulton/Archive by Getty Images; Hulton/Archive by Getty Images

212 The Granger Collection

213 © David Kohl/AP/Wide World Photos; © Bob Jordan/AP/Wide World Photos; © Alex Wong/Getty Images

214 © Private Collection/Christian Pierre/SuperStock; The Granger Collection

215 © Werner Forman/Art Resource, NY

216 © Art Resource, NY; © Werner Forman/Art Resource, NY; © Dagli Orti/Museo Naval, Madrid/The Art Archive

217 © Dagli Orti/Museo Naval, Madrid/The Art Archive

218 © Wei Yan/Masterfile; © Bruce Coleman Inc.

219 © Anat Givon/AP/Wide World Photos

220– © Axel Koester
221

222 © Bill Brooks/Masterfile

223 © Michael Rosenfeld/Stone/Getty Images

224 © Peter Christopher/Masterfile; Photo by Scott Bauer/ Agricultural Research Service/U.S. Department of Agriculture; Photo by Scott Bauer/ Agricultural Research Service/U.S. Department of Agriculture

225 © Alan L. Detrick/Photo Researchers, Inc.

226 © Matthew Borkoski/Stock, Boston, Inc./PictureQuest

227 © Alfred Eisendstaedt/TimePix/Getty Images

228 © Patrick Fagot/Photo Researchers, Inc.; Photo by Scott Bauer/Agricultural Research Service/U.S. Department of Agriculture

229 Photo by Jack Dykinga/Agricultural Research Service/U.S. Department of Agriculture

232 Photo by Jason Vick, NAR/Courtesy, Aerospace Industries Association; Photo by Joseph Baron/Courtesy, Aerospace Industries Association

233 © Walt Disney/Courtesy, The Everett Collection; Courtesy, Alfred A. Knopf Books for Young Readers; Photo © Eric Cahan/Courtesy, Alfred A. Knopf Books for Young Readers

234 © Scott Gries/Getty Images; © Warner Brothers/Courtesy, The Everett Collection

235 © Wendy Carlson; © Charles Dharapak/AP/Wide World Photos

236 © Ron Edmonds/AP/Wide World Photos; © Gerd Ludwig/NGS Image Collection

237 Courtesy, Intel Corporation

238– The Nelson-Atkins Museum of Art, Kansas City,
239 Missouri (Gift of the Friends of Art) F77-34; Photograph by Mel McLean

240– Photos by Hillel Burger; © President and Fellows
243 of Harvard College

244 © Miramax, Courtesy, The Everett Collection

245 © Paramount/Courtesy, The Everett Collection; The Everett Collection; © Walt Disney/Courtesy, The Everett Collection

246– © Walt Disney/Courtesy, The Everett Collection
247

248 TM & Copyright © 20th Century Fox Film Corp. All rights reserved/Courtesy, The Everett Collection; © Universal/Courtesy, The Everett Collection

249 © Walt Disney/Courtesy, The Everett Collection

250 © Universal/Courtesy, The Everett Collection; © Dreamworks/Courtesy, The Everett Collection

251 © Paramount/Courtesy, The Everett Collection

252 The Granger Collection; Courtesy, The Sherlock Holmes Museum, London

253 Courtesy, The Sherlock Holmes Museum, London

254 © Hammer/Kobal Collection; © Eileen Tweedy/Art Archive/Kobal Collection

255 © Universal/Kobal Collection; The Granger Collection

256 © 2003 CBS Worldwide Inc. All Rights Reserved./Courtesy, The Everett Collection

257 © HBO/Courtesy, The Everett Collection; © USA Network/Courtesy, The Everett Collection; © NBC/Courtesy, The Everett Collection

258 © Mary Altaffer/AP/Wide World Photos; © Yui Mok/AP/Wide World Photos

259 Getty Images; © Jim Cooper/AP/Wide World Photos

260 © Kevork Djansezian/AP/Wide World Photos; © Mary Altaffer/AP/Wide World Photos

261 © G. Schuster/Zefa/Masterfile

262 © James Veysey/CameraPress/Retna Ltd.

415

263   © Richard Drew/AP/Wide World Photos
264   © Photograph by Hickey-Robertson/Gift of Alexander Iolas/The Menil Collection, Houston/© The Joseph and Robert Cornell Memorial Foundation/Licensed by VAGA, NY
265   © Edward Owen/Art Resource, NY/© The Joseph and Robert Cornell Memorial Foundation/Licensed by VAGA, NY
266   National Gallery of Canada, Ottawa/© The Joseph and Robert Cornell Memorial Foundation/Licensed by VAGA, NY; © Art Resource, NY/© The Joseph and Robert Cornell Memorial Foundation/Licensed by VAGA, NY
267   Lindy and Edwin Bergman Joseph Cornell Collection, 1982.1843/The Art Institue of Chicago/© The Joseph and Robert Cornell Memorial Foundation/Licensed by VAGA, NY; Digital Image © The Museum of Modern Art/Licensed by SCALA/Art Resource, NY/© The Joseph and Robert Cornell Memorial Foundation/Licensed by VAGA, NY
268   Photofest; © Walt Disney/Courtesy, Everett Collection
269   © Kevork Djansezian/AP/Wide World Photos
270   © William Thomas Cain/Getty Images
271   © Nick Ut/AP/Wide World Photos; © Thomas Hoepker/Magnum Photos
272   © Kevork Djansezian/AP/Wide World Photos
273   Photo courtesy of Community Church, Malta, Austria; © Shizuo Kambayashi/AP/Wide World Photos
274   © Pierre Tremblay/Masterfile; North Wind Picture Archives
275   Art Resource, NY
276– Illustration from The Last Resort, copyright 2002
277   Roberto Innocenti, reprinted by permission of The Creative Company, 123 S. Broad Street, Mankato, MN 56001
278– Artist, Judith Cheng
283
284   My Friend Rabbit. Copyright © 2002 by Eric Rohmann. Reprinted by permission of Roaring Brook Press, a division of the The Millbrook Press, Inc. All rights reserved; Illustration from Alphabeasts, by Wallace Edwards, is used by permission of Kids Can Press. Illustration copyright © Wallace Edwards 2002.
285   From Daisy Comes Home by Jan Brett, copyright © 2002 by Jan Brett. Used by permission of G.P. Putnam's Sons, a division of Penguin Young Readers Group, a member of Penguin Group (USA) Inc., 345 Hudson St., New York, NY 10014. All rights reserved.
286   Illustration from Henry Builds a Cabin by D.B. Johnson. Copyright © 2002 by D.B. Johnson. Reprinted by permission of Houghton Mifflin Company. All rights reserved.; From Rap a Tap Tap: Here's Bojangles—Think of That! by Leo and Diane Dillon. Published by the Blue Sky Press, an imprint of Scholastic Inc. Copyright © 2002 by Leo and Diane Dillon. Used by permission.
287   Illustration by E.B. Lewis from Talkin' About Bessie: The Story of Aviator Bessie Coleman by Nikki Grimes. Published by Orchard Books, an imprint of Scholastic Inc. Illustration copyright © 2002 by Earl Lewis. Used by permission; Illustration copyright © 2002 by Aki Sogabe. All rights reserved. Reprinted from The Boy Who Drew Cats by Margaret Hodges by permission of Holiday House, Inc.
288   The Granger Collection
289– Artist, Chet Jezierski
299
300– Artist, Gary Torrisi
301
302– Artist, Meryl Treatner
311
313   Department of Homeland Security/AP/Wide World Photos
314   © Dave G. Houser/Houserstock; © Kevin Frayer/Canadian Press/AP/Wide World Photos; © David Young-Wolff/PhotoEdit
315   © David R. Austen/Stock, Boston/PictureQuest
316   © Peggy & Yoram Kahana/Peter Arnold, Inc.; © C.C. Lockwood/Bruce Coleman, Inc.
317   © Ken Heyman
318   © Thomas Hoepker/Magnum Photos
319   © Bill Foley/Bruce Coleman, Inc.
320   © Jeff Hester and Paul Scowen, Arizona State University/NASA; © Andreas Feininger/Time Life Pictures/Getty Images; © Alfred Pasieka/Science Photo Library/Photo Researchers, Inc.
321   © Chip Simons; © Adrian Myers/Taxi/Getty Images
323   Hulton/Archive by Getty Images
325   © The Museum of Modern Art/Licensed by Scala/Art Resource, NY
327   © Beth Kaiser/AP/Wide World Photos; Stapleton Collection/Bridgeman Art Library
328   © White Light
329   © 1990 Amon Carter Museum, Fort Worth, Texas, Bequest of an artist
330   © David Young-Wolff/PhotoEdit; © Justin D. Pyle/U.S. Army/Getty Images
331   NASA/Science Photo Library/Photo Researchers, Inc.; © Manfred P. Kage/OKAPIA/Oxford Scientific Films, Ltd.
332   Department of the Interior, National Park Service/National Archives at College Park
333   Gernsheim Collection/The Harry Ransom Humanities Research Center/The University of Texas at Austin; AP/Wide World Photos
334– © White Light
335
336   © Henri Cartier-Bresson/Magnum Photos
337   © Arnold Newman/Getty Images; © Elliott Erwitt/Magnum Photos
338   © White Light
339   CBS Photo Archive/Hulton/Archive by Getty Images; © Max Nash/AP/Wide World Photos
340   © Frans Lanting/Minden Pictures
341   Digital Vision/Getty Images; © Don W. Fawcett/Visuals Unlimited, Inc.; © Kjell B. Sandved/Photo Researchers, Inc.; © E.R. Degginger/Bruce Coleman, Inc.; © George Bernard/Animals Animals; © Don W. Fawcett/Visuals Unlimited, Inc.; © Joy Spurr/Bruce Coleman, Inc.; © Don W. Fawcett/Visuals Unlimited, Inc.
342   Digital Vision/Getty Image; © Gosner/Visuals Unlimited, Inc.; © E.R. Degginger/Bruce Coleman, Inc.; © Don W. Fawcett/Visuals Unlimited, Inc.; © Kjell B. Sandved/Visuals Unlimited, Inc.; © Don W. Fawcett/Visuals Unlimited, Inc.; © Viola's Photo Visions, Inc./Animals Animals; © Kerry Givens/Bruce Coleman, Inc.; © Barbara Strandova/Photo Researchers, Inc.; © Damir Frkovic/Masterfile
343   Digital Vision/Getty Images; © Richard Hutchings/Photo Researchers, Inc.; © Kerry Givens/Bruce Coleman, Inc.; © Don W. Fawcett/Visuals Unlimited, Inc.
344   © Picture Finders Ltd./eStock Photo; © Peter S. Thacher/Photo Researchers, Inc.; © Connie Coleman/Stone/Getty Images; © John Elk III/Bruce Coleman, Inc.
345   © Hans Madej/Bilderberg/Peter Arnold, Inc.; © Laurent Rebours/AP/Wide World Photos; © Paul Harris/Stone/Getty Images
347   © Brian Lawrence/Superstock
348   © Jean Paul Nacivet/eStock Photo; © Hjalte Tin/Bilderberg/Peter Arnold, Inc.
349   © Art Wolfe/Photo Researchers, Inc.
352   © Walter Bibikow/Danita Delimont, Agent
353   © Steve Vidler/eStock Photo
354   © C.C. Lockwood/Bruce Coleman, Inc.; © Sime/eStock Photo
355   © Fritz Polking/Bruce Coleman, Inc.; © H. Reinhard/Bruce Coleman, Inc.; © H. Reinhard/Zefa/Masterfile
356   © Nik Wheeler/Danita Delimont, Agent; Superstock; © Roland Weihrauch/AP/Wide World Photos; © Efrem Lukatsky/AP/Wide World Photos; © B. Lundberg/BIOS/Peter Arnold, Inc.
357   © Paul Stepan-Vierow/Photo Researchers, Inc.; © David Hanson/Stone/Getty Images; Superstock; © Frank Fournier/Woodfin Camp & Associates, Inc.
360   © David Lees/Getty Images; © Jeff Greenberg/eStock Photo
361   © Steve Vidler/eStock Photo; © James Baloq/Stone/Getty Images
362   © Richard Passmore/Stone/Getty Images; © Tomas Muscionico/Contact Press/PictureQuest
363   © Michael Busselle/Stone/Getty Images; © Adam Woolfitt/Woodfin Camp & Associates, Inc.
364   © Yngve Rakke/The Image Bank/Getty Images
365   Superstock; © Sigfried Tauquer/eStock Photo
366   © Robert Frerck/Woodfin Camp & Associates, Inc.; © Gregory Wrona/Panos Pictures; Digital Vision/Getty Images
367   © Vatican Museum and Galleries, Vatican City, Italy/Bridgeman Art Library; © Reunion des Musees Nationaux/Art Resource, NY
369   © Labat JM/Photo Researchers, Inc.; © Private Collection/Christopher Wood Gallery/Bridgeman Art Library
370   © Reunion des Musees Nationaux/Art Resource, NY
371   Keystone/Hulton/Archive by Getty Images
372   © Yves Logghe/AP/Wide World Photos
373   © Ariel Skelley/Masterfile
374   © A. Ramey/Woodfin Camp & Associates; © Tomas del Amo/The Viesti Collection; © John & Lisa Merrill/Danita Delimont, Agent; © David Young-Wolff/PhotoEdit
375   © Susan Sterner/AP/Wide World Photos; © A. Reininger/Woodfin Camp & Associates
376   AP/Wide World Photos
377   © Damien Lovegrove/Science Photo Library/Photo Researchers, Inc.
380   The Everett Collection
381   © Hulton/Archive by Getty Images; © Alfred Eisenstaedt/Time Life Pictures/Getty Images
382   Hulton/Archive by Getty Images; Photo by Universal Studios/Courtesy Getty Images
383   © ABC/Courtesy The Everett Collection; Hulton/Archive by Getty Images
393   © Bill Haber/AP/Wide World Photos